DATE DUE

DEMCO 38-296

The Peoples of the Middle Niger

The Peoples of Africa

General Editor: Parker Shipton

This series is about the African peoples from their origins to the present day. Drawing on archaeological, historical and anthropological evidence, each volume looks at a particular group's culture, society, and history.

Approaches will vary according to the subject and the nature of evidence. Volumes concerned mainly with culturally discrete peoples will be complemented by accounts which focus primarily on the historical period, on African nations and contemporary peoples. The overall aim of the series is to offer a comprehensive and up-to-date picture of the African peoples, in books which are at once scholarly and accessible.

Already published

The Sona and their Neighbours*
David Beach

The Berbers*
Michael Brett and Elizabeth Fentress

The Peoples of the Middle Niger*
Rod McIntosh

The Ethiopians*
Richard Pankhurst

The Egyptians*
Barbara Watterson

In preparation

The Swahili
Mark Horton and John Middleton

The Nubians
W. Godlewski and S. Jacobielski

The Black Peoples of Southern Africa
Timothy Maggs and W. Guest

The Peoples of Kenya
John Middleton

* Indicates title commissioned under the general editorship of Dr David Phillipson of Gonville and Caius College, Cambridge.

R

The Peoples of the Middle Niger

The Island of Gold

Roderick James McIntosh

BLACKWELL *Publishers*

)sh to be identified as author of this work
h the Copyright, Designs and Patents Act
1988.

blished 1988

10 9 7 5 3 1

Publishers Inc.
350 Main Street
Malden, Massachusetts 02148
USA

Blackwell Publishers Ltd
108 Cowley Road
Oxford OX4 1JF
UK

Library of Congress Cataloging-in-Publication Data

McIntosh, Roderick J.
    The peoples of the Middle Niger :   the island of gold / Roderick
James McIntosh.
        p.   cm. – (The peoples of Africa)
    Includes bibliographical references and index.
    ISBN 0–631–17361–7
    1. Ethnology–Mali. 2. Ethnology–Senegal. 3. Ethnology–Niger River
Valley. 4. Mali–Social life and customs. 5. Senegal–Social life and
customs. 6. Niger River Valley–Social life and customs. 7. Niger River
Valley–Antiquities. I. Title. II. Series.
GN652.M25M35   1998
305.8′009662–dc21   98–10817
                                                                          CIP

British Library Cataloguing in Publication Data
A CIP catalogue record for this book is available from the British Library.

Typeset in 11 on 12½ pt Sabon
by Ace Filmsetting Ltd, Frome, Somerset
Printed in Great Britain by MPG Books Ltd, Bodmin, Cornwall

This book is printed on acid-free paper

This book is dedicated to my wife, Susan Keech McIntosh

ROD BUMOJERE

Contents

List of Plates   ix

List of Figures   x

List of Maps   xi

Series editor's preface   xiii

Preface   xv

Acknowledgements   xxiii

Timeline   xxv

1   **The Island of Gold**   1
    Sad tale of the *Office du Niger*   1
    The original civil society: heterarchy versus hierarchy   6
    Synoecism and layered transformations   10
    Historical imagination   22
    Island of Gold   30

2   **The Dry Basins of the Middle Niger**   34
    Triumph of the wind: the Azawad   38
    Views of the stone-using communities   48
    Adaptations to the drying Méma   57
    Palaeoclimate   66

3   **Historical Imagination: 4100 BP**   81

4   **Peoples of the Four Live Basins**   88
    Autochtones of the Upper Delta: Bozo and Marka   89

Pastoral cycle of the Macina: the Fulani 106
Rainfed and *décrue* agriculture on the Erg of Bara:
    Bambara 115
Desert-river clash at the Lakes Region-Niger Bend:
    Songhai and Tuareg 120

5 **Historical Imagination: 300 BC** 131

6 **Penetration of the Deep Basins** 140
From stone to iron, from gatherer to farmer 145
Founders of Jenne-jeno 155
Economy of the Early Middle Niger 161
Settlements of the first colonists 166
Specialists in a realm of their own 176

7 **Historical Imagination: AD 400** 182

8 **Prosperity and Cities** 190
Mounds of the Lakes Region and Niger Bend 190
Mature Jenne-jeno 199
Precocious urbanism 203
Distant relations 213
Monuments and emerging polities 219

9 **Historical Imagination: AD 1000** 234

10 **The Imperial Tradition** 240
Global climate turned upside-down 241
Demographic cataclysm 244
The Middle Niger and the Great Empires 250
Island of Gold 267
The imperial tradition: power from authority 281

11 **Historical Imagination: AD 1472** 287

12 **Resilience of an Original Civil Society?** 294

Glossary 304

Bibliography 307

Index 340

Plates

1.1	Satellite image mosaic of the Middle Niger	19
2.1	Salt caravan approaching Timbuktu	36
2.2	Eroding lake deposits in the Malian Sahara (Haijad, Taoudenni Basin, 23° N)	37
2.3	Archaeological survey of the deflated Azawad plain	38
2.4	Satellite photo of the El Ahmar palaeochannel and Azawad dune system	44
2.5	Kolimbiné corridor of western Mali: imagining palaeochannel environments in the fourth millennium BP	59
2.6	Satellite photo of the recharged Fala de Molodo and the fringing fields of the Office du Niger	65
4.1	Jenne town at high flood and duststorm at low water (double)	92/3
4.2	Bird's-foot delta south of Lake Débo	107
4.3	Albedo halo around Timbuktu	124
5.1	Roundé Siru levee (near Jenne). This *marigot* and the one immediately east of Jenne are reputed to be home to one of the highest concentrations in all Mande of *faaro* water spirits	132
6.1	Aerial view of Jenne-jeno, with satellites to the north	159
8.1	Terracotta statuette	212
8.2	Tondidaro megalith field before its destruction at the hands of Clérisse	222
10.1	Middle Niger statuette with buboes	249

Figures and table

2.1   Articulated activities of early specialists   56
2.2   Holocene palaeoclimatic sequence and stable-unstable
      mode shifts   70
4.1   Annual climate and subsistence cycle   91
4.2   Placement of villages and fields on the Erg of Bara   118
5.1   Eponymous pioneering hunter   136
8.1   Idealized tumulus and cross-section of El-Oualadgi   225

2.1   Table of climate and geomorphological events   72/3

Maps

0.1	The Middle Niger	xvi
1.1	The Office du Niger in the Middle Niger	2
1.2	The Middle Niger mix of northern and southern Mande	16
2.1	AZAWAD: dead delta landforms and sites	35
2.2	Ancient hydrology: southern Saharan palaeochannels	59
2.3	MEMA: dead delta landforms and sites	60
2.4	Middle Niger palaeoenvironmental reconstruction	78
4.1	Live delta landforms and sites of the UPPER DELTA, MACINA, and ERG OF BARA	90
4.2	Transhumance routes of the Fulani	109
4.3	Live delta landforms and sites of the LAKES REGION-NIGER BEND	121
6.1	Later prehistoric sites and locations in West Africa	143
6.2	Jenne-jeno and its excavation	156
6.3	Prehistoric settlement dynamics in the Dia hinterland	169
6.4	Jenne-jeno urban cluster	174
8.1	Timbuktu and Gourma Rharous surveys	195
8.2	Part 1: Sites and landforms of the Timbuktu Survey region	196
	Part 2: Sites and landforms of the Gourma Rharous Survey region	197
8.3	Clustered specialist settlements within 4 km of Jenne	208
10.1	West Africa during the Great Empires with trans-Saharan and Wangara trade routes	251
10.2	Ibn Sa'id's Island of Gold	271
12.1	Successor states to Songhai	298

Series Editor's Preface

The Peoples of Africa series has been designed to provide reliable and up-to-date accounts of what is known about the development and antecedents of the diverse populations in that continent, and about their relations with others near or far. It is hoped that the series will enjoy a wide readership in many parts of the world, including Africa itself.

This series has counterparts relating to other continents, and it may be appropriate to discuss here aspects specific to a series dealing with Africa. Africa is a continent of contrasts – not only in its physical environments and in the life-styles and economies of its peoples, but also in the extent to which writing has influenced its development and recorded its past. Parts of Egypt have one of the longest histories of literacy in the world; on the other hand, some interior regions – notably in south-central Africa – remained wholly unrecorded in writing up to a hundred years ago. The historical significance of this contrast has been both varied and far-reaching.

The books in this series variously combine perspectives of archaeology, anthropology, and history. It will be obvious that someone studying the past of a non-literate people will adopt techniques very different from those that are at the disposal of historians who can base their work on written sources. The relevance of archaeology is by no means restricted to non-literate contexts, but it is clearly a preeminent means of illustrating even the comparatively recent past in those parts of Africa where writing was not employed. It may be less obvious to those not familiar with Africa that non-literate peoples were by no means ignorant of their past, traditional knowledge about which was often preserved and orally transmitted through several generations, albeit not infrequently subject to change – conscious or unconscious – in the light of contemporary circumstances. Further clues about the non-literate African past can be obtained from studying the distributions and interrelationships of modern languages. Each of these approaches presents its own problems, and has its own potential to illustrate particular aspects of the past.

Each volume in the series is a specialist's attempt to condense, and to order, a large and diverse body of scholarship on a way of life. The series describes both changes and continuities, relating historic processes occurring at all levels of scale, from the domestic to the intercontinental. The changing definitions and self-definitions of peoples, in the light of new communications and sensitive ethnic and national politics, pose difficult problems for theory and description. More often than not it is debatable where, and when, one population ends and another begins. Situating African societies flexibly in time and space, and taking account of continual movements, anomalies, and complexities in their cultures, these volumes attempt to convey some sense of the continent's great variety, to dispel myths about its essential character or its plight, and to introduce fresh and thoughtful perspectives on its role in human history.

Parker Shipton

Preface

The Island of Gold

The peoples of West Africa's Middle Niger occupy an awesome, ravaged landscape. The Niger's vast interior floodplain was, for twenty millennia (and unquestionably much longer), a battlefield contested by violent wind, raging flood, and unpredictable, torrential rains. Yet these forces sculpted an environment that is among the most diverse and productive in the world. The Middle Niger is a vast alluvial garden abutting the bleak Sahara.

The social ecology of this alluvial garden is one, preeminently, of accommodation. This human landscape might be expected to have been a minefield of ethnic mistrust and aggression. Indeed, as the desperate conditions of the eighteenth and nineteenth centuries sadly demonstrated, that potential for conflict was always there. Yet, for millennia, ethnic accommodation nourished the creative tensions and productive genius of the Middle Niger peoples. That genius produced some of sub-Saharan Africa's most spectacular prehistoric and historic achievements. Black Africa's earliest cities sprang from that source of innovative tension.

For early urbanism on a vast (170,000 km^2) arid-lands floodplain, one is tempted to evoke Mesopotamian models. Yet the peoples of the Middle Niger long resisted the rigid, oppressive social ranking and wealth inequalities that dominate our traditional view of the Mesopotamian social landscape. Equally, they avoided the monopolizing, despotic power tendencies of Sumerian or Babylonian statecraft.

This book is about deep-time resistance to monopolized, coercive power. It is, equally, about deep-time sources of successful

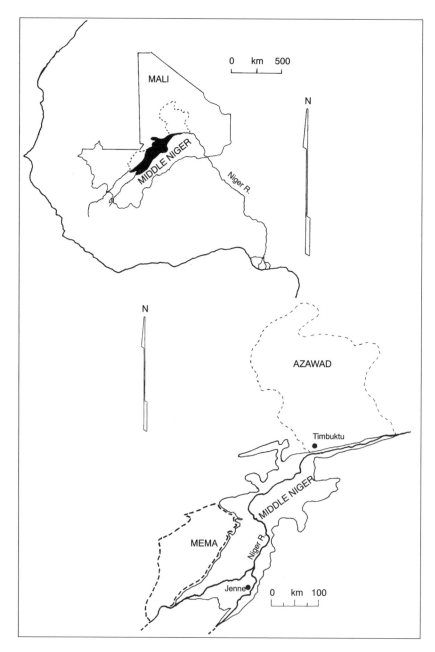

Map 0.1 *The Middle Niger*

social plurality. The two themes have, of course, danced together intimately over the millennia.

Most peoples of the Middle Niger divide themselves into ten major ethnic groups. Among these, the Bambara (Bamana), Songhai, and Fulani rank among West Africa's most populous. Others sort themselves into many smaller groups. Some of these are specialized by occupation (such as the Somono deep-channel fishers). Others, still, are the artifacts of the political and religious turmoil of the last few centuries. Among the last are the Rimaïbe, former clients of the Fulani. Within all this diversity is the unavoidable conclusion of an ancient and still-vigourous tolerance for the other in our midst. The great prehistoric and historic innovations of the people of the Middle Niger came about because they invented deep values of accommodation. These were the values underlying working rules of creative synergy that served them well through millennia of climatic and economic change.

This is a book about environmental responses and economic adaptation. It is also, and equally, about values of ethnic accommodation and repugnance for control hierarchies. That is, it touches upon prehistoric motivations. Ancient intentionality is, of course, impossible to dig out of the ground. Such motivations can only imperfectly be understood from the late-appearing, highly politically-edited, class-biased written traditional histories and Arab chronicles. Yet, one can speak of a landscape of ancient beliefs and, especially, profound notions of authority. Such a landscape of beliefs runs parallel to the physical, political, and social landscapes occupied by any peoples. It is in the historical transformations of the latter that we find proxy evidence for the world of beliefs. It is a core proposition of this book that a certain constellation of symbolic and ideological rules persisted from very deep time. To be sure, this was persistence with creative adaptation to changing circumstance.

As for creative adaptation: we must appreciate the deep-time values if we are to understand the trajectory of change in these peoples' histories. Indeed, it is a central thesis of this book that one must explore these deep-time values if one is to understand the precociousness of the region's political, social, and economic achievements.

Those achievements are among the most exciting of world prehistory and history. Indeed, the peoples of the Middle Niger take the stand as some of the most persuasive expert witnesses for the proposition that scholars have seriously sold short global history.

Can we really appreciate the true genius of past peoples by concentrating our efforts on the prehistory of a few, privileged parts of the globe? Do the achievements of the Near East, Europe, the Yucatan peninsula, and Andean South America sufficiently encompass the creative genius of all the world's peoples?

At issue is the implicit assertion of many scholars that the really key processes of the past all took place first elsewhere (especially the Near East and Europe). In this view, there were only a limited number of possible courses that led to the beginnings of agriculture, urbanism, commerce and industry, social stratification, and the appearance of complex forms of political organization. These courses were pioneered and trailmarked by a relatively few core cultures.

Has the use by archaeologists and historians of traditional categories of analysis, traditional interpretive models and research agendas restricted our ability to reconstruct the past of most of the globe's peoples? Or can the study of truly original theatres of past processes and adaptations, such as the Middle Niger, help us to transcend entrenched traditional interpretations?

The achievements of the peoples of the Middle Niger show, unambiguously, that the experience of world prehistory is much more diverse (and exciting) than the traditional map of progress in prehistory would allow. There are those who would, still, defend the marginalization of African archaeology. Now they must contend with the originality and indigenous origins of Middle Niger trade, cities, and polities.

Equally, those who would marginalize Africa's later history must now contend with the Middle Niger peoples' original solution to the global (and very modern) conundrum of counterpoised power. Who holds power as society becomes more complex? How is authority redeployed as scales of interactions magnify? What is to keep the few from lording coercive power over the many? The oral traditions and foundation legends of the Middle Niger reveal ancient and stable agencies of local resistance to despotism.

To paraphrase the transcendentalist essayist, Emerson, on genius, great havoc makes the Middle Niger among our originalities. Not only are the early towns of Jenne-jeno, Dia, Akumbu and many more yet to be excavated the earliest so far identified in sub-Saharan Africa, they are also formed from a mold quite distinct from that of, for example, Sumerian *tell* temple-towns or Hellenic Aegean city-states. These cities spread out over a floodplain superficially similar to Sumeria. However, far from servicing a centralized, coercive state, as we would expect from our Mesopotamian model of preindustrial urbanism, they thrived under non-hierarchical, heterogeneous rules of authority and functional pluralism.

In historic times, these traditions of dispersed authority threw up a persistent challenge – the need to invent new forms of governance – to the ruling dynasties of Ghana, Mali, and Songhai. In response, these expansive polities took the truly original form, not of kingdoms or centralized states, but of what the eminent historian, Nehemia Levtzion, now calls "over-kingdoms."

The peoples of the Middle Niger were the wealth of empire contested by these novel polities. Similarly, the famous trans-Saharan gold traffick would be grafted onto riverine trade networks. In the Middle Niger, these networks were perhaps a millennium older. For these and many other reasons, the people of the Middle Niger are a privilege – and also an unusual challenge – to study.

Because of that challenge, I have had to organized this book in a novel manner. The introductory chapter (chapter 1) broaches the continuing themes that bind together, as powerfully five millennia ago as today, the disparate peoples of this physical and demographic mosaic. The most enduring theme is the tendency to heterarchy and resistance to hierarchy. The determinedly small scale of political institutions is not an impulse to chaos. In fact, the people of the Middle Niger have experimented for millennia with values of multiple, small-scale, counterpoised authority analogous to those now promulgated actively by political advocates of Civil Society theory.

There is, among the peoples of the Middle Niger, a constellation of venerable notions of authority and models of causation in the world. These are the core values that persist through many millennia of changing climate and social circumstances. These systems of belief are, ultimately, responsible for the persistence in the history of this region of synoecism, or layered transformations with continuity. It is a region that has had a long and innovative history long before it became the "Island of Gold," the label by which it was known to the outside world for the greater part of the present millennium.

Unfortunately, the constellation of values is exceedingly difficult to describe in a Western vocabulary. For this reason, I have decided upon an experimental narrative style for every odd-numbered chapter following chapter 1. In each of these odd-numbered chapters, I begin with a brief bridge between the archaeological or historical events or circumstances described in the chapter immediately preceding. I attempt, then, to express through historical imagination the style and flavour of the oral traditions, masking performances, and family and hero legends pertaining to the values most illustrative of these epochs of Middle Niger history. Without historical imagination to make quick the motivations of the past, history and archaeology are just the driest dust that blows.

Thus, chapter 3 takes a view from the locale near to the future Timbuktu (northern Middle Niger). The story takes place on a day in 4100 BP. Fisherfolk, plant-growers, and herders find it to their mutual advantage to come together to share a long camp for part of each year. As their terminal stone age way of life undergoes the transformation that will result in precocious specialization, so too must their ability to accommodate others who are quite different. In this, hunters play a special role. Some life is blown into the dry archaeological cadaver of late stone age palaeoclimate, settlement patterns and lifestyle of the preceding chapter 2.

Chapter 5 presents a vignette at a levee near the future Jenne (southern Middle Niger) in the year 300 BC. A hunter arrives. A spirit helper leads him to a lush landscape newly opened for colonization by a six-century long dry episode. Formerly it was a permanent lake or insalubrious swamp. A variety of occult circumstances helps him decide when and where to move his community from an increasingly distressed Sahara margin. Chapter 5, thus, introduces many of the occult beliefs and ancient notions of sacred landscape that will be picked up and elaborated in subsequent historical imagination chapters. This is a landscape that must be navigated by the skilled "Man (or woman) of Crises." Peregrinations across this landscape are supremely dangerous, but are the only way to harvest power. Chapter 7 surveys the same locale in *c.*AD 400. It is the fluorescence of urbanism. In that year, the peace of the heterogeneous community is severely tested. The scene for this crisis is set in the preceding chapter 6 by a settlement pattern analysis of ancient Jenne's satellite mounds and by a reconstruction of the many productions corporations that settled them. Chapter 7 explores the values by which conflicts are resolved. Once resolved, the urban prosperity described in chapter 8 can take hold.

The caravan trade out of Timbuktu (AD 1000) is the backdrop to chapter 9. I use historical imagination to describe the distress of the community after a series of droughts and poor flood years. Those low water conditions prevented the arrival of the grain boats from Jenne. The final historical imagination chapter (chapter 11) finds the great Songhai empire conqueror outside the gates of Jenne in AD 1472. He has been frustrated in his seven-year siege. He must make an accommodation with the same *faaro* water spirit visited by the pioneer hunter in chapter 5.

Historical imagination can be good and instructive fun. However, the meat of this history of the Middle Niger is in the even-numbered archaeological and historical chapters. Chapter 2, "The Dry Basins of the Middle Niger," describes the mosaic of fluvial, lacustrine, and desert landforms of the two dead basins. These two basins (of the six making the Middle Niger) are now so desiccated as to be occupied only by a light dusting of pastoralists. A reconstruction of palaeoclimates (since *c*.20,000 BP) explains the transformation of a landscape once as fertile as the other four river-rich basins are today. How the late stone age peoples adapted to this volatile climate, ultimately founding specialized, but articulated communities, is a tale tied intimately to beliefs of how hunters take control of the dangerous life-forces of their landscape.

Chapter 4 takes us on a brief excursion to the present. The many ethnic groups of today's vital Middle Niger are complemented by a number of craft or artisan corporations. These entities are of primary importance to our story here. They are true corporations in the anthropological sense. They are self-defined groups with a shared history and shared sense of belonging, for whom group property is held in common and who make decisions as units. The Middle Niger corporations are the jealous keepers of well-defined domains of authority – the key to heterarchy in the Middle Niger. The identity of these smiths, leatherworkers, oral historians, etc. cross-cuts ethnicity. Under certain circumstances, a Bambara and a Marka smith will feel greater affinity to one another than to their ethnic brethren. Such counterpoised loyalties are a foundation of heterarchy. The four active-hydrology basins are composites of tightly packed microenvironments. The chapter reviews the, frankly, scanty evidence of origins of each ethnic group and the archaeological reconstruction of when they first entered the live basins.

In chapter 6, I make an attempt to reconstruct the nature of "proto-Mande" society during the first millennium BC. This is a critical period of immigration and mixing of several peoples of northern Mande (from ancestral Soninké stock of the southern Sahara), southern Mande (who claim their origins from so-called Old Mande "Heartland"), and now-extinct (?) autochthonous swamp-dwellers. The colonists brought with them recent innovations in iron smelting, agriculture, and pastoralism. The germ of later cities – their trading function and their clustered form – dates to these centuries. Components of clusters may have been occupied separately by different occupation or ethnic groups. The art historical and archaeological evidence from sites such Jenne-jeno (founded *c.*250 BC) suggests a separate, and powerful occult status for blacksmiths.

By the middle of the first millennium AD, large settlements and trade flourished in all four live basins of the Middle Niger (chapter 8). A climatic upturn recharged the environment of least one of the now-senescent basins, the Méma, as well. There, cities and kingdoms burgeon – and then extinguish almost overnight. Long-distance trade expands into the Sahara and far south to the gold-bearing forests. Late in the first millennium AD, funerary monuments (tumuli and megaliths) suggest the dawning of relations of inequality among the peoples and classes of the Middle Niger. This perhaps anticipates the emergence of the secular dynasts who will lead the Mali "over-kingdom" (and its several rivals) to imperial glory.

We explore this imperial tradition of the great savanna polities in chapter 10. The turn of the present millennium is a time of global climatic chaos. It is a time of demographic crisis in the Middle Niger. As Ghana, Mali and Songhi rise, older structures of non-centralized authority are significantly transformed, but never completely decline. Islam intrudes. Eventually, the new religion asserts itself. Onto the older trade networks, with the Middle Niger as their fulcrum, Arabo-Berber merchants graft the trans-Saharan luxury trade. The world now knows the Middle Niger as the Island of Gold.

The book's epilogue begins at 1599. That was the pivotal year of the failed attempted to retake Jenne (and so to kickstart imperial might) by the king of a much enfeebled Mali. Failing to take that southern gateway to the Middle Niger, Mali slips into obscurity. Songhai rule becomes more and more nominal. The Middle Niger sinks into a era of political turmoil. With political chaos comes unwelcome attention from outsiders – desert Tuareg, Bambara from Ségou, Islamic reformers, Tukulor conquerors from the Middle Senegal and, of course, the imperial French. These are sad centuries, true. However, the creative vitality of the Middle Niger peoples continues, unabated, in the face of rapacious invaders and social engineering monstrosities, such as the piety villages of Sékou Amadou's theocracy, or the impressed-labour hamlets of the Office du Niger .

So let us begin where the book ends, with the grand failure of colonial France's attempt to social-engineer heterarchy out of the Middle Niger.

Acknowledgements

My first words of thanks go to the people of Jenne and to various officials and friends in Bamako. The team keeps coming back to the Middle Niger, again and again, because of the steady support of old friends in Jenne – my deepest thanks go to Dani and Yama Traouré, Jaje Traouré, Petit Baba Traouré, Hama Bocoum, all the members of the Amis de Djenné and of "Patrimoine Djenneé," and to the staff of the Mission Culturelle de Djenné. The field research benefited from the dedication and cheerfulness under hard conditions of our excavation and survey crew members at Jenne and at Dia. I would rehire each and every one, no exceptions. They know from the emotional good-byes at the end of every season just how deep is our affection. And, of course, no progress could have been made without the many site supervisors and field specialists, Malian and expatriate, who have worked with us over the years (Sékou Bertie, Mamadou Cissé, Mary Clark, Nafogo Coulibaly, Youssouf Kapapo, Adria LaViolette, Brain McHenry, Charlie McNutt, Michael Petrèn, Paul Sinclair, and Karol Stoker, and various Peace Corps volunteers).

I wish to give particular acknowledgement to two friends who also happen to have joined me as co-directors of the later years of the Middle Niger research – Dr Téréba Togola (now Directeur National des Arts et de la Culture, until recently the head of archaeology at the Institut des Sciences Humaines) and Dr Boubacar Diaby (head of the Mission Culturelle de Djenné).

To the many officials in Bamako, and in the Dia, Jenne, Kayes, and Timbuktu Cercles who have made possible 20 years of survey and excavations at Jenne, Dia, Timbuktu, and the Kolimbiné Valley, my profound thanks. Too many helped in too many ways to mention here, but I would like to mention with gratitude the Director and Assistant Director of the Institut des Sciences Humaines, Drs Kléna Sanogo and Mammadi Dembélé, and the head of the Musée National, Dr Samuel Sidibé. Over the years the research has benefited enormously from the good will and support of American Embassy personnel, and in particular from the personal interest of several outstanding Ambassadors, heads of Peace Corps – Mali, and the heads of the USIS bureau.

I am pleased to acknowledge with gratitude and personal affection the continuing interest in the specific research at Jenne-jeno (where he joined us for the beginning of the 1977 season) of the archaeologist-President of Mali, Dr. Alpha Oumar Konaré, and of the distinguished historian, his wife, Dr. Adam Ba Konaré. Mali is indeed fortunate to have these visionaries at the helm.

This book is the product of conversations, specific and general, and of critiques of early draft sections by my many generous African and africanist colleagues. I mention here those who have most influenced the evolution of my ideas, with apologies to those whom I may have inexcusably neglected to list: R. Bedaux, D. Benjamin, G. Brooks, D. Conrad, C. Crumley, J. Devisse, B. Frank, S. Haidera, J. Hunwick, T. Insoll, P. Jacobberger, D. Konate, S. Kostof, N. Levtzion, M. Maas, K. MacDonald, A. McDougall, P. McNaughton, R. Mauny, P. Munson, N. Petit-Maire, M. Raimbault, B. Riley, R. Roberts, D. Robinson, A. Schmidt, P. Shipton, G. Tappen, J. D. van der Waals, R. Vernet, and J. Webb.

My deepest thanks go to my wife, Susan Keech McIntosh. This book is really a tribute to her synthetic mind and to her hard-headed command of the masses of prehistoric data coming out of the Middle Niger and the subcontinent generally. To her we owe entirely the comparative ceramic sequence and phase chronology of the various regions of the Middle Niger, those archaeological anchors for all levels of interpretation. In this book, the placement of the Middle Niger within broader cultural developments derive from her 15 years of cumulative syntheses of West African prehistory, covering the vast span of time from the late stone age through the early historical centuries. Much of the discussion in this book about alternatives to chiefs and states and to a way of looking at the historical trajectory of complex society that would place centralization as inevitable reflects her own ideas on these issues. And, of course, she rediscovered the Middle Niger as the Island of Gold in an historian's *coup fr force*.

As the reader sill soon see in the pages that follow, without her synthetic genius, this book would be only a hollow shell.

Timeline

Before Present (BP) dates (approximate)

8500 BP	Azawad fully recovered from late Pleistocene hyperaridity
7500 BP	Human colonization of the Azawad
7000–6000 BP	Cattle pastoralism appears
6500–5500 BP	Fullest Azawad occupation (Beginnings of specialist communities?)
5000 BP	(Initial plant domestication in the southern Sahara?)
4500 BP	End of pluvial conditions in dry basins Colonization of the Méma (from Hodh, Azawad?)
4100 BP:	**Chapter 3: Clustered Specialists**
4000 BP	Tichitt sequence begins Azawad progressively abandoned
3500 BP	Possible articulated specialist "pro-clusters" in the Méma Specialist production (axes, blades, beads) at Saharan localities near the northern Middle Niger (Lagreich; Ilouk)
3000–2700 BP	Appearance of iron smelting
2900–2600	Douentza tumuli
2500 BP	Méma environmental and demographic stress (beginning of depopulation?)

| | (Early penetration of the Macina and Upper Delta?) |
| 2300 BP | Foundation of large Méma clusters – Akumbu and Boundou Boubou |

Before Christ (BC) Dates / Anno Domini (AD) Dates

300 BC	**Chapter 5: Hunter Scouts of the Upper Delta**
300 BC	Foundation of Jenne-jeno (Upper Delta) and Dia (Macina)
AD 300	Demographic explosion in the four live basins
AD 400	**Chapter 7: The Corporate Life of Smiths**
AD 5th century	"Island of Gold" exchange relations with greater West Africa (Bambouk gold production?) Intensive clustering at Upper Delta and Macina cities Founding of large Niger Bend settlements (e.g., Timbuktu?)
AD 7th century	(Appearance of first tumuli/megaliths in Lakes Region?)
AD 690	Traditional date for foundation of Gao (Songhai capital)
AD 8th century	Occupation specialists in recognizable ("casted") form
*c.*AD 850	Rural abandonment begins in Dia hinterland Population maximum at Jenne-jeno and its hinterland (Ghana Empire hegemony over Méma and Lakes Region?)
AD 10th century	Early in-migration of Fulani pastoralists Beginning of abandonment of Lakes Region sites (Buré gold production?)
AD 1000	**Chapter 9: Timbuktu Shipping**
AD 1055	Almoravids wrest Awdaghost (Tegdaoust) from Ghana

AD 1076	Almoravids temporarily overwhelm capital of Ghana
AD 1100	Beginning of demographic decline in Macina and Upper Delta
AD 11–12th centuries	Beginning of contraction of Jenne-jeno's hinterland
	El-Oualadji constructed
	Prolonged droughts at Saharan entrepôt (e.g., Tegdaoust)
AD 13th century	Early in-migration of Bambara
	Méma an independent kingdom under *Tunkara*
	Abandonment of many large Méma settlement clusters
AD 1240	Battle of Krina – founding of the Mali Empire
AD 14th century	Creation of the Somono
AD 1320s	Mali Empire at maximum extent
AD 1370–1400	New waves of Fulani pastoralists
AD 1400	Jenne-jeno abandoned by this date
AD 1433	Tuareg hegemony over Timbuktu (Mali weakening)
AD 1464	Sonni Ali Ber begins Songhai expansion
AD 1468	Sonni Ali Ber conquers Timbuktu
AD 1472	End of Songhai siege of Jenne

| AD 1472 | **Chapter 11: Sonni Ali Ber and the *Faaro*** |

AD 1528–29	Askiya Mohammed deposed; end of Songhai expansion
AD 1591	Battle of Tondibi: Moroccan invasion
AD 1599 (April)	Mali fails to retake Jenne; end of the Mali Empire
AD 1670	Biton Coulibali (Ségou) pushes into Upper Delta and Macina
AD 1700	Bambara are a significant presence in Erg of Bara
AD 1712	Ségou Kingdom takes the southern Middle Niger
AD 1760	United Tuareg clans ravage the northern Middle Niger
AD 1787	Early phase of serial siege of Timbuktu by Tuareg
AD 1818	Sékou Amadou founds his theocratic state, the *Dina*

AD 1828	Middle Niger visited by Rene Caillié
AD 1862	El Hadj Umar's Tukulor invade Middle Niger
	End of Dina
AD 1866	Jenne falls to the Umarian state
AD 1893 (April)	Archinard takes Jenne
	Tukulor state collapses
AD 1894 (June)	Joffre takes Timbuktu
AD 1910s	Office du Niger conceived
AD 1932	Office du Niger incorporated
AD 1947	Markala barrages completed
AD 1958	République Soudanaise
AD 1960	République du Mali
AD 1968–(85?)	Sahel Drought
AD 1991	Democracy in Mali

1

The Island of Gold

Sad Tale of the Office du Niger

The central themes of this book have persisted as layers of transformations. Only a deep-time, millennia-scale assessment of these themes allows us to understand who the peoples of the Middle Niger are today. The Middle Niger is the great interior floodplain of the River Niger. Just as today the roughly 55,000 km² annually inundated flood-lands (the so-called "live delta") are an ecological lure to a great diversity of peoples, in the distant past the allure of a swamp and lake-land covering easily three times the area was no less. We pick up this book's central themes at least 5,000 years ago. And they are just as vigourous today. Today we celebrate the economic and social revival that has followed in the democratic wake of the 1991 popular overthrow of the 23-year despotic statism of the Moussa Traoré regime and the second round of democratic elections in 1997. For a good example of the continuing vitality of these themes, let us step back (a wee step in the scope of this book) to the early decades of the twentieth century. This excursion into recent history allows us to see how the deep-time realities of the Middle Niger hydrology and environment and, most especially, the values of its diverse peoples contributed to the spectacular failure of a huge French colonial development scheme.

During the first half of the twentieth century, colonial France devoted vast resources – corvée recruitment, private and state investment, and metropolitan prestige— to the Office du Niger irrigation scheme. The military penetration of the Middle Niger took place in the 1890s. Soon afterwards, engineers signaled the potential for moveable mechanical dam (barrage) and irrigation

Map 1.1   *The Office du Niger in the Middle Niger*

technology to bring many hectares of the hydrologically senescent southwestern Middle Niger into homogenized, monocrop agriculture. This is the southwestern sector of the great "dead delta," the Méma, that will play such a large role in the channeling of Saharan peoples into the hydrologically active parts of the Middle Niger at the time of the late stone age desiccation of the Sahara.

The Office du Niger scheme began modestly in the 1910s with studies focused on the potential for large-scale cotton production. The aim was to protect the French textile industry from the vagaries of American cotton imports. By the next decade, the project had become a colonial administration within itself, driven by the egoism of its chief architect and promoter. This guiding light was Monsieur l'Engineur Emile Bélime, superciliously christened "maître africain de l'eau" – "Bélime, African master of the waters"![1] African? Scarcely. He was scarcely even master of his own megalomania: by the late 1920s, Bélime dreamed of some 1,850,000 hectares irrigated by the great barrages of the Sansanding region (including Markala and Sotuba). The labor for his vast project was to be provided by between one and 3.5 million relocated peasants. Bélime's was a dream of masses toiling over fields planted, in roughly equal measure, in cotton, vegetables, and high-yield Asian rice.[2] Asian rice, *Oryza sativa*, is far less tolerant of climatic variability than the locally valued and locally domesticated *Oryza glaberrima* . This wished-for granary of the French Soudan was to be linked to the Mediterranean ports by a trans-Saharan railway some 3,270 kilometres long. For commercial interests in France, the investment potential was staggering.

Most analyses of the Office du Niger debacle concentrate on the press-gang conscription of the second portion of the colony's annual military contingent. Diverted for labor under conditions of extreme deprivation, the second portion became a lodestone for hatred of colonial rule. Published studies look at the dictatorial administration and at the near-universal resistance of tens of thousands of villagers relocated by forced marches to Bélime's reengineered efficiency villages within the project.[3] Equally

---

[1] Quoted in Denis Escudier, "Qui avait intérêt à créer l'Office du Niger?," *Afrique Histoire*, 9 (1985), p. 35.

[2] Commissariat de l'Afrique Occidentale Française, *L'Aménagement Hydraulique et la Mise en Valeur de la Vallée Moyenne du Niger*. Document for the 1931 Exposition Coloniale Internationale de Paris, (Commissariat de l'Afrique Occidentale Française, Paris, 1931); Amido Magasa. *Papa-Commandant à Jeté un Grand Filet Devant Nous. Les Exploités des Rives du Niger 1902–1962*, (François Maspero: Paris, 1978); A. T. Grove, *The Niger and its Neighbours*, (A. A. Balkema: Rotterdam, 1985), pp. 162–3, 196–7, and Figure 69.

[3] Myron Echenberg and Jean Filipovich, "African military labour and the building of the Office du Niger installations, 1925–1950," *Journal of African History*, 27 (1986), pp. 533–51; Pierre Herbart, *Le Chancre du Niger* (Gallimard: Paris, 1939); Magasa, *Papa-Commandant à Jeté* .

important to the themes of this book is the fact that expensive, areally extensive technologies (mechanized irrigation and production, monocropping in vast fields) applied to crops with low-tolerance of variability in rainfall, flood, and, local pests is a strategy of Western efficiency particularly unsuited to the landform and climatic diversity and inherent unpredictability of the Middle Niger.

That very diversity and unpredictability had, in fact, been quite satisfactorily dealt with by the indigenous peoples for millennia by an alternative strategy of diversity, or compartmental tasks within a generalized strategy. But the focus of the venerable sustainability strategy that made the Middle Niger the true granary of precolonial West Africa was the local village despised of Bélime. Monsieur l'Engineur wrote "Nous devons nous décider à désintégrer cette cellule économique stérile qu'est le village indigène" – (We must be steadfast in our resolve to break up that sterile economic cell that is the indigenous village).[4]

And what was the legacy of this way of thinking? By 1948, two massively costly dams could manage the irrigation only of 20,460 hectares worked by 22,850 demoralized and disease-ridden people. Far from the one or more millions of contented, high-productivity peasants once envisioned, by 1962 only some 42,000 highly taxed sharecroppers remained at the Office du Niger. Because of the destruction of villages of origin and the brutality of relocation, these mixtures of Bamana (or Bambara), Marka, Mossi, and others now are considered by other Malians to be a separate ethnic group. Today they are invested with a new ethnic name – the *toubabou diongwou*, "the captives of the Whites."[5]

The colonial power was quite correct about the potential richness of the Middle Niger. It was, however, dead wrong about how to proceed. The Office du Niger was so vigourously resisted and failed utterly to conquer the landscape because of ignorance of managed diversity and the historical inappropriateness of despotism. In this book, I try to show that millennia of experience with a productive but unpredictable landscape reinforce a well of deep-time values that nurture articulated diversity and that underlay resistance to concentrated power.

The sad tale of the Office du Niger illustrates most of the themes that have persisted over many millennia. First, the Middle Niger

---

[4] Quoted in Escudier, "Qui avait intérêt," p. 36.
[5] Ibid, p. 36; Magasa, *Papa-Commandant à Jeté* , pp. 83–97.

is a land of great productive potential. Yet, its highly changeable, highly variable climate and the tight packing of very different landforms and soil groups have demanded exploitation by articulated, but highly independent corporate groups. The ability of these componential corporate groups to massage the diversity of the physical environment is a theme, obviously, of great importance to any debates about sustainable development of the Middle Niger.

Second, ethnicity is an inescapable fact of life along the Middle Niger. Yet, (as we have seen with the construction of the *toubabou diongwou*) corporate identity is contingent and highly flexible.

Third, the glue of the Middle Niger ethnic mosaic is a shared (or better, differentially participated in) corpus of deep-time values, a symbolic reservoir of beliefs and canons of authority. Elements of this symbolic reservoir have undergone layers of transformation since late stone age times. But certain values do persist, and they are the key to peaceful and appropriate behavior between different groups.

It cannot be stressed too much that the concept of a symbolic reservoir, as used in this book, should not call up echoes collective archetypes or unchanging, unconscious, hard-wired mental structures. Mande scholars, be they historians, anthrapologists, or art historians, feel increasingly comfortable with the idea of reservoirs of symbols and ideologies that provide a persistent, often centuries-long trajectory to social action and culture change. The emphasis is upon change and upon the processes by which interacting (and competing) components of a highly heterogeneous society appropriate authority and reinvent beliefs about the historical framework of their present condition. Symbols are the currency of negotiations about meaning. Symbols are a community's metaphors that serve as calls to action in a changing world. And the reservoir image is particularly apt for the Middle Niger where, for millenia, beliefs and peoples have passed in and out of the highly permeable membranes between neighboring cultures.

And fourth, these key values allow us to understand why, from the earliest moments for which we possess archaeological evidence, the Middle Niger was, preeminently, a landscape of social and political heterarchy. One of the most persistent values is resistance to vertical power hierarchies. The arrogance of coercion has had a very uncertain history here. Let us look first to the principle of heterarchy.

The Original Civil Society: Heterarchy versus Hierarchy

With the end of the Cold War, a vast speculative literature has sprung up around the question of Africa's political future. At this critical transform in global relations among nations, is it an inevitability that Africa will continue down the path of absolutist states? Must Africa conform to the model of rigid bureaucratic statism imported from the metropolitan nations (especially France) and refined into the coercive, one-party socialism of the 1960s through 1980s? Or, as some now argue, can all citizens of African nations achieve a form of self-determination by local forms of Civil Society? The ideal of the Civil Society encourages the local evolution of pluralistic complexes, many competing interests in society that, together, challenge the power-seeking impulses of the state.[6]

The debate about Civil Society in Africa too often mires in an economic reductionist retreat into Marxist–Capitalist rhetoric.[7] Some, indeed, are so attached to the traditional nation state that they assert that the avatar of political and social anarchy has already descended upon the continent. For them, Africa is harbinger of post-Cold War global chaos.[8] Not all, happily, are so pessimistic. Opposed is a new breed of pluralists who argue that, while the

---

[6] Edward A. Alpers, "Africa reconfigured: Presidential Address," *African Studies Review* , 38(2) (1995), pp. 5–7; Robert Fatton, Jr, "Africa in the age of democratization: The civic limitations of Civil Society," *African Studies Review*, 38(2) (1995), pp. 67–99; John Keane, Introduction and "Despotism and democracy; The origins and development of the distinction between Civil Society and the state, 1750–1850," in *Civil Society and the State; New European Perspectives*, John Keane ed., (Verso: London, 1988), pp. 1–32; Irving Leonard Markovitz, "An uncivil and critical view of Civil Society in Africa with some considerations of the formation of new social structures in Senegal." Paper presented at the conference on Civil Society in Africa. Truman Institute, The Hebrew University of Jerusalem, January 1993; and "Constitutions, Civil Society, and the *Federalist Papers*." Paper presented at the symposium "On the Making of the New Ethiopian Constitution," Inter-Africa Group, Addis Ababa, May 1993; Donald Rithchild and Naomi Chazan (eds), *The Precarious Balance. State and Society in Africa,* (Westview: Boulder, CO, 1988).

[7] See Ellen Meiksin Wood, "The uses and abuses of Civil Society," in *The Socialist Register, 1990*, Ralph Milinand (ed.) (Monthly Review Press: New York, NY, 1991), pp. 60–84.

[8] Robert D. Kaplan, "The coming anarchy," *The Atlantic Monthly* 273 (2) (1994), pp. 44–76 and *The Ends of the Earth: A Journey at the Dawn of the 21st Century*. (Random House: New York, 1996).

nation state has the undeniable absolutist tendency to squeeze the independence of autonomous elements of society, Africa has a demonstrated talent for giving birth to a multitude of local-interest agencies. Most of these are not economic in origin. Local interest may be vested in kin groups, territorial units, voluntary or craft "sodalities," age-groups, occupation corporations, religious sects, or even in individuals invoking older or reinvented sources of power such as witchcraft or other, less freighted forms of occult authority. Fear of state terrorism or a loathing of state regulation can be a powerful goad to decentralization.

The local details of these autonomous, overlapping, and competing interests will emerge from the history of each particular situation. On the plane of general theory, however, we should concentrate on processes of pluralism and integration. Together, these overlapping and competing interests form a political landscape of factions, multiple lines of authority that can effectively resist the state. Civil Society celebrates decentralization. Civil Society celebrates the creative tensions and strength that arise out of the interconnectedness of networks of overlapping, articulated authority. Factions resist the tendency to elaborate vertical power control (hierarchy) of the state. Factions control the tendency to aggregation of other factions. Resistance and the strength of the horizontal web of authority derives not from independence, but from the interconnectedness of the segments, each autonomous in their appropriate spheres (heterarchy).

Many believe that the establishment of Civil Society is an obligatory condition for the promulgation of full human rights in Africa.[9] This belief makes the search for precolonial antecedents more than merely academic.

The Civil Society debate is vigorous, but is rather conducted in a deep-historical vacuum. Proponents of Civil Society in Africa would be heartened if they knew more about long historical trajectories. The archaeology and earliest history of many parts of the continent, and of the Middle Niger most especially, show unambiguously that Africa has long lived its own versions of Civil Society.

The evolution of early polities and the rise of precocious urbanism

---

[9] Ronald Cohen, "Endless teardrops: Prolegomena to the study of human rights in Africa," in *Human Rights and Governance in Africa*, Ronald Cohen, Goran Hyden, and Winston R. Nagan (ed.) (University Press of Florida: Gainesville, 1993), pp. 29–32.

in the Middle Niger has become the focus of alternative thinking about the emergence of complex society in Africa.[10] The focus of much of this book will be upon the emergence of large-scale, complex entities – cities and territorial polities – in which the horizontal integration of multiple small-scale agencies of authority is emphasized at the expense of mechanisms of coercive, vertical power.

There are, then, two important questions for continuing interpretation as we look at historical trajectories of dispersed authority: what historical processes encourage plural, overlapping agencies of decision-making, identity-formation, or mobilization of social action (as opposed to homogenizing control-hierarchies of classic state formation theory)? And what provides the integrative glue to compartmentalized authority?

The dominating themes of social and political organization in the Middle Niger are of authority distributed widely among many agencies. These are cross-cutting associations exercising ritual and secular authority. Such agencies become the focus for effective resistance to centralization by elites seeking to impose rigid social stratification and exclusive (despotic) political leadership. The Middle Niger example, however, is just one of many around the continent. Africa is, in a very real sense, in the vanguard of a larger, if belated, acknowledgment by archaeologists and historians that heterarchy as a model of social and political organization is at least as effective as hierarchy in dealing with problems of decision-making and information distribution.

Hierarchy is undeniably a fine way to concentrate decision-making in the hands of a few. Those privileged few can then implement their decisions with dispatch through the agency of the centralized bureaucracy. But is a hierarchy always the best means to deal with complex issues? Did our classic High Civilizations always provide the most expeditious, most appropriate response to climatic change (where gradual or cumulative changes lead up to threshold effects) or to the highly complex interactions of fluid, multi-ethnic mosaics or massive in-migration situations?

Hierarchies can, in fact, be notoriously slow to recognize the need for change and to make decisions. Slow to decide, quick to implement. The very privileges of the elites' exalted position in

---

[10] Esp., Susan Keech McIntosh (ed.), *Excavations at Jenné-jeno, Hambarketolo, and Kaniana, Inland Niger Delta, Mali. The 1981 Season*, (University of California Press: Berkeley, 1995), pp. 360–98; and McIntosh (ed.) *Pathways to Complexity: An African Perspective* (Cambridge: Cambridge University Press, 1998).

society can, in fact, be a powerful brake to responsive change. Hence, there is a nascent literature about the flexibility inherent in heterarchies. This is the flexibility of response to rapid change in environment or to population movement or to scale changes of regional political integration.[11] Flexibility, or "a society's capacity for revitalizing its organization and developing coping strategies"[12] is just one advantage.

Complexity, or the integration of multiple and diverse components can actually be enhanced. Heterarchy can be the cradle, the nurturing field for multiple self-organizing systems that each counterpoise and check the power of the others. With the right "contract" for peaceful access to services, specialization can be encouraged within a "generalized economy"[13] – encouraging precisely the strength through interconnectedness within a horizontally elaborating system advocated by the champions of Civil Society. Boundaries of appropriate spheres of authority must be well-defined and respected. The competition linking overlapping spheres must be channeled or massaged (not checked) by tradition and by canons of good will. If these integrative conditions are met, local institutions of sub-group representation and decision-making such as craft corporations, kinship groups, and territorial groups can actually be strengthened.

The Middle Niger is a case-study in these processes. Here, heterarchy worked as a stable alternative to hierarchy when Middle Niger cities such as Dia or Jenne-jeno emerged and thrived independent of the stimulus of the Arab or Mediterranean worlds. Heterarchy bound together the diverse corporate groups at Jenne-

---

[11] Heterarchy is defined by Carole Crumley as "the relations of elements [of complex society] to one another when they are unranked or when they possess the potential of being ranked in a number of different ways." See "Heterarchy and the analysis of complex society," in *Heterarchy ande the Anaysis of Complex Societes*, Robert Ehrenreich, Carole Crumley, and Janet Levy (eds.) (American Anthropological Association, Washington, DC, 1995), p. 3; see also Steve Barnett, "Futures; Probable and plausible," *Anthropology Newsletter* 37(7) (1994), p. 52; Carole L. Crumley, (ed.), *Historical Ecology. Cultural Knowledge and Changing Landscapes,* (School of American Research: Santa Fe, NM, 1994); Fekri Hassan, "Population ecology and civilization in ancient Egypt," in Crumley, *Historical Ecology* , pp. 155–181.
[12] Hassan, 'Population ecology', p. 159.
[13] Roderick J. McIntosh, "The Pulse Model. Genesis and accommodation of specialization in the Middle Niger," *Journal of African History* 34(2) (1993), pp. 181–220.

jeno (ethnic groups, subsistence producers, artisans, and merchants). Such ties encouraged the expansion of specialization from the 250 BC foundation of the town to its abandonment in *c.*AD 1400. Heterarchy accommodated a substantial population in the tens of thousands.[14] Heterarchy provided a viable means of social integration that allowed settlement pattern to shift from a landscape of dispersed (or seasonally attracted) producer hamlets of the last millennia before the Present Era to the clustered urbanism of the Middle Niger. And most importantly for the enterprise of cross-cultural comparisons, heterarchy allows us to recognize and appreciate far more dimensions and forms of variability in organizational complexity than did our prior obsession with centralized, hierarchically organized chiefdoms and states.

The Middle Niger's deep past forces us to recognize that courses to complex society were far more varied than we had imagined even twenty years ago. Africa's urban and social complexity experience can no longer be relegated to peripheral status merely because it does not replicate, or lags chronologically behind, the "universal" processes we thought we understood from the Near East. The Middle Niger shows clearly that those old interpretive traditions that emphasized hierarchy and coercive concentration of power in the hands of an increasingly remote elite simply cannot do justice to the real complexity of the human experience.[15]

Synoecism and Layered Transformations

This book deals directly with the charge that our traditional models for the rise of cities, states, and stratified society do not ad-

---

[14] Roderick J. McIntosh and Susan Keech McIntosh, "A la recherche du diagramme fondateur de la Djenné préhistorique," in *Djenné. Une Ville Millénaire au Mali*, R. M. A. Bedaux and J. D. van der Waals (eds.) (Rijksmuseum voor Volkenkunde: Leiden, 1994), pp. 54–63 ; Susan Keech McIntosh and Roderick J. McIntosh, "Cities without citadels: Understanding urban origins along the Middle Niger," In *The Archaeology of Africa; Foods, metals and towns*, Thurstan Shaw, Paul Sinclair, Bassi Andah, and A. Okpoko (eds) (Routledge: London, 1993), pp. 662–41.

[15] Roderick J. McIntosh, Susan Keech McIntosh and Téréba Togola, "Archaeology of the 'Peoples Without History,' " *Archaeology* 42 (1) (1989), pp. 74–80, 107.; Roderick J. McIntosh, "Early urban clusters in China and Africa; The arbitration of social ambiguity," *Journal of Field Archaeology*, 18 (1991), pp. 199–212.

equately encompass the true diversity of these processes in the past. Has our reliance upon the better researched record from the Near East and Europe really enabled us to appreciate the full ingeniousness of past peoples of the world?[16] Many historians and archaeologists are heavily invested in the values of (stadial) progress and competition that underlay the traditional models. To them, this book's themes of heterarchy and alternative courses to urbanism, production, and the complexification of society might be terribly threatening. We can anticipate concentrated resistance from the Neo-Evolutionists and from scholars taking a strict construction of historicity.

To the Neo-Evolutionists, it makes little tactical sense to devote archaeological field resources or historians' efforts to a "marginal" part of the globe, such as the Middle Niger. The really important processes of the past are better known elsewhere. Its proponents advance neo-evolutionism as the global paradigm for progressive changes in society from small-scale egalitarian hunting-gathering communities to the urban state. Its most vocal apologists insist upon a step-wise (stadial) progression of band, chiefdom, and state (to use the simplest step-wise scheme). Progress is driven by a "primary motor" of population growth under economic constraints.[17] Population growth leads to subsistence intensification. The resulting production risks and competition lead to larger scales of economic and political integration and to ever elaborating social stratification.

In this view, known levels of population density correspond to predictable stages of new technological innovations (production intensification) and political economy. Happily or unhappily, the Middle Niger is just one of many instances around the globe in which the predictions do not appear to hold out. However large or dense the population of the vast alluvium, the peoples of the Middle Niger remained studiously indifferent to new methods of subsistence intensification. (This contrasts markedly to their record of

[16] R. McIntosh, et al. 'Peoples Without History', pp. 76–7, 80.

[17] Allen W. Johnson and Timothy Earle, *The Evolution of Human Societies. From Foraging Group to Agrarian State*, (Stanford University Press: Stanford, 1987); Timothy Earle, "The evolution of chiefdoms," in *Chiefdoms: Power, Economy and Ideology*, Timothy Earle (ed.,) (Cambridge University Press, Cambridge, 1991), pp. 1–15; critiqued in Bruce G. Trigger, *A History of Archaeological Thought*, (Cambridge University Press: Cambridge, 1989), pp. 289–303. See Stephen K. Sanderson, *Social Evolutionism* (Blackwell: Oxford, 1993).

artisan and manufacturing innovations.) Nowhere do we find the mechanized irrigation or large fields worked by corvée labor known from other Old World arid-lands floodplains. Applied to the high productivity rice systems of the Middle Niger's Upper Delta, traditional practices can either be considered primitive and archaic (characterized by one archaeobotanist as "essentially unchanged from the earliest period of rice exploitation"[18]). Or, these practices can be considered to be a remarkably sophisticated, if determinedly small-scale response to a high-risk situation. Such sophistication can have developed only after a long period of experimentation.[19] The former opinion has just a hint of Monsieur l'Engineur Bélime to it.

The Middle Niger confronts the Neo-Evolutionists' predictions in a second, spectacular way. Since the 1970s, archaeology demonstrates the early (and indigenous) appearance of true towns, large populations, long-distance trade and production specialization. However, the elites, coercive state apparatuses, and celebration of monumentality develop only hesitantly, at the very end of a long process of alternative social complexity. The componential communities of the late stone age and their descendants, the populous but clustered cities of the floodplain fly in the face of such predictions.

These cities are the settlement expression of the heterarchies of the Middle Niger political landscape. Heterarchies, likewise, are more the product of accommodation and pluralist cooperation, rather than of social Darwinist competition. It is a fundamental thesis of this book that such accommodation and pluralist cooperation would not have been so stable, nor so successful, had there not been an enduring concept of authority that made horizontal complexity possible. Deep-time notions of authority underwent multiple layered transformation, to be sure. Layered transformation – of authority, of symbols, of ideology, and of the material world – is this book's meta-narrative, the deep storyline embedded in the narrative of all aspects of the social history of

[18] David R. Harris, "Traditional systems of plant food production and the origins of agriculture in West Africa," in *Origins of African Plant Domestication*, Jack R. Harlan, Jan M. J. de Wet and Anmn B. L. Stemler (eds) (Mouton: The Hague, 1976), p. 342.

[19] Roderick J. McIntosh and Susan Keech McIntosh, "Early Iron Age economy in the Inland Niger Delta (Mali)," in *From Hunters to Farmers. The Causes and Consequences of Food Production in Africa*, J. Desmond Clark and Steven A Brandt (eds), (University of California Press: Berkeley, 1984), p. 159.

the Middle Niger. Layered transformation will be the substitute for the progress and competition meta-narratives of neo-evolutionism.

Yet, we can anticipate that this interest in deep-time transformations of the symbolic and ideological world will spark a second line of resistance. The very theme is abhorrent to those committed to a strict construction of historicity. Historicity: what sources can allow authentic interpretation of the world of social and political organization and, especially, the world of beliefs, beyond the so-called ethnographic present? Historians with the recorded thoughts and reflections of the ancients can do it. First, of course, they must become critics of the social history of literacy. Can the same be done by interpreters of oral traditions? How much now extinct cognition can be tickled out from the dry dirt, stone, and potsherds of archaeology? Therein lies a enormous debate between archaeologists and some scholars, such as Herzfild[20] who dismisses any interest in the deep time as, at best, a search for "survivals" or "archaisms." The debate also goes on among prehistorians themselves.

This book joins a long tradition of Africanist revolt against small-minded atemporalism. Jan Vansina[21] has made perhaps the most vigorous methodological parry against those who would dismiss this as the search for "social fossils," or for the indefensible "pristine." Vansina's approach is broadly comparative. He reconstructs millennia-long traditions of political thought in equatorial Africa – and the language and institutions thereof – for an "ethnographic baseline" of *c.*AD 1900. From that departure point, he judiciously works back to an "ethnographic proto-baseline" of *c.*2000 BC.[22]

I find Vansina's methodology and operating assumptions convincing. But, then again, I have been immersed for many years in a similar exercise in the equally extensive Mande country of West Africa. Here, the effort is to expand, but also go beyond functionalists' explanations of adaptive strategies, by looking at decision-

[20] Michael Herzfild, *Anthropology Through the Looking-Glass. Critical Ethnography in the Margins of Europe*, (Cambridge University Press: Cambridge, 1987), esp. 8–11, 73–5.

[21] Jan Vansina, "Deep-down time: Political tradition in Central Africa," *History in Africa* 16 (1989), esp. 356, and *Paths in the Rainforests. Towards a History of Political Tradition in Equatorial Africa*, (University of Wisconsin Press: Madison, 1990).

[22] Vansina, "Deep-down time," pp. 342, 358–60.

making and canons of authority, the community-sanctioned right to make decisions. Decisions must make sense in terms of the deep-time rules. Such rules are the more profound organizing principles that give historical trajectory to cultural models of how the world works and to the evolving social construction of reality.

In this project, archaeologists have their material culture probes into deep time. Archaeologists are, however, partially dependent upon oral tradition and ethnohistorical sources from later times to flesh out that material skeleton. And it is here that the concept of the layered transformation comes into play: as we look well into the past for the instrumental symbols, myths, legends that are the very stuff of these profound cultural models, it becomes evident that we are dealing with a highly dynamic process.

These myths and material symbols are the instruments of legitimation, of invention of tradition, of moves to gather power, and of countermoves to resist hierarchy. Symbols can shift in meaning. They can be recombined or decoupled – but only according to the rules or concepts of authority, propriety, and sacrality that give historical trajectory and general continuity to these processes.

How, then, to investigate these deep-time layered transformations to the trajectories of cultural rules? An interesting informal consortium of archaeologists, art historians, and linguists have pioneered, in two very different regions of West Africa, the concept of the symbolic reservoir. Those working in the Mandara region of northern Cameroon and northeast Nigeria[23] deal in the dynamics of a spectacular ethnic mosaic. Among the peoples of the Mandara, this pluridisciplinary group looks at issues of selective permeability of boundaries. How do symbols retain or change meaning as they

---

[23] Marla Berns, "Symbolic reservoirs, sacred ceramics, and linguistic complexity in the Gonola Valley, northeastern Nigeria." Paper presented at the Dynamic Symbolic Reservoirs in Deep Time panel, 1993 annual meeting of the African Studies Association (Boston); Nicolas David, "The archaeology of ideology: Mortuary practices in the Central Mandara Highlands, Northern Cameroon," in *An African Commitment: Papers in Honour of Peter Lewis Shinnie*, Judy Sterner and Nicolas David (eds) (University of Calgary Press: Calgary, 1992), pp. 181–210; Scott MacEarchern, "'Symbolic reservoirs' and inter-group relations: West African examples," *The African Archaeological Review*, 12 (1994): 205–24; Judy Sterner, "Sacred pots and 'symbolic reservoirs' in the Mandara Highlands of Northern Cameroon," in *An African Commitment: Papers in Honour of Peter Lewis Shinnie*, Judy Sterner and Nicolas David (eds) (University of Calgary Press: Calgary, 1992), pp. 171–79.

pass through the porous cultural membrane at frontiers between people? How can we explain the loyalties to a persistent, two-millennia core of values and symbols shared selectively by peoples of very different linguistic, ethnic, and socio-political scales? In Greater Mande, archaeologists and art historians invoke the symbolic reservoir to deal with emerging complex society.[24] Under what circumstances do sub-groups in society dip into a venerable reservoir of beliefs and symbols in order to appropriate validating, legitimating legends and ensignia? What sets the syntax of "corporate discourse" in complex society? How is art constructed as metaphors around which social action crystallizes in a multi-componential community?

This is a particularly important experiment in whether or not archaeologists and art historians can function in the world of ancient symbols and ideologies. The Middle Niger, by the first millennium BC, at very latest, was the cauldron into which two or three distinct symbolic constellations were poured and in which something quite new was brewed. The Middle Niger forms the transition between the northern Soninké sphere and the southern Malinke "heartland". From the Saharan north, the lands of the "ancestral Soninké" communities, came one ideological system (or cluster of related systems). Up from the more wooded savanna at the present Mali–Guinea frontier, came peoples who claim ancestral loyalties to the "old Mande heartland" so celebrated in the later Sunjata traditions of the founding of the Mali empire. And Kevin MacDonald is quite correct to remind us not to forget the autothonous traditions of West Africa.[25] These are the small, mobile communities, the "Red Men" of Bozo and Nono traditions. The autochthons may have claimed the Middle Niger well before the second or first millennia BC. These communities may have been

[24] Roderick J. McIntosh and Susan Keech McIntosh, "Dilettantism and plunder: dimensions of the illicit traffic in ancient Malian art," *UNESCO Museum*, 149 (1986), pp. 52–7; and "Ancient terracottas before the Symplegades gateway," *African Arts*, 22(2) (1989), p. 77; and Roderick J. McIntosh and Susan Keech McIntosh " From *siècles obscurs* to revolutionary centuries on the Middle Niger," *World Archaeology* 20(1) (1998), p. 156; ; Patrick McNaughton, "Things change, but can they stay the same." Paper presented at the Dynamic Symbolic Reservoirs in Deep Time panel, 1993 annual meeting of the African Studies Association, Boston.

[25] Kevin MacDonand, *Socio-Economic Diversity and the Origins of Cultural Complexity along the Middle Niger (2000 B.C. to A.D. 300)*. Dissertation, University of Cambridge, 1994, pp. 37–8, 40, and Chapter VI.

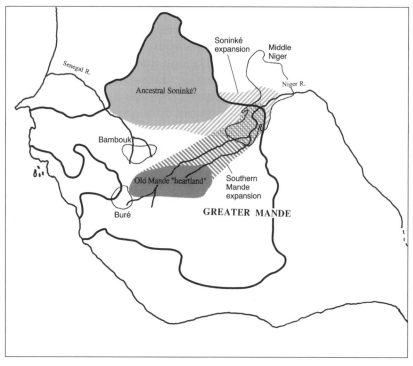

Map 1.2   *The Middle Niger mix of northern and southern Mande*

absorbed by later colonists, but their symbols and beliefs surely were not eliminated wholesale.

What we now know as the Mande symbolic reservoir is a product of many millennia of selective mix and continuous (directed) invention. As mixing ground of northern and southern ancestral communities, the Middle Niger produced the most fertile symbolic upwelling.

As a bare-bones, working definition of symbolic reservoir, I use the term to indicate the fluid landscape of ideologies, symbols, and myths that gives evolving complex societies their structured dynamism over deep time. The symbolic reservoir is that wellspring of symbols and ideologies into which different sub-groups of a society dip in order to extract, craft, and visually display a legitimating tradition to serve their own sectional interests. From this reservoir they find appropriate strategies from the past to deal with today's social or environmental crises. It is the place of mixing of symbols percolating in from adjoining traditions. The idea of the symbolic reservoir is simply a device to focus investigation on the mechanisms by which certain defining symbols or beliefs undergo constant reinvention over the centuries, always welling up from a deep fount of core values.

It is one thing to recognize the enduring-while-changing history (layered transformations) of certain elements in a symbolic reservoir. It is quite another to understand what lies behind the particulars of symbols and legends that are the stuff of appropriation, manipulation in legitimation sequences, and negotiation in the dynamic workings of complex society. In other words, certain symbols or perceptions of the physical or social environment can crystallize social action only if there is a deeper organizing principle that gives a historical trajectory to the society's social construction of reality.

These unspoken, core notions of how the world works that lie behind the daily functioning of the symbolic reservoir are extremely difficult to know. Such notions cannot, of course, be assumed to be extrapolatable, wholesale as it were, from the ethnographic or ethnohistorical record. But, paradoxically, if fully articulated and made explicit by society's members, those core notions become negotiable and thus lose their power as the givens of history to bind peoples together. In a pluri-ethnic mix such as the Middle Niger, it is these integrative notions that are of critical interest. Deep-time values are historical reality.

Can the workings of the symbolic reservoir be understood when the actors cannot be interviewed? We can give two examples of deep-time, core notions that were made known only by the persistence of archaeologists. The first is the ancient (back to the Neolithic) Chinese notion of shamanistic authority. Chang[26] sees shamanistic beliefs transformed into Bronze Age despotic kingship and, on the other hand, transmitted (recognizable but much transfigured) by Holocene migrants to the New World.[27] A second example from Egypt is the notoriously amorphous, but indispensable notion of *ma'at* – justice, truth, rightness in perpetuity, described by Kemp[28] as "the whole correct order of the universe." *Ma'at* was critical to the conceptual

[26] Kwang-chih Chang, *Art, Myth, and Ritual. The Path to Political Authority in Ancient China* (Harvard University Press: Cambridge, MA, 1983), pp. 44–8, 56–63 and *The Archaeology of Ancient China* (Yale University Press: New Haven, 1986). 4th edn, pp. 414–22.

[27] David Freidel, Linda Schiele, and Joy Parker, *Maya Cosmos. Three Thousand Years on the Shaman's Path*, (William Morrow and Co.: New York, 1993).

[28] Barry Kemp, *Ancient Egypt. Anatomy of a Civilisation*, (Routledge: London, 1989), p. 266.

evolution of Archaic Egyptian kingship (although its Predynastic expression is still poorly known). It was later appropriated by Akhenaten, for example, and given new meaning as a revelation about the nature of the godhood. Akhenaten's manipulation was a classic case of reinvention for legitimation of a deep-time notion.

This book explores what gives trajectory, what fundamentally structures the deep-time dynamism of complex cultural situations. The Middle Niger is a preeminent arena for an exploration of the principles that provide self-ordering regularity and a degree of pre-dictability to a fundamentally complex, highly volatile human and physical landscape. And so, the symbols, the myths, and legends and ideologies are just one, albeit a highly critical dimension of the how the many domains of complexity overlap and interact. Happily, there is a powerful (if curiously underused) concept that allows us to describe temporal (and processual) continuity within the highly complex interactions of various environmental, ecological and social agencies: synoecism.

When one looks at the clustered urban complexes of the Middle Niger, or at the ancient regional exchange systems that preceded the classic Berber-organized trans-Saharan trade, or at the heterachical networks of authority out of which the great sudanic "over-kingdoms" of Ghana, Mali, and Songhai grew, one sees synoecism at its finest. One sees the kinds of synoestic processes best described by Kostof[29] for the genesis of towns such as Sienna, Athens, or Calcutta. These communities grew as layered transformations out of the coming together of earlier villages (the physical) and earlier scale and administrative principles (the processes). Kostof's use of synoecism is non-directional (non-teleological). He emphasizes the process of recognizing the shapes and organization of prior settlements in the later urban landscape and reinvented organization of the descendant communities. The novel organism emerges from the spontaneous synthesis of the diverse old, whose signatures continue to be recognizable. This is a formulation of synoecism much more useful for this book than the stadial uses of,

---

[29] Spiro Kostof, "Urbanism and polity: Medieval Siena in context," *International Laboratory for Architecture and Urban Design. 1982 Yearbook.* p. 69; and "Junctions of town and country," in *Dwellings, Settlements and Tradition*, Jean-Paul Bourdier and Nezar Alsayyad (eds). (University Press of America: Lanham, MD, 1989), pp. 120–1 and pers. com., 1990. The term symoecism has a venerable history of refrence to the coming together of plural (foreign, alien) components of the city (state): Aristotle, *Politics* 1303ª.28 and Thucydides II. 15 and I. 24.

Plate 1.1   *Satellite image mosaic of the Middle Niger (courtesy of Pat Jacobberger Jellison).*

for example, Paul Wheatley[30] for Bronze Age Chinese cities or, even, an Oswald Spengler[31] speaking of universal stages of civilization. Here we will not be looking for synoecic stages on a more-or-less deterministic path to a predictable ultimate form.

I would argue strongly that one can only understand the history of the diverse peoples of the Middle Niger by embracing the nested landscape concept of synoecism. At first view, the physical, climatic, social and ideological landscapes of the Middle Niger might appear confused and even chaotic. The Middle Niger might, at first

---

[30] Paul Wheatley, *Pivot of the Four Quarters*, (Aldine: Chicago, 1970), p. 324, see also 30).

[31] Oswald Spengler, *The Decline of the West*, vol. II (A.A. Knopf: New York, 1926–8), 2 vols, p. 101.

blush, appear to defy a synthetic historical understanding. However, those landscapes are overlapping and dynamically interacting transformations of earlier forms. The historical process can be understood if we use a concept such as synoecism to cast off our old disciplinary blinders that kept, for example, archaeologists fearing to tread on the paths of symbols or historians wary of making speculations about deep-time reconstructions of notions of authority.

The synoecism concept makes us keep firmly in mind the fact that various dimensions of complexity interact in mutually transformative ways. The physical landscape, expressed by the very individual personalities of the six basins of the Middle Niger, is a classic synoecic product. The agencies of wind and water have sculpted the mosaic landforms of these basins. But the alternations of pluvial and dry periods lasting decades, centuries, or millennia have been so dramatic that the distribution of those landforms represents a complex layering of geomorphological transformations. And the Office du Niger is but a recent example of human agency in the transformation of the physical environment. The ten major and several minority ethnic groups, and many subsistence and occupational corporations have exploited the Middle Niger since late stone age times – these all have contributed layer upon layer of anthropogenic transformation.

We can describe palaeoclimate history as a synoecic process. So, too, are the generation and accommodation of ethnic and corporate groups, of farming, fishing, and pastoral practices. We must bring a synoecic analysis to classic settlement patterns – how people distribute themselves over the landscape and how, spontaneously, the first true towns emerged from these settlement dynamics at places such as Jenne-jeno and Dia. It becomes apparent that all these dimensions are interacting together recursively and at a variety of scales. As the preceding discussion of symbolic reservoirs made clear, a critical component of the dynamic mix is the world of ideas and myth and symbols together with notions of authority. People react to change, not in the "objective" world, but in the world as they perceive it. Cultural models are a powerful filter to perception. Their models of causation are cultural – the social construction of reality. All archaeologists and historians and art historians and palaeoecologists have ever done is to try to make sense of the incompletely preserved remains of past action upon multiple aspects of the world as socially constructed by people now long dead.[32]

---

[32] R. McIntosh and S. McIntosh "From siècles obscurs", p. 159.

It may be pushing the concept, but the various research projects concerned with the physical and social evolution of the Middle Niger have also been synoecic in their great interactive diversity. Archaeology is just an example. There is a very strong Malian imput into research priorities, even though much of the funding for archaeological research comes from the outside. The Malian research center, the Institut des Sciences Humaines, has issued and acted on very clear research and applied priorities. The Malian priorities have been regional survey and inventory, salvage archaeology at sites already looted by or under imminent threat by antiquities pillagers, and local education *sensibilisation* campaigns to build local pride in the past, however remote. Individual Malian archaeologist have conducted world-standard surveys and excavations. Téréba Togola's Méma project has revealed the late stone age roots to urbanism. Among the expatriate researchers, the Middle Niger has benefited enormously not just by the infusion of hard cash, but especially by the overlap and creative tension of different national research styles – French, Norwegian, English, Dutch, Polish, American, Belgian, and Swiss.[33] The Middle Niger, along with Madagascar and the Cameroon Grasslands, has been well served by the insights raised at the boundaries of different national research styles.

This diversity in archaeology describes only one dimension of Middle Niger research. Historians themselves are a diverse crowd – Arabists and post-colonial, "big empire" *griot* tradition and village-level collectors of oral traditions. So, too, are art historians (from high art terracotta specialists to students of bricolage and casted artisan technologies), and linguists, and even the natural scientists studying palaeoclimate and palaeobotany, geomorphology and desertification, modern landuse and ancient crops still employed.

The good news is that this extension of the concept of synoecism to research about the Middle Niger describes well the interactions between disciplines. Africa is already in the relatively advantageous position of having soft disciplinary boundaries. For example, the *Journal of African History* is a major organ for the publication of archaeological finds. Historically, the spectacular diversity and causal complexity of the Middle Niger has encouraged an exaggeration of this tendency. The reality of cooperative thinking – of real interpretive

[33] Roderick J. McIntosh, "Archaeological research in francophone Africa," in *Encyclopaedia of the History of Archaeology,* Timothy Murray (ed.) (Garland Press: New York, forthcoming).

pluralism[34] – is greater here than perhaps anywhere on the globe. Indeed, I lay the inspiration for this book happily at the feet of several wildly successful meetings of MANSA, the Mande Studies Association, and, before that, the shamelessly interdisciplinary "Deep Sahelian Civilization" panels of the mid-1980s, organized at the African Studies Association meetings by Thomas Hale and Paul Stoller.

The bad news is that the density of researchers, in any field, is still far too low in all parts of the Middle Niger. Some important regions of prehistoric urbanism or of dense late stone age occupation (by early specialists making the kinds of experiments with local grains that would lead to domestic rice, fonio, and perhaps stocks of sorghum and millet) have never been visited by an archaeologist. Too many old men and women – the irreplaceable libraries of rural Africa – pass on to another world without their stories being curated. And the most despicable news is that looting of archaeological sites and stripping of today's villages of their cultural treasures – all these acts of out-and-out cultural rape – are of epidemic proportions. An insatiable international market for antiquities and art is to blame.[35] No amount of goodwill and synergistic interaction among scholars of various disciplines will prevail if archaeological sites, a major class of evidence for the remarkable urban civilization of the Middle Niger, are erased forever before serious scientific examination can even begin. This potential tragedy is a very real possibility because of the cupidity and recklessness of the international antiquities traffick.[36]

Historical Imagination

However threatened the past of the Middle Niger, it has a spectacular heritage. The Middle Niger was a cradle of important crop domestication and, very probably, of precocious specialization dur-

---

[34] Roderick J. McIntosh, 'Early urban clusters', pp. 209–11; R. McIntosh and S. McIntosh "From Siècles obscurs", p. 158-159

[35] Michel Brent, "The rape of Mali," *Archaeology* 47(3) (1994), pp. 26–31, 34–5; Roderick J. McIntosh, "Plight of ancient Jenne," *Archaeology* 47(3) (1994), pp. 32–3; and R. McIntosh and S. McIntosh, "Dilettantism and plunder" and "Symplegades gateway"; Peter R. Schmidt and Roderick J. McIntosh, (eds), *Plundering Africa's Past*, (Indiana University Press: Bloomington, 1996), esp. chapters by McIntosh, Sidibé and Papageorge Kouroupas.

[36] Roderick J. McIntosh, Téréba Togola, and Susan Keech McIntosh, " The good collector and the premise of mutual respect among nations," *African Arts*, 28(4) (1995), pp. 60–9, 110-12.

ing the later millennia of the late stone age. During the last millennium BC, the region nurtured some of Africa's oldest metallurgy. As we shall see, early iron working is in part a story of technology and, in part, a growth industry in manipulating the most dangerous occult forces. The clustered hamlets of the pre-metallurgical communities gave rise to the wealthy and highly populous Middle Niger cities, without demonstrable outside help. Urbanism appears around the beginning of the Present Era. One of these has recently been christened in a popular French-language magazine: "Djenné-Djeno, berceau de l'Afrique occidentale"[37] (Jenne-jeno, cradle of West Africa). That's pushing it a bit, but these towns and the Niger riverine and the long-distant luxury commerce they serviced certainly played a major role in nurturing and sustaining the later trans-Saharan gold and salt trade. Jenne-jeno is the best investigated, but not necessarily the oldest or even the largest. The Middle Niger, for its riches in people, and in crops, and in manufactures, was contested ground for the great West African "empires" – Ghana, Mali and Songhai. Because of these accomplishments, archaeologists and historians have made great efforts to popularize their discoveries.[38] There has recently been a rush of film, television and print media exposés of the pillaging of the region's heritage. Despite this, the past glories of the people of the Middle Niger are still imperfectly known to the interested public.

It is to this readership that this book is principally addressed. Parts of this book are written in a novelistic style. I take just a moment to explain why I resort to historical imagination. The purpose of *The Peoples of Africa* series is not to provide yet another vehicle of tightly focussed scholarly publication. Rather, the series editors enjoin the authors to present readable yet scholarly and up-to-date accounts of African peoples, from their origins through historical times. The trick is to integrate several disciplines to tell this story: archaeology, history, ethnography, and the natural sciences. The intended, wide audience is anyone interested in a celebration of one of the world's most innovative and vibrant congeries of

[37] Hélios Molina and Jean-Stéphane Vincent. "Trafic de biens culturels: Le Mali se rebiffe," *L'Aladin* (October, 1995), p. 21.
[38] E.g., Susan Keech McIntosh and Roderick J. McIntosh, "Finding West Africa's oldest city," *National Geographic Magazine*, 162 (1982), pp. 398–418; and "Pompei de l'Afrique Noire," *GEO (France)* 47 (1983), pp. 36–51; Rogier M. A. Bedaux and J. D. van der Waals, *Djenné, Une Ville Millénaire au Mali*, (Rijksmuseum voor Volkenkunde: Leiden, 1994); see Time-Life Books, *Africa's Glorious Legacy* (Time-Life Books: Alexandria, VA, 1994), pp. 80–110.

peoples. To tell this story, every odd-numbered chapter after this introduction will contain a story of historical imagination. These will be my attempt to add an archaeologist's unspoken to the historical narrative of the chapter immediately preceding. Such a structure for this book is absolutely necessary for two purposes.

The first is that an archaeologist such as myself develops an extra intuition over some twenty years of intimate familiarity with a prehistoric landscape and with the tactile absorption of hundreds of thousands of artifacts. This intuition is an interpretive second sense about the threads of causation tying together the prehistoric material. This second sense is entirely subjective and grows despite enormous evidentiary holes. The very best archaeologists (Mortimer Wheeler, Mary Leakey, Leonard Woolley) are famous for translating that extra intuition into brilliant methodological leaps. The historical imagination segments here are my way to communicate my extra intuition about the whys of Middle Niger history. Historical imagination allows me to insert that extra dimension of past motivations so sadly missing in much archaeological and historical writing.

The second, and most important reason for historical imagination is that it is my way to take certain key narrative themes of the Mande people's view of themselves back to an archaeological time before the literal timeframe of the classic oral traditions. Historical imagination conveys the Middle Niger peoples' own assessment of what animates their souls and what is important in their history. The peoples of the Middle Niger call this perception and oral performance of history *kuma koro* ("ancient speech") and hold it to be very powerful.

I use historical imagination, writing a short segment of fiction, to "imagine" the salient, underlying processes and —most importantly – motivations that account for the continuity within layered transformations of Middle Niger history. Much of this historical imagination deals with a domain untouched or imperfectly documented by the material evidence. Central to past motivations was (and continues to be today) the world of occult beliefs and the all-important supernatural competencies of the Middle Niger (and greater Mande) "Men (and Women) of Crises." These are the persons charged by their communities to make decisions in time of change and crisis. The decision-makers have awesome authority.

These are the artisans charged by society to speak the words or fashion the masks, or "power bundles" (*boli*), or terracotta representations of powerful gods, ancestors or kings, or to create out of earth and fire that dangerous iron avatar of the forces that animate the world. In other words, with historical imagination I try to convey a sense of the Middle Niger rules of action, transformation, and canons of authority that give meaning to all decisions and that stand behind all social action. These are the core values. These are the fluid mechanics of the Middle Niger symbolic reservoir. Only by the novelistic style of historical imagination do I have any hope of conveying to the reader what the people of the Middle Niger themselves consider to be the essence, the all-critical core of their history.

Each historical imagination chapter describes a single episode, a short moment in time, as witnessed from one of two critical Middle Niger locations. The first location is from the bank north of the stream (*marigot*) immediately north of Jenne. This happens to be the location of the later historical village of Roundé Siru, famous as the home of Sekou Amadou, as an Islamic student. There he learned such abiding hatred for the Muslim notables of Jenne – a hatred that, in his maturity was to plunge the Middle Niger into fanaticism. The second location is atop one of the largest archaeological sites in the Niger Bend of the Middle Niger, the 24-hectare site designated W-13,[39] on the banks of the massive Al Ahmar dry channel (*wadi*) east of Timbuktu. From these vantage points in the Middle Niger's far north (the Lakes Region and Niger Bend) and the fertile southern basin (the Upper Delta), we see the history of the peoples of the Middle Niger in another dimension of its detail.

Style is the first problem for an author of historical imagination when that author has been born outside these societies. The vast and rapidly growing corpus of Mande oral traditions[40] is performed

---

[39] Susan Keech McIntosh and Roderick J. McIntosh, "Archaeological reconnaissance in the region of Timbuktu, Mali," *National Geographic Research*, 2(3) (1986), pp. 307 (figure 2), 315–17.

[40] Only some of the most important examples: Myeru Baa and Mahmadou L. Sunbunu. *La Geste de Fanta Maa. Archétype du Chaseur dans la Culture des Bozo,* (CELHTO: Niamey, 1987); Youssouf Tata Cisse and Wa Kamissoko, *La Grande Geste du Mali* (Karthala: Paris, 1988) and *Soundjata. La Gloire du Mali,* (Karthala: Paris, 1991); David Conrad, "Searching for history in the Sunjata epic: The case of Fakoli," *History in Africa* 19 (1992), pp. 147–220; Germaine Dieterlen and Diarra Sylla, *L'Empire de Ghana. Le Wagadou et les Traditions de Yéréré* (Karthala: Paris, 1992); Jean-Marie Gibbal, *Les Génies du Fleuve* (Presses de la Renaissance: Paris, 1988); John Johnson, Thomas A. Hale, and Stephen Belcher, *Oral Epic in Africa: Vibrant Voices from a Vast Continent,* (Indiana University Press: Bloomington, 1996); John Johnson, *The Epic of Son-jara. A West African Tradition,* (Indiana University Press, Bloomington, 1986); L. Kesteloot, C. Barbey

in a style (rather, in a collection of styles) quite beyond anything in the Western tradition. What genre does the West have that is even close? What would best convey the core values, the meta-narrative thrust of this literature? For me (archaeologist though I am), the Mande style is something between the "modern memory poetics" described by Paul Fussell in his *The Great War and Modern Memory*[41] and Emerson's[42] transcendentalist project to write the natural history of the intellect. Even these are inadequate approximations of Mande narrative.

The great stories told by the Mande *griots* are, collectively, a natural history of the Mande soul. Emerson's belief that the only thing of value in the universe is the active soul – a subjective consciousness and the conscious subject that animate objective reality – sounds a very Mande sentiment. But our Middle Niger "Men of Crises" would have no conceptual frame of reference for Emerson's political agenda of philosophical freedom and democratic individualism. Similarly, Fussell's biographical danger legend and his conflation of topography and psychology (the modern condition as "confluent acne of the wasteland under the wall of Ypres"[43]) are all very Mande ways of putting across their version of history. But no "Man of Crises" would be caught dead as actionless, subordinated, and paralyzed by anxiety as the modern Western hero! There is also not a little hint of an early (opiated) Tennyson (or a mature Coleridge) in the traditions of the water spirits (to whom the Songhai conqueror Sonni Ali must treat in chapter 11!).

There is a serious second difficulty in writing credible historical imagination. A part of the Mande conception of authority and real power in the world is simply out of bounds to outsiders. Sometimes it is too dangerous to speak of certain forms of supernatural competence. Certainly it is pure nonsense to divulge these secrets of power to foreigners or scholars, whose occupation it is to broadcast knowledge. It is sometimes too dangerous to share all secrets about how to roam the freighted space of wilderness. Only a fool

and S. M. Ndongo, "Tyamaba, mythe Peul," *Notes Africaines* 185–6 (1985), pp. 1–72; D. T. Niane, *Sundiata. An Epic of Old Mali,* (Longman: London, 1965).
[41] Paul Fussell, *The Great War and Modern Memory,* (Oxford University Press: London, 1975), esp. pp. 35, 310–26.
[42] Robert D. Richardson, Jr, *Emerson. The Mind of Fire,* (University of California Press: Berkeley, 1995), esp. pp. xi and 249–51.
[43] Guy Chapman, quoted in Fussell, *Great War*, p. 326.

would divulge knowledge of how to find and partake of the occult forces curated within the sacred landscape.

The Mande adept "floats on a sea of secret expertise that outsiders have no right to learn about".[44] And, indeed, I have no desire to trespass. However, there is much freely spoken in the traditions of what motivated the decision-makers of the Middle Niger past. These are the oral traditions of the great empire founders, those of the settling of Middle Niger towns or villages, those held as corporate property by the artisan corporations and *nyamakalaya* [45] (ancient, "casted" producer-transformer corporations). Historical imagination allows me to tie the three great power and authority themes of the Middle Niger peoples to the deep chronological anchor provided by archaeology.

These three themes are the very core of Mandeness. They are so potent that they are shared by other Middle Niger groups, such as the Songhai and Dogon, who are not linguistically classified as Mande. Each theme will be developed in the pre-historical imagination pages of each of the odd-numbered chapters. The first and best studied of these is *nyama* : that notion of the highly-dangerous vitalizing force of the world that can be packaged and made even more potent by acts of transformation. The second is *dali-ma-sigi*: those heroic quests over the sacred landscape made for the purpose of accumulating greater authority in the world of human affairs. The last is *Mande Onomasticon* : the notion that greater Mande, including and in many cases augmented in the Middle Niger, is a network of power locations, a spatial blueprint of power in three dimensions.

Hunters were perhaps the first to deal in vast quantities of *nyama*. They may have pioneered the concept of *nyama* that is the shared trait of the many Mande subgroups of the Middle Niger to this day. *Nyama* has been defined by many in subtly different, all complementary ways. It is one of those cultural concepts that defies precise, abbreviated definition in any Western language. There are undoubtedly many other nuances that are amongst the most jealously guarded secrets of "*nyama* – practitioners", the *nyamakalaw*, today, such as members of the *Komo* power association. *Nyama* is all of these things: it is the malign, if, improperly controlled

---

[44] McNaughton, *Mande Blacksmith*, p. xvi.

[45] David C. Conrad and Barbara E. Frank. "Contradiction and ambiguity in Mande society," in *Status and Identity in West Africa: Nyamakalaw of Mande*, David C. Conrad and Barbara E. Frank (eds) (Indiana University Press: Bloomington, IN, 1995), pp. 1–23, see also ix–x.

energy that flows through all animate and inanimate things.[46] It is
the "energy of action" released by any act.[47] And my personal
favorite is McNaughton's[48] equation of *nyama* with occult energy
as the source of moral reciprocity (human-to-human, and human-
to-all earth forces). For McNaughton, it can be not created, only
augmented; in his notion, *nyama* "is a little like electricity uncon-
strained by insulated wires but rather set neatly into a vast matrix
of deeply interfaced social and natural laws."

The common theme of the earliest expressions of *dali-ma-sigi* is
the voluntary removal of the hero to the wilderness. For it is there
that *nyama* runs rampant and chaotic. This is not an exile for community transgressions. For the good of the stressed community, the
hunter makes this dangerous tour of powerful locations, there to kill
the proprietary spirit animals taking the form most frequently of buffalo, hyena, crocodile, or snakes. Killing the guardian animal liber-
ates vast masses of *nyama* that only the most able hunter could control
and frees well-watered lands for hunter-led migration. The snake may
be secretly followed to water by the hunter. The snake may even succor
the famished hunter with milk from its tail – this also figures in non-
Mande Fulani migration myth.[49] The snake may willingly guide the
hunter. But the important point, one not lost on the next generations
of adventurers such as entrepreneur smiths and power-seeking dynasts,
is that one must know how to navigate the sacred landscape. What,
then, is the cultural map of the power of place?

The Mande mapping of the power of place, in which the Middle
Niger with its abundance of *nyama* –replete locales plays such a prominent part, goes beyond a simple two dimensional map of power localities. For Greater Mande we can talk about an evolving notion of
authority expressed as a spatial blueprint of the covenantial assimilation of power. Mande itself is a grid in space, the nodes of which
describe a vertical axis of sacrality. This map contains vital information about the viability of various geomorphological features under

---

[46] Sarah C. Brett-Smith, *The Making of Bamana Sculpture. Creativity and Gen-
der,* (Cambridge University Press: Cambridge, 1994), p. 38.
[47] Charles Bird, *The Songs of Seydou Camara,* (African Studies Center,
Bloomington, 1974), pp. vii–ix; Charles Bird and Martha Kendall, "The Mande
Hero", in *Explorations in African Systems of Thought* , Ivan Karp and Charles
Bird (eds) (Indiana University Press, Bloomington, 1980), pp. 16–17.
[48] Patrick McNaughton, *The Mande Blacksmith. Knowledge, Power and Art in
West Africa* (Indiana University Press, Bloomington, 1988), pp. 16, see also 15–21.
[49] Kesteloot et al., "Tyamaba."

different climatic conditions. In this sense, the study of Mande social memory most closely approximates the biblical study of Onomasticon.

The issues of historicity in biblical scholarship apply also to our study of the Mande sacred landscape. To what degree are traditions recorded at a later date (the Deuteronomist traditions) reliable records of a spatial view of sacrality that goes back to the early Iron Age (early Israelite) or, better still, Middle Bronze Age?[50] Are there special signatures to the sacrality of sites or features that will alert the excavators to their special role during certain periods? In the biblical tradition, onomasticon can simply be a listing of contemporaneous sites mentioned in the Bible or ancillary sources. However, increasingly, onomasticon has come to mean the study of power localities as mnemonics of deep-time memory of the relative power of households or lineages associate with those places.[51] So here I will use the term *Mande Onomasticon* for the study of the Mande as a network of power localities. There may be a proper Mande term for this conception of social memory – and it may be too secret ever to have been leaked out to scholars!

A sacred mapping of the landscape's power, drawn in important sites and ceremonial roadways, is not unique in world prehistory. The Maya "Milky Way" *sacbeob* , the network of roads linked pilgrimage procession centers in the Yucatan; in North America, the Anasazi and Hopewell had "White Paths" uniting communities in commerce and symbolically replicating a spiritual (origin myth?) landscape.[52]. However, it is my intuition that the *Mande Onomasticon* will prove unusually exciting for the potential of the adepts navigating this sacred landscape to augment and to change the very nature of occult power by their acts of invention and transformation. Those adepts come from all walks of life, all stations in society. The Mande world of the Middle Niger is never rigid, never

[50] Amihai Mazar, *Archaeology of the Land of the Bible. 10,000 to 586 B.C.E.*, (Doubleday: New York, NY 1990), pp. 348–52.

[51] Victor H. Matthews and Don C. Benjamin, *The Social World of the Bible, 1250–587 B.C.E.* (Hendrickson Publishers: Peabody, MA, 1993); Robert R. Wilson, *Geneology and History in the Biblical World* (New Haven, CT: Yale University Press, 1977).

[52] On the Maya – Freidel, Schele and Parker, *Maya Cosmos*, pp. 76–8; on the Anasazi–Kathryn Gabriel, *Roads to Center Place: A Cultural Atlas of Chaco Canyon and the Anasazi*, (Johnson Publishing Co.: Boulder, CO, 1991) and John Wicklein, "Spirit paths of the Anasazi," *Archaeology*, 47 (1) (1994), pp. 36–41; and on the Hopewell–Bradley T. Lepper, "Tracking Ohio's great Hopewell road," *Archaeology*, 48 (6)(1995), pp. 52, 56.

the *chasse gardée* (exclusive hunting preserve) of a privileged, elite class of rulers.

From crisis to crisis, over the several millennia that are the arena of this book, certain core values were symbolically reaffirmed, appropriated, manipulated, and reinvented by Mande "Men of Crisis", who move through and themselves create enormous packages of occult power by transforming the sacred landscape. They harvest power from the dangerous symbolic landscape. They thereby acquire the authority and the knowledge to deal with climate change and social change. "Men of Crisis" is a deeply entrenched Mande concept that almost certainly goes back to the late stone age genesis, initially with hunters, of the concept of specialist holders of occult and social authority.[53]

Thus, after the review of the late stone age evidence from two of the six Middle Niger basins in the next chapter, we use our historical imagination in chapter 5 to follow a hunter as he enters the drylands of the deeper basins, newly emerged during the severe dry period of *c.*300 BC to AD 300. He has left his community at the now dry Saharan fringe – a community increasingly in crisis (chapter 3). He must act. He must decided whether to migrate and to set up permanent settlement on this new fertile alluvium. His decision-making authority, his animal guides to that decision, and his negotiations with the local spirits make sense only within the value context of the Mande model of the world.

Through the millennia, new specialists, new adepts at acts of transformation (such as smiths, or speakers of oral histories (*griots*) or leather workers) and, finally, the new secular dynasts of Ghana, Mali and Songhai, reinvent these core notions of the foundation of authority. Each act of reinvention simply adds a new layer to the transformed, but recognizable core values. To each of their acts of cultural transformation and continuity, we apply, in turn, our historical imagination.

Island of Gold

It remains only to explain the title of this book. There's the word that strikes terror in the heart of every archaeologist. Gold. Men-

---

[53] Youssouf Cissé, "Notes sur les sociétés des chasseurs Malinké," *Journal de la Société des Africainistes,* 34 (1964); 175–226.

tion of gold cannot but evoke in the popular mind the basest Indiana Jones image of archaeologists' motivations. This is an image that cross cuts cultures. On more than one occasion while excavating Jenne-jeno, we shuffled onto the site in the dawning light of a new day, only to see the smashed remains of some urn or pot we had been forced to leave incompletely excavated and unlifted the day before. Clearly some souls in the nearby town of Jenne found it difficult to believe that we were doing all that work just for potsherds and charcoal samples of old cookfires. Indeed, it is the well-justified fear of every archaeologist that rumours of gold and other riches will bring on an army of looters to destroy forever the scientific knowledge of the past obtainable only by stratigraphic excavation. With the accelerating destruction of Middle Niger sites to feed the aforementioned international traffick in terrracottas, we do not need another acceleration of the rape of Mali's cultural heritage.

Yet, there is sound evidence that gold passed through Jenné-jeno by the seventh to ninth centuries AD.[54] Gold and other precious metals and stones have inestimable value to archaeologists as proxy measures for the growing complexity of society, the rank and status stratification of communities, the unequal access of a few in society to monetary or ideological (sumptuary) wealth, and to the importance of long-distance commerce. Many important syntheses of West African history begin with the commerce in gold out of the Western Sudanese mines of Bambouk and Buré, across the great desert to the western Islamic entrepôt and courts of North Africa.[55] Once, these histories were virtually unanimous in attributing the rise of the first two of the great West Africa "empires", Ghana and Mali, to the growth and control of that traffick in gold out of Wangara, or the Island of Gold. In these histories, the Island of Gold was unquestionably the Bambouk and Buré mining regions of upper Guinea, southwestern Mali and far eastern Senegal.[56]

Since the late 1970s and early 1980s, two things have happened to shake this tidy picture of civilization brought from "centers of radiation" in the Arab north and east. No longer can scholars claim that outsiders had to shake complacent and isolated West Africa

---

[54] S. McIntosh, *Excavations*, p. 267.
[55] For example, E. W. Bovill, *The Golden Trade of the Moors*, (Oxford University Press: Oxford, 1970); Basil Davidson, *A History of West Africa, 1000–1800*, (Longman: London, 1977), pp. 20–46.
[56] Ibid, map 9, p. 42 and p. 46.

out of (in the French archaeologist Raymond Mauny's terms) a level of development comparable to the northern European Halstatt (early Iron Age) in the southern Saharan and northern savanna and scarcely out of the Neolithic in the forest.[57] The first was the publication in 1981, by Susan Keech McIntosh, of a reassessment of Wangara in the *Journal of African History*. She argued that the real Island of Gold, that lured Arabo-Berber caravans across the sandy wastes and many European explorers to their premature deaths, were the Middle Niger *centers* of the gold trade rather than the mines at the *source* of the gold.[58] The Island of Gold was the Wangara of the Arab chroniclers, or the Palolus of the Europeans.

The second event, and strongest support for the Middle Niger as the Island of Gold was the archaeological discovery of cities dating at least to the earliest centuries of the Present Era. These cities did not stand alone. Archaeology demonstrates a contemporaneous long-distance trade throughout the grasslands of West Africa. There was an even earlier development in West Africa of specialists and production corporations. This evidence forms a major part of the story told in this book. These discoveries removed the major "negative evidence" support for Bambouk / Buré as the Island of Gold of al-Idrisi's (AD 1154) and Ibn Sa'id's (AD 1286) accounts. The earlier dismissal of the Middle Niger was based on the argument that the vast inner delta of the Niger was a backwater, without becoming a trade axis until the fourteenth century.[59]

Today, most historians accept the Middle Niger as the Island of Gold.[60] Some would compromise. They see the Island of Gold of the Arab chronicles, with their imperfect and hearsay knowledge of West African geography, as a conflation of the Middle Niger centers of gold trade with the distant production area.[61] A few still hold with the gold fields.[62] But the former near-unanimous identifi-

[57] Raymond Mauny, *Tableau Géographique de l'Ouest Africain au Moyan Age*, Mémoire no. 61 (Institut Fondamental de l'Afrique Noire: Dakar, 1961), pp. 541.
[58] Susan Keech McIntosh, "A reconsideration of Wangara/Palolus, Island of Gold," *Journal of African History*, 22(1981), pp. 145–58.
[59] Ibid, pp. 146–7.
[60] E.g., John Fage, *A History of Africa*, (Unwin Hyman: London, 1988, 2nd Edn), p. 58.
[61] John Hunwick, "Gao and the Almoravids revisited: Ethnicity, political change and the limits of interpretation," *Journal of African History*, 35 (1994), pp. 263–4.
[62] Abdoulaye Bathily, *Les Portes de l'Or. Le Royaume de Galam (Sénégal) de l'Ere Musulmane au Temps de Nègriers*, (Harmattan: Paris, 1989), p. 174.

cation by historians of the Island of Gold as Bambouk/Buré has evaporated.[63] In its place is a certainty of the capital importance of the Middle Niger for understanding the early history and prehistory of indigenous processes such as urbanism, long-distance trade, and state formation (and the alternative form of socio-political and productive complexity, heterarchy).

All these achievements— the populous cities, the specialists producing their manufactures for distant markets, novel forms of complex governance invented centuries before the "empires" of Ghana and Mali – all these were the genius of the peoples of the Middle Niger. The populations of the vast inner delta of the Niger did not need the gift of civilization from northern traders, clerics and (by the eleventh century) invaders drawn to the lands south of the Sahara by the lustre of gold. All these accomplishments came into being long before the trans-Saharan gold commerce. These are the real riches, riches beyond lucre, of the Island of Gold.

[63] S. McIntosh, "Wangara/Palolus," p. 145.

2

The Dry Basins of the Middle Niger

To the casual visitor, the Azawad is a sea of sand and monotony. Few, however, casually visit this northernmost and least forgiving of the six Middle Niger basins. To those with reason to be there, the Azawad sands tell very different stories of change and lost prosperity. For our purposes, the Azawad serves as an introduction to the layered transformations that crafted the Middle Niger landscapes. This basin also illustrates the often difficult lives of its inhabitants.

To the local population of Moors and Tuareg, the Azawad whispers subtle potential. If the rains come and if one knows how to read soil and relief, the herds of camel and goat can survive and even multiply. Landmarks on a horizon that would be featureless to any casual visitor guide Tuareg-led caravans wending south from Taoudenni and Teghaza. These salt mines have, for many hundreds of years, been a source of wealth augmenting (however meagerly) the ambulatory, bare-bones life of the desert-dwellers. The caravans' destination is Timbuktu, a city astride dune and river.

Timbuktu is a town at the frontier of the Niger's dead and live deltas. It is a city long wounded by conflict between desert Tuareg and riverine Songhai. The conflict has roots sunk centuries, if not millennia deep. It has sprouted again, briefly, in the early 1990s. A violent Sahara-based Tuareg separatist movement (Front Islamique Arab pour l'Azawad) was resisted in Timbuktu by an *ad hoc* civilian militia, provocatively named in Songhai, the "Owners of the Land."[1] Thus, the contest for dominance continues today between desert-born and river-sired peoples, as it has for centuries, and for millennia.

[1] Howard W. French, "In a faraway place, living with fear," *New York Times*, January 30, 1995, p. A6.

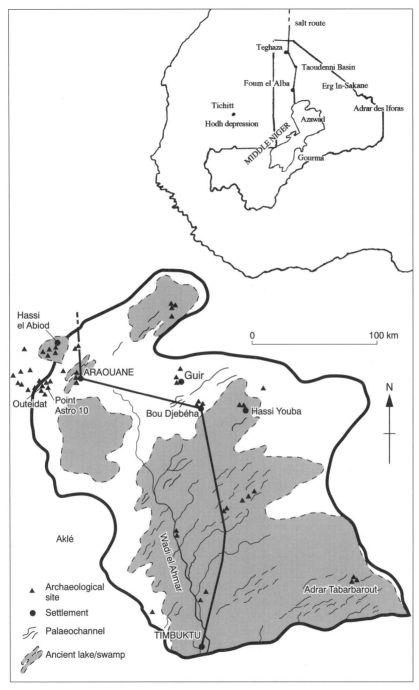

Map 2.1   *AZAWAD: dead delta landforms and sites*

Plate 2.1   *Salt caravan approaching Timbuktu.*

To the natural scientist, the Azawad sand plains (and the related Taoudenni palaeolake depressions further to the north) tell of the eventual triumph of wind over rain and flood. The Azawad is a mosaic of river, swamp, lake, and wind-borne deposits. So, too, are all six Middle Niger basins. Layered transformation is the best description of the cumulative effects of alternating agencies of rain, river, and desiccation that caused the complex interweave of microenvironments throughout the Middle Niger. In the northernmost basin the wind appears to take perverse pleasure in savaging testaments to wetter times.

In the palaeolake region of Taoudenni, dunes trail downwind from tall columns of eroded lake deposits. South, in the Azawad proper, ancient shallow lakes (playas), permanent streams, and once-generous rains left behind carpets of freshwater shell mixed with bones of massive perch, catfish, and crocodile. However, for five millennia, the wind has dominated. Each basin of the Middle Niger is a tight clustering of microenvironments, each rapidly shifting in

Plate 2.2   *Eroding lake deposits in the Malian Sahara (Haijad, Taoudenni Basin, 23°N) (courtesy of Nicole Petit-Maire).*

potential with a volatile climate. The Azawad will serve to introduce the prehistoric populations' adaptive strategy that led, eventually, to today's distinctive and synergistic accommodation of modern groups in the four live basins. The people of the Middle Niger have risen to the challenge of that environmental volatility by producing a web of specialized, but articulated occupations. Archaeological survey in the Azawad provides the earliest evidence of this adaptation to palaeoclimatic surprise and opportunity.

To the archaeologist, the Azawad is a legend in knapped stone and pottery of the people expelled from a once earthly Garden by the serpentine dunes. (Like the biblical Mesopotamia of the metaphor, this basin was an anomalous riverine and lake landscape interrupting the semi-arid monotony of the Holocene Sahara.[2]) Let us look first at what we know of the earliest inhabitants of the Middle Niger.

[2] E. Schulz, "The Taoudenni–Agorgott pollen record and the Holocene vegetation history of the Central Sahara," in *Paléoenvironnements du Sahara. Lacs Holocènes à Taoudenni (Mali)* Nicole Petit-Maire (ed.) (Editions CNRS: Marseille, 1991), pp. 143–58.

Plate 2.3   *Archaeological survey of the deflated Azawad Plain.*

Triumph of the Wind: The Azawad

For much of the colonial period, unsettled relations with the Tuareg confined archaeological exploration to the relatively safe vicinity of military posts or to wells along the salt route. The finds were intriguing. Stone age deposits crowded the margins of long dried lakes and swamps. At these sites, fish, animal and human bone mixed with lithics, ceramics, and bone harpoons.[3] After Malian

[3] Raymond Guitat, "Carte et répertoire des sites néolithiques du Mali et de la Haute-Volta," *Bulletin de l'Institut Fondamental d'Afrique Noire* (B), 34 (4) (1972), pp. 896–925; Raymond Mauny and F. Poussibet, "Nouveaux sites à harpons et faune subfossile de l'Azawad (Saharien malien)," *Notes Africaines*, 93 (1962), pp. 1–5; Michel Raimbault, "Les faciès néolithiques du Sahara malien avant l'aridification," *Actes du 116ᵉ Congrès National des Société Savantes*, (Editions

independence, with the distractions of the Sahel Drought (1968–85?) and the Tuareg unrest, research remained sporadic. However, recent work in the Azawad and in the other dry Middle Niger basin, the Méma, has yielded evidence that challenges many archaeologists' most dearly held expectations.

Most archaeologists expected that all these late stone-using communities, to one degree or another, were engaged in a generalized economy of lake-shore fishing and the hunting of aquatic mammals, crocodile and tortoise.[4] The gathering of wild plants and grains would be an important supplementary task. Such communities should leave behind sites marked by a relatively similar scatter of bone harpoons, grindstones, fishbone, and pottery (decorated with diagnostic dotted-wavy lines). Exactly such remains had been described, during colonial times, at sites such as Araouane, Hassi Youba, and Guir.

These were the expectations to underlay the first systematic regional survey in 1964 by the Swiss archaeologist, Allain Gallay. Gallay went into the Araouane hinterland (near Outeidat) and to the extreme southeast (Adrar Tabarbarout) for the principal purpose of thoroughly collecting a "typical" aquatic Azawad site.[5] Indeed, he searched for and found many sites with just those char-

---

du Comité des Travaux Historiques et Scientifiques: Paris, 1992), pp. 85–7; Théodore Monod and Raymond Mauny, "Découverte de nouveaux instruments en os dans l'Ouest africain," *Proceedings of the Third Panafrican Congress of Prehistory and Quaternary Studies* (Livingstone) (Chato & Windus: London, 1955), pp. 242–7. For an overview of this and related southern Saharan basins, see Robert Vernet, 'Préhistoire des bassins affluents de la rive gauche du fleuve Niger', in *Vallées du Niger,* (Editions de la Réunion des Musées Nationaux: Paris, 1993), pp. 63–74.

[4] Gabriel Camps, *Les Civilisations Préhistoriques de l'Afrique du Nord et du Sahara* (Doin: Paris, 1974), pp. 221–56; Gabriel Camps, "Extension territoriale des civilisations épipaléolithique et néolithique dans le nord de l'Afrique," *Acts of the Sixth Panafrican Congress of Prehistory and Quaternary Studies* , H.-J. Hugot (ed.) (Les Imprimeries Réunies: Chambéry, 1967), pp. 284–7; John E. G. Sutton, "The Aquatic civilisation of middle Africa," *Journal of African History,* 15 (1974), pp. 527–46; Andrew B. Smith, "The neolithic tradition in the Sahara," in *The Sahara and the Nile,* Martin A.J. Williams and Hugues Faure (eds) (A.A. Balkema, Rotterdam: 1980), pp. 451–66.

[5] Alain Gallay, "Quelques gisements néolithiques du Sahara Malien," *Bulletin de la Société des Africainistes,* 36 (2) (1966), pp. 167–208; Alain Gallay and Eric Huysecom, "Un site néolithique de l'Adrar Tabarbarout (Sahara malien oriental)," *Bulletin de la Société Préhistorique Français,* 90 (5) (1993), pp. 357–64.

acteristics, such as his classic bone-harpoon Point Astro 10 site. However, rather than being typical, Point Astro 10 proved an exception among a bewildering variety of sites. The mystery deepened when he found sites of different types scattered over the same dune slope or dried lake (*playa*) edge.

Great variability of sites is not what archaeologists expected to find in the Azawad. Late lithic-using peoples were supposed to have been culturally and industrially conservative. (Africanists prefer the term late stone age (LSA) over the Neolithic – a term freighted with European connotations of agriculture, settled village life, ground stone tools, and ceramics.) Their conservatism, so prehistorians reasoned, locked them into a uniform and highly generalized way of making a living from the lakes and swamps of the Azawad. This presumption of a monotonous, glacially changing way of life was further shaken by the results of eight extensive geomorphological and archaeological expeditions, headed by Nicole Petit-Maire. From 1980 to 1988 she directed the Missions Paléoenvironnements du Sahara Occidental et Central [6] and she takes credit for the project's innovative multidisciplinary approach.

Because of this project, we have, for the first time, detailed description of the sites' climate and local environment. The Missions Paléoenvironnements team comprised geologists, geomorphologists, palaeobotanists, palaeozoologists, physical anthropologists, and archaeologists. They looked at the fish, aquatic mammals, reptiles, and shellfish that frequented nearby lakes and streams, as well as the resources of the surrounding steppe grasslands. Together, these spe-

---

[6] Nicole Petit-Maire, "Homo climaticus: Vers une paléoanthropologie écologique," *Bulletin de la Société Royale Belge d'Anthropologie et de Préhistoire*, 97 (1986), pp. 59–75 and (ed.), *Paléoenvironnements du Sahara, Lacs Holocène à Taodenni*, (Editions CNRS: Paris, 1991); Nicole Petit-Maire and Jean Riser (eds), *Sahara ou Sahel? Quaternaire Récent du Bassin de Taoudenni (Mali)*, (Marseille: CNRS, 1983); Nicole Petit-Maire, J. C. Celles, Dominique Commelin, G. Delibrias, and Michel Raimbault, "The Sahara in northern Mali. Man and his environment between 10,000 and 3500 years BP," *The African Archaeological Review*, 1 (1983), pp. 105–25; Jean Fabre and Nicole Petit-Maire, "Holocene climatic evolution at 22–23°N from two palaeolakes in the Taoudenni area (northern Mali)," *Palaeogeography, Palaeoclimatology, Palaeoecology*, 65 (1988), pp. 133–48; Michel Raimbault, "Pour une approche du néolithique du Sahara malien," *Travaux du Laboratoire d'Anthropologie et de Préhistoire des Pays de la Méditerranée Occidentale*, (1990), pp. 67–81; the radiocarbon determinations reported by this project convincingly date the range of time for prehistoric occupation at from 7000 to c.3500 BP. However, there are too few samples to convincingly date any one individual site, or determinations were run on materials, such as shell, that yield very large error factors.

cialists refined our appreciation of the local and regional effects on local populations of Holocene wet periods (pluvials) of 8500–3000 BP[7] that alternated with periods of sharp desiccation.[8] The last such wet period ended some 4000–3000 years ago. The familiar Sahara has been in the ascendant ever since. (This paleoclimatic sequence will be brought up again later, when we attempt to unravel the chronology of human occupation in the sister dead-delta, the Méma.) These sites were recorded over a vast area between the Taoudenni basin to the far north, east to Erg Ine Sakane on the west flank of the Adrar des Iforas, and the Azawad proper. Research included 19 sites near Hassi el Abiod, at the northernmost frontier of the Azawad (19°30' N latitude) and several more along and east of the Timbuktu to Araouane camel route (recorded in 1983). The archaeologist attached to the team, Michel Raimbault, characterizes the Azawad "néolithique" as a period of extreme diversity.[9]

Without question, the Holocene wet period environment was as rich as the Middle Niger has known for some 20,000 years. By 8500 BP, the Azawad was an enormous, 90,000 km^2 marshy (paludial) and lake (lacustrine) basin[10] of the 170,000 km^2 Middle Niger total. The natural scientists confirmed the presence of plants and animals from different biological provinces: Senegal-Atlantic, arboreal-savanna, and southern tropical. Rainfall was five to ten times (or greater) that of today. Also, precipitation was better spread throughout the year, in contrast to today's tropical monsoonal pattern of a single, very short and intense rainy season. The Azawad became an extremely rich and varied biotope, in Petit-Maire's words, "a true biological crossroads."[11]

The research of the Missions Paléoenvironnements documented

---

[7] I will use the convention of the *Journal of African History* for BP and BC / AD dates. Dates before the first millennium before the Present Era will be designated BP, unless the reference is to a specific calibrated radiocarbon date (Cal BC).

[8] Dominique Commelin, Michel Raimbault and Jean-François Saliège, "Nouvelles données sur la chronologie du Néolithique au Sahara malien," *Comptes Rendus de la Académie des Sciences, Paris*. Série II, 317 (1993):, pp. 543–50.; Susan Keech McIntosh, "Changing perceptions of West Africa's past: Archaeological research since 1988," *Journal of Archaeological Research*, 2(2) (1994), pp. 167–73; Vernet, 'Préhistoire des bassins', p. 68.

[9] Michel Raimbault, "Les récentes missions du C.N.R.S. dans le Sahara Malien (1980-1985)," in *Recherches Archéologiques au Mali*, Michel Raimbaul and Kléna Sanogo (eds) (Kathala, Paris, 1991), p. 124.

[10] Ibid., p. 65.

[11] Petit-Maire and Risier, *Sahara ou Sahel?*, p. 415; see also Wim Van Neer, "Holocene fish remains from the Sahara," *Sahara*, 2 (1989) pp. 61–8.

the luxuriant life that once teamed in each microenvironment of this now dead delta. The team revealed the broad principles of landform organization for the prehistoric Azawad environment, principles that are valid for the four live basins today.[12] The Holocene history of the Azawad is the overlapping transformation of distinct local ecologies: lacustrine, seasonal playas and marshes, palaeo-channels, semi-arid steppe.

Lacustrine   As early as 12,000 BP, flood waters from a rejuvenated Niger breached the massive dune barriers erected during the Late Pleistocene (upper latitudes' glacial mode) hyperarid period. In stark contrast to this most sterile of deserts today, many bodies of permanent water dominated the landscape. In the deepest parts of the Azawad (and even more dramatically to the north, in the Taoudenni basin, and east at Erg in-Sakane) there were large permanent lakes. Some of these were over 500 km² in area.

For millennia, these were freshwater. Some were fed by rainfall; some were recharged by groundwater exposed by low relief. During the best of times, the lakes were home to abundant perch, tilapia, and catfish; to several species of water turtle, crocodile, hippo, and a water python that could grow to an alarming four meters.

Not all, however, could remain freshwater in what was, after all, still a semi-arid precipitation and evaporation zone. Niger overflow fed most of the seasonal Azawad lakes (*playas*) and creeks (*marigots*). Seasonally, high river floods filled the vast network of interdunal corridors between the massive late Pleistocene (longitudinal) dunes covering most of this basin.

Seasonal playas and marshes   Lake and swampland temperature, salinity, and oxygen levels can be recorded by silica-shelled algae (diatoms), mollusks, and bivalve crustaceans (ostracods). These tiny organic documents demonstrate that long periods of fresh, well-oxygenated water were periodically interrupted by high evaporation. During recessions of the larger lakes to the north of the Azawad proper, salty crusts and nodules of halite or calcite formed at the edges of these stagnant, playa-like bodies of water.

---

[12] Pierre Rognon, "L'Evolution des vallées du Niger depuis 20.000 ans," in *Vallées du Niger* , pp. 48–51; Patricia Jacobberger, "Mapping abandoned river channels in Mali through directional filtering of thematic mapper data," *Remote Sensing of Environment*, 26 (1988), pp. 161–70; L. Kervran, "Le cours fossile du Niger," *Notre Sahara*, 10 (1959), pp. 53–8; Nicole Petit-Maire and Mireille Gayet, "Hydrologie du Niger (Mali) à l'Holocène ancien," *Comptes Rendus de l'Académie des Sciences de Paris*, Série II, 298 (1) (1984), pp. 21–3.

The Azawad backswamps and interdunal corridors were quite different from the lakes in that they were home to thick, permanent-swamp (paludial) vegetation. These backswamps were vast low-lying regions inundated each year by flooding (ultimately from the Niger). The annual floods probably extended north of Hassi el Abiod only during the exceptional year. However, for much of the 90,000 km² Azawad, interdunal depressions and chains of paleolakes held water for most, if not all months of the year. Swamp and interdunal ponds served as nurseries for great shoals of fish that thrived upon the abundant vegetation of marshes. Hippo, crocodile, and at least two species of water-dependent antelopes (*Tragelaphus* and *Kob*), as well as African water buffalo (*Syncerus caffer*) roamed the swamps.

The shallows would have been prime environments for wild, edible grasses, some of which were ancestral to domesticated sorghums, millets, fonio, and African rice (*Oryza*). Other important wild grasses (*bourgou* – *Echinochloa stagnina; kreb* – *Panicum laetum* ; *Brachiaria deflexa*) were extensively gathered even after the beginning of agriculture. These wild grasses still constitute a major part of the diet in the Middle Niger. Sadly, not nearly enough archaeology has been done in the southern Sahara and Azawad (and even fewer projects include routine plant recovery techniques, such as flotation) for us to know the true chronology for the emergence of agriculture out of late stone age gathering practices.[13] The systematic searches around Araouane by Gallay and Hassi el Abiod by the Petit-Maire team are unusual. We need a far more elementary survey of the river channels that would have been natural corridors from movements of peoples as the Azawad became true desert.

Palaeochannels The annual flood was spread throughout the Azawad by a network of palaeochannels extending over 180 km north–south, by 130 km east–west. Most channels served to distribute Niger flood water brought into the Azawad by a great palaeochannel, the Wadi El-Ahmar, 1200 m wide at its southern (Niger Bend) end.[14] The channel's 70–100 km northward mean-

---

[13] Jack R. Harlan, "Wild grass seeds as food sources in the Sahara and sub-Sahara," *Sahara* , 2 (1989), pp. 69–74; Roderick J. McIntosh, "African agricultural beginnings," in *The Archaeology of Sub-Saharan Africa: An Encyclopaedia*, Joseph O. Vogel (ed.) (Garland Press: New York, 1997), pp. 409–11.

[14] Rognon, "Evolution," p. 51 and figure 7, p. 49; Jean Risier and Nicole Petit-Maire, "Paléohydrologie du bassin d'Araouane à l'Holocène," *Revue de Géologie Dynamique et de Géographie Physique*, 27 (3–4) (1986), pp. 205–12; S. McIntosh and R. McIntosh. "Archaeological reconnaissance, Timbuktu," pp. 305–7, 315–17.

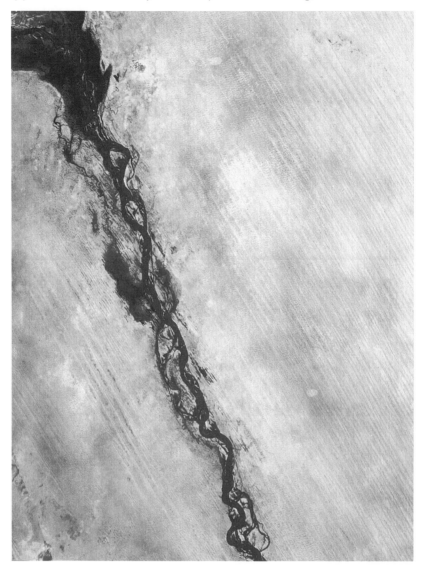

Plate 2.4   *Satellite photo of the El Ahmar palaeochannel and Azawad dune System.*

dering is clearly traced on satellite images and aerial photos. During the Holocene lacustrine period, the major palaeochannels must have been permanent. From the finds of a 1.6m long perch (*Lates niloticus*) that will not tolerate stagnant conditions, we know that well-oxygenated water flowed in the larger palaeochannels during much of the Holocene pluvial. We see an illustration in the Diaka *marigot* that services the Macina basin today. Most other channels probably dried for several months of the year, as do the majority of the *marigots* in the live basins of the Middle Niger today.

The scores of palaeochannels visible on air and satellite photos have not yet been visited by archaeologists, much less systematically surveyed. The revealing exception was a total survey of the proximal (southern) 13 kilometers of the Wadi El Ahmar. Survey began at its point of departure from the Niger floodplain, about three kilometers east of Timbuktu.[15] There are a hundred doctoral dissertations just waiting in the Malian Sahara. The lack of prior interest in these fossil channels is all the more curious because they would have been a natural route for peoples pushing south to the four still-viable basins of the Middle Niger when modern Saharan conditions set in.

Archaeologists have recently been asked to think about the implications of adaptation to a tightly interwoven mix of micro-environments within and along the palaeochannels.[16] Let us imagine, for a moment the mosaic of environments confronting those communities. Palaeochannels were lined by levees, often in series, erected in clays or sands by the floods. The levees would have supported a tall, varied grass and a rather heavily treed (riparian) environment. Within the channels proper, fish-rich depressions and sand or clay bars and banks would have emerged with the seasonal decline in the water level. In experiments that led to full plant domestication, these features would have been perfect for the incipient recessional plant cultivation (preferential harvesting, tending, protection of grasses in the soils exposed by receding flood waters).

The aforementioned paludial backswamps, as well as permanently dry features such as dune crests and higher elevation plains would also have been no great distance from the palaeochannels. The fauna of these distinct environments would have been within walking distance for the hunters of these communities.

Semi-arid steppe   Away from stream-side and lake-side was the broad grass and lightly treed steppe. The non-inundated Azawad plains would have experienced the spectrum of botanical person-

---

[15] S. McIntosh and R. McIntosh, "Archaeological reconnaissance, Timbuktu," pp. 302–18.

[16] R. McIntosh, "Pulse model," pp. 181–200.

alities, from rather heavily wooded savanna (during pluvial conditions) to marginal grass and thorn shrub. Relief on the grasslands was undulating, reflecting the underlying late Pleistocene parallel dune system. For millennia, the steppe was home to giraffe, elephant, rhino, lion, several species of savanna and sahel antelope – and, less certainly, to wild cattle (*Bos taurus*) and zebra.

In our enthusiasm for Holocene lacustrine adaptations, the importance of these steppes for stone-using peoples is too often overlooked. At the northern margin of the Azawad and in the Foum el Alba region, there is a curious delay of nearly two millennia to the commencement of human occupation. The northern palaeolakes fill at 9,500–9,000 years ago. But where are the people who should be exploiting the aquatic resources? By *c.*7000 BP, this dune landscape was stabilized by the regular rains and by the resulting grass cover: the swampy interdunes develop a characteristic red-brown palaeosol. Only then do we find communities in any appreciable density. The treed grasslands were the domain of hunters. The grasslands were also certainly supportive of the domestic cattle tended by at least some late stone age communities after the *c.*7000 BP bioclimatic optimum. By this date, human occupation was widespread, intensive, and, burgeoning.[17]

The various water bodies and landforms above are not segregated into neat precincts. All Middle Niger basins are mosaics comprised of most landforms just described, in differing proportion, mixed as if by some diabolical random principle. In fact, that principle is layered transformation. The mixture of microenvironments (Petit-Maire's biogeographical crossroads) would have supported a high diversity of plant and animal resources. That diversity is more than matched by the site-to-site variability and high density of archaeological sites carpeting those same landforms.

---

[17] Petit-Maire, "Homo climaticus," p. 66; Susan Keech McIntosh and Roderick J. McIntosh, "From stone to metal: New perspectives on the later prehistory of West Africa," *Journal of World Prehistory*, 2 (1) (1988), pp. 94, 97–101; Vernet, 'Préhistoire des bassins', figure 2, p. 66. There is a single (anomalous?) early radiocarbon date of 6090–5590 BC for Hassi el Abiod, and Raimbault remarks (in "Industrie lithique," in Petit-Maire and Risier, *Sahara ou Sahel*, pp. 319–22) that there was clearly a culturally distinct, "epipalaeolithic" occupation of the Foum el Alba region, some 150 km north of the Azawad as early as the seventh millennium BC. The critical point, still, is that serious colonization of the Azawad was delayed by one or two millennia after the recharging of the northern Malian lakes.

From the extensive surveys of Gallay and the Missions Paléoenvironnements , we have some feel for the diversity of sites in two parts of the Azawad.[18] From the differences in lithics and in food remains at various sites, it is likely that different activities predominated at different sites.

There are areally extensive sites on the dune–lake interface, sites with scores (or hundreds, in some cases) of bone harpoons, thick with fish and aquatic mammal bone. Other, nearly identical sites, but with negligible numbers of bone harpoons, can be found deeper within the interdunes and within the interiors of the backswamps and playas. The former may have been the camps of semi-sedentary fishermen and hunters of crocodile, hippo, and turtle. The latter were possibly the camps of more specialized fisherfolk. Both types of sites appear to have been the home, either for one or a very few repeat visits of a large community, or of smaller bands that revisited these preferred locales over and over. Yet another distinctive type of site is the shell and bone midden (archaeologists import the term *kjökkemmödding*). These range in area from 10 to 60 m². Some middens abound in lithics and bone tools. Others yield few tools. Although the middens are rarely more than a meter high, the quantity of fish, mollusk, and large aquatic faunal remains found there suggest a location of seasonally extended occupation.

Sites with grindstones (for plant processing) are abundant in the far north, far less so around Hassi el Abiod or the central Azawad. In some cases, the grindstones were very abundant and other tools far less so. It is hard to escape the conclusion that gathering and collecting of wild plant remains must have constituted a majority occupation at this type of site. It is uncertain at what period peoples of these communities began to dedicate themselves to local plant resources. Archaeologists debate whether the process was accelerated or inhibited by dramatic dry spells, such as the southern

---

[18] This diversity of Azawad sites and the issue of specialization and intergroup differences is assessed by Vernet, "Préhistoire des bassins," pp. 68–70 and Jean Devisse and Robert Vernet, "Le bassin des Vallées du Niger: Chronologie et espaces," in *Vallées du Niger,* (Editions de la Réunion des Musées Nationaux, Paris, 1993), p. 17. In broader, (southern) Saharan perspective, Vernet terms 4000 BP the "date charnière," the "turning or fulcrum point" for expansion of diversity – Robert Vernet, "Le Néolithique récent dans le sud-ouest du Sahara," in *Environmental Change and Human Culture in the Nile Basin and Northern Africa until the Second Millennium BC* , L. Krzyzaniak, M. Kobusiewcz, and J. Alexander, (eds) (Poznan Archaeological Museum: Posnan, 1993), p. 92, 94–5.

Sahara experienced at 6500–6000 BP or 4500–4000 BP.[19] In time, the grass and vegetable gatherers of the community may have concentrated preferentially on a few grain species. In so doing, they began a long experimental process in which they slowly shifted from opportunistic gathering to weeding, irrigating, and even sowing. With these steps they began down the long path to domestication of the major cereals such as sorghum, millet, and African rice.

Beyond these differences, Azawad sites show enormous differences in their flaked stone tool assemblages. At most sites, tools are made of the same materials. Therefore, these differences cannot be explained solely by raw materials used. Some basic forms are identical over wide areas (e.g., all-purpose scrapers at Foum el Alba and Hassi el Abiod). Taken as a whole, however, lithics vary significantly between sites within the same surveyed region.[20] The numerous blades, backed bladelettes, arrow and lance points were probably used by the hunters of grassland grazers. Other assemblages suggest several variations on a theme of a generalized toolkit. These assemblages would have been useful for those engaged in aquatic hunting and fishing or processing plants. Ceramics can be abundant at some sites, rare at others and, like lithics, display great diversity in predominating form and decoration.[21] What, then, do we make of all this diversity?

Views of the Stone-Using Communities

Systematic survey is a basic tool of the archaeologist.[22] It is a strategy of exploration in which all sites are recorded (all site types; all peri-

---

[19] Ibid., p. 93; S. McIntosh and R. McIntosh "From stone," p. 100; S. McIntosh, "Changing perceptions," pp. 169–70; Roderick J. McIntosh, "African agricultural beginnings,"; Vernet, 'Néolithique récent', p. 93.

[20] Michel Raimbault, "Industrie lithique," in *Sahara ou Sahel?*, Petit-Maire and Riser (eds), pp. 317–41; Raimbault, "Pour une approche," pp. 67–81.

[21] Dominique Commelin, 'Céramique', in *Sahara ou Sahel?*, Petit-Maire and Riser (eds), pp. 343–66.

[22] The basic arguments for systematic survey and for the use of probability theory in its design are given in: Roderick J. McIntosh and Susan Keech McIntosh, "Les prospections d'après les photos aériennes: Régions de Djenné et Tombouctou," in Réunion des Musées Nationaux, *Vallées du Niger*, pp. 234–43; S. K. Fish and S. Kowalewski, *The Archaeology of Regions,* (The Smithsonian Institution Press: Washington DC, 1990); for an analogous floodplain situation, see Steve Falconer and Stephen Savage, "Heartlands and hinterlands: Alternative trajectories of early urbanism in Mesopotamia and the southern Levant," *American Antiquity* 60 (1) (1995), pp. 37–58.

ods). Ideally, the survey team covers every landform in a broad region, in its totality, by foot. Unfortunately, in the Azawad, we lack even a single such ideal survey. Still, we have the beginnings of an impression of human occupation patterns during the lacustrine phases and after the onset of final desiccation. That impression is of a rather dense, largely mobile population skilled in the exploitation of the riches of their environment. These communities did so in a way that shows appreciation of the resource personality of each microenvironment.

The Azawad demonstrates a high site density, extraordinary diversity of sites, and the distribution of several sites of quite different personality on the same landform. Often several sites of very different character cluster very close together. There are four ways to interpret this pattern: eponymous and evolutionary, facies, seasonality, and articulated specialization. Differences of opinion on the four options go to the very core of generational or national traditions of field research and interpretation.

The true story will never be sorted out until the Azawad is covered by many more systematic surveys. Until lithic assemblages are analyzed by style, function, and tool task, and until sites are dated to far greater precision, interpretation of prehistoric activities and mobility will remain speculative. The last is especially important. Knowing the dates of a site's occupation is fundamental to any argument of contemporaneous or sequential occupation of neighboring sites. The issue of sequential or simultaneous occupation of nearby sites is important to all, but is critical to at least two of the views of stone-using communities. In my opinion, these two (seasonality nested within articulated specialization) are most consistent with the best available evidence for the Late Stone Age settlement history of the peoples of the Middle Niger. Others demur.[23] For the moment, we must be content to discuss the four options and let future research sort the fact from the speculation.

The first way to approach the late stone age of the Azawad is to ignore diversity altogether. This approach I call eponymous and evolutionary. It is eponymous because the characteristics of one or a small cluster of type sites overwhelms the diversity of remains at later discovered sites within a very broad region. This view is also evolutionary because these sites are typically seen to represent stages in a progressive sequence from less developed to more complex social or economic forms. The Sahara is the testing ground for one of the discipline's most seductive grand interpretations of a prehis-

[23] Michel Raimbault, pers. com., December 2 1992.

toric way of life. During the early 1970s, africanist archaeologists developed the argument that a successful, aquatic-based adaptation swept the Sahara from sources in the upper Nile or Rift Valley regions.[24] This adaptation was more successful than preceding scattered (epipalaeolithic) hunting, but its very success would delay advancement to the "neolithic" domestication of plants and animals. This thesis is assimilative and diagnostic.

According to its classic formulation, peoples moving from the east, perhaps as early as 9,000 years ago, brought with them characteristic ceramics and bone tools. Most significantly, they brought a knowledge of how efficiently to exploit the riches of the newly green Sahara. They assimilated local peoples as the wave spread through and south of the highlands (massifs) of the central Sahara. Often they colonized and exploited the lakeshores and swamps that the Holocene rains had created of areas long abandoned during the late Pleistocene hyperarid phase. This aquatic civilization (nicknamed the "Aqualithic") came to be recognized by its diagnostic artifacts. These diagnostics were bone harpoon, ceramics with a wavy-line or dotted wavy-line decoration, and an aquatic subsistence base. Others added polished stone hachettes (small axes or adzes), stone bracelets, and globular pottery. Significantly, some archaeologists complain that the lithic assemblages were of a "disconcerting poverty."[25] As a consequence, lithics were considered to be of little value for an evaluation of the Aqualithic culture area. For those writing syntheses of African prehistory, the Azawad bone harpoon, lake and swamp sites became the eponymous Aqualithic communities.[26]

Unhappily, grand industrial constructs such as the 'Aqualithic' predispose researchers to see the similarities of a few privileged artifact types (and thus to speak of overall homogeneity).[27] The

---

[24] Gabriel Camps, *Les Civilisations Préhistoriques de l'Afrique du Nord et du Sahara*, (Doin: Paris, 1974), pp. 221–56; Gabriel Camps, "Extension territoriale des civilisations épipaléolithique et néolithique dans le nord de l'Afrique," *Acts of the Sixth Panafrican Congress of Prehistory and Quaternary Studies*, (Dakar, 1967) (Chambéry: Les Imprimeries Réunies, 1972), pp. 284–7; Sutton, "Aquatic civilisation," pp. 527–46.

[25] Camps, *Civilisation Préhistoriques*, p. 231.

[26] Ibid., pp. 254–6; Smith, "Neolithic tradition," p. 452.

[27] Two examples, from utterly thorough researchers who have themselves recorded inter-site artifact differences: François Paris, Alain Person, and Jean-François Saliège, "Peuplements et environnements holocènes du bassin de l'Azawagh oriental (Niger)," in Réunion des Musées Nationaux, *Vallées du Niger*, p. 388; and Vernet, "Préhistoire des bassins affluents," pp. 71–3.

equally important, but statistical variability in assemblages is sub-ordinated.

More recently, scholars have begun to play closer attention to differences in lithic assemblages. Variability can be measured broadly across the Sahara or regionally. Variability is revealed by more exacting studies of ceramic or lithic percentages and faunal or botanical studies of the communities' food supply.[28] Intensive local studies of lithics and other remains are now available from widely separated regions, the Egyptian Western Desert, the Hoggar massif of Algeria, Azawagh Valley of Niger, and the Tilemsi Valley of Mali.[29]

Again and again, this detailed research shows that broadly shared attributes in ceramics (such as the wavy-line decor) or in one or two tool types are simply not persuasive enough to explain away significant differences between sites. Intersite differences can be plotted in the tool assemblage composition, geographical preferences for site location, and the animal remains left behind. The human ecology of these sites is different. Within the limits of precision afforded by radiocarbon dating, some of the different stone-using communities show signs of being genuinely contemporaneous. Most importantly, they may have had contact with each other. This is an interpretation very much at odds with the classic eponymous and evolutionary formulation. Rather than one extraordinarily homogeneous "culture," highly successful, highly assimilative and, from 9,000 to perhaps 3,000 years ago, steadfastly conservative – we now appear to have a frenzy of local adaptations.

Only more intensive survey will tell us if we, too, can character-

---

[28] The two principal works are MacDonald, *Socio-Economic Diversity* and J-P. Maitre, "Notes sur deux conceptions traditionelles du néolithique Saharien," *Libyca*, 20 (1972), pp. 125–36; see also, Vernet, "Préhistoire des bassins," pp. 69–70 and S. McIntosh and R. McIntosh, "From stone to metal," pp. 97–102.

[29] Thanks to MacDonald, *Socio-Economic Diversity*, p. 3 and pers. comm., 1994 for bringing this growing literature to my attention (MacDonald's supporting study of Méma lithics follows). Western Desert: Thomas R. Hays, "An examination of the Sudanese Neolithic," in *Proceedings of the 7th Panafrican Congress of Prehistory and Related Studies*, A.Berhanou, J. Chevaillon, and J.E.G. Sutton (eds) (Provisional Military Government of Socialist Ethiopia, Ministry of Culture: Addis Ababa, 1971), pp. 85–92; Hoggar: J.-P. Maitre, "Schémas d'evolution culturelle, I. Note sur la répartition régionale des décors céramiques néolithiques sahariens," *L'Anthropologie*, 83 (1979), pp. 584–601; Azawagh: Paris, Person and Saliège, "Peuplements et environnements," p. 388; Tilemsi: Marianne Cornevin, *Archéologie Africaine. A la Lumière des Découvertes Récentes* (Maisonneuve et Larose: Paris, 1993), pp. 99–102 and Smith, "Neolithic tradition," pp. 460–3.

ize the apparent variability of sites in the Azawad as evidence of many adaptations. That is not what is predicted by the second interpretive tradition: multiplying facies. The second way of looking at these sites is genetic and normative. In this tradition, the function of tools and the details of a past peoples' way of life and of their ecological adaptations are largely irrelevant.

The attempt to define facies is unquestionably more rigourous than the search for the Aqualithic. The exercise is still one of selective forgiveness of variability. In the facies approach, one looks for a single or (more commonly now) a restricted cluster of shared lithics in local assemblages or for shared ceramic designs and pot forms. These clusters define facies. In the Sahara, the defining tools or decorative marks are called *fossiles directeurs*, or diagnostics. The facies are coherent and integral over time and space. Facies represent the material culture signature of a "people" who shared a common set of norms for making pots and tools. Facies would be long lasting and would change rarely for internal reasons. Change is due more often to outside influences, either to migration or (with more difficulty) to diffusion in of new ideas. Thus one can trace the genetic affinities of newly appeared facies. Boundaries between facies are marked by slowly permeable cultural membranes.

Gallay explains the differences in his sites near Araouane as reflecting three successive facies.[30] The archaeologist attached to the Missions Paléoenvironnements, defines five lithic facies from the Azawad and locations north and east.[31] Dealing with the same sites, another archaeologist defines four facies on the basis of the ceramics.[32] The pottery is, if anything, more diverse than the lithics. The five lithic facies cover at least two segments of the Holocene. Other localities, such as Bou Djebéha, have material so different they could not possibly be attached at any of these five facies.

The Missions Paléoenvironnements archaeologist, Raimbault does acknowledge the effect on the assemblage composition of "different geo-economic contexts" and the "reflections of synchronous groups."[33] Unfortunately, ecological and demographic diversity is at fundamental odds with a stadial, genetic, and normative conception of prehistory. Liberated from this facies way of approaching sites in the Azawad, there are two other approaches that can

[30] Gallay, "Quelques gisements," pp. 204–6.
[31] Raimbault, "Industrie lithique," pp. 317–41.
[32] Commelin, "Céramique," pp. 343–66.
[33] Raimbault, "Industrie lithique," pp. 331–2.

accommodate and, indeed, they predict high variability among contemporary sites.

The third interpretation begins with the presumption of seasonality – close seasonal adaptation and high seasonal mobility. All but the most sedentary communities (that is, everyone before people became utterly reliant upon agriculture) will have a component of seasonal movement to their yearly calendar.[34] In some cases, the community will pick up as a whole a few or many times during the year. In other instances, parts of the community will fission off during one or more seasons and will unify at a predictable time. Seasonality predicts that sites on different landforms within a group's territory will have the tools and food remains appropriate to the season's resources. All sites within a group's territory will also have some elements common to that single people's identity.

The Azawad sites have not been recorded in a manner that would allow us to specify types of sites and numbers of sites by landform. Nor have botanical or faunal materials from those sites been analyzed in such a way as to test the seasonality thesis. One needs to know the functional definition of the entire toolkit. One must also know the proportional efforts put into the different resources of each microenvironment in the sites' vicinity. With luck, one can determine the seasonal signature of each resource. The last is difficult, but not impossible. For example, some fish (such as *Alestes*) are highly seasonal in their habits. High counts of newborn or very young animals in the faunal remains can give accurate estimates of the months during which a site was used.

Seasonality has not been considered in the Azawad, but has at a series of broadly contemporaneous (or slightly earlier) sites in the northern arch of the Hodh depression in Mauritania.[35] Although distant from the Middle Niger, Tichitt region of the Hodh is central to a discussion of the first peoples to enter the live basins. Ceramics made by the first colonists to the deepest of those live basins, the

---

[34] For a general introduction to seasonal settlement analysis, see Karl W. Butzer, *Archaeology as Human Ecology. Method and Theory for a Contextual Approach.* (Cambridge University Press: Cambridge, 1992), pp. 230–43, esp., figure 13.1, p. 236 and figure 13.2, p. 238. For a classic Mesoamerican application, Richard S. MacNeish, *The Science of Archaeology?*, (Duxbury Press: North Scituate, MA, 1978), pp. 124–70.

[35] Augustin Holl, *Economie et Société Néolithique du Dhar Tichitt (Mauritanie)*, (Editions Recherches sur les Civilisations, ADPF: Paris, 1986); Augustin Holl, "Subsistence patterns of the Dhar Tichitt, Mauritania," *The African Archaeological Review*, 3 (1985), pp. 151–62.

Macina and Upper Delta, are more similar to Hodh pottery than to any other late stone age ceramics.[36] And, some of the late stone-using pastoral and agricultural communities of the second dry basin, the Méma, probably migrated in after *c.*3500–3300 BP from the Hodh.[37]

The varied sites around Tichitt have submitted to all the interpretative fashions: Aqualithic homogeneous, sequential facies, and most recently they have been labeled the components of a two-season exploitation round. Holl considered the substantial masonry sites high atop a 60-meter escarpment overlooking an old lake bed. He then looked at the ephemeral scatters on the sandy flats and interdunal depression within the bed of the lake itself. The Tichitt lake rose and fell dramatically by season. During the wet season, inhabitants of the large sites grew domesticated millet and kept large herds at the settlement. During the hard dry season the group fissioned off. One part gathered wild grain and fished at the receding banks of the lake (another, presumably, drove the cattle to greener pastures).

Seasonality is a temptingly elegant interpretation, but in the Tichitt case it has come under considerable criticism.[38] A seasonality hypothesis requires a large series of internally-consistent absolute dates to establish contemporaneity of all sites in the seasonal round. If, from 4,000 to 2,000 years ago, the Dhar Tichitt environment was changing fast and desiccation made life quite unbearable, then even a few hundred years could have seen dramatic changes in ecology and the settlement system. Just such a sequence of eight stages had earlier been posited by Munson. In a rejoinder to Holl's seasonality, Munson questions why Holl arbitrarily lumps together all the region's radiocarbon dates from 46 sites in an 660 km² area. Munson (and many others) is reluctant to accept a hypothesis that posits a state of cultural stasis for some 2,000 years. Could there really have been no

---

[36] Susan Keech McIntosh, *Excavations*, pp. 362–3.

[37] MacDonald, *Socio-Economic Diversity*, pp. 105–6.

[38] Patrick Munson, "Debate about 'Economie et Société Néolithique du Dhar Tichitt (Mauritanie),' " *Sahara* 2 (1989), pp. 106–8; Alfred Muzzolini, "A reappraisal of the 'Neolithic' of Tichitt (Mauritania)," *Journal of Arid Environments*, 16 (1989), pp. 101–5; and especially, MacDonald, *Socio-Economic Diversity*, pp. 108–11 and "Tichitt-Walata and the Middle Niger: evidence for cultural contact in the second millennium BC," in *Aspects of African Archaeology. Papers from the 10th Congress of the PanAfrican Association for Prehistory and Related Studies*, Gilbert Pwiti and Robert Soper (eds), (University of Zimbabwe Publications: Harare, 1996), pp. 429–40.

adjustments to a demonstrably worsening climate? Holl hurts his case by simply assuming that all Tichitt sites, no matter their landform position, size or economic component, are homogeneous. The seasonality thesis requires a demonstration of a single group's intersite variations – with functional, adaptive explanations by season.

Munson provides perhaps the most significant argument against seasonality as the only explanation for the differences in Tichitt sites. He argues, "There is however, or at least should be, a corollary assumption, which Holl does not consider, namely that contemporary sites occupied by members of the same social group and located in the same physiographic situation and at the same seasons would be expected to show very similar subsistence activities. This is not the case."[39] Sites of different size classes, located on the same landform (plateau-top, in this case) yield quite different economic evidence. How might the interpretation of the Tichitt material shift if we change the assumption about the identity of those communities? Can we exclude the possibility of contemporary sites occupied by members of *different social groups* and located in the same or adjacent physiographic situations?

With that question we introduce the possibility of a fourth interpretation of the Azawad communities: articulated specialization. The reader will recall from discussion of Gallay's Arouane survey, the high density of sites on the same or adjacent landforms. These sites show great variability in tools, presence of grinding stones, ceramics, and in fish, animal or shell remains. And yet they also show similarities in several elements, such as polished stone axes, stone bracelets, a few pottery decorations, and several types of stone tools (but not all). The fourth interpretive alternative combines a spin on the seasonality theme with the possibility of interacting communities of specialists.

According to this fourth interpretation, the Azawad would, through time, have evolved into a landscape of subsistence specialists. The specialists – fisherfolk, hunters of the steppe, pastoralists, and perhaps incipient gatherer-cultivators – regarded themselves as "ethnically" different, yet maintained frequent and complementary relations with other groups.[40] Site variability in the Azawad reflects the seasonal movements and activities of several communities. These communities defined their interest in the same landform in terms of different resources, different seasons of the year, when it was useful

---

[39] Munson, "Debate," pp. 107–8.
[40] R.McIntosh, "Pulse model," pp. 181–220; see Devisse and Vernet, "Le bassin," p. 17.

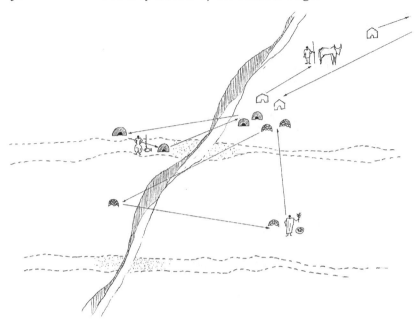

Figure 2.1   *Articulated activities of early specialists
(Courtesy of Matt Harvey)*.

for them to occupy that landform. Just as importantly, the communities were articulated. They exchanged the fruit of their labour freely against the surplus of other groups. Different communities may very well have found it useful to set up camp nearby the camps of others, at least for short periods.

If participated in amicably, this system would have the effect of sharing the wealth. It would also help to smooth out the environmental stresses that were a constant fact of life in the later stages of Saharan desiccation. This system would have provided the addition advantage of allowing each group to turn their attention more and more to their particular slice of the ecological pie. Those skilled in the tending of herds could devote more of their time to the transhumant search for pasturage. Those skilled in fishing could depend more on others for the grains of their diet. Those skilled in the gathering and processing of wild plants could devote more time to the preferential harvest and storage of certain species. These, eventually, will be domesticated.

This alternative provides an explanation for the proximity of varied sites: articulation in a predictable system of exchange. We would expect to find differences between communities because of their specialist activities and because of style used to signal a separate identity. Other items are widely exchanged or widely emulated. And so, Raimbault muses that the similarities within differences he sees in northern Malian lithics and ceramics may reflect "synchrony of different groups".[41] The perfect characterization of articulation of early specialists – by a dedicated proponent of the facies explanation!

This model of articulated, segmented communities has a built-in prediction of increasing specialization. Its corollary is increasing interdependence among partners in this landscape of exchange. Increasing interdependence may mean that communities elect to remain close to each other for longer periods as time progresses. That dynamism contrasts with the argument of cultural stasis that sometimes lies at the heart of the seasonality thesis. It is an argument of internal dynamism that relieves the archaeologist of always having to look for external sources of change (migration, stimulus diffusion).

The appeal of this thesis is that it provides a long continuity to a system of relations among equivalent specialized groups that remains, still today, a signature of the people of the Middle Niger. Unhappily the articulated specialization alternative is, as yet, completely untested in the Azawad. Now, however, there is recent supporting research from the second dead basin of the Middle Niger. From the Méma (and from the Gourma, far at the southeastern margin of the Middle Niger) there is some of the best evidence from anywhere in the Sahara that late stone-using groups had begun to diverge in their subsistence activities, and yet lived in proximity to one another for at least part of each year. We turn now to that second basin, and to the story of climate change that can be traced there.

Adaptations to the Drying Méma

Occupation ends in the Azawad at between 4,000 and 3,200 years ago. Abandonment of this basin (and of the Taoudenni and Hodh Depressions, or the Adrar des Iforas) leaves one of the grand questions of Middle Niger prehistory. Where did these people go when

[41] Raimbault, 'Industrie lithique', p. 322 and 'Pour une approche', p. 70; see also, Danilo Grébénart, Relations inter-éthniques Saharo-sahéliennes dans l'Ouest africain durant la préhistoire finale et la protohistoire', *Préhistoire et Anthropologie Méditerranéennes* 4 (1995), p. 122.

the climate turned against them? Prehistorians have traditionally looked to the Méma for the answer. The reason is found in any map of the ancient hydrology of the southern Sahara. As well as being, hypothetically, ideal landscapes for the emergence of specialist producers and for close-contact relations of complementary reciprocity between them, these palaeochannels would have been the last water sources to dry out. Climate oscillations during the last several millennia BC would create a 'pulse' of population movement north and south along these long fossil channels. The model predicts that, with the final Saharan desiccation, communities most closely related to the Azawad (or more northerly Malian), or Tichitt, or Tilemsi Valley refuge groups would be ejected into the hinterland of these corridors' southern reaches.[42] Indeed, during the colonial period, archaeologists searched for classic Aqualithic sites along the lower course of Méma palaeochannels. When the triumph of the wind was complete in the rest of the Sahara, these now fossil corridors would still have been a chain of shallow lakes, with quite extensive seasonal floodplains. There, at sites such as Kobadi and Kolima, they recorded abundant bone harpoons, a thick litter of fish, crocodile, hippo bone, and wavy-line pottery.[43]

Even without the drama of Azawad depopulation, the Méma site of Kobadi alone would have fired archaeologists' interest in the Méma. The site is a long, thin (360 m by *c*.30 m.) heavy scatter on a levee fronting one of the major, and now senescent palaeochannels (the Bras de Nampala). Very recently Raimbault conducted his usual thorough testing of several locations within the site.[44] His locations yielded more than 100 burials of individuals of a characteristic

---

[42] MacDonald, *Socio-Economic Diversity*, pp. 273–5 and "Tichitt-Walata." For the end of the Azawad and Taoudenni Basin sequences, see Commelin, et al., "Nouvelles données," pp. 543–50.

[43] Monod and Mauny, 'Découverte', pp. 242–7; Raimbault, "Pour une approche," p. 80.

[44] Michel Raimbault, *Sahara Malien: Environnement, Populations et Industries Préhistoriques*, Thèse d'Etat, Université de Provence, 1994; and "Le gisement néolithique de Kobadi (Sahel malien) et ses implications paléohydrologiques," in *Changements Globaux en Afrique Durant le Quaternaire. Passé-Présent-Futur*, H. Faure, L. Faure, and E. S. Diop (eds) (Editions de l'ORSTOM: Paris 1986), pp. 393–7; Michel Raimbault and Olivier Dutour, "Les nouvelles données du site néolithique de Kobadi dans le Sahel malien," *Travaux du Laboratoire d'Anthropologie et de Préhistoire des Pays de la Méditerranée Occidentale*, (1989), pp. 175-83; Michel Raimbault, C. Guérin and M. Faure, "Les vertébrés du gisement néolithique de Kobadi (Mali)," *Archaeozoologia*, 12 (1987), pp. 224–7.

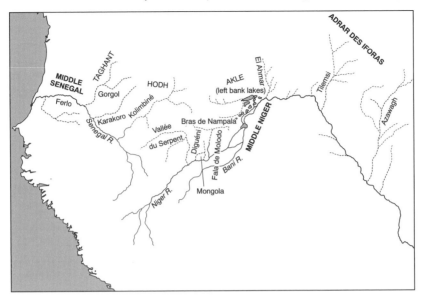

Map 2.2   *Ancient hydrology: southern Saharan palaeochannels*

Plate 2.5   *Kolimbiné corridor of western Mali: imagining palaeochannel environments in the fourth millennium BP.*

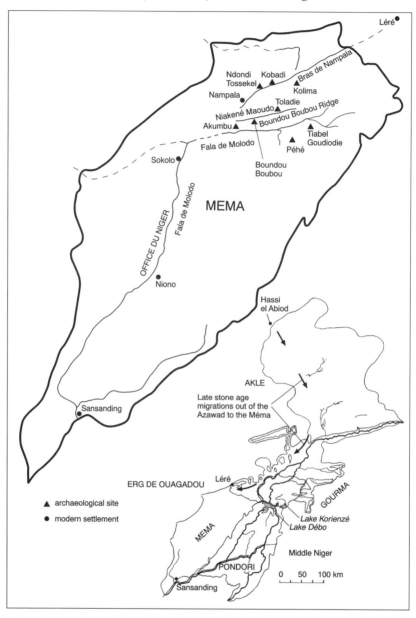

Map 2.3   *MEMA: dead delta landforms and sites*

archaic form (Mechtoïd, known also from Hassi el Abiod). There was evidence of fishing (catfish and Nile perch, *Lates*), and hunting (hippo, tortoise, crocodile, and the swamp-adapted antelope, *Sitatunga*). The site provided radiocarbon dates bracketing occupation between *c.*3,800 and 2,200 years ago. The dates, and the slightly earlier dates for Tiabel Goudiodie (4500–4300 BP) neatly place the beginning of known Méma occupation at the very close of habitation in the surveyed parts of the Azawad.

Two aspects of Kobadi are quite unlike the aquatically oriented Azawad sites. The first is the remains of domesticated cattle. We have known for some time that domestic cattle (and perhaps later, sheep and goat) come into the Sahara at around 6000 BP.[45] The usual Aqualithic argument has been that this was a minority pursuit by groups primarily interested in aquatic resources. Pastoralism became a majority pursuit only when climatic conditions became seriously degraded. However, there are several Saharan sites with abundant cattle remains, but few with remains of cattle, fish, and hunted animals all tossed together. Kobadi is one of those rare sites. So, were the inhabitants doing a bit of everything? A closer examination of the proportion of body parts has led another researcher, Kevin MacDonald, to the conclusion that the cattle was traded in from elsewhere.[46] That elsewhere is the second surprise about Kobadi and its neighbours. MacDonald and his Malian collaborator, Téréba Togola, believe that exchange relations existed by 3500–3300 BP among neighboring groups with different subsistence specializations and identities .

In order to understand why the Méma is the best support so far uncovered from prehistoric Africa for the articulated specialization hypothesis, we must briefly look at the survey data upon which MacDonald bases his conclusions. It is his conviction that these data show that the region was home to multiple contemporaneous groups. These communities were distributed, not in discrete spatial packages with centres and jealously attended frontiers, but in local mosaics of peoples and their adaptive strategies. Of these mosaic he writes that "high degrees of economic specialization require high degrees of interdependence."[47]

[45] S. McIntosh and R. McIntosh, "From stone to metal," pp. 97–102; Andrew B. Smith, "Cattle domestication in North Africa," *The African Archaeological Review*, 4 (1986), pp. 197–203.
[46] MacDonald, pers. comm. 1992 and *Socio-Economic Diversity*, pp. 114–15, 273–5.
[47] Ibid., p. 30.

The MacDonald–Togola survey of 1989–90 is the most systematic in the history of archaeological surveys of the Méma. Some colonial period searches for sites were conducted rather haphazardly in the vicinity of the massive historical sites of Péhé, Kolima, and Toladie.[48] Other extensive Iron Age site inventories were made by non-archaeologists during hydrological prospection or development projects and by prehistorians as part of Mali's national site inventory.[49] By the 1980s, more than two hundred Iron Age sites had been plotted and perhaps a half-dozen excavated (to varying degrees of care). However, only three late stone age sites had been investigated: Kobadi, Tiabel Goudiodié (a low shell midden on the banks of the Fala de Molodo), and the deeply stratified Kolima Sud.[50] The late stone age was rather the odd man out. Curious, since Kobadi was so often cited as a classic, late Aqualithic site.

In 1989–90, MacDonald and Togola combined regionally extensive systematic survey with excavation at deeply stratified sites to provide a chronological anchor.[51] These researchers retested the three meters of deposits at Kolima Sud and at another site, "Akumbu LSA." These were two of 28 stone age sites (out of a total of 137 sites) found within their survey region. The sites ranged from ex-

---

[48] Raymond Mauny, *Tableau Géographique*, pp. 97–100, 103–4; Georges Szumowski, "Fouilles au nord du Macina et dans la région de Ségou," *Bulletin de l'Institut Fondamental d'Afrique Noire (B)*, 19 (1957), pp. 224–58; Pierre-Bernard Fontes, Alain Person, and Jean-François Saliège, "Prospection de sites archéologiques de la région des lacs du delta intérieur du Niger (1980)," in *Recherches Archéologiques au Mali: Les Sites Protohistoriques de la Zone Lacustre*, Michel Raimbault and Kléna Sanogo (eds) (Paris, Agence de Coopération Culturelle et Technique: Karthala, 1991), pp. 34–7.

[49] Yves Urvoy, head hydrologist for the Office du Niger inventoried 80 "tumuli" (in fact, they are settlement sites) between Sokolo and Niafunké, see Mauny, *Tableau Géographique*, p. 97. The Centre International pour l'Elevage en Afrique plotted over 700 archaeological mounds north of the live deltas of the Middle Niger, of which most are in the Méma, see CIPEA, *Evolution de l'Utilisation des Terres et de la Végétation dans la Zone Soudano-Sahelienne* (CIPEA: Addis Abeba, 1981), p. 11; site inventory survey conducted by Téréba Togola and Michel Raimbault, "Les missions d'inventaire dans le Méma, Kanéri, et Farimaké" (1984–1985), in Raimbault and Sanogo, *Recherche Archéologique*, pp. 81–98.

[50] Ibid., pp. 81–98; Guitat, "Cartes et répertoire," (separate map) .

[51] The survey results are reported in: MacDonald, *Socio-Economic Diversity*, pp. 72–93; Téréba Togola, *Archaeological Investigation of Iron Age Sites in the Méma, Mali*, PhD Dissertation, Rice University (1993), pp. 38–64; Kevin MacDonald and Win Van Neer, "Specialized fishing peoples in the Later Holocene of the Méma region (Mali)," *Annales du Musée Royal de l'Afrique Centrale, Sciences Zoologiques*, 274 (1994), pp. 243–51.

tensive surface scatters to mounds stratified up to three meters, with areas from 0.25 ha. to more that 12 ha.

What most stood out was the high variability in lithics and ceramics. MacDonald has identified at least four ceramic traditions and has demonstrated, within the precision of current dating techniques, that at least some of these were contemporaneous. Faunal collections at these sites show significant differences. Some display a generalized exploitation of hunted, fished and herded resources. Others (with affinities to the 1250–850 BC Chebka/Arriane phase at the Tichitt sites) show an emphasis on domestic cattle or sheep and goat. Still others (with affinities to Hassi el Abiod) are dominated by fish, hippo, and crocodile and some have only fish or only shell fish. Some of those specialized sites are on the same levee as Kobadi, not terribly far away.

The pattern of tightly packed, highly varied sites recalls the hypothesis of articulated, specialist groups presented above. Here, at sites such as Kobadi and Kolima Sud, we have strong evidence for exchange among the groups. The herding communities traded cattle for fish. There appears to have been a general circulation of tiny polished stone axes (hachettes), stone arm rings, and drilled stone or shell beads, and even the exchange throughout the Méma of pre-worked lithics of jasper, siltstone, schist, and dolorite from distant sources.[52] These signs of exchange among specialists are all the more convincing because, in a similar survey in the dry Gourma of the eastern Middle Niger, MacDonald was able to document neighboring specialists *conspicuously without* neighborly relations of reciprocity and commerce.[53]

Significantly, there are a handful of later stratified sites, occupied primarily during the first millennium AD, but with lithic deposits at their fringes. These sites are prime candidates for a continuous transition, during the later first millennium BC, from stone-using to iron-using. However, compared to the numbers of pure late stone age sites and to the great proliferation of first millennium AD sites, these transitional sites are relatively rare. This is not at all the exception in West Africa. In 1995, Téréba Togola excavated these transitional levels at Akumbu.[54] There, he found a new type of ceramic, the

---

[52] MacDonald, *Socio-Economic Diversity*, pp. 50–62, 114–15, 227.
[53] Ibid, pp. 249–51; Kevin C. MacDonald, Téréba Togola, Rachel Hutton MacDonald, and Cecilia Capezza, "International news; Douentza, Mali," *PAST, The Newsletter of the Prehistoric Society*, 17 (4) (1994), pp. 12–14.
[54] Téréba Togola, pers. com., 1995.

highly distinctive, thin-walled "chinaware," or fineware paste pottery of the earliest occupations of the Macina (Dia) and Upper Delta (Jenné-jeno).

Thus, we have a curious – and complex – pattern of prehistoric occupation in the Méma. There are few sites demonstrably earlier than *c.*4500–4000 BP. There is a floruit of stone-using communities around 3500–3300 BP (with population injections from the Hodh and the Azawad). Then the region suffers an apparent sharp fall – off of population at *c.*800–500 BC (despite a final infusion of Tichitt folk at mid-millennium). Demography shows understandable signs of great stress during the 300 BC to AD 300 dry episode, of which we will speak later. An iron age explosion follows in the first millennium of the Present Era. At the close of that millennium, population dives precipitously. Oscillation of settlement density probably marched in step with oscillations of climate. Steep demographic declines probably mirror the incremental strangulation of the major palaeochannels that once kept the Méma every bit as viable as the Upper Delta or Macina today. The geomorphology of the Méma is a good illustration of the pulses of climate that swept the entire Middle Niger.

The Méma is roughly 25,000 km² of delta and aeolian deposits. This dry basin is framed to the northwest by the massive dune system called the Erg de Ouagadou and to the northeast by the live parallel dune system called the Aklé (separating the Azawad Basin from the low relief Méma). To the east is the Macina basin. The Méma Basin is crossed by three major palaeochannels that trend roughly southwest to northeast. The first of these (from south to north) is the Fala de Molodo. Furon[55] considered this to be a relict of a Pleistocene channel of the Niger leading north and then west of the present Méma all the way into the Hodh depression. The second is the Niakené Maoudo, separated from the Fala de Molodo by the ironpan covered sandstone hills of the Boulel and Boundouboubou Ridges. Finally, the Bras de Nampala crosses the extreme west of the Méma. These palaeochannels are defunct today. However, in the past, each encroached upon the framing dunes and erected complex systems of high levees interspersed with seasonally flooded pans and playas. These features indicate very clearly that, periodically, they were very powerful streams that changed channel often. They all fed large backswamp regions. The evidence

---

[55] Raymond Furon, "L'Ancien delta du Niger," *Révue de Géographie Physique et de Géologie Dynamique*, 2 (1929), pp. 270–3.

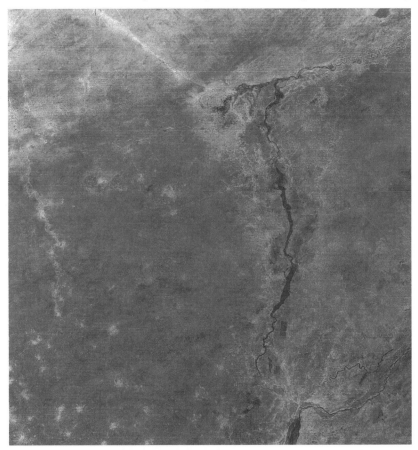

Plate 2.6 *Satellite photo of the recharged Fala de Molodo and the fringing fields of the Office du Niger (courtesy of Pat Jacobberger Jellison).*

that this senescent hydrological system had not been too badly degraded excited and delighted colonial engineers. The Fala de Molodo was selected to be artificially recharged as the hydrological spinal cord of the Office du Niger.

These landforms are the legacy of the dynamic climate history of West Africa. Researchers have only recently pieced together the minutiae of local sequences in a few localities (still far too few). Palaeoclimatologists compared the results with the lake-level record from the East African Rift Valley and to global-synchronous data generally. In effect, the coordination of the archaeological record of settlement and demographic change with the palaeoclimate record is among the best on the continent. We turn briefly to that climate record. Its effect on the peoples of the Middle Niger was always dramatic, and sometimes devastating. Surely, many of the enduring institutions of the inhabitants reflect the legacy of millennia of responses to this source of risk, surprise – and prosperity. These institutions ultimately provided highly adaptive, highly stable solutions to the potential conflicts of different ethnic or producer groups occupying this highly changeable semiarid tropical floodplain.

Palaeoclimate

Park[56] has examined the record of historical and present-day variability in rainfall and floods along the Middle Niger's close cousin, the Middle Senegal Valley. This kindred floodplain sits astride roughly the same rainfall zone (150 to 800mm). Like the Middle Niger, the Middle Senegal depends upon rainfall in the same distant Guinea Dorsal highlands for its annual floods. Park concludes that unpredictability – indeed, chaos – so strongly characterizes the historic and prehistoric climatic regime that no amount of knowledge of past trends will ever enable local peoples to manage that variability by means of storage or trade of foodstuffs.

Park's conclusions are of central relevance to thinking about how present and past populations adapted to the stressful requirements of the Middle Niger's tropical semi-arid climatic regime. He falls on the pessimistic end of a spectrum of researchers looking at the long-term record of West African climate for evidence of global periodicities. Park is reacting to recent failures to predict, for example, the end of the Sahel Drought[57]. By falling back on chaos

[56] Thomas K. Park, "Early trends towards class stratification: chaos, common property, and flood recession agriculture," *American Anthropologist*, 94 (1) (1992), pp. 91, 97–8.

[57] Hugues Faure and Jean-Yves Gac, "Will the Sahelian drought end in 1985?," *Nature*, 291 (1981), pp. 475–8; C. K. Folland, T. N. Palmer, and D. E. Parker, "Sahel rainfall and worldwide sea temperatures, 1901–1985," *Nature*, 320 (April 17 1986), pp. 602–7; P. Pestiaux, J-C. Duplessy, and A. Berger, "Paleoclimatic variability at frequencies ranging from 10-4 cycle per year to 10-3 cycle per year – evidence for nonlinear behavior of the climate system," in *Climate, History, Periodicity and Predictability*, Michael R. Rampino, John E. Sanders, Walter S. Newman and L.K. Königsson (eds) (Van Nostrand Reinhold, New York 1987), pp. 285–99; Nicole Petit-Maire, "Palaeoclimates in the Sahara of Mali," *Episodes*, 9 (1) (1986), p. 15.

theory, he asserts his belief in a very fundamental unpredictability. His prediction is that Middle Senegal populations would have responded by a property-based hierarchy and a mechanism by which populations most at risk can be physically moved away in times of threshold crises.

On the other end of the spectrum are those who are convinced of some degree of active local response to climate shifts and anomalies.[58] In this view, prediction of specific dry or wet events is less important than the cumulative social memory of climate change. In other words, sustainability for these prehistoric and historic populations meant curating experience over the centuries with precipitation and flood deviations. Sustainability also meant maintaining decision-making institutions and ways to spread the risk widely.

The 1980s and 1990s saw an unprecedented sophistication of models of general atmospheric circulation principles and of orbital and solar forcing mechanism . We have a qualitatively new understanding of teleconnections linking global climates. Fairbridge, among most palaeoclimatologists, is confident of soon achieving the "breakthrough" insight into the causes of climate change.[59] The Saharan and Sahelian historical, geomorphological, and lake level records of climate have made a significant contribution to this revolution in palaeoclimatic understanding.

Data from these arid tropical regions represent a rare low lati-

[58] Roderick J. McIntosh, Joseph Tainter, and Susan Keech McIntosh, *Global Change in History and Prehistory*, Columbia University Press: New York, 1998.
[59] Rhodes Fairbridge, "Monsoons and paleomonsoons," *Episodes,* 9 (1986), p. 143; the literature on global synchrony and forcing mechanisms is vast and heavily specialized, but of most interest to readers of this book will be J. E. Kutzbach, "The changing pulse of the monsoon," in *Monsoons,* Jay Fein and Pamela Stephens (eds) (Wiley: New York, 1987), pp. 247–68; J. D. Hays, John Imbrie, and N. J. Shackleton, "Variations in the Earth's orbit: Pacemaker of the Ice Ages," *Science*, 194 (4270) (1976), pp. 1121–94; COHMAP Members, "Climatic changes of the last 18,000 years: Observations and model simulations," *Science,* 241 (1988), pp. 1043–52; J. E. Kutzbach and F. A. Street-Perrott, "Milankovitch forcing of fluctuations in the level of tropical lakes from 18 to 0 kyr BP," *Nature,* 317 (1985), pp. 130–4; and H. E. Wright, et al., *Global Climates since the Last Glacial Maximum,* (University of Minnesota Press: Minneapolis, 1993), esp.ch. 2, pp. 5–11, ch. 3, pp. 12–23, and ch. 19, pp. 514–35; for more on the relevance to archaeologists of these hypotheses of global synchronies, see Susan K. McIntosh and Roderick J. McIntosh, "Current directions in West African prehistory," *Annual Review of Anthropology,* 12 (1983), pp. 219–25; and S.McIntosh and R.McIntosh "From stone to metal," pp. 92–7.

tude record of climate change to be compared against the better documented records from the middle and upper latitudes. These data come in three dimensions that should be mentioned briefly. The present Sahara has not always been so. The record of wetter times (pluvials) and alternating arid episodes, and of the all-important rate of climate shifts and oscillations, is a pluri-dimensional one best served by long-term, extensive regional, multidisciplinary projects. Two of these in the Sahara deserve particular attention: Paralleling the spectacular results of the Missions Paléoenvironnements du Sahara *Occidental et Central* in northern Mali is the Frankfort and Cologne Universities' Besiedlungsgeschichte der Ost-Sahara (or B.O.S. – "History of Population Dynamics in the Eastern Sahara") . The focus of this project was split between a long transect through the western Egyptian, Libyan, and Sudan deserts and, more recently, the Sahel of Burkino Faso and northeast Nigeria[60]. The second dimension is the continent – scale or sub-continent – scale syntheses of climate change since c. 50,000 BP.[61] The scale of these synthetic data compilations make them particularly useful for climate modeling purposes. The final dimension is represented by more tightly focussed, individual river basin or lake basin research in the Senegal River Valley, the Lake Chad floodplain,

---

[60] Rudolph Kuper, "Sahel in Egypt: Environmental change and cultural development in the Abu Ballas area, Libyan Desert," in Krzyzaniak, Kobusiewicz, and Alexander, *Environmental Change,* pp. 213–24 and "Agyptem am Rande des Sahel," *Archäologie in Deutschland,* 2 (1988), pp. 18–22; Katharina Neumann, "The contribution of anthracology to the study of the late Quaternary vegetation history of the Mediterranean region and Africa," *Bulletin de la Société Botanique de France,* 139 (1992), pp. 421–40; Aziz Ballouche and Katharina Neumann, "A new contribution to the Holocene vegetation history of the West African Sahel," *Vegetation History and Archaeobotany,* 4 (1995), pp. 31–9.

[61] Among many: F. A. Street-Perrott and R. A. Perrott, "Holocene vegetation, lake levels and climate of Africa," in Wright, et al., *Global Climates ,* pp. 318–56; Robert Vernet, *Climats Anciens du Nord de l'Afrique,* (Harmattan: Paris, 1995); Anthony T. Grove and A. Warren, "Quaternary landforms and climate on the south side of the Sahara," *Geographical Journal,* 134 (1968), pp. 194–208; Michael R. Talbot, "Environmental responses to climatic change in the West African Sahel over the past 20,000 years," in *The Sahara and the Nile,* Williams and Faure (eds), pp. 37–62; Pierre Rognon, "Essai d'interprétation des variations climatiques au Sahara depuis 40,000 ans," *Révue de Géographie Physique et de Géologie Dynamique,* 18 (1976), pp. 258–64; F. A. Street and Anthony T. Grove, "Environmental and climatic implications of late Quaternary lake-level fluctuations in Africa," *Nature,* 261 (1976), 387–8.; A.-M. Lézine, "Late Quaternary vegetation and climate of the Sahel," *Quaternary Research,* 32 (1989), pp. 317–34.

the extraordinary rain-gauge situation of Lake Bosumtwi (Ghana) and, of course, the middle course of the Niger[62].

In general, there is undeniable synchrony across the Sahara and Sahel of the climatic episodes discussed below (embracing, therefore, the Middle Niger). However, perhaps the most exciting research of the past decade emphasizes the "regionality," or local variants in the record. This is the reality on the ground that archaeologists must deal with: palaeoclimatic alternations at different scales, creating constantly-shifting microenvironments at the local scale. Prehistorians study the adaptations of past peoples to, in Vernet's words, "un paysage-mosaïque, succession de micro-milieux liés étroitement à des conditions locales variables à l'infini (a mosaic landscape, of micro-ecologies tightly linked to an almost infinitely-variable local climatic history").[63] How best to adapt to these conditions of infinite potential – but of high risk and low predictability? One way is Park's extreme stratification and coerced outmigration option, that is, hierarchy and centralized control. Or, there is Hassan's alternative that emphasizes a "society's capacity for revitalizing its organization and developing coping strategies"[64] – the very heart of heterarchy. Our ability to decide between these options improves as we better understand the nature of long-term climate oscillations.

Many of the landform modeling events one observes in the six basins of the Middle Niger can only be dated relatively. However, some events can be related with some confidence to phenomena or climate episodes dated absolutely in other parts of West Africa. While the general rule is that Middle Niger weather has always been highly variable, it is now clear that there have been different degrees to that unpredictability. Some periods had relatively less surprise (*c.*300 BC to AD 300; most of the first millennium AD; the later eighteenth century AD through about 1830; *c.*1860–1910). Others are marked by apparent spurts of high short-term or even

[62] For the last, see especially, A. Grove, *Niger*, esp. pp. 29–58; Jean Gallais, *Le Delta Intérieur du Niger, Etude de Géographie Régionale*, Mémoire No. 79 (Institut Fondamental de l'Afrique Noire: Dakar, 1967); Roderick J. McIntosh, "Floodplain geomorphology and human occupation of the upper Inland Delta of the Niger," *Geographical Journal*, 149 (2) (1983), pp. 182–201; Patricia Jacobberger, "Geomorphology of the upper inland Niger delta," *Journal of Arid Environments* 13 (1987), pp. 95–112.

[63] Vernet, *Climats Anciens*, p. 28, see pp. 76 and 147; see, also Cornevin, *Archéologie Africaine*, p. 43.

[64] Hassan, "Population ecology," p. 159.

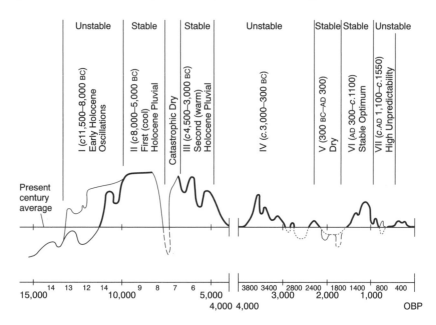

Figure 2.2   *Holocene palaeoclimatic sequence and stable-unstable mode shifts*

interannual variability (13,500–10,000 BP; *c.*3000 to 300 BC; AD twelfth to sixteenth and the mid-eighteenth centuries). These trends in the Middle Niger are entirely in line with recent global palaeoclimatic interpretations that emphasize abrupt mode-shifts (threshold events, sometimes called frequency domains or variability bands) from relative stability to high climate oscillation and back again, or from one kind of stable mode to another.[65]

The situation is further complicated by the fact that humans have to respond to three time-scales of variability. Unpredictability may dominate our perspective at a time-scale of 100 years or even of 1000 years. That need not make us forget that, at a prehistorian's perspective of 10,000 (or more) years, there have been significant humid and dry phases (each of greater or lesser stability).

[65] Jeffery S. Dean, "Human behavioral response to environmental change in the prehistoric American Southwest," in R. McIntosh, et al., *Global Climate Change*,; Robert Dunbar, "Climate variability during the Holocene: An update," in Ibid,; Fekri Hassan, "Abrupt Holocene climatic events and cultural responses in Africa," in *Proceedings of the 10th Congress of the Pan African Association for Prehistory and Related Studes* (University of Zimbabwe Publications: Harare, 1995), (Cambridge University Press: New York, 1996), pp. 83–9.

Local conditions during phases at all three time-scales provided constraints to human activity. Constraints, yes, but new potential for innovations in economy, technology, and social organization also appeared with these significant mode-shifts. We are very fortunate in semi-arid West Africa that, within the last 10–15 years, researchers have reached strong consensus on the broad outline of these long-term, mode-shift phases.[66] We can link geomorphological events in the Méma (and elsewhere in the Middle Niger) to those phases.

The erection of the Boulel Ridge laterite cap and the erosion at the edge the Ridge to form the flanking ironpan peneplain date to the alternative dry and wet episodes of *c*.40,000 to 20,000 BP. This laterite will one day be the foundation ore of the blacksmiths' prosperity. Undoubtedly, some of the deep floodplain deposits that underlie the mosaic of Middle Niger surface features date to the high alluviation of that period and even earlier. The first datable features are the massive erg systems of Ouagadou and Aklé. These dunes are part of a remarkable system of longitudinal dunes forming a continuous field from the Atlantic to the Qoz of Sudan. The Méma, Azawad, Niger Bend, and Erg of Bara sand fields are part of this continental dune system's Sahelian fringe. The broad dates for dune erection (referred to by geomorphologists as the Ogolian) are 20,000 to 15,000 BP.[67]

During the dry maximum (for approximately two millennia after 18,000 BP) both the Niger and Senegal ceased to flow through their middle valleys. Well-sorted alluvium, its path unimpeded by vegetation, was transported long distances by the winds. Temperature decreased by 3°–7° C. Most of the Sahel and Sahara was hyperarid and the desert's southern limit was as much as 400 kilometers to the south. It is very probable that vast sheets of earlier unconsolidated alluvium covering the entire Middle Niger were heavily deflated during this period. The deep excavation of the backswamps in the northern part of the Méma and, especially the Pondori of the Upper Delta, would date to the Ogolian.

The large dune sands were reddened (the first stage of soil-formation) when conditions improved during the early Holocene (mode I of table 2.1). Improvement may have begun as early as 13,500 year ago. However, the last few centuries of the Pleistocene were

[66] Roderick J. McIntosh, "The Mande weather machine and the social memory engine," in R. McIntosh, et al. *Global Climate Change.*
[67] Vernet, *Climats Anciens*, pp. 54–62; Grove, *Niger*, pp. 33–8.

Table 2.1 Climate and geomorphological events

Period	Conditions	Middle Niger Landforms
Mid–Late Quaternary	Alternating wet-dry	Laterite covering older alluvium at MN periphery and Boulel Ridge
40,000–20,000 BP	Pluvial (arid intervals)	Deeply bedded alluvium within all basins
20,000–13,000 BP	Hyperarid (Ogolian)	Massive parallel dunes (Ouagadou, Bara, Aklé); many basins deflated
Holocene I Early Holocene Oscillations		**HIGHLY UNSTABLE**
13,000–10,000 BP	Severe oscillations	Begin dune reddening
Holocene II First (Cool) Holocene Pluvial		**STABLE**
10,000–7500 BP	Pluvial	Paléo-Débo (?) covers southern basins; Niger and Bani meander; rivers deposit deep alluvium and high levees; river breaches Erg of Bara; (Fala de Molodo flows into Hodh?)
c.8,000 BP	Dry millennium	First white-yellow dunes
Holocene III Second (Warm) Pluvial		**MODERATELY STABLE**
6500–5000 BP	Pluvial	Niger-Bani find present channels
Holocene IV (Transition to Present Conditions)		**QUITE UNSTABLE**
4500–4100 BP	Dry	White-yellow dunes
4,100–2500 BP	Rapid oscillations	Dunes and levees reworked; lakes decline to swamps, many disappear; progressive disorganization of stream networks; "pulse" recharge of palaeochannels
Holocene V "Big" Dry	**STABLE**	
300 BC–AD 300	Dry	Irreversible desertification of Azawad; (first occupation of Macina and Upper Delta?)
Holocene VI Recent Optimum		**STABLE**
AD 300–700	Improving precipitation	Expansion of distributary system
AD 700–c.1000	Optimal conditions	
Holocene VII High Unpredictability		**UNSTABLE**
AD 1000–1200	Rapid oscillations	

AD 1200–1500	Severe droughts	Further degraded distributary system
c.AD 1550–1630	Wet (with dry interruptions)	1592, 1616, 1618–39: high flooding
c.AD 1630–1860	Generally dry	1640–4: severe drought 1670s & 1680s: severe drought 1738–56, 1770s, 1790s: severe droughts 1820–40: sustained dry 1860? to early 1900: wet phase most of 1910s: drought comparable to Sahel Drought 1950–1958: wet phase 1972–(88?): Sahel Drought

those of rapid and relatively dramatic oscillations.[68] In the Ghanaian forest we possess a remarkable rain-gauge lake recording precipitation during this time. Lake Bosumtwi rises and falls after 13,000 BP. The lake is stable and high after 9200, a stability matched at least by mid-eighth millennium BP by most Saharan lakes.[69] Rainfall increases on the order of +300 to +400mm in the central Sahara. By 9000 BP, this increased precipitation created an environment of lakes, frequent perennial streams and lush grass steppe. Petit-Maire estimates that the northern boundary of the Sahel travels some 1,000 kilometers to the north.[70] Despite this, we have no

[68] Nils-Axel Mörner, "Short-term paleoclimatic changes: observational data and a novel causation model," in *Climate, History, Periodicity and Predictability*, Michael R. Rampino, John E. Sanders, Walter S. Newman, and L.K. Königsson (eds), pp. 264–5; Alfred Muzzolini, "Les climats au Sahara et sur ses bordures, du Pléistocène final à l'aride actuel," *Empuries*, 47 (1985), p. 16; Rognon, "Essai d'interprétation," pp. 264–6.

[69] Anne-Marie Lézine and H. Hooghiemstra, "Land-sea comparisons during the last glacial-interglacial transition: pollen records from West Tropical Africa," *Palaeogeography, Palaeoclimatology, Palaeoecology*, 79 (1990), pp. 326–8; F. A. Street and Anthony T. Grove, "Global maps of lake-level fluctuations since 30,000 yr BP," *Quaternary Research*, 12 (1979), pp. 98–9; Michael R. Talbot and G. Delibrias, 'A new pleistocene-Holocene water-level curve for Lake Bosumtwi, Ghana', *Earth and Planetary Science Letters*, 47 (1980), p. 341.

[70] Nicole Petit-Maire, "Interglacial environments in presently hyperarid Sahara: Palaeoclimatic implications," in *Paleoclimatology and Paleometerorology: Modern and Past Patterns of Global Atmospheric Transport*, Margaret Leinen and Michael Sarnthein (eds), NATO Advanced Science Institutes, Series C: Mathematical and Physical Sciences, no. 282, (Kluwer Academic Publishers: Dordrecht, 1987), p. 652.

evidence that humans moved into the southern Sahara and Sahel before about 7000 BP.

Indeed, there is no evidence from this first Holocene pluvial of human occupation in the Méma or in any of the four live basins of the Middle Niger. As conditions improved, the Niger carried a significant sand and sediment load and meandered widely. This may be the period during which a significant portion of the Niger discharge was carried by the Fala de Molodo (and by the Vallée du Serpent to the west), perhaps as far as the southern Hodh depression. We can only be sure that most prominent fluvial features of all basins date to this period (channel deposits, the meander scars, dune degradation, and major levees).

It is entirely possible that a lake (or, at least, seasonal swamps) covered much of the Méma. As in the Azawad, those landforms not under water were covered by wooded savanna or treed steppe and were home to such large mammals as giraffe, rhino, and elephant. Geomorphologists have also assumed that permanent water filled the Macina and the Upper Delta from the Erg of Bara to the Pondori during much of this period. Indeed, there has been more presumption than proof that a massive and stable Lake Paléo-Débo covered the entire southern Middle Niger as late as 4500 BP (and perhaps even as late as the early first millennium before the Present Era).[71] The present Lakes Débo and Korientze would be all that remains of that larger lake's slow recession. The debate about Paléo-Débo's existence, extent, permanence, or seasonality echoes the polemics about the Holocene lake in the Chad basin, the so-called MegaChad. It is a debate of central importance to the peopling of the southern "live delta" basins of the Middle Niger. A Paléo-Débo lake certainly would explain the lack of evidence for late stone age occupation in those basins. So, too, however, would heavy rates of alluviation (deeply covering remains of seasonal occupation) and of stream migration (erasing that evidence).

---

[71] Devisse and Vernet, "Le bassin," fig. 3, p. 16 and fig. 4, p. 17; Vernet, *Climats Anciens,* p. 117; Jean Tricart, *Reconnaissance Géomorphologique de la Vallée Moyenne du Niger,* Mémoire de l'Institut Fondamental d'Afrique Noire, no. 72 (IFAN: Dakar 1965), pp. 25–7, 74; Gallais, *Le Delta Intérieur,* p. 100; Sharon E. Nicholson, *A Climatic Chronology for Africa: Synthesis of Geological, Historical and Meteorological Information and Data,* PhD Thesis, University of Wisconsin (Madison, 1976), pp. 52, 70–1; however, see counter arguments in Jacobberger, "Geomorphology," pp. 95–112 and McIntosh, "Floodplain geomorphology," pp. 191–2.

Lake Bosumtwi goes into deep regression at *c*.8000 BP, consistent with drops in most Saharan lakes sometime between 8000 and 6500 BP. The Ogolian dunes are reworked or remobilized by the wind in many places. This is the first (and most severe) of two or three episodes of dune remobilization that left a legacy of small yellow or white dunes trailing away from the reddened late Pleistocene dunes.

By 6,500 BP the second Holocene Pluvial had begun. Permanent streams filled with large perch (*Lates niloticus)* coursed through the Azawad as far as 350km north of Timbuktu. This basin is lacustrine up to 19°20′N as late as 5500 BP and remains so to the south as late, perhaps, as the last millennium BC. Conditions during this second pluvial are different, however. Overall temperature steadily becomes warmer. Many geomorphologists are convinced that climatic conditions oscillated in the Sahel far more than during the first Holocene Pluvial. Precipitation is strongly seasonal and torrential (monsoonal), rather than spread more-or-less evenly throughout the year. The Niger and its many active *marigots* in the Méma returned to levels of activity near those of the first Pluvial. The increased sediment load and increased tendency to seasonal flood left a double legacy of meandering channels and multiple levees in the deeply modeled floodplain.

These oscillations apparently pick up pace and intensity at *c*.5000–4000 BP, in broad synchrony with changing tropical monsoonal circulation and precipitation changes around the globe (beginning of mode IV. of table 2.1). Lakes Chad, Bosumtwi and Tichitt all fall at that time.[72] The southern Sahara has begun its decline, with oscillations, to modern conditions. By 3500 BP the Second Holocene Pluvial is at an end.

As Saharan conditions declined, the affected peoples must have intensified experimentation with new habits of food production. This might have led, in some cases, to plant domestication. Others may have turned to increased mobility and transhumant pastoral-

---

[72] Jean Maley, "Les variations climatiques dans le bassin du Tchad durant le dernier millénaire: nouvelles données palynologiques et paleoclimatiques," *Acts of the Congress of the International Union for Quaternary Research*, (IUQR: Christchurch, 1973), p. 175; Patrick Munson, "Archaeological data on the origin of cultivation in the southwestern Sahara and their implication for West Africa," in *Origins of African Plant Domestication*, Jack Harlan, Jan M. J. de Wet and Ann B. Stemler (eds) (Mouton: The Hague, 1976), pp. 187–209; Talbot and Delibrias, "Pleistocene-Holocene," p. 341; Street and Grove, "Global maps," pp. 102–3.

ism. Others, undoubtedly, migrated to the better watered south. It would be quite incorrect to envision a unidirectional, massive flight. Rather, it is likely that oscillations in climate encouraged several "pulses" of population movements north and south, especially along the many palaeochannels. Saharan lakes were transgressive again at 4100–4000 and from 3500 to 3000 BP (the period of occupation of Kobadi), and periodically (but briefly) during the first millennium BC. But by 3000–2500 BP, even shallow playa–lakes such as that near Tichitt had essentially disappeared. Lake Chad was at its present level.

There is a developing consensus that, worldwide, the period around 500 BC (2500 BP) was one of major shift in climatic mechanism[73] (mode V). Many parts of the Middle Niger may still have been swamp (with a fair share of water-borne diseases) before the late first millennium BC. We lack any evidence of late stone age occupation in the deep floodplain basins, although there is evidence that semi-sedentary fisherfolk passed through the live deltas to the Gourma by 4000 BP.[74] That changes rapidly. There is a flood of colonization, probably from the Méma and Azawad (and Hodh and Tilemsi Valley) into the Macina, Upper Delta, and Gourma coinciding with a significant dry period beginning at least 300 BC and ending c.AD 300. Mode V rainfall is estimated at below −20 percent of the AD 1930–1960 average. Lakes in the Chad basin drop or disappear forever. The Senegal discharge is so low that sea water invades the Lower Senegal and Ferlo Valleys.[75] Even a half-millennium of low floods in the deepest basins would have allowed sufficient occupation for a substantial accumulation of debris at permanent hamlets and villages. Thus were founded the habitation mound, or *tells*, that are the signature of precocious urbanism in the Middle Niger. That mounding would have put settlements above most floods when conditions again began to improve. Unfortunately,

---

[73] Jean Maley, "Mise en evidence d'une péjoration climatique entre *ca.*2500 et 2000 ans BP en Afrique tropicale humide," *Bulletin de la Société de Géologie Française,* 163 (3) (1992), pp. 363–5; Mörner, "Short-term," pp. 257–8, 266; Vernet, *Climats Anciens,* p. 126.

[74] MacDonald, *Socio-Economic Diversity,* pp. 249–51.

[75] Ann-Marie Lézine and Joel Casanova, "Pollen and hydrological evidence for the interpretation of past climates in tropical West Africa during the Holocene," *Quaternary Science Review,* 8 (1989), pp. 45–55; J. Monteillet, Hugues Faure, P. Pirazzoli, and Annie Ravise, "L'invasion saline du Ferlo (Sénégal) à l'Holocène supérieur (1900 BP)," *Paleoecology of Africa,* 13 (1981), pp. 205–15.

in the Méma, this period appears to translate for the latest of the late stone-using peoples to a time of extreme stress and diminished population.

From *c*.AD 300 to 700 precipitation rises to +20% of the 1930–1960 average (mode VI). The good rains last at least until AD 1000 and perhaps as late as the mid-twelfth century. We will see that these dates coincide with a population and urban explosion in the Méma and in the live deltas alike. Early in the present millennium, however, climate turns capricious, and ugly, and highly unpredictable. Lake Chad is moderately high in the second half of the first millennium AD but declines precipitously at AD 1000–1150, rises again, then declines severely at *c*.1300. Bosumtwi recovers slowly during the first millennium AD from a lowstand of several centuries beginning at 300 BC, but after AD 1000 suffers regression as severe as any since 13,000 BP. The lake recovers somewhat, then is low again by the thirteenth century. West African conditions were good and quite stable during much of the first millennium AD, probably even quite excellent in exceptional floodplains such as the Middle Niger. After that, stress and surprise are the order of the day. Variability on the order of 50–150 years accelerates considerably after AD 1100 and remains so until at least AD 1610.

After that date, we begin to have better resolution on that variability. Oral traditions and historical records of droughts, floods, and their legacy of human suffering become available. West African conditions are similar to those of the present century. However, from the mid-sixteenth century to the eighteen century wetter conditions (on average) in West Africa corresponded to the Little Ice Ages of the northern latitudes.[76]

However, with the appearance of historical documentation we can see clearly the factor of local variability within the broad Sahel. From Webb's[77] excellent reconstruction of southern Mauritanian

---

[76] Peter J. Lamb and Randy A. Peppler, "West Africa," in *Teleconnections Linking Worldwide Climatic Anomalies,* Michael H. Glantz, Richard W. Katz, and Neville Nicholls (eds) (Cambridge University Press: Cambridge 1991), pp. 126–128; Sharon E. Nicholson, "The methodology of historical climate reconstruction and its application to Africa," *Journal of African History,* 20 (1979), pp. 42–8; George Brooks, "A provisional historical schema for Western African based on seven climate periods (*c*.9000 BC to the 19th century)," *Cahiers d'Etudes Africaines,* 26 (1986), pp. 43–62 and *Landlords and Strangers: A History of Western Africa, 1000-1630,* (Westview Press: Boulder, CO, 1992), pp.7–9.

[77] James L. A. Webb, *Desert Frontier. Ecological and Economic Change along the Westrn Sahel. 1600–1850* (University of Wisconsin Press: Madison, WI, 1995).

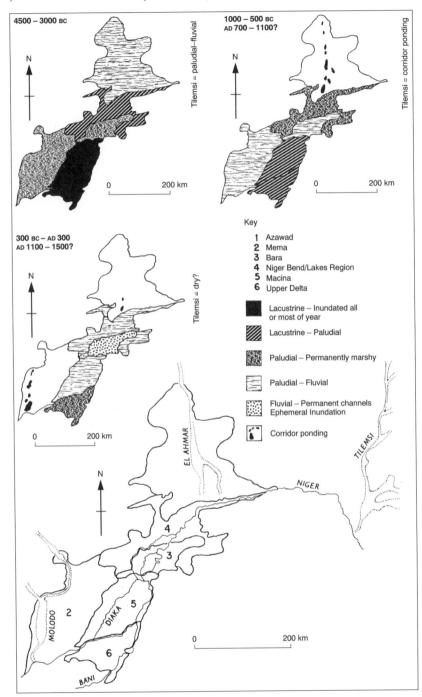

Map 2.4　Middle Niger palaeoenvironmental reconstruction

historical climate, we see that a generally wet late sixteenth and early seventeenth centuries (with ecological zones shifted some 200–300 km to the north of today) gives way in the 1640s to increasing aridity. With aridity comes the shift south of camel pastoralism, the crowding out of Black sedentary farmers, and (most importantly) the creation of new ethnic classes at the zone of pastoralist–farmer tension. Decades of the seventeenth and eighteenth centuries may have been wetter than today. Webb shows that these were, nevertheless, times of famine and distress because the local productive strategies were still geared to the higher precipitation levels of almost a half-century before. Thus, social memory of climate did a disservice to these distressed populations.

This record has clear implications for interpreting the struggle of the prehistoric peoples of the Middle Niger to adapt to their dynamic environment. That environment is a blend of climate (alternating at several time-scales), the mosaic of landforms (the layered transformation of basic lacustrine, paludial, riverine and aeolian themes), and the varied human communities staking claim to various productive territories.

The salient characteristics of today's climate and flood regime are high interannual variability and the difficulty of prediction from year to year (much less at longer perspectives). Those characteristics can, with some confidence, be extrapolated back into prehistoric time. Year-by-year variability can further be transposed over oscillations of wet and dry episodes of a 10–30 year duration. Those oscillations are felt locally at a time perspective of 100 years, that is, within the memory of the living members of a village. They are further transposed over oscillations (of anything from 150 to 400 years, for example) that can be felt only at a time perspective of 1,000 years. Examples of such variations are the wet spell correlated with the so-called Little Ice Age (AD 1550–1840) or the dry centuries between 300 BC and AD 300. These in turn are transposed over oscillations at the 10,000 year perspective (e.g., the rapid lake rises and falls of *c.*4500–2500 BP or the two Holocene Pluvials).

The lesson for the prehistorian and historian working within these long-term perspectives is that environmental stress, surprise, and unpredictability were constant realities for the inhabitants of the Middle Niger. Do differences in tool assemblages, faunal remains, and settlement location reflect a precocious development of specialists linked together by habits of regional exchange? If so, we will have evidence for one quite successful adaptation to climatic surprise.[78] If so, and if the emergence of specialists does not entail the emergence of elites, we have the beginnings of a long-successful Middle Niger brand of heterarchy. Who makes the decisions affecting inter-group relations? Who keeps the peace within communities? Who keeps the peace as communities without recognized kinship ties increasingly come into contact? The earliest, most archaic oral traditions of the Middle Niger (and, indeed, of greater Mande) strongly hint at a special authority invested in the hunters. This authority at the dawn of heterarchy may have been foundational to deep-time Mande notions of power.

Those oral traditions and a bit of historical imagination call us back to the parallel dune landscape just north of the later city of Timbuktu. The year is 4100 BP.

---

[78] Argued more fully in McIntosh, "The Pulse Model."

3

Historical Imagination: 4100 BP

Archaeology is tedious; it's hot, dusty, and it's literal. Yet, there can be moments of exquisite revelation when artifacts and oral traditions are combined judiciously with a bit of historical imagination. Let us return by a different path to some of the themes of the preceding chapter by imagining a scene in the year 4100 BP, viewed by an observer standing at the future location of site "Wadi-13" (not far from present-day Timbuktu.)

They're back. Things have returned to what they once were. Yet they are different also, different in where they live, in their speech, in the way they plait their hair.

Things are better now. But change has penetrated the bones of the land. The rains had forgotten this land for so long. So, too, did the river. It took generations for the worst to arrive. And then most of the people left the dunes for good. First the grandfathers said that neither they, nor their fathers and grandfathers, had ever seen the long ponds between the dunes dry, even for parts of the year. Then the long ponds dried for many months each year. They began to fear the same for the great stream that snakes north from the great wide water a half day's walk away. The annual rise in the level of the stream came later and later each year. Then it came no more. No rains, no flood spilling out between the dunes. Just the big winds during both hot and cold seasons; sand blowing up and around the concave carcasses of great interior rivers.

The hippos left. The crocodile and big turtle fled. The fish, one of which would feed a camp for a week, never came out of the wide river. There would be no sweet marsh plants, no water deer or waterbuck mincing through the muddy waters, only the dune antelope and mean porridge made of the spine and nettle grass.

But now, most everyone has returned after the long dry spell. Returned to a land that, before, has only ever seen humans come to wander by, never to settle down, peripatetic for so long that there is no memory of who once claimed rights to the long pond, or to a desired section of the great stream. No matter, the rules are different now.

Once the rains were gentle. Once they fell over most of the year and nurtured thick grass on the dunes, a forest of trees on the stream and pond banks. Now the rains come with violence. The rains are, as ever, welcomed with joy at the end of the desperate dry season. The people will rejoice when they return in a few weeks. Now, however, their return is heralded daily by vast walls of dust that choke, blind, and terrify the herds. The rains are torrential now. When they come in earnest, they sweep away the feeble grasses of the dunes leaving great barren gullies. Sand heaps in the beds of the once plentiful streams, making barriers to the rise later in the year of the flood waters from the great river to the south. It is the rise of those waters at the end of the rains that saves the land. The floods return stronger and stronger each year. Partial health is returning to the land.

The land is healthier, but the differences are profound. When the flood has receded, the winds that scorch howl in from the barren dunes and rocky cliffs of the far north. Then the people are reminded. This is no longer the land of water. Now the desert has its say – perhaps a little less one year, a little more the next. The hippo are returning, and so, too, the swamp antelope. The crocodile are back, and there are fish in abundance. But not so the fish it took a grown man to carry. Still, with the flow of the waters in and out of the long ponds, the fish that have returned are in some ways even easier to catch than ever before. Or perhaps the fisherfolk are just more adept.

One would have hesitated, before, to describe any of the people as "fisherfolk." But things are different now. Everyone still hunts a little. Everyone gathers the sweet grasses that grow deep in the long ponds. And everyone fishes a little when the pools left by the declining long ponds writhe with trapped catfish and tilapia. But now some spend most of their days at it and they use more than the rude shell fishhooks and bone spears that have been used since time began. Nets and baskets. Nets come in a bewildering variety of sizes and shapes. Hand-held triangular nets, long nets stretched over the width of wide streams Baskets and nets – all these are used at different seasons, for different kinds of fish and in different parts of the streams and long ponds. Their use is dictated by a logic so complex it is known only to the fisherfolk. Only the fisherfolk gather together in such numbers at the beginning of the falling waters to build the barriers at the opening of the long ponds. Those openings form natural traps between the dunes and the streams travelling, not north at this season, but south. At the barriers they catch the oil-rich *Alestes* by the millions.

Only the fisherfolk know how to smoke these tiny fish and, at the same time, to gather the oil. Smoked fish and ceramic pots of oil are used for trade with others at the long camps. Only the fisherfolk take on the hippo. Only they have the permission of the water spirits to kill these most ferocious of the water beasts, feared more even than the crocodile. And after he has killed his first hippo, a young fisherman can select a bride from the growers.

"Growers" – these are another innovation. In the time of the infinite lakes and marshes, people had always gathered grasses, roots, and grain from the water"s sides and depths. The plants were used for bedding, for baskets, for rope. They were eaten in great quantities and in great varieties. Even then, camps would have moved far more frequently had it not been for the anchor of the sandstone grindstones needed to grind the grain and the pots in which it was boiled.

Now the growers are just that. Before this, the people gathered as they could and moved from stand to stand of grain or from patch of thick roots to fruiting trees. Now the growers save seed. They do still gather many plants. They know better than any others where to find a desired plant. They know how rich or poor will be its yield if the rains are bad or late. They know what will happen to a subsequent stand of grain if, one year, the growers leave behind the tallest plants. Now, however, the growers in the dune country spend more and more of their time with the grains that grow naturally on the dunes' banks after the waters drop. Where these grow wild, the growers weed and sometimes bring water in pots to the higher reaches of the stands. The growers take specially selected seed to the long camps. And after weeks of blessings and prohibitions of behavior, they plant. One seed to a hole. In each hole, a sacrifice of an *Alestes*. Bond of land and water, grower and fisherfolk.

All around the long camp are fields of experiments in several of the dune-side plants. Some need only the rains. Some grow only where the floods have been. Some do better, some never delight the growers. The growers here are especially disappointed in their efforts with the wild grains of the deepest long ponds, those that grow only in full water. For they have heard from the herders who travel for months at a time, that other growers far to the west and south live in great prosperity on the seeds of the water grain alone.

Some of the growers spend months in distant, short camps following the declining waters. But even they spend far longer in the long camp than fisherfolk and herders. Some grower families have begun never to leave the long camp. Now they make their huts out of curved banks of clay, like a pot, rather than of stick and mat, as before, or of bundles of grasses, as do the fisherfolk and herders.

The people here can scarcely credit other accounts of the herders. Especially suspect are the reports that the long camps of those southern water-grain growers are many times larger than the long camps here in the dune country. The long camps are the domain of the growers. When the fisherfolk and herders set up hot season camp next to the growers, all obey the light persuasions of the grower's headman – and the far weightier warnings of the hunters from the fisher, grower, and herder clans. Strange men these hunters. They are the most traditional of us all, yet they walk with the spirits where none other can even imagine. Look at how they chastise those looking to cause trouble between, say, herder and grower. Even that is done under the veil of their new fearsome powers.

Those who spend the least amount of time at the long camp, and who are in some ways the least welcome, are the herders. Once everyone hunted the grazers. Then appeared a people who delight to travel long distances with the most docile of the grazers. At the rains and when the waters are high or in early recession, the herders move away with their cattle, sheep, and goat. They know full well that this is a time of terrible disease for the herds. But as the heat increases and the grasses burn off the tops of the dunes, the herders return. They are welcome for the milk they trade. They are welcome for stories of other peoples far distant. Their return is welcome for the useful, beautiful stones and the salt they bring to trade for the fish oil and for the grain of the growers.

But some herder families have been banned from this long camp forever for allowing the cattle to stray before the harvest into the dune-side fields. And by the time the rains come, their herds will be trampling the muds that are all that is left of the once deepest long ponds. The herds will scare away the fish the fisherfolk hope to catch in the shallows. The herds will trample the last of the wild water-grains the growers' children have been sent to gather. All will be as content to see the herders leave at the first rains as they are each year upon their arrival.

Where fisherfolk, growers, herders' and the elusive hunters went during the great dryness is hard to say. They must have gone a great distance to survive. And when they returned, they were a changed people. Yet their traditions dip into deepest memory. That wisdom recalls a time when the land was rich beyond dreams. Ponds were more like lakes. It was a time when no one had to work and the great fish leapt into the arms of those walking the shores of long ponds between the dunes. Their traditions claim that all people were one. All spoke the same language, revered the same water python spirit, called each other brother and sister, auntie and uncle.

Yet, even with the change, or perhaps because of it, the people are content now. The great dryness is finished, That is, finished except for an occasional year of no rain or late flood – just to remind the people that the desert is still there, still waiting. The land has become rich again. The water python is important, to be sure, but more important in the daily lives of the people are the many new spirits that have revealed themselves, particularly to the hunters, on their recent journeys. The form of these spirits are kept as each people's deepest secret. To each in their own way, the spirits have revealed the land's inner bounty: of fish – to the fisherfolk; grass – to the growers; or beast – to the herders. With the help of the spirits, with long hours now spent tending one type of field, or finding the best waterholes for the herds, or devising new ways to glean the precious oil from the shimmering silver blanket of fish covering the banks of streams, the land is in many ways as generous now as in most remote memory.

Things are much as they once were, but the people are no longer one. Nowhere is that more evident than during this hot season when all come together in the long camps. Children of growers, herders, and fisherfolk mingle and run together and poke fun of mild disdain at garbled pronunciations, misused words, and mangled grammar. Growers and fisherfolk speak in tongues closely related. The herders learn a second language for their stay at the long camps. Sometimes it is useful to have a secret language, as is shared by the hunters of all three groups, but the children tend to absorb any language, any dialect, and pronunciation. Not that one could mistake grower and fisherfolk. All may wear the same shell beads, hang about their necks the same tiny ritual polished axehead, and wear a stone dagger in a leather sheath bound to the outside of the left forearm. All women and young men may beautify their eyes or hands with the green, red or blue stone and powders brought back by the hunters and herders. But a grower would never allow her daughter to dress her hair in the fisherfolk style. All boast distinctive scars of faces and backs, distinctive shapes of pots, distinctive tools leaning against the walls of their dwellings. One would never mistake whose hut one had entered in the long camp.

The hot season: season of the long camps, of the largest assemblages of different peoples, season of the greatest strains on fresh food. But also the season of peace, of trade, of exchange of grain against oil against that fat sheep to be consumed next week at the wedding feast. Exchange of stories of distant peoples. Exchange of worries and hopes for the prosperity of next year's fields or flocks. The long camp is a time of contentment. Things are as they once were, but the people are content with the differences.

Why bother with these historical imagination chapters? So often the dry stones and bones of archaeology are simply inadequate to the prehistorian's real job of unearthing the deep-time roots of historical processes and social institutions. We use historical imagination to bridge from the highly fragmentary material remains of the past to the institutions known from oral traditions and ethnography, institutions that have undergone multiple transformations to arrive at their current state. There is no "essentialism" here, nor arguments for cultural relicts. Historical imagination is just that: imagined stories made up in the mind of a prehistorian as an attempt to translate his or her intuitions about what were the vital concerns of once-living peoples.

I believe the late stone age world of the southern Sahara was one of profound innovation precipitated by the crises of climatic stress and mass migrations. That innovation was the accommodation (and, indeed, encouragement) of interlocking ethnic and occupational specialization. I believe this social ecological accommodation encouraged the seasonal magnetism of specialist communities that will eventually lead to clustered urbanism. I believe the early Mande world was also one of resistance to nascent centralization – to the Big Men or early chieftaincies developing in other parts of the world. We can understand the persistence of that resistance by looking at those who were sanctioned to transform symbols to express new forms of authority[1] during periodic crises. Who had the community's consent to make decisions? Who counteracted the disruptive threat to community posed by increasing social differentiation? In Mande terms, who acted as "Men of Crises",[2] tapping the power of place to claim authority? Crises are periods of changing circumstances that can as easily lead to opportunities and cultural elaboration as to collapse of cultural systems. From crisis to crisis, certain core values were symbolically reaffirmed, as this society of specialists celebrated overlapping and persuasive authority, yet resisted coercive power.

The crisis we saw in chapter 2 played out during the last few millennia before the Present Era along the shallow interdunal lakes and streams of the Azawad (as elsewhere in the Sahara). After c.4500 BP, climate trended to desiccation. Population density rose. Sites increasingly showed evidence of seasonal specialist exploitation. Specialists gravitated together for exchange and, seasonally, came together in segmented, but articulated communities.[3] In a physical landscape undergoing deep disruptions and transformations, there appear here the first perceivable innovations in values of community that will in time come to be the signature of being Mande. The peoples of the Middle Niger are at a crossroads: crisis can be resolved by conflict, warfare, and new despotic institutions. Or a new heterarchical community can prevail. All depends upon the invention of new styles of authority.

Nothing in the archaeology predicts who would have the authority to maintain peace between segments of these articulated communities or to lead their migrations when the desert prevails. I'll put my money on the hunters. The sources concur that hunters form the first secret society to cross-cut kin loyalties.[4] In terms de-

---

[1] After S. Nanda *Cultural Anthropology*, (Belmont, CA: Wadsworth, 1994) p. 289.

[2] Cissé, "Notes," p. 190.

[3] R. McIntosh "Pulse model," pp. 200–5, 212–14.

[4] Cissé, "Notes," 175–6, 182; S. McIntosh "Blacksmiths and the evolution of political complexity in Mande society: an hypothesis," SAR Advanced Seminar paper, p. 18; Hunters' cross-cutting loyalty to their society: Cissé, "Notes," pp. 176–9, 186; G. Cashion *Hunters of the Mande: A Behavioral Code and Worldview Derived from the Study of their Folklore* 3 vols. PhD dissertation, Indiana University, 1984, pp. 13, 81, 102, 115, 310–16.

fining their own moral code, the Mande hunter has no country. Hunters must have these transcendent loyalties because they deal in vast quantities of *nyama* (the earth's and all living things' fundamental life force).

Indeed, they are credited with pioneering attempts to control those dangerous life-energies of their animal or human prey.[5] *Nyama* may still be at a purely extractive stage, but the moral imperative to manipulate notions of purity and guardianship of social equilibrium will persist through transformations at the hands of smiths, secular dynasts and, arguably, into modern civil society democracy. Hunters pioneer notions of authority predicated upon *nyama* . And so, too, they invent institutions of closed-membership power associations and magical, sumptuary objects of dangerous power (bow and arrow, whistle, *boli*-horns and packets, amulets and bracelets, sacks of herbs and medicines). In this, are they simply reinventing even older traditions of the hero who "floats on a sea of secret expertise that outsiders have no right to learn about?"[6] This is entirely possible. What is new is their authoritative mediating role: mediating between the community and strangers, between ordered settlement and the wilderness, and within the community between alliance-bound families, clans, and occupation groups. When this new formulation of authority works, specialization can explode.

These early Middle Niger peoples have invented one of the fundamental values of the Mande world: horizontal authority. Not coercion, rather persuasion is used to contest inherited or imposed leadership. This is the key to deep-time traditions of resistance to political economies of monopoly, and to concentrations of power.

The hunter epics suggest that horizontal authority emerged as a solution to our formative crisis. As guardians of social equilibrium, hunters were duty bound to preserve alliances between villages and accords between a community's sub-groups.[7] Hunter's authority in prehistory derived from the horrible sanction of *nyama* as used to maintain peace between the emerging occupationally defined groups. With open exchange, society became increasingly segmented horizontally. The Middle Niger has begun a long journey down the path of heterarchical segmentation to the astonishing human mosaic that prevails today.

[5] Cashion, *Hunters*, p. 309; Cissé, "Notes," 182, 187, 205–7; P. McNaughton, *Mande Blacksmiths* , pp. 16–17, 41–3.

[6] McNaughton, *Mande Blacksmiths*, p. xvi.

[7] Cissé, "Notes," 194–5, 199, 204; McNaughton, *Mande Blacksmiths*. p. 10.

4

Peoples of the Four Live Basins

This chapter is about the many dimensions of landscape in the annually flooded basins: the clay dominated Upper Delta and Macina to the south and, to the north, the "sandy" Erg of Bara and Lakes Region-Niger Bend. We continue to examine the physical landscape and the dynamic processes responsible for landform evolution. But landscape also comprises people. We examine where they are found today and where they were in documented history and why. Landscape is also the Middle Niger people's social memory of how they came to be as separate and interacting peoples. This last point, the historical production of social space (and thereby of ethnic or corporate identity), is a growth industry in human geography and social history.[1] It is also a source of great anxiety for anyone attempting, as I do here, to stride off upon the thin ice of ethnic origins.

Outdated and outmoded though it may be, Will Durant's *The Story of Civilization* still extrudes some universal gems. Durant speaks of the deep social landscape history, but dubious historicity, of one particularly cohesive Asian people: "Japanese origins, like all others, are lost in the cosmic nebula of theory ... Here, as elsewhere, a mingling of diverse stocks preceded by many hundreds of years the establishment off a new racial type speaking with a new voice and creating a new civilization."[2] If the first memories of Japanese social landscape are murky, in the Middle Niger they are

---

[1] "The production of human spatiality," of D. Gregory, *Geographical Imaginations*, (Blackwell: Oxford, 1994). p. 4. or the "rich deposit of myths, memories, and obsessions" of S. Schama, *Landscape and Memory*, (New York: Knopf, 1995), p. 14.

[2] Will Durant, *The Story of Civilization: Part I. Our Oriental Heritage*, (Simon & Schuster: New York, 1954), p. 831.

more nebulous, more protean still. When one occupies a dynamic, complex, often unpredictable physical and social environment, however, such nebulousness can armor one in great endurance and resilience.

Autochtones of the Upper Delta: Bozo and Marka

Of the four live basins of the Middle Niger, the annual floods are most dramatic in the Upper Delta.[3] The lives of the signature peoples of the Upper Delta, the Bozo fisherfolk and the rice cultivators, the Marka, are most directly tied to the floods. The Upper Delta roughly forms a triangle of some 6,000 km². The long hypotenuse to the north is defined by the Niger River. This is also the frontier with the Macina. (This last term can be used loosely to refer to the entire delta south of Lake Débo.) To the east are the Paleozoic sandstones of the Bandiagara Plateau. Separating the alluvium and sandstone is a narrow highland strip of Pleistocene clays and sandy-silts (Bénédougou). The Bénédougou and the clays and loams forming the southern border of the Upper Delta are capped in places by lateritic crusts. These laterites were presumably the iron ore sources for prehistoric blacksmiths.

The late Pleistocene dry phase had its usual dramatic effects in this basin. By *c.*20,000 BP, the Niger and Bani rivers had ceased to flow in the present region of Lake Débo. A strong dune system formed, the Erg of Bara. When precipitation improved during the early Holocene, the rejuvenated rivers were thus blocked. The Niger eventually breached the parallel dunes in channels known now as the Bara-Issa, the Sebi-Marigot, and the Issa-Ber. Before that, however, the rivers were dammed and formed a massive Lake Paléo-Débo, of which Lakes Débo and Korientzé are vestiges. It is impossible at present to decide between two hypotheses about Paléo-Débo. Either the lake was massive, stable and covered the entirety of the Upper Delta and Macina until perhaps as recently as 4500 BP (some even argue as recent as 2500 BP). Or, permanent flooding of the Upper Delta occurred only during the earliest Holocene, but was of relatively short duration.

---

[3] The best single source on Middle Niger floodplain dynamism is Jacques Quensière, Jean-Claude Olivry, Yveline Poncet and Jean Wuillot, "Environnement deltaïque," in *La Pêche dans le Delta central du Niger*, Jacques Quensière (ed.), (ORSTOM: Paris, 1994), pp. 29–80.

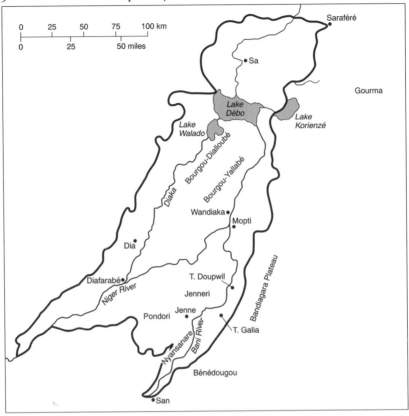

Map 4.1   *Live delta landforms and sites of the UPPER DELTA,*
MACINA, and ERG OF BARA

There is slightly more support for the latter hypothesis. The geomorphological mosaïç of the Upper Delta must have been many millennia in the making. The principle dynamic at work has been the shift of the Niger and Bani to the east.[4] The Niger abandoned the Diaka channel in the Macina before assuming its present chan-

---

[4] Yves Brunet-Moret, P. Chaperon, J. P. Lamagat and M. Molinier, *Monographie Hydrologique du Fleuve Niger*, ORSTOM Monographies Hydrologiques, no. 8 (Paris: Institut Français de Recherche Scientifique pour le Développement et Coopération, 1986), II, p. 33; C. Voute, "Geological and morphological evolution of the Niger and Benue valleys," *Annales du Musée Royale de l'Afrique Centrale*, 40 (1962), pp. 196–8; Yves Urvoy, *Les Bassins du Niger*, Mémoires de l'Institut Fondamental d'Afrique Noire, no. 4, (Dakar, IFAN, 1942), pp. 60, 83; Grove, *Niger*, p. 43.

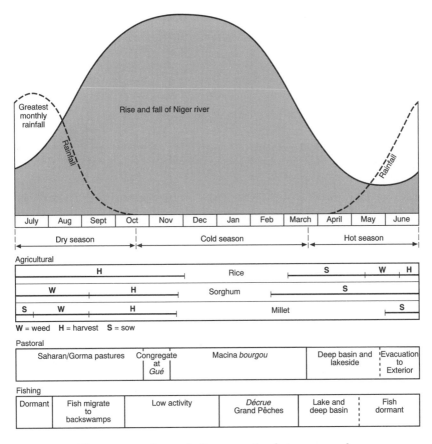

Figure 4.1   *Annual climate and subsistence cycle*
(after Imperato 1972)   McIntosh: Peoples of the Middle Niger
Fig 4.1

nel. The Bani joined with the Niger, also, after the late Pleistocene dry period.

Aeolian features are quite minor in the Upper Delta and Macina, compared to the last two basins we have examined. The exceptions to this are a large isolated red dune north and west of Jenne and a smattering of smaller white and yellow dunes. The smaller dunes can be dated to the Holocene's shorter dry periods (probably *c.*8000 BP and 4500–4000 BP). The large dune was breached several times during the early Holocene. Before the rivers could run free of the dune, however, a swampy depression formed upstream of the dune. This depression is the rich rice country now known as the Pondori and its proximity undoubtedly contributed to the success of the principal historical town of the Upper Delta, Jenne. During this pluvial, a meandering Niger created multiple meander scars and

Plate 4.1a and b (above and opposite)   *Jenne town at high flood and dust storm at low water (4.1a courtesy of Merrick Posnansky).*

levees as the river migrated right up to the northern edge of the red dune. The river shifted to the north much later. South and east of the Pondori, the Bani formed a massive levee. This highland feature (the Nyansanare) is much favored today by Bambara growers of rainfed millet and *décrue* (recessional) sorghum. The high levees would also have been a source of trees for firewood and for iron smelters' charcoal.

To the observer crossing on foot, the Upper Delta landscape can be mind-numbingly monotonous. Monotony only superficially masks a diverse, indeed chaotic, distribution of landforms in this, as in all the live basins of the Middle Niger. The human exploitation of those landforms is rendered more chaotic still by the unpredictable rainfall and flood regimes. Indeed, the two salient characteristics of semi-arid tropical climate and flood regimes are high interannual variability and unpredictability. These characteristics conspire to force fishing, agricultural, and pastoral systems to be highly adaptive to stress and surprise. These systems must adapt as well to those gradual changes and to the mode shifts we

reviewed in the section on long-term climate change: so gradual or rare are those last sets of environmental changes that they are barely discernible within the lifetime of an individual.

Climate records for a principal floodplain town illustrate these realities for the people of the Upper Delta. Mopti receives an average of 540 mm of rain over roughly 48 days. The majority of the rain falls during the torrential months of July, August, and September.[5] During the years 1936–64, the annual total ranged from 962 mm (1952) to 360 mm (1947). Eleven years had rains of greater than the mean-plus-one quarter. Seven years had rains of the mean-minus-one quarter (without any regular oscillations or regular clustering of good or bad years). Typically, there are two hot periods of

[5] Gallais, *Delta Intérieur* p. 51; Jean Gallais, *Le Delta Intérieur et ses Bordures: Etude Morphologique.* Mémoires et Documents du Centre de la Documentation Cartographiques et Géographiques, no. 3, (Paris: Centre National de la Recherche Scientifique, 1967), pp. 65–66.

the year (May – maximum 40.9° – and October, even hotter!), interrupted by a minor cooling brought on by the rains in August. The greater relief comes during the true cool season from end-November to end-February. The season of SW monsoonal winds runs from May to October. The more dramatic NE Trades blow from November to April.

The season of annual inundation is transposed over the seasons defined by temperature and precipitation. The summer rains are followed in September through November by the rise of the flood. There is significant interannual variability in flood height (with an interannual variability of maximum flood of >1 meter). From year to year it is impossible to predict the date of arrival and of the flood's evacuation. Lastly, the floods transport a highly variable sediment and soluble-materials load; sediment and discharge, of course, control the year-to-year personality of the Upper Delta distributaries. Some years they can incise their beds; other years they can abandon channels and shift dramatically over the landscape (avulsion).

Unpredictability in these several aspects of the Niger and Bani flood are of more than academic interest to the local population. Slight differences in flood height can make dramatic differences in the total area flooded. Minor flood differences can dramatically affect what parts of the floodplain can be put into crops.[6] The "average" flood reaches the south of the Upper Delta between mid-September and mid-October. The Niger crest reaches Mopti between October 20 and December 10. The Bani flood reaches that station three weeks later. This lag between the rivers has a curious effect on the flow of flood waters into the broad backswamps. The role of the *marigots* (distributaries) is to channel the rising waters quickly to the deep back basins. Several of the major Upper Delta *marigots* flow first south from the Niger, only to reverse current south to north when the Bani tops its banks. An average volume of water of 70 km³ enters the Middle Niger below Lake Débo. The Niger contributes 50 km³ and 20 km³ is contributed by the Bani.[7] The estimated volume of flood water evacuated downstream from Lake Débo is 36 km³. The difference is lost to evaporation, evapo-transpiration by vegetation and to the subterranean water table. Between 1.8 and 4.9 million tons of sediment are deposited in the

---

[6] Gallais, *Bordures*, p. 84; Brunet-Moret et al., *Monographie Hydrologique*, II, pp. 132–6, 164–5.
[7] Gallais, *Delta Intérieur*, p. 56.

Middle Niger each year. The alluvium accumulates in an annual lens of sediment of between 0.07 mm to 0.2 mm. (*c.*1 meter in 5,000 years). The Upper Delta has a very weak slope (<5 cm/km).

The flood is the major event of the dry season. The fortuitous timing of the Middle Niger inundation allows an unusual potential for human exploitation. The post-inundation lushness of the floodplain is in stark contrast to neighboring southern Saharan and Sahelian regions at the same time of year. The Middle Niger rains and flood have a highly complex effect upon the mosaic of landforms and gradations of relief. Mosaic is an understatement. The situation is an eerie mirror to Henry Wright's characterization of Mesopotamia: "When ... man-made factors compound the varied natural situation on the surface if the Euphrates geosyncline, then the physical environment becomes so complex that it defies detailed interpretation."[8]

The most important effect is to create potentials for exploitation that are defined in very different fashion by the specialist occupation groups. In the description of each live Middle Niger basin I will describe one or two groups per section as "signature" or most numerous for each. I wish to emphasize that the presentation of these groups by the basin they dominate is in essence an artificial device. I have had to make excesses of simplification in an attempt to organize, in some coherent fashion, a tour of the complex mix of present-day groups. With regret, this will be a far too brief introduction to the many modern ethnic groups and occupation-defined castes. In fact, each basin is itself a mosaic of ethnic groups, as are many if not most of the villages and towns of the Middle Niger. Several bordering groups, such as the Bobo, Mossi, or Dogon, have a significant presence in some villages, but cannot be described fully here. In all of this, we risk sacrificing an appreciation of how intricately the web of inter groups dependence is woven. Gallais describes a human geographer's reaction to the Middle Niger ethnic mosaic:

> On a plain without major obstacles, liberally served by rivers and relatively homogeneous [*sic*] in its major landforms, we find an astonishing diversity to the human population. This is especially rare in the Sahel-Savanna, where more often ethnic distribution provides the fundamental unit of division of space. This is a plain easily travelled and without obstacles to cultural and political movement

[8] Henry Wright, *The Administration of Rural Production in an Early Mesopotamian Town*, University of Michigan Museum of Anthropology: Papers no. 38, (University of Michigan Museum of Anthropology, Ann Arbor, 1969), p. 9.

and influences or to ethnic assimilation. Not only is the population highly diverse. Also, no one ethnic group dominates absolutely.[9]

Two demographic dynamics in particular strike those undertaking syntheses of the modern ethnographic situation. The first is the long historical proximity of many groups; the second the excessive fragmentation within the ethnic groups.[10] This fragmentation is particularly noticeable in the case of the two groups with the traditions of longest occupation in the floodplain. The Bozo fisherfolk recognize among themselves four dialectical (and sometimes ecologically specialized) sub-groups. The Marka rice growers divide themselves into three sub-groups. (And one finds multiple sub-groups among the anciently related Dogon inhabiting the eastern periphery of the Upper Delta.)

The annual floods, of course, make the Middle Niger the scene of dramatic migrations of fish. The fish stocking the floodplain display fantastic differences in size, breeding habits, and schooling or solitary personality. Fishing has traditionally been the specialization of the Bozo. We begin with this group held by tradition to have been the first to enter the deep basins of the Middle Niger.[11] Let us postpone, until the conclusion of this section, the tricky issue of their first archaeological appearance.

Ironically, by calling them Bozo we use an outsider's (Bambara) term to lump together four or five linguistically distinct groups of fisher and aquatic–hunting folk. All are united by a shared tradition that they are the first peoples of the deep basins of the Middle Niger.[12] The approximately 60,000 Bozo of the Upper Delta and

---

[9] Ibid., p. 25.

[10] Jean Gallais, *Hommes du Sahel* (Paris: Flammarion, 1984), p. 25; Lars Sundström, *Ecology and Symbiosis: Niger Water Folk*, Studia Ethnographica Upsaliensia, no. 35 (Uppsala: Institutonen för Allmän och Jämförande Ethnografi vid Uppsala Universitet, 1972), pp. 164–8.

[11] Jean Daget, "La pêche dans le Delta central du Niger," *Journal de la Société des Africanistes*, 19 (1949), pp. 1–79; Gallais, *Delta Intérieur*, I, pp. 78–82, 106–8 and II, pp. 413–65; Gallais, *Hommes*, pp. 23–7, 48–72; Bokar N"Diaye, *Groupes Ethniques au Mali* (Bamako, Editions Populaires, 1970), pp. 418-41; Sundström, *Ecology*, pp. 15-72; Ibréhima Kassibo, "Histoire du peuplement humain," in *La Pêche dans le Delta central du Niger*, Jacques Quensière (ed.), (ORSTOM: Paris, 1994), pp. 81–92.

[12] Gallais, *Delta Intérieur*, p. 78; Gallais, *Hommes*, p. 48; Monteil, *Une Cité Soudanaise, Djénné. Métropole du Delta Central du Niger*, p. 30. However, in a few Middle Niger locations traditions tell of Bozo diplacing earlier settlements of Dogon: Sundström, *Ecology*, p. 49; MacDonald and Van Neer, "Specialized fishing peoples," p. 244.

Macina are divided by preferred environment. The traditionally more isolated Bozo are deep swamp dwellers (Sorogo of the Upper Delta, Pondo-Sorogo of the Macina from Lake Débo to Dia). Two "river Bozo" (the Tié of the Niger and Diaka near Diafarabé and the Kélinga upstream of Diafarabé) have historically been more influenced by aggressive neighbors.

The 10,500 Upper Delta Sorogo boast the most archaic dialect. At the very least, their dialect is understood with most difficulty by other Bozo. Sorogo live in isolated small villages of between 200 and 300 persons located on the banks of deep interior *marigots* or on artificial tells deep in the Pondori. These "swamp Bozo" possess the most archaic hunting implements (spears and harpoons). They also preserve the most elaborate rituals of the hunt. Such archaic rituals are used not just for large aquatic species, but also for marsh adapted antelope, hyena, and elephant. One thousand, five hundred live in Jenne. Town Bozo have adopted several non-fishing occupations, including blacksmithing, masonry, and pottery making.

The two river groups have traditionally been less jealous of their political and linguistic independence. Historically, they have been less willing than the Pondo-Sorogo to withdraw into the refuge of the deep swamp when a new group tries to assert hegemony. The Tié and Kélinga are more likely to have been used as boatmen by other groups. They also use the large deep channel nets. In their occupation as rivermen they are not to be confused with the Somono.[13] Many Bozo were forcibly incorporated into this boat transport and deep-river fishing group. However, the river Bozo retain their original language and ties of distant kinship and ritual to all other Bozo. The Somono are more caste than distinct ethnic group. Significantly, they lack the distinction of a separate, identifying language.

Many place the origin of the Somono during relatively recent times (by the fourteenth century, or even as late as the seventeenth to eighteenth centuries).[14] Somono appear to be the product of an

---

[13] Gallais, *Hommes*, pp. 28, 50; N'Diaye, *Groupes*, pp. 439–41.

[14] E.g., Tal Tamari, "The development of caste systems in West Africa," *Journal of African History*, 30 (1991), p. 235. See also, Adria LaViolette, "Women craft specialists in Jenne. The manipulation of Mande social categories," in *Status and Identity in West Africa. Nyamakalaw of Mande*, David C. Conrad and Barbara E. Frank (eds) (Indiana University Press: Bloomington, 1995), p. 172; Richard Roberts, *Warriors, Merchants and Slaves. The State and the Economy in the Middle Niger Valley, 1700–1914*, Stanford University Press, Stanford, 1987, p. 70.

explicit enterprise of redefining the notion of specialists that, in chapter 10, we shall label the Imperial Tradition. The essence of the Imperial Tradition is the process by which a new class of Mande political rulers stripped authority from formerly dominant occupation groups, in part by breaking them up. Somono may have been entirely an artifact of this tradition, a group created wholesale from among the captives of the Mali Emperor or of the Bamana kingdom of Segou. Those states would have been in need of boatmen more pliant and less likely simply to run away than the Bozo.

What made the Bozo so elusive, so resistant to the imperial and later traditions of remolding the indigenous concept of ethnicity, was their ephemeral presence on the landscape. They are unusual in the Middle Niger for their habits of mobility. This mobility is borne of the Middle Niger fishing cycle and of the seasonal need for communities to fission into remote camps. Fish are dormant and hard to catch in the season of low water. As the waters begin to rise in August and September, they swim the network of *marigots* to reach the vegetation-rich backswamps. There they breed, multiplying spectacularly. It is at that season that the Bozo of the interior tend to dissipate to the high borders of the deep basins. During the long winter months the fish prepare for the reverse migration with the onset of *décrue* (flood recession at the beginning of January). With *décrue*, the Bozo begin their slow movement back to the depths of the backswamps.

The *décrue* begins the most dramatic of the three fishing campaigns – the *grandes pêches* . Vast shoals of the tiny, oil-rich *Alestes leuciscus* begin at this time to leave the deep basins. Inevitably the shoals are accompanied by many carnivorous fish. During the dry season, the Bozo build artificial levees, dikes, and barrages within the swamps to channel the run of *Alestes* . The fish runs can be continuous for several kilometers and often take several days to pass the family-manned barrages. The fishermen stand at the opening of the barrages with handheld nets. In the larger *marigots*, co-operative fishing is needed for 10-30 meter nets.

This *Alestes* season of January and February is followed, at the beginning of March, by a focus upon the declining ponds of the floodplain. Often 150 canoes (*pirogues*) will assemble for the large, collective efforts of this season. It is then that the Bozo count upon help from neighboring Marka and Rimaïbé. The collective fishing is under the tight control of the ritual chiefs, the *dyi tuu*. The *dyi tuu* are believed to be the keepers of ancient pacts made between the first colonists of the floodplains and the water spirits (*faaro* or *ba-faaro*). As the floods decline fully (March and April), efforts turn to exploitation of the banks of the lakes (especially Débo and Walado). There is large-scale migration to lakeside and to the major *marigots* feeding those lakes. This is the time, particularly, for the use of harpoons and for long surface lines of fishhooks.

Such is the cycle of the principal *grandes pêches* of the fisherfolk's year. Individuals or families will also take any opportunity to harpoon the massive perch (*Lates niloticus*). This prized fish averages 4–5 kilograms, but can often reach 40 kilograms. Harpoon is also used for manatees (which are attracted to the lush *Echinochloa-bourgou* vegetation of the swamps) and for crocodile, caïmon, and the occasional hippo.

The Bozo tend not to farm. The exception to this rule is the planting of fonio (*Digitaria exilis*) used in many of the inter-ethnic rituals at which their leaders officiate. They will, however, regularly help the Marka, the preeminent cultivators of the deep floodplains.[15]

The rice harvests come, conveniently during the high flood, when the fish are hardest to catch. Although linked by strong traditions of common origin, what separates Bozo and Marka most is specialist occupational knowledge. Both focus on the aquatic sphere of the Middle Niger: Bozo on the fauna, Marka on the floral.

It is at the beginning of the rice agricultural year that the special knowledge of the Marka comes into play. Gallais[16] inventories the environmental stresses that bedevil the Marka. The all too common surprises of flood and rain can, in a week, strip away a year's hard work and leave whole villages desolate. These include premature, late, or excessive flooding. The Marka fear irregular rains (too soon or not soon enough, too little, too little at the start of the rains when the fields must be prepared). Rice-eating birds, fish and insects are their unrelenting foes. To counter all these forces, the Marka have a large and venerable store of predictive knowledge and ritual aids. This practical and occult knowledge is evoked for the simultaneous cultivation of many varieties of African rice (*Oryza glaberrima*). These many varieties vary by length of germination and preference for flood level and, of course, yield.

Significantly, the traditional Marka do not sow the highest yield varieties exclusively. Their specialist knowledge is employed in decisions concerning how many and what varieties to sow, at what

---

[15] Gallais, *Delta Intérieur*, I, pp. 109–11; Gallais, *Hommes*, pp. 23–30, 95–7.
[16] Ibid., p. 96.

time of the planting season. Long, narrow fields are laid out along the range of progression in the slope of the rice basins. Different rice varieties are sown at different sectors of the fields.

The year of the Marka begins between the middle of June and early July. The first of several sowings is completed as the light rains are due. The latest rice can be sown up to mid-August. The extremely time-consuming stoop labour of weeding has begun in July. The floods enter the paddies at the end of August or early September. Harvest of the fastest germinating varieties begins in mid-October. The real harvest is underway by the end of October and continues often into December. January through June are the months for threshing and for travel to markets to sell.

This annual cycle structures the lives of 27,000 of the 66,000 Marka of the Macina and Upper Delta. These, the most traditional rice growers, live in artificially built-up mound (*tell*) villages of c.430 inhabitants in the middle slopes of the floodplain. Others form a small majority in the towns of Mopti, Jenne, San and Dia. Another 16,000 live along the eastern borderlands around San (the Bénédougou). It is very likely that these border Marka played an important role in the development of long-distance exchange that nurtured the earliest cities of the Upper Delta.

The Marka divide themselves into the Marka *pi* (black) and the Marka *dié* (white). The latter are mixed with other Soninké and may have been in the Middle Niger only for several centuries. The older Marka have taken this name (Marka = Mali-Ka = Men of Mali) to celebrate their conversion to Islam to the time of the Mali empire.[17] However, they retain sentimental ties to an older name, Nono. This is particularly the case for the 15,000 rice farmers of the Jenneri (the higher, sandier plains within 30 km north of Jenné) and the Pondori. These are widely considered to be the most traditional of the rice growers. Clans of these Nono-Marka claim to be the oldest neighbors of the Bozo. One Bozo clan, the Tanapo, is noteworthy for the number and variety of ritual rights within their purview. It is these traditional Nono-Marka that have the closest ritual and mutual-aid alliances with the Sorogo.[18] Such alliances are played out in exchanges of labor with the net against stoop labor in the fields. Not surprisingly, they share with the

[17] But, see Boubacar Diallo, "Les Soninko," in *Vallées du Niger* , Réunion des Musées Nationaux, (RMN: Paris, 1993), p. 134.
[18] Ibid., p. 48; R. McIntosh, "Pulse model," pp. 209–11; Sundström, *Ecology*, pp. 52–5, 162–7.

Sorogo mythologies that place them, respectively, as the first and second autochtones of the Middle Niger.

The origin myths do not help us to sort out the full truth of the earliest settlement of the Upper Delta. We can only look forward to the day when sufficient archaeology has been done in the region. Only then might we be better able to sort through several origin hypotheses. The first, preferred by conceptual Lumpers,[19] argues that the self-imposed label of Bozo was attached rather late. In this view, long epochs passed before these people began to see themselves as a distinct group. Long into prehistory there had been a single, if amorphous, fisherfolk who also collected plants, hunted and perhaps tended small stock. Self-identification was by community or clan, at most. For most of their past we must speak of an aggregate of fisherfolk bound loosely by the common interests of the profession. The concept is evocative of the assimilative, diagnostic interpretation of the Aqualithic fisherfolk.

With the Lumpers we might imagine an earlier time characterized by several aquatic specialist communities (deep channel and lake, swamp, aquatic and highland hunters). The identity of the specialists began as segmentary, but merged more because of intensified contact and pressures from later groups. A common ancestral identity might have been invented as a convenient fiction.

The second hypothesis is really a variation on the first, but is far more inclusive. This thesis states that several of the Middle Niger ethnic groups fissioned from a much earlier unity. The unity was defined by the practice of a generalized economy. Ethnographers have long recognized the claims in oral tradition for common origin between the Bozo and the Nono[20] and the Bozo and the Dogon.[21] The Dogon inhabit the Bandiagara sandstone cliffs and surrounding lands immediately to the east of the Upper Delta. Nono and Dogon do not recognize common descent. However, it may be that

---

[19] Sundström, *Ecology and Symbiosis*, p. 163; For variations, see James L. Newman, *The Peopling of Africa*, (Yale University Press: New Haven, CT, 1995), p. 57 and Grove, *Niger and its Neighbours*, p. 143.

[20] For Bozo-Nono relations, see Jean Daget, "La pêche à Diafarabé," *Bulletin de l'Institut Fondamental d'Afrique Noire (B)*, 18 (1956), p. 16; Gallais, *Delta Intérieur*, p. 76; Gallais, *Hommes*, p. 48; Sundström, *Ecology*, p. 53.

[21] For Bozo-Dogon relations, see Germaine Dieterlen, *Les Ames des Dogon*, Travaux et Mémoires de l'Institut d'Ethnologie, no. 40 (Institut d'Ethnologie: Paris, 1941); Gallais, *Delta Intérieur*, p . 79; Marcelle Griaule, "L'Alliance cathartique," *Africa* 18, (1948), pp. 242–58; N'Diaye, *Groupes*, p. 247; Sundström, *Ecol-*

one of the two split from the Bozo earlier. In that case, the Nono and Dogon recognize common origin at no greater than one degree of distance. In addition to origin myths, Bozo and Dogon share strong relations based upon legends of more recent interaction (stories of mutual aid and alliances against common adversity). These bonds translate into rights of joking and insult, strong ritual obligations of reciprocal aid, and prohibitions against intermarriage and the shedding of blood. The three agree upon a symbolic representation of their alliance. Ethnicity is expressed as a triumvirate of grains. Each recognizes the mythical quality and equivalence of grains of fonio (the Bozo), millet (the Dogon), and rice (the Nono). This line of reasoning about ethnic or clan origins would be favoured by those who see regional demographic segmentation principally as a response to continuing or quite recent pressures (social, climatic, economic); the splits may be very recent but might nevertheless be justified by "venerable" oral traditions.

There is much speculation about joint Nono-Bozo origin because of the mutual intelligibility of archaic Nono and Sorogo dialects. They also share many rituals and totems. Certain collective fishing enterprises require not simply the joint participation, but also the ritual support of both. The strength and apparent antiquity of these bonds raises an important question that must be answered before one can accept the fission hypothesis. The question is pertinent equally for Dogon and Nono. Why would two agricultural groups (Nono and Dogon) have broken off from an aquatically based protogroup with a way of life most similar to the archaic Bozo? Perhaps certain communities within the earlier group spent more time gathering wild water plants. With their refined knowledge of the habits of these plants, they may have begun a process of domestication. Interest in wild plants has never waived. Ethnobotanists have found that many communities in the floodplain still regularly gather over a dozen species of wild plants (including wild rice, *Oryza barthii*). Perhaps another group increasingly specialized in the plants of the Middle Niger's highland features. This interest might have been critical to survival, particularly during episodes of low floods. Only later they migrated from the floodplain altogether. They then took a different name, the Dogon.

Or perhaps recent archaeology points to a possibility of a far more ancient division, with sustained interaction, between communities ancestral to these specialist ethnic groups. This is the domain of conceptual Splitters. Archaeologists and human geographers are becoming more comfortable with the principle of long, sustained interactions (only sometimes resulting in assimilation) or mosaics of specialist groups.[22] These specialists either developed *in situ* in the rich farm and fishing lands of the Middle Niger or, in a variation supported by excavated data primarily from the Méma, distinct groups entered the Middle Niger melting pot from distant points of origin. In this third scenario, around 2000 BC microlithic-using autochtonous groups (the "Red Men" of Bozo oral tradition, the counterpart in the savanna and sahel of the "pygmy" autochtones of the equatorial forest) welcomed the proto-Bozo fisherfolk, makers of the Méma Kobadi tradition ceramics. Later (*c.*1300 BC) the Ndondi Tossokel proto-agro-pastoralists (ancestors of the Nono-Marka) migrate from the Tichitt-Oualata regions (where they are identifiable as the makers of the Chebka-Arriane phase ceramics).[23] Claims of separate origin and of in-migration should not deflect us from the equally interesting claim of sustained interaction upon this ethnic and geomorphological mosaic.

Yet another fishing group also maintains some traditions of common origin, perhaps, or perhaps of boundary-effacing interaction, with the Bozo. Most scholars place the Songhai in an entirely different, non-Mande language family (the Nilo-Saharan). However, the Songhai sub-group called the Sorko claim that all the fisherfolk of the Middle Niger were once one people. Sorko, too, are harpoon hunters of crocodile, manatee, and hippo. They present us with other parallels with Bozo myth and prohibitions. Sorko tradition maintains that they are the issue of the marriage of a man of the water and a woman of red earth (agriculturist). In Bozo tradition, the red people are the Dogon, whom the Sorko also may not marry.[24] The connection here is very tenuous. The process at play may simply be attempts at myth invention once Bozo and Sorko came into contact. The purpose might have been to strengthen the possibilities for mutual aid of relations between fishing and agricultural specialists and between culturally distinct fishing communities.

Unfortunately, the support for a migration hypothesis is no firmer. According to this third thesis, groups entered the floodplain with

[22] Robert Vernet, " Néolithique du Sahel: Promlèmes spécifiques, éléments de synthèse et exemple du sud-ouest nigérien," *L'Anthropologie*, 100 (1996), p. 345; B. Diallo, "Les Soninko," p. 138.

[23] MacDonald and Van Neer, "Specialized fishing people," pp. 245–50; MacDonald, *Socio-economic Diversity*, pp. 37–48, 105–17, 196–7, 273–5; MacDonald, "Tichitt-Walata," pp. 429–40.

[24] Sundström, *Ecology*, pp. 91, 163.

subsistence economies already developed. They then had to enter alliances in order to enjoy neighborly peace and security. They underpinned those alliances with myths that provided the justification of timelessness.

I have dwelt on this issue of origin traditions to demonstrate the truth of Will Durant"s warning about the "cosmic nebula of theory." Not even the most universally held origin legends favor Lumpers over Splitters. The Tapama myth, to which we will return when discussing the founding of the city of Jenne, is perhaps the classic. In this myth, one finds universal recognition of the Bozo claim to first possession of the land and of the subsequent Nono right to use the land. By the extraordinary sacrifice of a virgin by the Bozo, the success and wealth of the Nono town was ensured. The Nono, of course, came into the region from elsewhere. Had the Bozo always been in the Middle Niger? Or were they migrants from elsewhere who, as Sundström argues, lacked a language of their own? He believes they were forced to borrow one from "some previous host population".[25] Some Bozo myth speak of an origin from the earth itself: the ancestors emerged from holes at Wandiaka (on the Niger downstream of Mopti) and Dia (on the Diaka in the Macina).[26] Or are such myths simply inventions, fabrications to bolster claims to ritual authority over the land and to the right to minister to the land and water spirits of the Middle Niger?

Perhaps one day archaeology will help us to sort through these three alternatives. There are certainly those who doubt even that and who would deny any validity to attempts to investigate the deep-time roots of belonging. We can only say with confidence that no *permanent* occupation has been found in the Upper Delta coeval with the most recent late stone age occupation of the Méma. Past that, however, we descend into the realm of pure speculation. "Proto-specializations" resembling the earliest economies of communities directly ancestral to Bozo, Nono, and Dogon might very well have been developed during the last few millennia BC. We have already seen in the Méma and perhaps the Azawad as yet highly ambiguous evidence that points in that direction. These specializations may have been encouraged by the climatic deterioration and stress of those millennia. And those same specializations may have encouraged the domestication of rice, sorghum, and millet.

---

[25] Sundström, *Ecology,* p. 165.
[26] Gallais, *Hommes,* p. 48; Sundström, *Ecology,* p. 49.

In the end, however, origin myths are just historical tales heavily edited to conform to how peoples wish to think of themselves and to present themselves to the rest of the world. The archaeologist's time can be put to far better use than looking for the origin of named ethnic groups, or looking too long for "proto-Bozo" or "proto-Nono." Rather, more progress has already been made by those archaeologists documenting the circumstances under which specialized economies developed in the late stone age. Then we can trace how those economies "translated" to the live basins of the Middle Niger during the earliest iron age.

Were the specializations as fixed and as ethnically exclusive as they appear to have been from historical times? Or did groups with generalized ways of life enter as a slow trickle from the southern Sahara, only to fragment later? It is hard to say. But it is certain that sustained diversification, *as a process*, has a long pedigree as the cultural signature of the Middle Niger. Gallais provides the classic environmental explanation for continued occupational fragmentation:

> However, one easily comes to the conclusion that these conditions of the physical environment maintain a cultural cradle in which the most surprising aspect is the specialization of production. Man is fisher, rice farmer, pastoralist. His activities rarely transgress the bounds of traditional practice. This specialization of production in the natural world is quite distinct from that produced by a system of castes. It is not maintained by an artificial hierarchy of activities and expectations based upon rights and pollution, as with the Indian caste system. It is less solid, less crystallized, and yet entirely solidly rooted.[27]

I hope to show that specialization is not just a functional adaptation to environment. It is also a state of mind, a fundamental cultural value, a defining element of the landscape of memory. In the Middle Niger, specialization has an origin deep in the realm of history verging into prehistory. There is no doubt that the live basins continued to provide fertile ground for specialization. Without doubt, the live basins enjoyed a long history as magnets for incoming movements of other specialists whom today we recognize as distinct ethnic groups. One example of the floodplain's ability to accommodate later additions can be seen in the case of the group dominating the plains of the Macina, the pastoral Fulani.

---

[27] Gallais, *Hommes*, p. 38.

Pastoral Cycle of the Macina: the Fulani

In overall physical organization, the Macina is less complex than the Upper Delta. As one enters the Macina from its western frontier with the Méma, one first traverses high sandy floodplain. Then, traveling east, floodplain of middle depth dominates the basin from west of the Diaka *marigot* to the Niger at the eastern margin of the Macina. North of the sandy plain (west of Lake Débo) one finds a low erg system (the southwestern appendix of the Erg of Bara). Deep basins flank most of the length of the Diaka. An important deep basin south of Lakes Débo and Walado covers *c.*150,000 ha. This is the Bourgou-Dialloubé (nearest the lakes) and Bourgou-Yallabé (to the southwest). Here the Fulani find the rich pasturage that sustains their herds during the last months of the dry season.

The Macina's deep basins are just the last occupied within a cycle of pasturages. The depth and availability of palatable, dry season vegetation increase from southwest to northeast. The higher elevation plains are a morass of channels, ponds, ancient levees, and dunes. These features are exaggerated in the eastern section, particularly (Pérou Kaïmankou and Pérou Dialloube). This tangle of microenvironments is clearly part of an ancient bird's-foot delta etched in clay and loamy sand as a larger Lake Débo receded to its present size. This is yet another argument against the thesis of a stable Lake Paléo-Débo. Such bird's-foot delta are more typically erected in large bodies of water that recede slowly, but steadily. They are less common in stable lakes that decline precipitously.

Two factors make the Macina a particular magnet for a group more recently arrived in the Middle Niger, the Fulani. The first is the bathymetric progression of Macina soils from the frontier with the dry plains of the Méma. As the dry season proceeds, the herds enter the Macina floodplain, in stages, from the high western border terraces to the lowest basins south of the lakes. Secondly, each depth progression provides the luxuriant growth of *bourgou* vegetation (an assemblage of middle and deep basin wild plants, dominated by *Echinocloa stagnina* and *Oryza barthii*).

We will probably never know whether the deeper parts of the Macina were once densely populated by Nono and Bozo.[28] Today these peoples are confined to the town of Dia and to rural enclaves nearby. This question is complicated by the Macina's large popula-

---

[28] Ibid., p. 32; Louis Tauxier, *Moeurs et Histoire des Peuls* (Paris: Payot, 1937), p. 9.

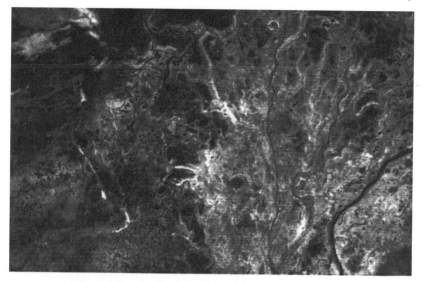

Plate 4.2 *Bird's-foot delta south of Lake Débo.*

tion of Rimaïbé. They are the servile agricultural attendants of the pastoral Fulani. Were they introduced to the Macina only as the Fulani moved in? Or, are they an amalgam of local Nono, Bozo, and others that were conquered and stripped of their original ethnic affiliation by the pastoralists? If the latter, the Rimaïbé represent the triumph of the Fulani's definition of the backswamps as *bourgou*. With their subjugation came the defeat of the autochthone's definition of the same features as riceland or fishing grounds. In the Macina, the winner took all, land, voluntary labor, and sense of separate ethnicity. Even the date for this process is uncertain. It was only at the beginning of the last century that the Fulani cleric-dynast Sekou Amadou reorganized the annual transhumant cycle.[29] His major triumph was to break the traditional authority of the clan-military heads (*Ardo*). Sekou Amadou founded villages of Rimaïbé and many free Fulani within the floodplain. It is not at all certain that the Rimaïbé population was at all significant before that time. However, it is still very much a possibility that the basic pattern of Rimaïbé settlement that we see today dates to the first penetration of the Fulani, well before the turbulent nineteenth century.

---

[29] William A. Brown, *The Caliphate of Hamdullahi, ca. 1818–1864. A Study in African History and Tradition* . PhD dissertation, University of Wisconsin, 1969.

The Fulani number some 132,000 in the Upper Delta and Macina.[30] Only in the Macina do they represent the majority (where the 68,000 Fulani represent 71% of the population). Fulani divide themselves into three classes. First in rank are the freemen. They are followed by casted "artisans" (merchants, bards, smiths, jewelers, butchers, carpenters, leatherworkers, and tanners). Last are those of formerly servile status, the aforementioned Rimaïbé. The last functioned principally to provide grain for nomadic Fulani herds during the stressful late dry season months and for the sedentary Fulani during the inundation season.

The closeness of dune and *bourgou* in the Macina satisfy the basic concerns of the sedentary Fulani. The middle floodplain slopes are the preferred village location for the sedentary Fulani. There they are away from the deepest backswamps, which must be conserved to sustain the assembled herds when the travelling Fulani return to the Macina. The village Fulani send most of their herd on the transhumance round. They keep with them only those milk cows (and their calves) needed to sustain the community. The middle floodplain provides a grass of poorer quality than the deep *bourgou*. Of equal importance here is the presence of sandy highland features. Less preferred are the *pérou* levees of clay or sandy loam. The village herd must be kept on high sand features. Sand levees and dunes retain the heat of the day during the cold months of the flood season and winter, when nights can be frigid. Grazing is limited on these small islands in the vastness of the Middle Niger flood. As long as there has been a sedentary population of Fulani, there has been a complementary need for the fodder and grain tribute of the Rimaïbé. This proximity of vegetated basin and sand highland (*bourgou* and *seno*) is the signature of the Niafunké region in the Lakes Region. A similar configuration of landforms blesses most of the Erg of Bara, and the Jenneri north of Jenne in the Upper Delta. However, the *bourgou* and *seno* association is by far the most extensive in the Macina.

The transhumant Fulani (and their 1.5 million cattle, half million goat and quarter million sheep) are the emblem of the Macina.[31]

---

[30] Gallais, *Hommes*, pp. 23–4, 32; Imperato estimates 163,000 transhumant and 250,000 sedentary Fulani for the entire Middle Niger, a figure that seems somewhat high: Pascal J. Imperato, "Nomades of the Niger," *Natural History*, 81 (1972), p. 33.

[31] For the transhumant cycle of the Fulani, see Gallais, *Delta Intérieur*, I, pp. 112–14, 119–61, II, 361–411; Gallais, *Hommes*, pp. 42–55, 74–94; Imperato, "Nomades," pp. 62–4, 67.

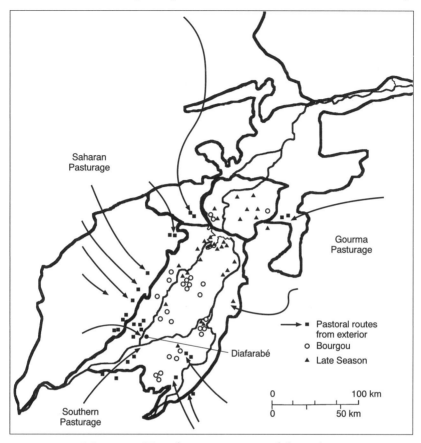

Map 4.2   *Transhumance routes of the Fulani*

Theirs is a complex year dictated by rain and flood. By the arrival of the first weak rains of June, the cattle are in distress. Most are crowded into the last remaining deep *bourgou* . The rest are grazing the banks of the Niger, the Diaka, and the lakesides. Too many cattle, too many clans, have been pressed too close together for too many dry months. Predictably, there is an escalation of clan-clan, Fulani-Tuareg, and pastoralist-farmer conflicts. Then, the floodplain begins to green over with the first serious rains of July. By mid-month a quite rapid transhumant movement evacuates the Middle Niger. It is rapid, centrifugal, and dispersive: the mobile Fulani have left for their traditional rainy season territories at the exterior of the Middle Niger.

The herds can travel up to 500 kilometers from their end-dry season starting point to reach these pastures. Six of these territories are to the sandy eastern margin or deep into the Gourma wastes south of the Bend of the Niger. Nine rainy season territories penetrate the sahelian sands west of the Méma (from Nara to Bassikounou) or are centered in the Méma itself. In the Méma, Fulani search out the old Holocene lake and swamp beds, the now-senescent channels and meander scars, and the loams of the degraded dunes. All these ancient fluvial and lacustrine features do their part to channel, pond, and preserve the sparse rains of summer. For that very short season, the Méma becomes a rich prairie.

The Middle Niger holds the key to the success of the entire Fulani agro-pastoral system. The allure of the floodplain is renewed at the beginning of flood recession. With the end, in September, of the late summer *doungou* rains, the distant prairies fast loose their appeal. The herds from 15 remote territories (including, most recently, three Tuareg groups) begin to congregate. As early as November, the herds are poised for their entry through the 17 traditional ports or passageways (*gué*) into the land of the *bourgou*. Each of the traveling herds of approximately 15,000 head form together under the authority of a "chief of cattle." The herds travel from their most distant point on the transhumant round to these ports, and thence through the Macina along fifteen well established paths (*burti*). As the herds gather before the *gué*, often waiting a month for permission to cross into the Macina, the *burti* paths can cross. Lines of authority of the traditional "chiefs of cattle" can become confused. Competing clan claims are often pressed by club or knife.

It is little wonder that, after the tensions of awaiting permission to enter, the Fulani consider the floodplain a temporal paradise. Passageways such as Diafarabé are passed with a riotous ritual marking the safe crossing of the Niger or Diaka by hundreds of thousands of cattle. By end-December or January the Macina is awash with cattle.

Once past the river, the herds begin a slow penetration. Grazing begins at the high sandy floodplain at the western frontier of the Macina. When all goes well, there is a slow, orderly descent (north and east) through successively deeper, *bourgou*-rich basins. January, February and March see the successive exhaustion of *bourgou* in the high and middle Macina. Grazing and standing water are sufficient. In this ideal scenario, the Marka and Bambara welcome "their" Fulani to the vicinity. The herds graze on the stubble of the recently harvested fields and some farmers even pay the pastoralists in grain for the favor of manuring next year's fields. By the end of March, the competition for resources grows appreciably. The hot season has begun. The herds coalesce around the deepest basins of the Bourgou-Dialloubé and Bourgou-Yallabé or flank the banks of the Niger and Diaka. Here the land is still green and the animals content. There could be no sharper contrast with the suffocatingly dry Sahel and northern savanna surrounding the Middle Niger.

The herds move every few weeks, deeper and deeper into the Macina, closer and closer to the lakes. Tensions grow as more and more animals crowd together. The same *bourgou* pastures are often claimed by different clans. The heat increases. Anxiety increases that, perhaps this year, the *bourgou* and water will not suffice for all. By April and June the crowding approaches the intolerable. Tensions build, and build . . . until the harbinger rains begin to fall. Then, all rejoice in the catharsis of movement.

Unfortunately, the long dry-season camps on the lake shores are not the only scenes of conflict. The July commencement of the *doungou* rains is the time of the rapid dispersal out of the floodplain. Movement separates the feuding Fulani clans. However, the early rains also signal the first sowing and weeding of the farmers' fields to the east of the Middle Niger. If the cattle trample or consume the tender sprouts, the herders must contend with the righteous wrath of those farmers.

Most serious farmer-pastoralist conflict occurs during the all too frequent years of insufficient rains. Friendship between farmer and cowherd quickly turns to violent enmity. Poor rains prolong the growing season. The harvest of millet, especially, can be delayed to late October, November, or even December. Insufficient rains have left the Fulani little option but to leave even the best grazing land of the Méma weeks before they would normally have done so. The desperate cattle crowd before the *gué* at the edge of the floodplain. The clan chiefs have little option but to give early leave to enter the Macina. There, the still unharvested millet fields are irresistible to the poor beasts. Year after year, the poor rains of the long Sahel Drought gave examples of bloody conflict of Fulani with peasants determined to save their grain.

Lastly, during the last few centuries the Tuareg and some Moors have pushed their herds further and further to the south. Now they mingle with the Fulani south of the large lakes, just at the moment of greatest late-dry season distress. The numbers of Tuareg are not large. Perhaps only some 3,000 congregate around Lake Débo. However, they are perceived as intruding ever more persistently, always unacceptably, into the traditional *burti* routes and clan-held *bourgou*.

The intensity of these conflicts internal to the Fulani transhumant cycle increased century after century in historical times. The situation became intolerable because of the violence done to the Fulani by Bambara immigrants from the south. Matters became intolerable when, during the seventeenth and eighteenth centuries, Bambara armies of Segou and the Bélédougou ravaged the Macina. Sekou Amadou revolutionized the life of the pastoral Fulani, in part, to respond to these affronts and, undoubtedly, to facilitate his dream of a purified Islamic state.[32] In 1818 he established his empire, the Dina, and organized the Fulani into 37 districts, or *leydi* . These he placed under new forms of chiefs, or *ardo* (who were firmly under submission to himself). His strategy was to compel the Fulani to accept his vision of the landscape by breaking the power of the traditional military-clan structure under cattle and pasturage chiefs. Often he had canals dug to set frontiers and resolve *bourgou* ownership disputes between clans and between members of *leydi*. He fixed the routes in and out of the Macina. He tried also to regularize the date of herd movement to reduce conflicts with the peasants.

Sekou Amadou's most disruptive reform was to force sedentarism on the Fulani. On pain of loss of water and *bourgou* rights, each family had to have a fixed abode. A significant part of the family had to remain in the Macina year-round. From nomadic camps sprung villages. With forced sedentarism came the entirely new problem of how to provision the herd of milk cows and their young. The problem was particularly acute when the annual flood arrived. The solution was one of more suffering. Captives of the wars to establish the *Dina* and unfortunates settled in the wrong place fed the expanded Rimaïbé class. Rimaïbé-grown grain maintained that part of the herds kept in the Middle Niger year-round.

As mentioned above, it is hard to know how large the Rimaïbé population was before the nineteenth century. They and other unfortunate captives are seldom mentioned in the local *ta'rikhs* and oral traditions. It is likely that a wholly or largely nomadic Fulani had need of relatively few in servile relationship to them. It is reasonably certain that the Fulani were largely nomadic when they first entered the Middle Niger. When they entered, and from whence, is open to much debate. A great deal of yet to be completed archaeology will have to supplement the historical record in order to resolve

---

[32] Sekou Amadou and the Dina period will be the subject of extensive treatment in a later chapter. For his reorganization of the *butri*, see Gallais, *Hommes*, pp. 54–5, 75–7.

this tricky issue of the arrival of the Fulani in the Middle Niger.

The arrival of the herdsmen is not welcomed in the revered local history of the Middle Niger, es-Sadi's *Ta'rikh es-Sudan* of 1656. For es-Sadi, the appearance of the unrestrained and bellicose Fulani marked the beginning of a period of chaos and poverty in the Macina and Upper Delta. In es-Sa'di's evocative language, the Fulani were responsible for "the oppression of [other ethnic groups of] the Macina, by their arrogance and by their tyranny they have sown troubles in all directions and in all places. Oh, the miserable men of God who have perished by the blow of these Macina Fulani. What riches have they unjustly stolen by pure violence".[33] Delafosse and Tauxier placed the entry into the Macina of the first clan, the Dialloubé, under Ardo Maghan Diallo, at *c*.AD 1400. Gallais's sources specify the date of entry at AD 1378.[34]

There is no possible way to verify these dates. It is interesting that these dates coincide generally with the period of severe droughts (roughly AD 1200–1400) that follows an equally long period of rapid climatic oscillations (AD 1000–1200) (see table 2.1). The oral traditions record that the first Macina Fulani came from the west. By west is probably meant the dry, and increasingly more desiccated Méma and Sahel between the Middle Niger and the Middle Senegal Valley and, indeed, a number of waterways, such as the Vallée du Serpent, would have provided convenient paths.[35] If these traditions have any basis in fact, then climate may be a partial answer to why they came in such disruptive numbers. The Middle Niger must have loomed before the first arrivals as a paradise of *bourgou*.

The Fulani's origin is a matter of pure speculation.[36] Colonial authors, such as Delafosse, reflected the prejudices of their era. He saw them as descendants of Jews or Judeo-Syrians forced across the Sahara from North Africa by the wave of Islam. Tauxier rejects this thesis and the thesis of Berber origin. His belief, instead, is that the Fulani represent travel-weary "Hamites" originally from Ethiopia. This Hamitic stream moved to the Nile, and thence across North Africa, where it was pushed to the bend of the Senegal in AD 736. At the Middle Senegal Valley, some intermarried with Serer to make the Tukulor. Others retained "racial purity" in the Ferlo Valley until,

[33] Es-Sa'di, *Ta'rikh es-Sudan*, trans. O. Houdas (Paris: Leroux, 1900), p. 411.

[34] Maurice Delafosse, Haut-Sénégal-Niger, (Paris: Larose, 1912), II, p. 223; Gallais, Hommes, p. 51; Tauxier, Moeurs , pp. 7–10.

[35] See Kesteloot, et al., "Les Peul," figures 3, 4, and 5.

[36] Gallais, *Delta Intérieur*, I, p. 87; Tauxier, *Moeurs*, pp. 7–115.

in the eighth century, the irresistible urge built to push eastward. They were still pushing into Chad in the nineteenth century.

How much can we trust this rather typical and highly speculative mixture of colonial-period racial and anecdotal history? Probably not very much. Unfortunately, more recent theses are no less speculative. At the moment, we have no very hard archaeological evidence to prove or disprove an alternative thesis by archaeologists who claim the Fulani as descendants of the pastoral peoples depicted in the "Neolithic" rock paintings of the Saharan Adrar des Iforas, Hoggar, and Tassili.[37] These paintings are of the so-called "Bovidien" period, presumed to date to the fourth through second millennia BC. The attribution of these paintings to a "proto-Fulani" is soundly rejected by other rock art specialists. Nevertheless, the ethnic group we now call the Fulani may have had its origin in the numerous late stone age communities that increasingly specialized in the tending of cattle (and sheep and goat). The lsa pastoralists first appear in Saharan archaeological contexts after *c.*7,000 years ago. The speculation will continue until far more archaeological research is undertaken on those early pastoralist communities.

There is, however, some consensus growing that Saharan pastoralists would have been squeezed out of the present desert regions by the first millennium BC. Some claim an immediate presence in the Middle Niger (at least by mid-first millennium AD).[38] Most authorities, however, postulate a "curing" period, a maturation of Fulani identity (a process which would include the complementary formation of Tukulor identity and of enmity relations with camel-tending Moors), in the Futa Toro. Once a self-recognized, if politically amorphous Fulani develop, they migrate eastwards and become a presence in the Méma and Macina some time between the tenth and fifteenth centuries AD.[39] Ethnic origins and early migration are the antithesis of high-precision history!

---

[37] Gabriel Camps, *Les Berbères. Mémoire et Identité* (Paris, Editions Errance, 1987), p. 41; Alfred Muzzolini, *L'Art Rupestre Préhistorique des Massifs Centraux Sahariens*, Cambridge Monographs in African Archaeology, no. 16 (Oxford: BAR, 1986), pp. 318, 323, 326; Andrew Smith, "New approaches to Saharan rock of the Bovidian Period," in *Environmental Change and Human Culture in the Nile Basin and Northern Africa until the Second Millennium BC*, Lech Krzyzaniak, Michal Kobusiewicz, and John Alexander (eds), (Poznan Archaeological Museum: Poznan, 1993), pp. 77–89; Christian Dupuy, "Trois mille ans d'histoire pastorale au sud du Sahara," *Préhistoire et Anthropologie Méditerranéennes*, 1992: 105–26.

[38] Dupuy, "Trois mille ans," p. 115.

[39] Kesteloot, et al., "Les Peul," pp. 181, 182; Newman, *Peopling*, p. 130.

Rainfed and Décrue *Agriculture on the Erg of Bara: Bambara*

We are on slightly more secure ground concerning the origin of the Bambara (also known as Bamana) of the dune system north of Lake Débo. Penetration of the Erg of Bara represents the final stage of the remarkable march of southern Mande speakers, a march linked to the successes of centralized and expansive Mande states, from Mali (thirteenth century) to Biton Coulibali's Segou (seventeenth century).

In some ways, the geomorphologial organization of the Erg of Bara region is the simplest of the six Middle Niger basins.[40] Simplicity would not be a cartographer's word, however. The Erg of Bara is dominated by the massive late Pleistocene (Ogolian) dunes. These dunes blocked the Niger at the beginning of the first Holocene Pluvial. The dune system is an attenuated western extension of the great Gourma Erg that occupies the vast desert south of the bend in the Niger. Lakes Débo, Korienzé and Walado remain as evidence of the large body of blocked water. These lakes frame the Erg of Bara region to the south. The structural trough they occupy and the sandstone Mountains of Goundourou to the southeast of the lakes are evidence of folding and faulting. Geologists date these events to the Eocene, at the latest. The large Lake Region lakes frame this basin to the northwest (Lakes Korarou, Tana and Kabara) and northeast (Lakes Aougoundou and Niangay).

The Erg of Bara represents a transition zone between the lush floodplains of the Upper Delta and Macina and the dunal wastes of the Lakes Region-Niger Bend. The dunes here are not actively moving. They are stabilized by a light cover of acacias and grass. That grass cover is restricted, however, by the 300–400mm rainfall average and by the Fulani and Tuareg herds. Dunecrests average 2–3 kilometers apart. Between are interdunal ponds, approximately one kilometer wide, that fill to 2–3 meters with the annual flood.

At the end of the Pleistocene hyperaridity, the rejuvenated Niger did eventually breach the high Ogolian dunes. Now the divided

---

[40] Brunet-Moret, *Monographie Hydrologique*, II, pp. 27, 31; Yvon Vincent, "Pasteurs, paysans et pêcheurs du Guimbala (Partie Centrale de l'Erg du Bara)," in *Nomades et Paysans de l'Afrique Noire Occidentale*, Pierre Galloy, Yvon Vincent et Maurice Forget (eds), Annales de l'Est, no. 23 (Université de Nancy: Nancy, 1963), pp. 35–157; Urvoy, *Bassins* pp. 48–9, 75–6.

river snakes through the region in several parts. The Issa-Ber and Bara-Issa issues out of Lake Débo; the Koli-Koli out of Lake Korienzé.

The dunes are cut by innumerable *marigots,* oxbows, interdunal lakes and ponds. The river cut through the dunes at a time of significantly higher discharge. Those rapidly moving waters became laden with sand and so migrated wildly. The very personality of the river changed: today, the Niger is only very mildly sinuous upstream of Lake Débo. Its channel is rather well delineated, with few parallel-running side channels, point bars, and the like. Below Débo, the fluvial system is classically anastomosing. Channels divide and reunite in a complex web like pattern. Sand bars are left behind as the channel migrates. Oxbow lakes stand exposed in a local dunal landscape. The heavier soils of the interdunal depressions support standing water well into the dry season. There are, however, fewer of the large deep *bourgou*-filled depressions here than in the Macina (or even the Upper Delta). This does not prevent the Fulani from coming into conflict with the agriculturists of the region. Armed conflict is no stranger to the millet and sorghum farmers of the Erg of Bara, the proudly martial Bambara.

The Bambara are presumed to have entered the Middle Niger at about the same time or slightly later than the Fulani. Delafosse[41] believed that they trickled into the Upper Delta in about the thirteenth century. This is a chronology that consciously links the spread to Lake Débo of a named southern Mande peoples with the expansion of the Mali empire. But the chronological divide is arbitrary. Were the Bambara really stopped at the southern shore of the lake for several centuries, perhaps until the successes of the Ségou empire-builders or were Bambara among the most northern pagan "Lamlam" mentioned by Arab chroniclers several centuries earlier?[42] Were the mound settlements of the first millennium AD Upper Delta and Macina exclusively Nono and Bozo (northern Mande-speakers), or did a slow trickle of Bambara begin long before Mali?

Whatever the answers to these intractable questions, we can

---

[41] Delafosse, *Haut-Sénégal-Niger*, I, pp. 283–9.
[42] Jean Devisse and Samuel Sidibé, "Mandinka et mandéphones," in *Vallées du Niger*, Réunion des Musées Nationaux, (Editions de la Réunion des Musées Nationaux: Paris, 1993), p. 146.

develop a rough outline of classic Bambara migrations into the Erg of Bara from their traditions and from the *ta'rikhs* of the towns peoples with whom they came into contact. The first pioneers were hunters. As were explorer hunters of the earlier groups, they were attracted by concentrations of game during the flood season on the non-inundated features such as dunes and levees.[43] Hunters were followed by a split–wave of farmer-soldiers. One group migrated north along the sandy plains of the Méma-Macina boundary, stopping at about the latitude of Dia. The second and numerically more important entered the Upper Delta with the permission of the Jenne Weré (traditional chief of that town). These Bambara settled the levee south of Jenne (the Nyansannari), as well as the isolated dunes of the Derrari and Femaye north and northeast of that city. More Bambara trickled along the sandy eastern frontier of the Upper Delta and northern Macina. They finally entered the Erg of Bara region, in numbers great enough to call attention to themselves, by the beginning of the eighteenth century.[44]

These farmer-soldiers founded small settlements joined in village federations or cantons. Each canton fell under the authority of a *fama*, a chief of the land and of battle. Bambara cantons fought the Fulani and fought each other. From the early seventeenth century the Middle Niger Bambara became increasingly allied with the *fama* of Ségou. In 1670, *fama* Biton Coulibali of Segou was able to push his direct influence up to Jenne. With the aid of the local Bambara, he imposed his conditions upon the Jenne Weré and *Ardo* of Macina.

The *ta'rikhs* record this as a time of infamy to which the Bambara made a considerable sad contribution. The seventeenth and eighteenth century Middle Niger was the scene of state-inspired economic chaos, pillage, crushing tribute, and forced population displacements. In the Erg of Bara region, confederations of fortified villages and satellite hamlets formed under the aegis of the city-states of Sa, Saraféré and N'Gorkou.[45] The Bambara population continued to rise. So did hostilities with Fulani and Tuareg neighbors. The Fulani theocratic dynast, Sekou

---

[43] Gallais, *Hommes*, pp. 52–3; Gérard Brasseur, *Les Etablissements Humains au Mali*, Mémoire de l'Institut Fondamental d'Afrique Noire, no. 83 (IFAN: Dakar, 1961), pp. 261–3.

[44] Vincent, "Pasteurs," pp. 50–8.

[45] Ibid., pp. 51, 144–9; Gallais, *Hommes*, p. 31.

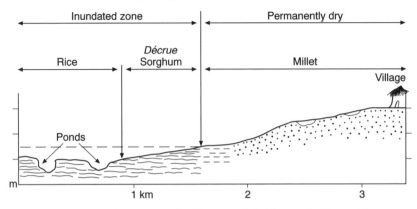

Figure 4.2   *Placement of villages and fields on the Erg of Bara*

Amadou, imposed a peace of sorts after 1818. A cement for that peace was to merge, in the same villages, newly sedentarized Fulani with conquered, but free, Bambara. Farmer-pastoralist conflicts could never be completely eliminated and (at a very local level) continue today.[46]

There are approximately 62,000 Bambara in the Middle Niger. Bambara form a majority of the population only in the Erg of Bara. They retain the same language and same preoccupation with millet as Bambara elsewhere in Mali. Here, however, we must understand several distinctive features. The Erg Bambara are unusual in their mixture of rainfed and *décrue* agriculture. Secondly, farmers and pastoralists are extraordinarily interdependent. Indeed, human geographers speak of an "agro-Peul" organization to the Erg of Bara calendar.[47]

The agricultural year begins with the late June rains.[48] At that time, the mobile segment of the Fulani population begins its transhumant dispersal. After the second good rains (usually in July), millet is sown in dunecrest fields around the villages. The lightly compacted, yellow-white sands of the dunes are easily worked and retain the early rains. They are, however, poor soils. Farmers anxiously pass a critical fortnight after sowing during which regular rains must fall or the crop will fail. The fields are weeded from

---

[46] Vincent, "Pasteurs," pp. 86–98.
[47] Hubert Gerbeau, "La région de l'Issa-Ber," *Etude d'Outre-Mer*, 42 (1959), I, pp. 51-8; II, pp. 91–108; Vincent, "Pasteurs," figure 5, p. 61.
[48] Ibid., pp. 43–6, 59–75; Gallais, *Delta Intérieur* , I, pp. 111–12, 331–52.

July to September. Harvest takes place from the end of September to early October. The rains of their region are, in principle, sufficient for a decent yield of millet. However, the irregularity of timing and amount of rain ensures that millet is the majority, but never the exclusive crop of the dunes.

The Erg of Bara Bambara watch the rise of the floods with anxiety. Due to the reservoir effect of the southern lakes, the waters rise slowly in July through January. High flood is from four to five weeks later than its arrival at Mopti. The interdunal spaces flood and become luxuriant with *bourgou* grasses (especially wild rice). The nomadic Sorko fishermen and hippo hunters travel the *marigots* at this season. At high water, the farmers plant sorghum in hand-irrigated fields above the flood.

Décrue begins in February. It is at this point that the Bambara have to perform an act of precise prediction in this environment of high interannual variability in flood timing and height. The young seeds are transplanted during March and April into the muddy sand-clay soils of the sides of the dunes. The lowest field must be above the flood height at September-October of the following year. The fields cannot be too low, or the high-water mark too high. If the position of fields is miscalculated, a significant portion of the crop will be lost before harvest. The ideal is to have the highest possible flood (in order to have fields far up the slope of the dune). The ideal flood would rise as slowly as possible (so as not to kill the sorghum planted the year before). Rarely is the Niger flood so cooperative.

Here at the northernmost extension of their distribution, the Bambara have been forced to diversify their farming. In addition to rainfed millet and *décrue* sorghum, the Bambara also plant rice in the deep ponds and *marigots*. As an important hedge against total crop failure, they contract with the local Fulani to tend their cattle. No groups in the region have forgotten the centuries of past conflict with fishermen and, especially, with pastoralists. Nevertheless, the drive for more subsistence insurance in this unpredictable environment ensures a fundamental degree of respect for occupational differences in the historical relations with other ethnic groups. In the words of Vincent: "Fishermen, farmers, and pastoralists subsist together by maintaining more or less good relations, without attempting to level differences of race and customs."[49]

[49] Vincent, "Pasteurs," p. 52.

Desert-River Clash at the Lakes Region-Niger Bend:
Songhai and Tuareg

The floodplain of the Middle Niger is capped to the far north and northeast by a region of lakes, dune cordons, and sandstone exposures. These features progressively funnel the river's waters into the narrow floodplain of the Niger Bend near Timbuktu. At Timbuktu, the floodplain has narrowed to a width of 10–15 kilometres. The floodplain is reduced to six kilometers wide at Gourma-Rharous. Somewhat arbitrarily, we shall take that town as the eastern limit of the Middle Niger. Here we return to the desert, full circle in the description of the Middle Niger basins. Today the river and desert struggle to dominate one another. That was the clash won ultimately in the Azawad by wind and sand.

The Lakes Region-Niger Bend is unusual for the numbers and complexity of laterite and rock exposures (sandstones, schists, quartzites, dolerites). More so than in the deeper southern basins, these exposures provide much of the organization of the region's lakes and dune features. The most important geological features are the sandstone Goundam Hills and laterized tabular late Tertiary (Continental Terminal) sandstone and clays of the Niger Bend. Rock exposures illustrate the long and continuing history of tectonic warping and faulting that has had a profound effect upon the river's history. The Niger has recently (in the geologist's sense of time) taken an impetuous turn. To understand this event we must take a broader look at the evolution of the region.

The entire Middle Niger has been subjected to deep subsidence (synclinal warping) at least from the Eocene.[50] The depression hosting the Upper Delta and the Macina is intimately linked with the Hodh and Araouane (comprised of the Aklé and Azawad) in a massive system of folding. Between the Upper Delta and Macina and the northern desert synclines is a system of smaller troughs and upwardly buckled (anticlinal) rock. These are the folds and troughs

---

[50] J.-P. Blanck, *Projet d'Amenagement de la Vallée du Niger entre Tombouctou et Labbezanga*, (Centre de Géographie Appliqueée, Université de Strasbourg: Strasbourg 1968), pp. 12–20; J.-P. Blanck, "Schéma d'evolution géomorphologique de la Vallée du Niger entre Tombouctou et Labbezanga (République du Mali)," *Bulletin de l'Association Sénégalese pour l'Etude du Quaternaire de l'Ouest Africain, Dakar*, 19–20 (1968), pp. 17–26; Brunet-Moret et al., *Monographie* , pp. 27–30; Tricart, *Reconnaissance* , pp. 18–20, 22–8; Urvoy, *Bassins*, pp. 21–35.

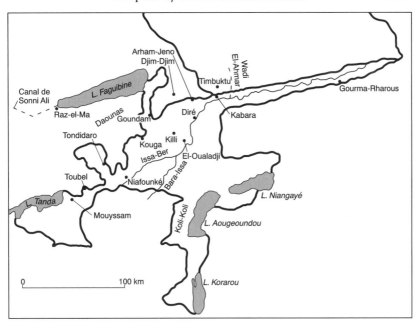

Map 4.3   *Live delta landforms and site of the LAKES REGION-NIGER BEND*

of the Lakes Region-Niger Bend that orient lakes and river. Tectonic activity picked up pace in the Middle Quaternary. Most dramatically, faulting opened up the east-west trench east of Timbuktu. And the Lakes Region-Niger Bend is far from dormant.[51] There has been recent uplift of the old beaches of Lake Faguibine and the extrusion of volcanic material in that lake's vicinity. The result of faulting and folding from at least the Eocene to present is a series of sandstone plateaux and hills on the left bank of the Niger. These rise up to 70 meters above the lakes they frame to the east. Related fields of less extensive hills dominate the lakes of the right bank and the Daounas area west of Lake Faguibine.

These sandstone features played a curious role during the late

[51] Théodore Monod and G. Palausi, "Sur la présence dans la région du lac Faguibine de venues volcaniques d'âge subactuel," *Comptes Rendus de l'Académie des Sciences de Paris*, 246 (1958), pp. 666–8; Jean Riser, Anne-Marie Aucour and Fousseyni Toure, "Niveaux lacustres et néotectoniques au lac Faguibine (Mali)," *Comptes Rendus de l'Académie des Sciences de Paris*, Série II, 10 (1986), pp. 941–3.

Pleistocene hyperarid period. There were major disruptions to the large ENE-WSW oriented parallel dunes being modelled from the thick earlier Niger alluvium. These, of course, are the familiar red dunes (Ogolian). The Lakes Region dunes are part of the Erg of Bara, that barrier to the Niger when its flow returned at the beginning of the Holocene. In the Erg of Bara as in its continuation in the Azawad, the parallel dune system is continuous. Here, however, the 20–30 kilometer-long dunes were blocked to the west of each of the Goundam hills. Some of the troughs thus formed were further excavated by subsidence (eg., Lake Faguibine).

When the flood waters returned in earnest at the beginning of the first Holocene Pluvial, the troughs were linked by dune-breaching *marigots*. The lakes filled rapidly. The wave of inundation swamped the Azawad (to the evident delight of the late stone age fisherfolk poised to take advantage of that lush lacustrine environment). During the Holocene climatic optima, the lake system of the Niger's right and left banks were more extensive than today. Excess water spilled from Faguibine. That flood travelled west into the multiple troughs of the Daounas. The excess from the Lakes Region very possibly spilled into the distant Hodh depression. We can trace the water's path through a structural depression, the "canal de Sonni Ali Ber" leading from Raz-el-Ma to Bassikounou. The canal forms the northern boundary of the Lakes Region. It has plainly visible channels and meander scars witnessing its recharge from the Niger during the middle of the present millennium.[52]

The star event of the early Holocene, however, took place to the east. Volumes of excessive early Holocene flood travelled along the east-west interdunal depressions and, especially, along a long tectonic trough following the orientation of the dunes. Eventually, the waters begin to erode away the barrier quartzites, gneisses, and schists at Bosakalia and Tosaye. These sills in time submitted to the flood. The Niger spilled over into another system altogether. The river gradually gave up its march to the north, joining the Lower Niger fed from the Adrar des Iforas via the Tilemsi Valley.[53]

---

[52] Ibrahim Songoré, "Présentation géographique," in *Recherches Archéologiques au Mali*, Raimbault and Sanogo (eds), (Karthala, Paris, 1991), pp. 223; Tricart, *Reconnaissance*, p. 60; Urvoy, *Bassins*, p. 31.

[53] Blanck, *Projet*, p. 15; Tricart, *Reconnaissane*, pp. 33–5, 57, 63–4; Urvoy, *Bassins*, pp. 76–7, 83–5; there is, however, a persistent minority voice agruing that the joining of the upper and lower Niger valleys was far more ancient: see, G. Beaudet, R. Coque, Pierre Michel, and Pierre Rognon, "Y-a-t-il eu capture du Niger?," *Bulletin de l'Association des Géographes Françaises*, 445–6 (1977), pp. 215–22.

The reorientation of the Niger was not strickly speaking a "capture." It was, rather, a natural shift in the river's course. This shift, of course, has dramatic consequences. Not the least of these consequences was the progressive atrophying of the Azawad. With time, there was a diminution in the role of the several northward trending channels of the Niger Bend. These are the now senescent channels that depart the left bank from Timbuktu to Gourma-Rharous for the Azawad interior. They ceased being free-running streams and became seasonal embayments during wetter decades or centuries. Today, palaeochannels such as the El Ahmar are the site of pathetic ponds left behind only after the exceptional flood. Further inland, the high sand-load had the effect of reducing the number of *marigots* emanating from the major feed palaeochannels. These *marigot* could no longer feed the once well-organized fluvio-lacustrine system in a dunal landscape. After only a few dry years during which northern lakes and interdunal spaces were not refilled, the linking *marigot* would be blocked for all time by blown sand. The effects of these processes are augmented by the desiccating sands blown through the dead Azawad. The same clash of fluvial and aeolian processes are very much alive in the Lakes Region-Niger Bend. Since the end of the first Holocene Pluvial, certainly, the desert has dominated somewhat.

The Holocene wet periods were interrupted (probably at 8000 BP) by a significant dry episode. The top 1–3 metres of the parallel dunes were remobilized. Fields of three meter north-south parabolic, barkhan and nebkha dunes marched over the whole of the Lakes Region-Niger Bend, probably dating to this event. Humid conditions returned. The river returned to the paleochannels north of the river. The newly assertive waters seriously undercut and degraded the edges of dunes in the Timbuktu vicinity. The river's victory was short-lived. After c.4500 BC, the river was shut off from its more northern channel within the Niger Bend. Its high bed load was deposited as multiple point bars, low levees and scrolls in the floodplain. And, today, overgrazing of the dunes' sparse grass and destruction of acacias results in new fields of barkhans and nebkhas.

Satellite imagery confirms the depressing story of expanding halos of irretrievably degraded soil around Lakes Region-Niger Bend villages. The Sahel Drought has only aggravated a long historical process of human-aided desertification and gradual atrophy of the lake system.[54] Except for Faguibine at 620 km², the

[54] Brunet-Moret et al., *Monographie*, pp. 12–23; Songoré, "Présentation géographique," pp. 222–3.

Plate 4.3   *Albedo halo around Timbuktu (courtesy of
Pat Jacobberger Jellison).*

right bank lakes (in km², Niangaye = 350, Aougoundou = 90, Do
= 135, Gakoreï = 45, Gourou-100 and Haribongo = 60) are generally larger than those of the left bank (Tanda = 92, Kabara = 22,
Horo = 20, Fati = 35, Télé = 70, again in km²). At highstand, the
interlocking right bank lakes are refilled along the lake chain from
year to year. In years of low flood, only the lakes near the Bara-
Issa (eg., Niangaye, Aougoundou, Do) might receive any water.
In years of high or low flood, the lakes fill fast. Unhappily for
local farmers, infiltration and high rates of evaporation cause them
to empty quickly. These are the worst flood conditions for *décrue*
sorghum. Millet growing is also a risky proposition because of
low average precipitation (Niafunké = 315 mm, Goundam = 240
mm, Timbuktu = 195 mm). In the struggle of desert against river

cultures, the deck is stacked against the region's farmers and fisherfolk, the Songhai.

The origin of the Songhai is known in broad stroke. The details, however, are steeped in tradition and *post hoc* wishful thinking.[55] The story begins in the Songhai heartland downstream of Gao. Most scholars believe them to have been the first to occupy the river and floodplain. Above Gao, however, the first immigrants encountered voltaic-speaking autochtones, (related to Koromba and Gourmantché). These the Songhai assimilated while investing their more ancient magical powers of the water and land in the hands of the *Do* and *Korongou* castes. Some oral traditions place the home of the original Songhai in Mande country far to the west. The more received traditions claim they were always on the lower Niger. Rouch and others[56] have settled upon a distant migration from the east (perhaps from the Chad Basin along the Benue). Others look upon them as part of a Saharan migration of peoples adapted to a lacustrine way of life.[57]

Whatever the prehistoric origin, tradition focuses next upon the early settlement of Koukya (or Bentia). This community near the Mali-Niger border was the first settled town and principle market of these otherwise nomadic fishermen and hippo hunters. The town was overrun by Lamta Berbers in the seventh century. The invaders founded the despotic dynasty of Za (or Dia). Alternative readings claim the Dia to have been an earlier Mande peoples. Some Songhai submitted, but others began a trickle upriver that would end only at Lake Débo. At the big lake, they ran into a critical mass of Bozo occupying the same riverine niche. From Koukya, pioneer hippo hunters (*Sorko*) and riverside hunters (*Gow*) founded the town of Gao. By tradition, this took place in AD 690. In these same traditions, the ruler of Koukya converts to Islam in 1009 and moves his capital to Gao. The Songhai were under the sway of the Mali Empire

[55] Sékéné M. Cissoko, *Tombouctou et l'Empire Songhay* (Dakar: Nouvelles Editions Africaines, 1975), pp. 155–6; Boubou Hama, *Histoire des Songhay,* (Présence Africaine: Paris, 1968) ch. II.; N'Diaye, *Groupes*, pp. 215–22; Jean Rouch, *Contribution à l'Histoire des Songhay,* Mémoire de l'Institut Fondamental d'Afrique Noire, no. 29 (IFAN: Daka, 1953); Jean Rouch, *Les Songhay* (Presses universitaires: Paris, 1954), pp. 8–11; Z. Dramani-Issifou, "Les Songhay: dimention historique," in *Vallées du Niger*, (Edition de la Réunion des Musées Nationaux: Paris, 1993), pp. 151–61.

[56] Rouch, *Songhay*, p. 8; Sundström, *Ecology*, p. 78.

[57] Cissoko, *Tombouctou*, pp. 155–6.

by 1325. They broke away by *c*.1400. With the expansionist Sonni Ali Ber (1464–92), they consolidated an empire enclusive of the entire Middle Niger. The Songhai conquest of the Upper Delta took place in 1468. Their imperial history has left them even today in important, but isolated, merchant pockets as far upstream as Jenne.

The imperial peace in the Lakes Region-Niger Bend was broken by the Moroccan invasion of 1591. A political vacuum followed that date. And in the vacuum, the Songhai waged an increasingly desperate rearguard action against the Tuareg. The Tuareg Oullimiden from the Adrar des Iforar laid siege to Gao in 1680 and to Timbuktu in 1787. By the time of the earliest firsthand European accounts (eg., Caillié in 1828), the Tuareg had thoroughly disrupted the river trade. The Niger Bend agriculturists were held in their oppressive-tribute thrall.

The Songhai are a heavily hierachized people. They categorize themselves by occupation and status and, significantly, by territory.[58] The most important territorial distinctions are those made between the Fono Sorko of the Erg of Bara and the Faran Sorko of the narrow river downstream. Highest in status are the aristocratic Arma. All Arma today are the real or fictive descendants of Moroccans and their Songhai wives. Next in rank are the *borcin*, a social class composed of free farmers (*Gabiri*) and fisherfolk-harpoon hunters of hippo, crocodile, and manatee – the *Sorko*. Artisans form the next rank. They can be non-casted (*griots* and scholars, traders, jewelers, weavers) or strictly casted (blacksmiths, leatherworkers, other weavers, potters, butchers, and masons). Below all are the *banniya*, captives and slaves.

Sorko once specialized in the harpoon and trident hunting of large fish and aquatic animals. Sorko who follow the archaic trade are quite rare now. The *Gow* are virtually extinct as exclusive hunters. These were the pioneers of the Songhai upstream migration, followed to the new lands by farmers. *Sorko* farm today to a greater or lesser extent. They retain their status as "masters of the water" and are often confused with the Bozo.[59] They do still fish channel and *marigot* with a combination of harpoon, net, lure, and basket.

---

[58] Songhai terms for status groups or castes can shift significantly over the long expanse of their territory. The ones used here are most current in the western sector; N'Diaye, *Groupes*, pp. 213–39; Brasseur, *Etablissements*, pp. 113–42; Jean-Pierre Olivier de Sardan, *Les Sociétés Songhay-Zarma*, (Niger-Mali), (Karthala: Paris, 1984), pp. 27–132.

[59] For example, Songoré, "Présentation géographique," pp. 225–6.

The non-Sorko farmer will fish with small triangular hand nets the ponds remaining at *décrue* .

The ancient occupations have declined among all Songhai to such an extent that Sundström calls the ethnic group "indifferent fishermen."[60] Farming has fared little better due, in large part, to the siege of the desert. Songhai grow rice in the interdunal ponds and in the floodplain of the river. Sorghum grows along the banks of the degraded dunes. During good years, the grain thrives on the long shores of the Lakes Region lakes. Maturation is too often aborted by the rapid seasonal fall of those lakes. Songhai also grow millet, fonio and keep small herds of cattle, sheep, goat and camel. Productivity is just enough to keep villages self-sufficient. Historically the larger towns, especially Timbuktu, were dependent upon grain shipped from the granaries of the Upper Delta and Macina.[61] That dependence may only postdate the first millennium AD. During that more favored millennium, as we shall see, the Lakes Region-Niger Bend was far more densely populated.

In the early 1950s, the Songhai population of the Lakes Region-Niger Bend was *c.*79,000. They could boast an additional 8,500 in the Erg of Bara and 86,000 in the Gao administrative region (outside the Middle Niger). Compare this figure to the estimated 82,500 Tuareg, their traditional nemesis in the Lakes Region-Niger Bend. The numbers of herdsmen is augmented by an additional *c.*10,000 Arab-speaking Moors. The comparison allows us to appreciate the considerable pastoral component of our final live basin of the Middle Niger.

The origin of the Tuareg is as obscure, if not more so, than that of their Songhai neighbors. They are of Berber origin, speak a Berber language (*tamasheq*) and use a Berber alphabet (*tifinar*). They are more properly called the Kel Tamasheq after their ancestral language, at which point any certainty about their origin ceases. Most reconstructions place them as descendants of the so-called Libyco-Berber. Libyco-Berber is a generic term given to a cluster of Saharan groups with a history deep in the pre-Christian period.[62] The

---

[60] Sundström, *Ecology*, p. 76.

[61] Ibid., 74; René Caillié, *Travels Through Central Africa to Timbuktu and Across the Great Desert to Morocco: Performed in the Years 1824–1828*, (Colburn & Bentley: London, 1830), pp. 57–9.

[62] Camps, *Berbères*, pp. 48-91; Camps, *Civilisation Préhistoriques*, pp. 346-8; Muzzolini, *L'Art Rupestre*, pp, 308 and 324; N'Diaye, *Groupes*, pp. 10-16; Michael Brett and Elizabeth Fentress, *The Berbers*, (Blackwell: Oxford, 1996), pp. 206–8; Dupuy, "Trois mille ans," pp. 115–23.

ancestors of Tuareg were very probably related to the Garamantes of Herodotus. They may already have been a southern stream of the ancient Libyans (sometimes called paleo-Berbers). These are the so-called *guerriers libyens* (Libyan warriors) depicted on horse and war chariot in the Saharan rock art. Depictions in the art of battle and chase scenes demonstrate that relations with Black neighbors were already strained.

Once the Berber began to coalesce in language and custom, one division (the Sanhadja) gave birth to the Tuareg. Like many Berbers, they reckon (fictive) descent to the pre-Islamic princess Tin Hinan. Her pre-fifth-century AD tomb is purported to have been found at Ablessa in the western Hoggar.[63] We may never know a precise location of their origin. They may simply have been a later amalgamation of diverse southern Berbers. At some point they differentiated themselves from another camel-herding, Berber-speaking people of the southern Sahara, the Moors to the west of the Majabat al-Kubra.[64] As opposed to their considerable bellicose influence on the Middle Senegal, the Moors play a very minor role in the Middle Niger.

·Tuareg probably were reluctant participants in later waves of Saharan pastoralists pushed south by the inescapable worsening of the climate. It is always possible that the Fulani participated in a preceding wave. Tuareg from the Tilemsi Valley to the Lakes Region-Niger Bend share an oral tradition of dislocations in historical times. According to this tradition they were still in the Adrar des Iforas at the time of the strength of the Songhai Empire. They took advantage of the political chaos after the Moroccan invasion of 1591 to take root along the river and northernmost lakes.

Perhaps it was during the long sojourn in the Sahara that they took clientage over a large Black and sedentary farming population. The *Bella* (servile population) and *Harratine* (former slaves) form the lowest rung of this highly hierarchical society.[65] They live

[63] Camps, *Berbères*, pp. 202–3, 234; Mauny, *Tableau Géographique*, pp. 83–4.
[64] James Webb, *Desert Frontier*, (University of Wisconsin Press: Madison, 1995), pp. 14–25.
[65] Pierre Galloy, "Nomadisme et fixation dans la région des lacs du Moyen Niger," in *Nomades et Paysans de l'Afrique Noire Occidentale*, Pierre Galloy, Yvon Vincent et Maurice Forget (eds), Annales de l'Est, no. 23 (Université de Nancy: Nancy, 1963), pp. 11–34; J. Nicolaisen, *Ecology and Culture of the Pastoral Tuareg* (The National Museum: Copenhagen, 1963); Susan E. Smith, "The environmental adaptation of nomads in the West African Sahel: a key to understanding prehistoric pastoralists," in *The Sahara and the Nile*, Martin A. J. Williams and Hugues Faure (eds) (Balkema: Rotterdam, 1980), pp. 467–87.

in small villages where they grow wheat, millet, and sorghum. They also collect the many wild plants (including fonio and kram-kram) that supplement the milk-based diet of the nomadic free population. Above the Bella are the free artisans (*Inadan*), marabouts (*Kel Essouk*), and freemen (*Imrad*). Above all these are the artistocrats, the noble warrior *Imajaren*.

All who can eschew the sedentary life. It is the higher occupation to keep the herds and follow them on the annual transhumant cycle.[66] The year has three parts, divided very similarly to that of the Fulani. At the beginning of the rainy season (July, lasting until sometime in September) the herds move into the dunes. They travel from the lakes and river, going north of the Niger Bend into the Azawad and Aklé or south into the Gourma. The c.100–250 mm of rain allows a temporary cover of grass to the dunes. The herds move impressive distances. Some go as far as Araouane. In the dunefields they subsist on the pasturage around hand-dug wells. Elsewhere, the Tuareg herds are sustained by the grasses growing on rain-fed ponds in the old clay soils of the interdunal depressions.

Soon, however, the herds make the slow retreat to the lakes and river. The Tuareg pass through the southern part of the Azawad as early as March (the beginning of the cold season). When the cold season flood begins to recede, the herds enter the floodplain and the lake beds. They are on the relentless search for the *bourgou* that will nourish the herds until the rains begin again. It is at the beginning of the *décrue* that one finds most troubles between Tuareg and Songhai millet and rice farmers. No less epochal is the clash with their competitors for *bourgou*, the Fulani of the southern Lakes Region. The Tuareg-Fulani conflict has intensified during the past few centuries, as Tuareg have encroached more and more into the northern Macina as well.

No description of the Tuareg would be complete without mention of the *Azalaï*, the salt caravans. Twice yearly, long trains of camels burdened with thousands of bars of salt depart from the mid-Saharan salt mines of Taoudeni. They are bound for Timbuktu, the northern riverine port of the Middle Niger. The *Azalaï* traverses the bed of the El Ahmar palaeochannel as it cuts its north-south path through the red dunes. Today the caravaners are oblivious of the wealth of water that once flowed where they now trudge through sand. Along the southern trail they pass massive, long-forgotten

---

[66] See maps of the transhumant zones during the three seasons in Galloy, "Nomadisme et fixation," figures I, II, and III.

settlements from the last millennium. Littering their approach to Araouane are extensive scatters of late stone age pottery, bone harpoons and fish bone. Without doubt, the caravaners are oblivious to the archaeological remains of these stone age peoples. Where thriving communities once hunted, fished, and tended their herds, now there now is only desolation as far as the eye can roam. Those early people forsook the desert. Where they went is a story for the archaeologist to tell.

5

Historical Imagination: 300 BC

The story archaeologists tell of the exodus from the drying Sahara and penetration of the deepest Middle Niger basins is one of the world's great migration tales. But hoes and harpoons do not grow legs; pots do not march over the landscape as many archaeologists' texts would lead one to believe! Real people led quests of epic adventure and suffering in their search for their own promised land. One such quest led to the foundation of settlements on the low levees in the vicinity of a future Jenne.

They come in the tens of thousands, week after week. Now, as the waters have begun slowly to recede, they fight, peck, and shove in the hundreds of thousands for a place of rest from flight on the levee and dune crests just beginning to appear above the limitless horizon of water. From a distance, each dune takes on the appearance of a living thing, something in a perpetual motion of undulations and convulsions. Closer, one sees that the writhing is the frantic motion of thousands of wings and bodies jockeying for position.

The convulsions are the short flight of small segments of flocks in a temporary panic provoked by a circling hawk: tens of thousands of stork, cranes, pelicans, anhingas, darters, cormorants, herons, egrets, geese, and duck. Out in the shallow waters off the emerging levees are vast pink carpets of flamingo, wine and deep green prairies of ibis. This is the time of the winter migration out of Europe. One branch of the southern migration blankets the Nile Valley and the immense Sudd depression; the western branch winters on the teeming fish and insect life of the Middle Niger. But the birds will soon have to compete with others for the first islands of levee or dune to appear at flood fall.

Perhaps a century ago, years would pass without this levee ever rising above permanent water. The thick marsh grasses, dense stands of wild rice and sweet stalks of *bourgou* would grow on the tops of the levee at the season of the

Plate 5.1 *Roundé Siru levee (near Jenne). This* marigot *and the one immediately east of Jenne-jeno are reputed to be home of one of the highest concentrations in all Mande of* faaro *water spirits.*

lowest water. No people would come. There had been people long before, at other times when the waters dropped below the tops of dune and levee while the weather was still cold. Then, even the stream nearby dried completely at the end of the hot season. But they were passing hunters. They came alone or in groups of two or three. They came with stone-tipped spear and arrows to take the shy march antelope, the great fish of the shallows and the cold-stunned crocodile. And they came, of course, for the birds. The bravest used giant harpoons of bone, and tridents tipped with stone and poison to ambush hippo or the evil-tempered buffalo. They never stayed in one place for long. They only left ashes from their night fires and the bones of their prey to be swept away by the onrush of the next flood. When the waters rose again, these hunters went elsewhere.

The hunters returned first. As the declining waters exposed more and more dune and levee each year, the hunters descended deeper and deeper, each year a few kilometers more, into the deep floodplain. They took the same prey – the reedbuck and waterbuck, buffalo and crocodile on the dry land, hippo and giant catfish as they lolled in the shallows. They never stayed long at any one camp and they came in their twos and threes. But there were big differences also.

Many came with familiar-looking chert- and quartzite-tipped spears and with harpoons made of bone with multiple serrations on one or both sides. These made formidable weapons in the hands of these experienced men. But the new hunters, those that began to wade into these swamps perhaps a hundred years ago, carry iron: long thin spearheads ending in narrow tangs to insert into the long wooded spear shafts; evil-looking, heavy harpoons with collars in which to set the thick, stubby shafts. No longer is the hunt limited by the breakage of tips off spears, These hunters would die rather than loose the precious iron spear or harpoon heads. They are used over, and over, and over again. The hunters can stay in the floodplain many more weeks at a time now that they do not have to return to sources of stone to tip their weapons. And there are other differences.

Some among the hunters, those who came into the swamps earliest, watch the declining waters and emergence of dry land with more than a hunter's interest. Using a logic all their own, they set up solitary camps on these levees or dunes and stay for scores of days rather than the more usual handful. They hunt and fish as before. But instead of thanking the spirit of the slain animal for their luck and tossing into the water a part of each to keep the goodwill of whatever great water serpent or miraculous bird that claims sway over this stretch of the floodplain, now hours each day are spent calling forth other spirits. These others are more reclusive, but infinitely more powerful. Hunters with other things than the hunt on their mind, they spend hours watching the flight of birds over the dune or levee they have selected. Hunters in a land of abundance, they fast for days hoping for a sign from the shy spirits.

Sometimes they leave in disappointment. Often however, as this man has done here, they return year after year to try again and, finally, as has happened here also, the deeply hidden spirits consent to give the hunter a sign that he may be their bridge between their world of shadows, dampness, and perpetual time and his world of light and change. He takes the sign (a nodule of limonite or calcite, a crocodile plate, the ear bone of a monster fish) in a sack hung around his neck. He leaves as before and then, the waters rise again. He will return and he will bring with him the third great difference.

This time he is followed by children trudging through the mud with arms full of skins for the floor of huts; Women with babies and with heads loaded high with pots; and sheep, goat and cattle – beasts never seen in the swamps before. The birds hover behind them in their hundreds, catching the locusts and other flying insects sent into flight by the lumbering great hooves. Ibises and cranes fight for a perch on their thick necks, hoping for a feast of ticks and flies. Wives, children – families – have never before been seen this far into the marshland. The people intend to stay.

The first families came to this levee perhaps ten years ago. They were led here by the same hunter. He had asked the concurrence of the spirits years before that, but then came many years of dangerously high floods. The levee remained the home only to wild rice and, where a few centimeters touched the air for a few weeks, to the squabbling anhingas. The hunter was patient. The waters again receded, earlier and earlier each year and then the families came back. The first two years were good years. The families set up their rude huts of mud-faced mats spread over a beehive-shaped framework of saplings. The men of the several families stretched long nets across the mouths of channels crisscrossing the floodplain and, with great excitement hunted hippo and crocodile as had been done for millennia. The children scooped up the fish in ponds left behind as the waters dried from the swampland. The women and children harvested the wild plants of the swamp. The men prepared the fields and the women weeded and harvested the seed they brought with them from wherever to the west they came from. The harvests were good and some of this crop of fonio they ate. But much was used by the guide hunter in private rituals of thanks and future requests. This was, and still is, a sacred grain – as critical to the spiritual nourishment of these peoples as are fish, wild plants, and the flesh of the migratory bird for their physical nourishment. All was happy until the high floods came.

For two years the floods came as in former days. The people had to leave. They lost most of their small herd to the rapidly rising water and they just managed to escape with their lives and with their store of sacred seed. The first hunter kept the sacs with the sign from the spirits of this place. So did his son and the heads of one or two other families who had been accepted to the rituals. They would be back. This is a good place, with water and fish in the deep stream even during the hottest days of the driest season, with good rains to nourish the sacred crop. And with the protection of generous (if, at times, petulant) spirits of the land and water.

After the years of devastating floods, the families returned yet again and have been here ever since. Once or twice they had to find higher ground for a week or more during highest flood, but always the spirits welcomed them back. And now the families can see the smoke of camps at other dunes and levees across the swamps. On the dunes to the north and west are camps of peoples who fish very little, but who have large fields of millet and sorghum. On the wide levee of the great river to the south are peoples who spend their lives up to their waist in water. It is cold, hard work but when they harvest their rice all are just a little envious of the generosity of their spirits. And on the many small levees and tiny dunes between the great north and south rivers are many other camps of the fisherfolk.

The spirits are content and the land thrives. Families increase in number and more and more enter each year from the dry land. It is a welcoming land and the different peoples of the land are welcoming also. Fisherfolk far from their camps think nothing of asking for a sleeping skin and a fire in a camp of rice growers. Rice farmers, with time on their hands at that time of the year, know when to show up at the mud and stick barriers the fisherfolk have erected in the deep interior *marigots* to catch the vast schools escaping with the rushing waters. The two meet again at the harvest, when the fisherfolk pick up the long iron knives to gather together the rice. And they meet more and more often at camps known for the generosity of their guardian spirits when news has spread of the arrival of the workers in iron.

Those who work the iron are respected – even a little feared – and are eagerly sought after. Often they set small fires made extra hot by goatskin-serviced and small-boy-driven bellows to straighten and otherwise repair harpoons, knives, or hoes. It is a time of great excitement and even reverence when the fires are made large and extra hot. Then the smiths take the large blocks of rock-hard soil brought from the laterite terraces to the west and make, by miracle, brand new tools. Rumor has spread that some families of smiths will stay. They will have to cut many distant trees to fuel the furnaces. But even now the most ancient of the smiths is at the small, otherwise undistinguished Senuba *marigot* not far to the south.

Only the iron workers have the courage to call forth certain most secret powers. If the most hidden of the spirits agree to aid the fires that make iron from earth, it will be a sign that the land has finally accepted the people. If so, then the people will increase in numbers free of the bone-withering lack of food and the wasting, infant-devouring diseases they knew all to well in the western lands from which they fled not so terribly long ago.

All are filled with hope. The water has sent the occasional high flood to remind the people of the respect it demands. But the land has been more than generous. The smiths are to be feared because of the commerce they have opened with spirits infinitely more powerful than even the most powerful hunter's spirits of land and water. But the smiths can foresee a bounteous future here and that is why they will consider ending their long travels in order to settle here year round. The future of this place will hold spectacular things.

Another duty of ancient hunters was the *dali-ma-sigi*, or quest.[1] Most traditions agree that hunters pioneered the Mande initiative of the "knowledge quest,"[2] and hence are accorded eponymous credit not only for founding most Mande towns and for expand-

---

[1] S. Bulman, "The Buffalo-Woman tale: Political imperatives and narrative constraints in the Sunjata epic," in K. Barber and P. F. de Moraes Farias (eds), *Discourse and its Disguises. The Interpretation of African Oral Texts*, (Birmington: CWAS, 1989) pp. 171–5; Cashion, *Hunters*, pp. 240–3, 300–1, 321–2; Cissé, "Notes," pp. 184, 195–6; Conrad, D. "A town called Dakalajan," *Journal of African History*, 35 (1994), pp. 355–77; D. Conrad, "Blind man meets prophet," in *Status and Identity in West Africa: Nyamakalaw of Mande*, David Conrad and B. E. Frank (eds) (Indiana University Press, Bloomington, 1995), pp. 86–132; McNaughton, *Blacksmiths*, pp. (18), 71; P. McNaughton, "From Mande Komo to Jukun Akuma. Approaching the difficult question of history," *African Arts*, 25(2) (1992): 79–80 – *inter alia* !
[2] Cissé, "Notes," pp. 195–96, Cashion, *Hunters*, pp. 110–11, 240–3.

Figure 5.1 *Eponymous pioneering hunter*
(Courtesy of Matt Harvey).

ing the Mande world, but more importantly for symbolically defining Mande as a secret, energy-laden landscape to be traversed safely only by those most knowledgeable in the strange ways of *nyama*. Like the earliest cultures' heroes, such as Dinga[3] of the

---

[3] Germaine Dieterlen and Diarra Sylla, *L'Empire de Ghana. Le Wagadou et les Traditions de Yéréré* , (Karthala: Paris, 1992).
[4] Baa and Sunbunu, *Geste.*

Soninké or Fanta Maa[4] of the Bozo, one travels to powerful locations, there to kill the proprietary spirit animals taking the form of buffalo, hyena, crocodiles, or snakes. In the epics, this act frees well-watered lands for hunter-led migration. The snake may be secretly followed to water by the hunter. The snake may succor the famished hunter with milk from its tail, or may even purposefully guide him.[5] But later, the snake is usually killed for its superabundant *nyama*. It's head and skin become trophies added to other ancient hunter's symbols: bow and quiver,[6] ax,[7] horns,[8] and spear.[9]

Many of these symbols are transformed during a second Mande crisis[10] caused by new opportunities of sedentarism. Who has the authority to lay claim permanently to territory? Who says "We stop here!" when colonists saltate, like grains of sand, moving by leaps and bounds across the floodplains of the Niger and Senegal during the last centuries BC?[11] When Jenne-jeno, Akumbu, and Dia in the Middle Niger become true cities – who regulates relations between the growing number of artisan corporations defined by occult mysteries?[12] Increasingly, the role of the hunters and of their secret societies are contested by the smiths. We will leave the story of the smiths' transformation of *nyama* until the following chapter.

---

[5] Cashion, *Hunters*, pp. 172, 237, 263 note 21; Cissé, "Notes," p. 187; D. Conrad and H. Fischer, "The conquest that never was. II," *History in Africa*, 10 (1983): 61–2, 65, 67; McNaughton, *Blacksmith*, p. 17.

[6] Cashion, *Hunters*, pp. 177–8.

[7] Cashion, *Hunters*, pp.172; G. Dieterlen and Y. Cissé, *Les Fondements de la Société d'Initiation du Komo*, (Paris: Mouton, 1972), pp. 39.

[8] Cashion, *Hunters*, pp. 147–8; see G. Dieterlen, "The Mande creation myth," *Africa*, 27(2) (1957), p. 134.

[9] Cashion, *Hunters*, pp. 176–7.

[10] And this may explain the general disparagement of blacksmiths by hunters! – Cissé, "Notes," 180, 188; see McNaughton, *Blacksmiths*, p. 71; S. McIntosh, "Blacksmiths," p. 10.

[11] For the earliest history of these settlements and hypotheses about colonization of the Middle Niger and Middle Senegal, see R. McIntosh, "Pulse model," pp. 182–8; S. McIntosh, Roderick J. McIntosh, and Hamady Bocoum, "The Middle Senegal Valley Project: Preliminary results from the 1990–1991 field season," *Nyame Akuma*, 38 (1992), pp. 47–61. For a compelling model of movements (I use the term saltation) into unclaimed frontier situations, see I. Kopytoff, *The African Frontier*, (Bloomington: Indiana University Press, 1987) pp. 3–78.

[12] The competing occult specialists and their power associations are enumerated in Cissé, "Notes," pp. 188, 225; Cashion, *Hunter*, pp. 110, 152–3; McNaughton, *Blacksmiths*, p. 39.

What smiths and hunters do share, however, is the notion of the sacred landscape and of the occult-competent hero. The hero, be he (or she)[13] the eponymous ancestor or the founder of a great empire, is kept alive in oral tradition as the symbol, the crystallizer of communities' values and social action. The trick for the archaeologist is to add some empirical substance to the spirit of "ancient speech," *kuma koro*, stories of the heroes that represent the peoples' vision of their entire history:

> In a society boasting an unsurpassed level of oral art and consciousness, the epic ancestors remain as they have apparently been for many centuries, the means of identification for every stranger entering a town or village, and for every householder receiving strangers ... It is no exaggeration to say that regardless of gender, the ancestors described in *kuma koro* or "ancient speech" define the identity of each and every member of Mande society. Therefore, if the ancestors were to be forgotten, the fundamental essence of the Mande world – as it is perceived by the Mande people themselves – would disappear. For foreign scholars to maintain that it is not possible for Sunjata [founder of the Mali empire] and his companions to be known after so many centuries and that they and their deeds are entirely mythological (that their's is "imaginary history" as one colleague has phrased it), is to deny a fact of Mande culture: genuine reverence for the ancestors has kept certain aspects of the past more alive than could have been accomplished with the written word.[14]

All Mande heroes traverse a sacred landscape and few parts of Mande are as rich in power locales as the Middle Niger. In future chapters we will come symbolically to see the Middle Niger as a power grid, a grid made of nodes of high *nyama* potential defined on a vertical axis superimposed upon the two-dimensional geographical landscape. The founder of towns such as Jenne or Dia has the special competence needed to read and travel across this spatial blueprint of occult knowledge and, for the good of the people, to enter into covenential relations with the guardian spirits. Just how hunters and smiths, and later dynasts such as Sunjata, assimilate this power and knowledge can be quite different. We can

[13] David Conrad, "Mooning armies and mothering heroes: Female power in Mande epic tradition," in Ralph Austin (ed.), *In Search of Sunjata: The Mande Epic as History, Literature and Performance*, (Indiana University Press: Bloomington, forthcoming).

[14] Ibid., ms. p. 34.

begin to understand the logic of the late first millennium penetration of the deepest Middle Niger basins by looking at how this perceived landscape mingled with the functional obligation imposed upon the first colonizers by a changing climate and by the ecology of physical landforms.

6

Penetration of the Deep Basins

The first colonists' penetration of the Middle Niger deep basins was a case of response to a providential climate mode shift. One people's providence is another's purgatory and, paradoxically in the Middle Niger, those peoples are one and the same. The long dry episode that opens the Upper Delta and Macina to its first year-round habitation is the closure to the millennia of climate instability that, as we have seen in chapter 2, abused so badly the stone tool-using populations of the near-Saharan Azawad and Méma. I have argued in that chapter that migration, precocious specialization, and experimentation with seasonal clustering of communities were the human responses to the highly oscillatory climate mode that began around 3000 BC. Penetration of the deep Middle Niger basins and the (consequent?) beginnings of spectacular population growth were the signature of a new climate mode beginning around the middle of the last millennium BC.

However, climate tells only a fragment of the tale. The new, stable dry climate mode only encouraged and did not cause the expression of two themes critical to the penetration of the live basins of the Middle Niger by those first colonists. Those themes are domestication of plants and animals and the assignment of a curious status to blacksmith. Let us look first at the evidence for a significant climate shift, beginning at between 500 BC and 300 BC, and then sort out the consequent constraints or encouragements to these two vital processes.

In the latter half of the last millennium BC, West Africa endures a stable, very dry period of something just over a half-millennium in duration. Our best estimate is that rainfall was reduced to ±20 percent less than the present century average.[1] By the beginning of this dry period, the Saharan lakes and most palaeochannels have long gone senescent. By the end of this dry phase, sedentary peoples have not only moved into the apparently virgin, highly fertile floodplains of the Middle Niger and Middle Senegal Valley. These communities are moving rapidly towards urbanism.

This West African event appears to be part of a true global mode shift. Ice cores confirm that, for the upper and middle latitudes, the periods between 300 and 100 BC and AD 350–550 were colder than the Little Ice Age (the latter averages −1.0°C of the present century average; the former may have been as much as −2.5°C cooler).[2] At 600–500 BC, until *c*.AD 300, the Amazon suffers a major dry period, with attendant major hiatus in the archaeological record[3], and the Nile is much reduced.[4]

As we have seen above (chapter 2), we must resist the temptation to think of the Saharan late stone age as a good-neighborly Eden. In an idealized scenario, ancestral Mande hunters and gatherers inhabit a bountiful Sahel between and immediately north of the Senegal and Niger rivers. They rub shoulders with proto-Nilo Saharan (Songhai) fishermen and hippo hunters and with (peaceful) proto-Berber pastoralists. We now know that this paradiasical scene is illusion: the climatic stresses and conflicts induced by attendant migrations must have been the source of considerable tensions. It is the unusual resolution of these tensions that make this phase in the early history of the peoples of the Middle Niger of such interest.

Warfare and acts of forcible assimilation must often have proven the ultimate resolution to these tensions in many places. However, a pervasive alternative to competition is strongly suggested by the apparent interaction network cast by these migrants. Lines of commerce and communication are left open all along the southern Sahara during the first millennium BC. The early Mande are an extensively distributed, but still reasonably coherent language group, who only later sub-divide into the familiar Soninké, Bozo, and Nono (and Mande heartland – Bambara and Malinke). It is to this areally

[1] R. McIntosh, "Pulse model," p. 196; S. and R. McIntosh, "From stone," p. 94.
[2] Mörner, "Short-term," pp. 257–66.
[3] Betty J. Meggers, "Biogeographical approaches to reconstructing the prehistory of Amazonia," *Biogeographica*, 70 (1994), pp. 97–110.
[4] Fekri Hassan and B. R. Stucki, "Nile floods and climatic change," in Rampino et al., *Climate, History, Periodicity, and Predictability*, pp. 37–46.

extensive coherence that Brooks[5] attributes their successful spread and the vitality of their social institutions. Extensive areal communication is the key to the emergence, once iron technology comes on the scene, of the Mande magician-technicians.

In both the first manifestations of smiths and their crafts and in anomalous evidence for the migration routes through and within the Middle Niger we have hints of very deep roots to traditional Mande beliefs about occult power.

It would be impossible to overestimate the importance of these specialists. Smiths dabble both in the most vital powers of this world and in the most dangerous forces of the unseen world. The institution of the magico-technician had probably begun to take recognizable form centuries before the turn of the Present Era. In the first millennium AD, one would see the steady elaboration of separate corporate groups. Smiths were surely among the most prominent. Smiths were likely the first to reinvent, or to appropriate concepts of dangerous social power to be harvested and augmented by the occult creative act, adding a level of complexity to the extractive view of *nyama* pioneered by the hunters. It will be the task of oral historians and archaeologists together to estimate just how early smith groups conform to the often itinerant, slightly feared (if not already endogamous and casted) model that we have historically for the *nyamakalaw*, occupational castes for which the Mande are famous throughout West Africa. This theme will increasingly occupy our attention as the chapter precedes.

Much can be gleaned from oral traditions and historical place names about early movements at the edge of the Middle Niger.[6] Many of these movements preceded the founding of the first known settlements within the live basins. By the last millennium BC, various groups speaking reasonably mutually-intelligible dialects lived in the Méma, Azawad, and in neighboring regions. These dialects were most closely related to the earliest form of Soninké. These groups were innovative, they were mobile, and they already had an eye for the commercial advantage. They continued to be pressed hard by an environment become very unwelcoming by the end of the millennium.

---

[5] George E. Brooks, "Ecological perspectives on Mande population movements, commercial networks and settlement patterns from the Atlantic Wet Phase (ca. 5500–2500 B.C.) to the present," *History in Africa,* 16 (1989), pp. 26–32.
[6] S. McIntosh, "Reconsideration," pp. 154–7.

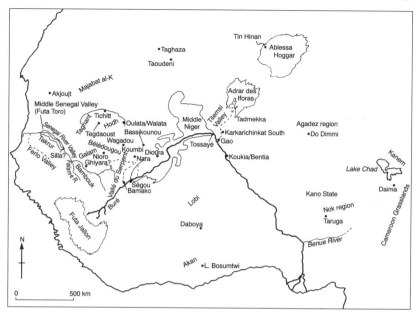

Map 6.1 *Later prehistoric sites and locations in West Africa*

Persistent traditions tell of dispersal from three centers. Nono claim to originate along the western frontier of the Méma (near Bassikounou). These incipient or already full agriculturists move into the Méma region of Dioura and, thence, to Dia. From Dia communities move into the deep basin of the Upper Delta. Nono found Jenne, Sansanding, and other early trade towns. Another wing of what can probably be recognized as archaic Soninké move from the Wagadou region of the Bélédougou west to the Senegal River Valley. There they found centers of trade and political dynasties that long acknowledge their parentage from Wagadou and Dia. Later Soninké rejuvenate commerce with these Senegal River Valley communities by at least one other trade diaspora westward from Dia.

Archaeology supports three essential elements of speculations about the sources of the earliest Middle Niger peoples. Those first to colonize the floodplain of the Middle Niger came from neighboring country to the north and west.[7] In the last millennia

[7] For the affinities of these peoples, as reconstructed from the earliest Middle Niger ceramics, see S. McIntosh, *Excavations*, pp. 360–4.

BC, one finds there a reservoir of peoples adapted to wetlands, but under pressure from a declining environment. Second, their response to ecological change was the (continued?) domestication of cereals and the use of cattle, sheep, and goat. And, lastly, not only were they iron-using, their smiths were already of transformed social status. Whenever and however they may have entered the deeper Middle Niger basins – in an almost imperceptible trickle, in regular waves, or as one (highly unlikely) human avalanche – the archaeology of their routes will increasingly reveal much about their occupations and beliefs.

On purely archaeological and ecological grounds, one would expect the north-south trending palaeochannels of the Sahara and Sahel to be natural reservoirs of climate distressed populations, the locations for their experiments with new domesticates and new occupation specializations, and (ultimately) corridors for their movements. And indeed, the traditions about the Mande perception of sacred space, in addition to mentioning discrete points, talk in detail about a fluid network of underground watercourses. These subterranean routes link the most sacred places with, especially, the Niger River.[8] At one level we have here a map of safe passage (of saltation from one isolated pond to another) across a severe drought landscape.

However, attempts to predict human occupation and climate response can fall to curious twists of evidence. Just north of the Middle Niger, slightly later in time, is the traditional home of the Ghana (or Wagadou) state of the Soninké. In the Ghana tradition, the fabulous snake Bida lives in an aquatic underground quarter (Mallaara) of the town of Koumbi.[9] This lair of the serpent is linked by a subterranean stream to another subterranean channel from Lake Faguibine (Lakes Region) to Nioro, *c.*220 kilometers to the southwest. These subterranean channels are further linked to the Vallée du Serpent paleochannel north and west of the Méma.

MacDonald's recent survey of the Vallée du Serpent yielded the completely unexpected results of abundant mid-Holocene macrolithic sites (7000–4000 BC). He also found lots of very recent iron and tobacco pipe-yielding localities (perhaps dating as late as the AD nineteenth century Tukulor incursion from the Middle Sen-

[8] Brett-Smith, *Making*, p. 129, fig. 23.
[9] Dieterlen and Sylla, *L"Empire*, pp. 55–7.

egal) – and virtually nothing between.[10] In a Sahelian archaeological landscape otherwise dense with late stone age sites along comparable palaeochannels, some powerful force prohibited occupation of a privileged environment. Perhaps the fear (universally understood among the Mande) of a traveling Bida overcame the desire for an inviting habitat!

This is but one of many examples from oral tradition and archaeology that collectively suggest that deep-time beliefs about sacred places and power prohibitions (expressed spatially) date to at least the moment of penetration of the deepest Middle Niger basins. Now we need the hard empirical tests of these interpretations.

Unfortunately, our weakest hard data link is the transition from late stone age adaptations to fully sedentary life. Our first good look at the life and economy of these colonists is at the Upper Delta archaeological site of Jenne-jeno and at Dia in the Macina. Unfortunately, even at the foundation of these sites, the most momentous of these transformations to the economy and changes in settlement patterns had already taken place. Their crops are already fully domesticated. Their smiths are very accomplished. For the moment, we have to go back in time and take a brief detour from the Middle Niger. In order to appreciate the earliest Middle Niger evidence, we have to look very briefly at the overall West African picture of the emergence of crops and herds and of the origins of iron smelting as a technical and a social act.

From Stone to Iron, from Gatherer to Farmer

Reconstructions of the date and circumstances of the appearance of iron in West Africa have long been highly speculative. That situation will persist as long as there are so few archaeological sites with the late stone age to iron age transition stratified in context.[11] The transition sites we possess are rather late. These include Daboya,

---

[10] K. MacDonald and P. Allsworth-Jones, "A reconsideration of the West African Macrolithic Conundrum: New factory sites and an associated settlement in the Vallée du Serpent, Mali," *The African Archaeological Review*, 12(1994), pp. 76–7.

[11] For the present state of the question of early iron in West Africa, see S. McIntosh, "Changing perceptions," pp. 173–7 and S. and R. McIntosh, "From stone," pp. 102–10; Nikolaas J. van der Merwe, "The advent of iron in Africa," in *The Coming of the Age of Iron*, Theodore A. Wertime and James D. Muhly (eds.) (Yale University Press: New Haven, 1980), pp. 463–506; D.Miller and Nikolaas Van Der Merwe, "Early

Ghana – dating to the last centuries BC;[12] Daima, Nigeria – AD fifth century[13]; and several caves in Sierra Leone and Liberia – end first millennium AD. Several early iron age sites in the Méma have abundant stone tools eroding out of their lower levels. These may provide us with hope, were it not for another problem.

Many of the Méma transitional sites might be expected to date to the mid-first millennium BC.[14] To this period date the earliest known West African sites with evidence of iron production: Taruga in the Nok region of Nigeria (600 or before BC), Do Dimmi (Termit Massif) in Niger (*c.*700 BC, with some arguing for thirteenth-century BC dates[15]), and the Agadez region of Niger (400–100 BC[16]). Unhappily, the calendrical dates for these sites cannot be given with a precision expected of most radiocarbon-based determinations. These dates fall within a dramatic period of flattening of the statistical curve used to calibrate our radiocarbon determinations. This curve is the statistical device used by archaeologists to find the true relationship between radiocarbon measurements and calendar years. Dates falling between 800 and 400 BC cannot be sorted out in any chronological order within that 400-year period.[17] This particular flattening of the radiocarbon calibration curve could not have come at a worse spot in our West African timeline. The flattening seriously cripples those who wish to ask not just when and where iron first appeared, but also how and why it spread apparently as quickly as it did.

---

metal working in Sub-Saharan Africa: A review of recent research," *Journal of African History* 35(1994): 6–10; T. Childs and D. Killick, "Indigenous African metallurgy: Nature and Culture," *Annual Review of Anthropology*, 22 (1993), pp. 320–2.

[12] François Kense, "The initial diffusion of iron to Africa," in *African Iron Working – Ancient and Traditional*, (Norwegian University Press, Bergen, 1985), pp. 16–17.

[13] Graham Connah, *Three Thousand Years in Africa*, (Cambridge University Press: Cambridge, 1981), pp. 146–7, fig., 6.10, cf. 137; Nicholas David, "History of crops and peoples in north Cameroon to AD 1900," in J. Harlan, J. M. de Wet and A. B. Stemler (eds.), *Origins of African Plant Domestication,* (Mouton: The Hague, 1976), pp. 223–67.

[14] T. Togola, "Iron age occupation in the Méma region, Mali," *The African Archaeological Review*, 13(2) (1996), p. 107.

[15] M. Cornevin, *Archéologie Africaine*, pp. 121–2.

[16] See S. McIntosh, "Changing perceptions," p. 173.

[17] The methodology of high precision calibration and the effect of curve flattening is explained in Susan Keech McIntosh and Roderick J. McIntosh, "Recent archaeological research and dates from West Africa," *Journal of African History*, 27 (1986), pp. 413–17; and S. and R. McIntosh "From stone to metal," pp. 106–7.

Those asking when and where have developed three hypotheses. The argument of independent invention has always been rather weakened because of the absence of a copper-based metallurgical tradition before iron use. No convincing case has yet been made that West African societies took the leap to full-blown iron smelting pyrotechnology without an intervening stage after simple kiln-firing of ceramics. In other parts of the world, the critical episode in this transitional "copper age" may come about purely by accident. Copper Age smiths begin to use iron ores as a flux to separate molten copper from its silica wastes.[18] First millennium BC copper production sites at Akjoujt[19] in Mauritania and the Agadez vicinity[20] appear to record the melting and simple working of metallic copper. This is metal production without smelting, by persistently late stone age, semi-nomadic pastoralists. The jury is still out on this hypothesis.

The second hypothesis, namely that iron spread into Sub-Saharan Africa from Meroë (Nubia) can also be dismissed. The furnaces at Meroë are just too recent (dating to the first two centuries AD) and of the wrong type (Roman-type slag tapping).[21]

Currently favored (but also with reservations) is the argument of a Punic or North African source of iron technology. This thesis asserts that fully mature iron smelting technology spread south

[18] R. F. Tylecote, "Furnaces, crucibles and slags," in *The Coming of the Age of Iron,* J. A. Wertime and J. D. Muhly (eds) (Yale University Press, New Haven, 1980), p. 183.

[19] Nicole Lambert, "L'Apparition du cuivre dans les civilisations préhistoriques," in *Le Sol, La Parole, et l'Ecrit,* C. H. Perrot, Yves Person, Y. Chrétien and Jean Devisse (eds.) (Société Française d'Histoire d'Outre-Mer: Paris, 1981), pp. 214–26; Nicole Lambert, "Nouvelle contribution à l'étude du Chalcolithique de Mauritanie," in *Métallurgie Africaines: Nouvelles Contributions,* Nicole Echard (ed.), Mémoire de la Société des Africanistes, no. 9 (Société des Africanistes: Paris, 1983), pp. 63–87.

[20] D. Grébénart, "Les métallurgies du cuivre et du fer autour d'Agadez (Niger), des origines au début de la periode médievale," in Echard, *Métallurgie Africaines,* pp. 109–25; David Killick, Nikolaas J. van der Merwe, R. B. Gordon and D. Grébénart, "Reassessment of the evidence for early metallurgy in Niger, West Africa," *Journal of Archaeological Science,* 15 (1988), pp. 367–94; S. McIntosh, "Changing perceptions," p. 173. For recent statements for the independent invention hypothesis, see Cornevin, *Archéologie Africaine,* pp. 116–22; and against, see D. Killick, "On claims for 'Advanced' ironworking technology in precolonial Africa," in *The Culture and Technology of African Iron Production,* Peter R. Schmidt (ed.), (University Press of Florida, Gainesville, 1996), pp. 247–66.

[21] S. and R. McIntosh, "Current directions," p. 242.

across the desert by the intermediaries of central and southern Saharan Berber tribes. The source would have been the iron age Phoenician colonies, such as Carthage and Leptis Magna, that were established from the ninth to seventh centuries BC. The timing is certainly possible. However, we have no hard evidence of how the technology passed into Berber hands[22] and, thence, to non-Berber societies to the south.

Perhaps there is no better illustration of the sterility of the prehistorian's quest for the "earliest" than the debate about the spread of metals. The emotions of the debate deflect our attention from two far more important questions:

1 Once in West Africa, how and why did it spread (and, as a corollary question, what was the nature of relations between iron-users and their stone tool-using neighbours)? As one can see from the dates above, the spread was anything but uniform. Even in superficially identical environments, large gaps exist in present evidence for iron's first appearance. The first colonists who entered the deep floodplains of the Upper Delta and Macina in the third and second centuries BC brought with them the knowledge of iron smelting. Considerable survey and excavation of the southern Lake Chad floodplain in Northeast Nigeria, southern Chad and northern Cameroon have not yielded radiocarbon dates for iron earlier than AD 400.[23] At most we can say that the spread of iron through West Africa was rapid, yet highly uneven. Future research will have to provide the local context of iron spread. Local causes may include the need for new tools to open previously impenetrable land to agriculture. Rapid penetration into some regions may be linked to the need to open large areas to cultivation. Clearly this is a point that needs clarification if we are to understand the mode of Middle Niger penetration (waves, saltation, or slow trickle). Need for iron intensified as population densities expand and larger numbers become sedentary. In other places, the critical factor might be the impact of trade and exchange for high quality iron and ores.

2 Why does the variation in early West African furnace types and

[22] There was Punic influence, by the sixth century BC, on the Akjoujt native copper industry, but the leap from this to iron smelting remains a long one. See Lambert, "L'Apparition du cuivre," p. 214.
[23] David "History of crops"; S. and R. McIntosh, "Current directions," p. 243.

smelting protocols so greatly exceed that documented elsewhere in the Old World? Prehistoric metal production in the Middle Niger (around Jenne and in the Lakes Region[24]), the Middle Senegal, Kano State (Nigeria) and the Cameroon Grasslands is far more diverse and is marked by an explosion of innovations in smelting and smithing technologies.[25]

Van der Merwe[26] writes that African smiths: "followed ideas which were highly observational and inventive, producing a wide variety of approaches, furnace designs, and smelting products." By the last centuries BC and first centuries AD, we see in West Africa an explosion in the smiths' inventory. We find simple bowl furnaces and large, elaborate bowl furnaces. We also find bellows-blown shaft furnaces and induced draft smelting. Near Soumpi, in the Lakes Region, we find sites with peripheral iron smelting and forging ateliers. Scattered cheek-by-jowl in the same locations are four quite different furnace types. Would the different furnace designs have required significantly different pyrotechnical knowledge? Are these furnaces sequential? Or were they contemporaneous? Did these evolve in place? Was there a demand for different qualities of smelt that had to be produced by very different smelting technologies? How much significance should we attach to the observation that one of these Lakes Region furnace types is found in only one place elsewhere, along the Middle Senegal Valley? This furnace is a shallow bowl with a raised central cylinder, presumably to encourage the slag to flow into a convenient ring. Are these cases of independent invention, or of very early, very long-distance contact between smiths?

Evidence of innovation in smelting technology enables us to look at the first colonists of the Middle Niger as anything but a technically conservative iron age peasantry. Innovation: the theme is pervasive in the evolution and spread of iron technology into regions such as the Middle Niger. The happy consequence of our new appreciation of African metallurgy as a web of perception, social process, and technical prowess is an ability to identify metals' roles in

[24] V. Chieze, "La métallurgie du fer dans la zone lacustre," in *Recherches Archéologiques au Mali* , Michel Raimbault and Kléna Sanogo (eds.), (ACCT: Karthala, Paris, 1991), pp. 449–55.

[25] D. Killick, "A little-known extractive process: Iron smelting in natural draft furnaces," *JOM: Journal of the Minerals, Metals, and Materials Society* 43(4) (1991), pp. 62–4; S. McIntosh, "Changing perceptions," pp. 176–7.

[26] Van der Merwe, "Advent," p. 486.

the emergence of specialization, of stratification of society, and in the evolution of potent concepts of authority.

Does an early tendency to innovate suggest the evolution in the Middle Niger, as across West Africa, of specialized iron production centers and the early presence of a corps of specialists? The evidence is thin, but it points in that direction. The Agadez sites in Niger begin as habitation sites with furnaces dispersed in almost haphazard distribution upon them. Production soon shifts to special function smelting sites with concentrations of furnaces. We will see a similar pattern to the smelting and smithing evidence from Jenne-jeno in the Upper Delta. This may be a first sign of a tendency towards secrecy and monopoly on the part of blacksmiths.

If so, it is highly significant. The monopoly of technical knowledge is intimately linked with the concentration and manipulation of magico-religious ritual and occult beliefs by blacksmiths in societies such as the Mande. The earliest and most persistent Mande oral traditions hold a key. They tell of how the blacksmith's secret knowledge of the smelt opens the door to the occult power that makes political action possible.[27] Occult beliefs are mostly lost to the archaeologist. However, there are archaeologically visible remains of technological innovation and concentration of production. In these remains we may have proxy measures of development in the political and religious realms. We will continue to scrutinize the blacksmiths for the first glimmerings of more elusive beginnings of changes to the very fabric of social and political structure.

The theme of smiths and their relation to emerging political power is one to which we will return at the end of this chapter. For the moment, we must shift to discussion of the origin of agriculture.[28] The origins of the need for those iron tools resided, at least partially, in new practices and demands of food production. And agriculture will permit unprecedented levels of sedentarism and population growth that appear most precociously, most spectacularly, in the Middle Niger. We must again begin with the larger West African picture and with a debate.[29]

The personalities of the various Middle Niger basins, some senescent and others fluvially active, are at the heart of a debate about

[27] S. McIntosh, "Blacksmiths."
[28] For the pan-African picture, see R. McIntosh, "Agricultural beginnings."
[29] The debate, with commentary, is found in Harlan, de Wet and Stemler, *Origins of African Plant Domestication* and in R. McIntosh and S. McIntosh, "Early Iron Age economy," pp. 160–3; see S. McIntosh, "Changing perceptions," pp. 167–71.

causes of plant domestication. The Middle Niger has long attracted those looking for the center of stone age experimentations leading to the domestication of a number of critical African cereals. These include fonio (*Digitaria exilis*), bulrush millet (*Pennisetum americanum*), African rice (*Oryza glaberrima*), and, perhaps, sorghum (*Sorghum bicolor*).

Portères[30] expounded the "primary variation" view. He argued that the live deltas of the Middle Niger are the critical areas for understanding the chronology and circumstances of domestication (of rice in particular). He reasoned that domestication took place in areas where today wild forms with genetically dominant characteristics abound. The opposing view was proposed by Chevalier,[31] according to whom, cereal domestication would take place under conditions of environmental stress. For Chevalier, one should search for the roots of agriculture in the processes that turned the formerly lush Méma and Azawad into now desiccated regions.

For the moment, the weight of opinion falls with Chevalier. Scholars side with him because of inference and not because of hard evidence. The four live basins of the Middle Niger simply lack evidence of a long late stone age occupation. The more likely candidates for those first to experiment with cereals are the members of communities under environmental stress, the same pressures that eventually pushed them out of the southern Sahara.

For several millennia, these people had to cope with unpredictable, oscillating and devastating conditions. As we have seen, such stresses would have become increasingly frequent after *c.*3000 BC in the broad basins of the Azawad and Méma. And the search must not ignore nearby Saharan palaeochannels, such as the Tilemsi Valley coursing south to Gao from the Adrar des Iforas. It is also possible that experiments with plant domestication had an even longer pedigree, beginning during the stable pluvial times of the middle Holocene. According to this alternative, agriculture is an entirely accidental outcome of intensive gathering, perhaps encouraged by the need for dry-season provisioning of the newly introduced herds of cattle.

---

[30] R. Portères, "African cereals: elusine, fonio, black fonio, teff, brachiaria, paspalum, pennisetum and African rice," in Harlan, de Wet and Stemler, *Origins of African Plant Domestication,* p. 445; see also R. Portères, "Vielles agricultures africains avant le XVIème siècle. Berceaux d"agriculture et centres de variation," *L'Agronomie Tropicale,* 5 (1950), pp. 489–507.

[31] A. Chevalier, *Le Sahara. Centre d'Origins de Plantes Cultivées* , Mémoire de la Société Biogéographie, no. 6 (Société Biogéographie: Paris, 1938), pp. 307–22.

These late stone age peoples made intensive used of a broad spectrum of resources in their environment. They developed a corpus of observations about the responses to local soil disturbances and "folk genetics" of annual grasses. Scheduling of seasonal movements or the degree of sedentarism may have changed independently of any considerations of the plant resources available in preferred locales. Perhaps the shifts in annual scheduling related to the demands of the herds (access to permanent water for calves, for example). Perhaps communities became more sedentary, or their round "simplified," with more specialized exploitation of other, entirely unrelated wild foods. We can only speculate about what support for this "optimal" thesis might come from future research.

At the moment, Chevalier's stress argument enjoys the weight of feeble evidence. The only unequivocal West African evidence for domesticated plants at late stone age sites comes from two rather late "stress" location sites. The first is Karkarichinkat South,[32] where we have potsherd impressions of two varieties of millet at *c.*4000–3500 BP. The second is Tichitt[33] at the northern edge of the Hodh. Here millet impressions are permanently fixed in pottery from 3000–2900 BP. Only at the latter has the argument been made for an *in situ* shift from a stable "aquatic" hunting and gathering economy. The oscillating, but progressive decline of the Tichitt lake encouraged the kind of experimentation under stress leading to a majority reliance upon a domesticated cereal.

From this rather spotty evidence two inferences can be made. The first is rather obvious. Systematic recovery of large macrobotanical samples by flotation and column sampling have not before been commonplace at excavations of southern Saharan and Middle Niger archaeological sites (with the exception of Jenne-jeno, Akumbu, and the Douentza area). Until flotation is standard procedure, we will remain as ignorant as we are today about the chronology and circumstances of the emergence of agriculture.

Second, West African plant domestication appears not to have been centric. Experiments with potential domesticates took place

[32] Andrew B. Smith, "Origins of the Neolithic in the Sahara," in Clark and Brandt, *From Hunters to Farmers*, p. 89.

[33] Sylvie Amblard and J. Pernès, "The identification of cultivated pearl millet (*Pennisetum*) amongst plant impressions on pottery from Oued Chebbi (Dhar Oualata, Mauritania)," *The African Archaeological Review* 7(1989): 117–26; Holl, "Subsistence," pp. 151–62; Munson, "Archaeological data," pp. 187–209; but, for doubts concerning the Tichitt evidence, see Robert Vernet, *La Mauritanie, des Origins au Début de l'Histoire* (Centre Culturel Français: Nouakchott, 1986), pp. 30–1.

over a long period over a large areal spread. Experiments probably took place in different environments within the sub-continent.[34] Belatedly, researchers in the Near East have recognized similar, non-centric patterns of domestication. In the southern Sahara and Middle Niger fringe, these experiments may have been in direct response to climatic deterioration. In others, communities may simply have elected to change their seasonal schedules of resource exploitation. Perhaps some scheduling decisions were indeed made to take advantage of increasing yields, potentials for a sedentary life, or storage capabilities of wild cereals. The more they "massaged" those cereals according to their knowledge of folk-genetics, the more they interfered with the soils in which those cereals grew. The more they fired the land, weeded, or allowed their neighbor's herds to manure, the more that strategy would pay off.

To what degree did these early agriculturists adopt pastoralism as their complementary pursuit? Were they pastoralists first? Did they only later split into complementary, specialized exploitation communities, with one tending the herds, the other growing the fodder that only later became human staple? To what degree did they ally themselves with intrusive, alien communities of sheep, goat, and cattle herders?

The details of agricultural origins are still debated. Any resolution will require much more dirt archaeology. However, we are on slightly firmer evidential ground for specialized Saharan pastoralism. Saharan pastoralism emerged after 7000 BP. Earlier, by 9500 BP at sites such as Bir Kiseiba and Nabta in the Egyptian western desert, local inhabitants of a drought-prone steppe had begun to manipulate wild cattle herds. By 7000 BP, however, standing water had become increasingly seasonal and often sporadically available throughout the Sahara. Pastoralism appears as a stable response to these climatic uncertainties. Smith and Gabriel document pastoralists' home bases and transhumant camps, sites at which herding was the majority specialist pursuit.[35]

After *c*.4000 BP, sites with abundant cattle remains are almost

---

[34] S. and R. McIntosh, "Current directions," p. 239.

[35] Baldur Gabriel, "Palaeoecological evidence from neolithic fireplaces in the Sahara," *The African Archaeological Review*, 5 (1987), pp. 93–103; Andrew B. Smith, "Origins of the Neolithic"; and "Cattle domestication," pp. 197–203. and *Pastoralism in Africa: Origins, Development and Ecology* (Ohio University Press: Athens, OH, 1992); see also A.Gautier, "Prehistoric men and cattle in North Africa; A dearth of data and a surfeit of models," in *Prehistory of Arid North Africa: Essays in Honor of Fred Wendorf*, Angela Close (ed.), (SMU Press, Dallas, 1987), pp. 163–87.

exclusively found to the south. There, they are clustered around the remaining Saharan lakes and ponded palaeochannels (Tichitt, Tilemsi, Agadez Basin) or the floodplain of Lake Chad. We have already seen specialist pastoralist communities identified in the first millennium BC Méma. A major question for the future will be the nature of relations between these pastoralists and their (semi-) sedentary farming or (semi-) mobile fishing and hunting neighbors. Did Saharan pastoralism under increasingly sub-optimal conditions encourage experiments with wild grains as herders sought ways to add a plant supplement to their diet? Plants add nutrition to milk (and blood) diet and are especially important for sustaining the fragment of the community left behind with the mild cows and calves when a herd is split during a long-range transhumance season.

What can we say about the varied peoples poised on the unflooded periphery of the live basins of the Middle Niger at about 300 BC? At that date, climatic conditions took a seriously dry turn. They brought with them fully domesticated animals as well as dryland cereals and African rice (probably domesticated in the swamps of the Azawad and Méma). They were perhaps still using stone tools before entering the far northern and western floodplains. However, they left those tools behind in preference to iron as they took the leap into the Macina and Upper Delta. They came in significant numbers. Their communities prospered and multiplied rapidly. No one yet has conducted excavations at sites on the donor borders of the deep alluvium. Rather, we draw these conclusions from Dia and Jenne-jeno, the principle sites of the deepest, most active of the live basins and from Akumbu in the Méma and far eastern extension of the Middle Niger at Douentza.[36] Were those first colonists specialized by subsistence occupation? It is quite likely that they were. Did they speak a generic "proto-Soninké" or an archaic Mande? Or had they already fragmented into a linguistic mosaic? Did they speak separate languages already recognizable as Bozo or Nono? Had they already begun to accord privilege and fearful respect to their blacksmiths? Do the Douentza tumuli dated to *c.*900– 600 BC indicate some nascent social or even political hierarchy amongst some? And just where did they come from? Let us see what inferences about these stubborn questions have been exposed in the lowest levels of Jenne-jeno.

---

[36] K. C. MacDonald, et al., "Douentza," pp. 12–14.

Founders of Jenne-jeno

Rarely have documentary sources and oral traditions been at greater odds concerning the founding of a sub-Saharan location of such importance. Rarely has archaeology had the opportunity to prove both so incorrect! The Upper Delta city of Jenne has had a commercial importance to the trans-Saharan trade long acknowledged by historians. The city's importance was first lauded in the seventeenth century by the local chronicler es-Sa'di: "it is because of this blessed city that camel caravans come to Timbuktu from all points of the horizon."[37] Curiously, the first mention of the city is not until 1447. In that year, the Genoese Antonio Malfante heard of this *civitate* (city-state) during a trip of commercial espionage to the North African city of Tuat.[38] By that date Jenne and Timbuktu were already linked. These were, respectively, the southern and northern terminus in transport along the Middle Niger riverine network. Merchants from these towns had for centuries trafficked in the items traded in the famous trans-Saharan exchange (the "Golden Trade of the Moors"). From forest and savanna to the south came gold, ivory, kola; and slaves. From the Sahara and beyond came salt, luxury manufactures, and manuscripts. Lubricating the trade were grain, smoked fish and meat, and fish oil. These last staples were the particular contribution of the lush floodplain of the Jenne vicinity.

After Malfante, the references to Jenne increase, both in Arab and European sources. The town is given unenthusiastic mention by later visitors, such as Leo Africanus in 1511. Because of their lukewarm descriptions and because of the late first mention, historians have acceded to the foundation date advanced by Delafosse.[39] He felt no need for an early commercial center in the southern Middle Niger. No need would have existed until the southern (Akan and Lobi) gold sources became at least as important as those in the headwaters of the Senegal River. The founding of Jenne was pegged at the late thirteenth to early fourteenth century.

---

[37] es-Sa'di, *Ta'rikh es-Sudan*, p. 23.

[38] The historical background to Jenne is found in Roderick J. McIntosh and Susan K. McIntosh, "The Inland Niger Delta before the Empire of Mali: evidence from Jenne-jeno," *Journal of African History* 21, (1981), pp. 2–8.

[39] Delafosse, *Haut-Sénégal-Niger*, I, pp. 269–70; see Mauny *Tableau Géographique*, pp. 115, 500.

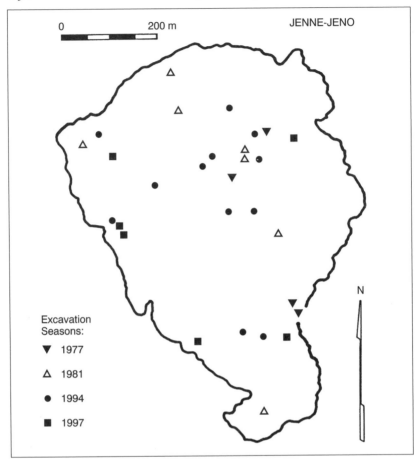

Map 6.2   *Jenne-jeno and its excavation*

This reconstruction was directly at odds with the oral traditions that were persistent enough through time and Islamization to be first recorded by es-Sa'di. These pre-Islamic traditions placed the founding of an ancestral Jenne in the eighth century. The ancestral town was called Zoboro, Joboro, Jenne-Siré, or Jenne-jeno – depending upon the (ethnic) preferences of the speaker. The conversion of a "king of Jenne" (that is, of the town's present location) took place in about AD 1106, according to these same traditions.

The historical reconstruction has tended to hold sway among historians. The apparent late date of the city dampened the interest of archaeologists in those mounds. That archaeological interest never really did develop, despite the discovery in the 1940s of terracotta statuettes on mounds near Jenne. A colonial teacher, Vieillard claimed to have found nothing of interest in his 1938 tests and peregrinations at Jenne-jeno. It is no small irony that, by his discouraging report, he helped to preserve the site from the untrained.[40] Perhaps there were just too many tumuli elsewhere in the Middle Niger. These held out the promise of rich burials that lured advocational archaeologists to the Lakes Region. Jenne-jeno remained reasonably free of looters' trenches and pits. The site remained unexcavated before major seasons of excavation, mechanical coring, and regional survey in 1977, 1981, 1994, and 1996–7 (and planned for 1998–9).[41]

The location of the site was no mystery and was known by its ancient name to the inhabitants of the descendant town. Three kilometres south of Jenne, the ancient site shared with modern Jenne the advantage of being in a broad clay channel of the Souman-Bani distributary. This major channel links the Niger and the Bani. At Jenne, the channel loses itself in a tangle of distributaries. One of these distributaries, the Senuba, flows along the western edge of the ancient site. The site and modern town are on the southern bevel of a large red ("Ogolian") dune. The location is significant. The dune is inundated by today's flood, but would have stood up above the perennially weak floods presumed to have been characteristic of the 300 BC to AD 300 dry episode.

Jenne-jeno commands a classic ecotone, or interlock of environmental zones. The site fronts the deep rice basin of the Pondori to the southwest. To the north are the *bourgou-seno* pastures of the red dune and Jenneri plains. To the south are the lightly treed highlands of the Nyansanari. Its inhabitants had moderate-draft river boat access to the Niger and Bani via the Senuba and nearby Souman-Bani.

Jenne-jeno's location was well placed. And although that location was no mystery, before excavations, the contradictory oral traditions were the only clues to its founding date. Scholars had no inkling about how the site grew, nor how its first inhabitants made their livelihood.

---

[40] Ibid., p. 102.
[41] 1977 season reported in S. McIntosh and R. McIntosh, *Prehistoric Investigations*; 1981 season reported in S. McIntosh, *Excavations*; the 1994 coring project is reported in Roderick J. McIntosh, T. Togola, P. Sinclair and S. K. McIntosh, "Exploratory archaeology at Jenne and Jenne-jeno, Mali," *Sahara*, 8 (1996), pp. 19–28.

The founding of Jenne-jeno appears to have been intimately linked to the final drying of the Sahara and Sahel that had become well progressed by *c*.300 BC.[42] The first colonists were there to stay. Occupation was extensive and year-round from the very beginning. The site was to remain occupied continuously for over 1,600 years, but only the first 650 years concern us here. For a few hundred years, the first colonists of the Upper Delta maintained stable habits of pottery production and economy. In the archaeologist's terms, this was a coherent phase, called (perhaps inelegantly) Phase I. Yet population rose throughout and Jenne-jeno expanded rapidly. Trade to the exterior expanded, and by at least AD 400 we can begin to speak of the site as the focus of an urbanized region.

The earliest occupation presents a curiosity. The palaeogeomorphology of the Upper Delta indicates that the annual flood had begun to decline from levels common to the first centuries of the last millennium BC. Most of the higher of today's submersible features (minor levees, small dunes) were probably permanently above water during most years. The drying continued during the next several centuries. Conditions were drier than today, yet the oldest traditions claim that fisherfolk were there first. The Tapama legend was mentioned previously: a fishing clan gives one of their daughters to be immured alive in a Nono community's wall – thereby ensuring the survival of permanent settlement (insurance against periodic high floods that would melt the wall foundations?) and cementing relations between the two groups.

There is a low levee on the east bank of the Senuba. We might have expected the first colonists to have located there, rather than on full floodplain. That appears not to have been the case. A similar aggressive colonization of lowlying floodplain was found at one other site (KNT 2), at least, in the Lakes Region. The first inhabitants settled an extensive sector that covers most of the centre and southeast of the site. Curiously, they would have had to build upon floodplain now well below inundation level. By the first centuries AD they had expanded the site north and founded an adjacent site (Hambarketolo) on floodplain even two meters lower.

It was not until early first millennium AD that the growing settlement crept over onto the Senuba levee. The move was successful

[42] The Jenne-jeno phase chronology is based on changes to ceramics, economy, and the appearance at the site of innovations in technology, imports, and house types. The three phases are: Phase I/II: 250 BC–AD 400, Phase III: AD 400–850, Phase IV: AD 850–1400.

Plate 6.1 *Aerial view of Jenne-jeno, with satellites to the north.*

only after the inhabitants built an artificial platform or revêtement (to deal with the rejuvenated floods?). Thus, in the last centuries BC and particularly the first centuries AD, the southern edge of the red dune would have resembled more a prairie than a deep basin floodplain. The first colonists found a location that remained dry for all but the infrequent year of exceptional inundation. The half millennium of occupation allowed deposits to accumulate sufficiently for the settlement to be above high water when conditions improved. However, Jenne-jeno grew horizontally as well as vertically. Studies by archaeologists of *tell* (settlement mound) formation on floodplains in Mesopotamia and elsewhere show that communities on dry floodplain expand very rapidly outward. The tendency is modified and growth is upward if they needed always to raise the level of current occupation above threatening floods. Jenne-jeno was at minimum 12 hectares by c.AD 300. Two hundred years later, its size had doubled.

The first inhabitants lived in rather solid huts of mud-covered mats lain over a framework of bent poles. By the end of the phase they had begun to build houses of solid coursed mud (tauf). From the very beginning they were fully iron-using. Not a single chipped stone tool has been recovered from the site. However, hundreds of sandstone grindstones were recovered from these deposits. The iron ore for the smelts at Jenne-jeno must have been from exposed laterite deposits along the eastern margin of the Middle Niger. These give us a picture of the antiquity and volume of trade to the exterior of the floodplain. The grindstones are of a restricted size and shape range. The lack of raw sandstone blocks and waste chips suggests that finished (or roughed-out) products were imported from the periphery of the stoneless floodplain.

These necessary, utilitarian imports were exchanged against the wealth of the Upper Delta – grain, smoked fish and meat, and oil. Other imports, such as a variety of stone beads, came from more distant Saharan sources. And there was another curiosity from a second- or third-century AD level. Locked into undisturbed context was a dark blue glass bead of east or southeast Asian manufacture of the Han period (206 BC to AD 220). Not too much should be made of a single isolated find, however secure the findspot. However, this bead may have been an incidental item in a trickle trade or even in a very early, Berber-organized trade across the Sahara. Much of this pre-"Golden Trade" commerce must have been in invisible items such as salt.[43]

And where did the colonists come from? They made a distinctive, well-made, fine-fabric ceramic with undoubted Saharan affinities. Their pots were small and twine-decorated, with simple open and closed rims, round bottoms. A good percentage have a fabric so fine we call it "chinaware" or fineware. The form of this pottery most closely recalls pots made at late stone age Tichitt in the late second and early first millennia.[44] Somewhat later than at Tichitt, a similar ceramic is used by the inhabitants at Kobadi and in the Méma. Contemporaneous with Jenne-jeno, sites with "chinaware" are Boundou Boubou and Akumbu in the Méma[45] and Soye, between Jenne and Mopti in the Upper Delta. We also found it on portions of the surface at fully three-quarters of the sites surveyed near Dia in the Macina.

The large number of sites with related ceramics is evocative. The aforementioned oral traditions claim that Nono from Dia asked permission of the nomadic Bozo already in the Jenne-jeno region for permission to found the settlement.[46] The oral traditions of even earlier Soninké diaspora prove uncannily close to the story told by

[43] S. McIntosh, *Excavations,* pp. 252–5, 390–3.
[44] Ibid., pp. 361–4.
[45] Téréba Togola, pers. comm. and "Iron Age occupation," pp. 91–110.
[46] S. McIntosh, "Reconsideration," p. 154.

early Iron Age ceramic affinities. The traditions tell of the founding of Dia by groups originating around Bassikounou, who traveled to the Macina via the Méma. The earliest Iron Age assemblage of the Méma, known from the excavation and extensive survey of Togola and MacDonald,[47] is very closely related to the Dia / Jenne-jeno pottery. Bassikounou is located in the center of the so-called "Hodh window". That region forms the break in the escarpments and plateaux that make the Hodh depression. This window is where the Vallée du Serpent palaeochannel once directed waters from the Niger into the Hodh.

Those same traditions tell of a western diaspora from Wagadou (just west of Bassikounou) to found settlements along the Middle Senegal River. Indeed, ceramics on the surface of villages of the first colonists of that floodplain are strikingly similar to the Jenne-jeno assemblage.[48] As in the Middle Niger, colonization of the Middle Senegal floodplain began not too long before the early centuries of the first millennium AD.

Oral tradition and ceramics may be imperfect documents. In this case, together, they tell a coherent story of large-scale population movements during the first millennium BC. Most movement was into the Sahel (and specifically into previously uninhabited parts of the Middle Niger) from source areas in the southern Sahara. Surely, there was no single epicentre for migration. However, the strongest candidate for a general source area is the plateaux country framing the Hodh, especially the Tagant and the Dhars Tichitt, Oualata and Néma.[49]

Economy of the Early Middle Niger

We can say quite a bit about how these early colonists made a living. The issue is important, not just because it allows us to reconstruct their way of life. Food surpluses from the deep basins of

[47] T. Togola, *Archaeological Investigations*, pp. 189–91, 196–200.

[48] S. McIntosh, et al., "Middle Senegal Valley," pp. 47–61.

[49] Robert Vernet, *Préhistoire de la Mauritanie. Etat de la Question*, (CNRS, Paris, 1993). For the lack of "neolithic" finds in the upper delta itself, see R. M. A. Bedaux, M.Dembélé, A.M.Schmidt, and J. D. Van Der Waals, "L'archéologie entre Bani et Niger," in *Djenné: Une Ville Millénaire au Mali*, R. M. A. Bedaux and J. D. Van Der Waals (eds.) (Rijksmuseum voor Volkenkunde: Leiden, 1994), pp. 41–53.

the Upper Delta and Macina were to become the foundation of an extensive riverine exchange system and a precocious urban civilization. The suite of animals, fish and plants exploited by the inhabitants of Jenne-jeno changed little during the millennium and a half of the site's occupation. That came as somewhat of a surprise. What changes we do see reflect presumed shifts in the environment. We can also discern the effects on the near floodplain of higher human population densities. The economy is an interesting – and stable even as the population grew – mix of wild and domestic. The economy was very generalized. However, that view may simply reflect the way the animal bone, macrobotanical remains, and fragmented fish parts effectively become churned together in archaeological levels.

The faunal remains[50] tell of a population that subsisted on wild resources (antelope, hippo, warthog) and domestic cattle and sheep and goat. Antelope are major components of the earliest deposits. The solitary, riparian to swampland adapted Kob (*Kobus kob*) predominates. Other antelope (reedbuck, bushbuck, and to a lesser extent, hartebeest) would have thrived on the lightly wooded, open-grass dunes and levees. Hunters apparently had a harder time finding these antelope after the close of Phase I/II. Their decline was perhaps due to growing numbers of settlements within the grazers' territories. Alternatively, rising floods and longer flood seasons after *c.*AD 300 perhaps wiped out many highland habitats.

There is domestic stock from the beginning of occupation. The goat or sheep appear to be a tsetse-resistant dwarf form. These dwarf forms do not easily support the long transhumant treks of the kind taken by Fulani mixed-stock herds today, raising several questions for future research. Were these dwarf sheep and goat bred by the pastoralists as they moved into floodplain regions still subject to tsetse infestation? Or was that resistance needed centuries if not millennia before in the southern Sahara? And does the appearance of bone of non-dwarf forms during the next phase (after *c.*AD 400–500) mean that the local population had established exchange relations with transhument pastoralists? That is, had local population outstripped the capacity of local pastures to maintain herds of sufficient size by mid-first millennium? It is impossible to determine whether the earliest cattle at Jenne-jeno are the drought-resistant humped form. If so, they were undoubtedly similar to the

---

[50] Kevin C. MacDonald, "Analysis of the mammal, reptile and bird remains," in S. McIntosh, *Excavations*, pp. 291–318.

Zebu or Sanga preferred by transhumant pastoralists today. Alternatively, the earliest cattle may have been the tsetse-resistant breeds used today in southern savanna and forest (*N'dama* and dwarf shorthorn). During Phase III (AD 400–850) there are at least two breeding populations represented. Were the two bred locally? Or do the faunal remains from the archaeological sites represent meat from locally tended herds, mixed with exchanged long-distance grazers?

The aquatic impression given by the wild assemblage of marsh antelope and hippo is reinforced by the reptiles and water birds. Among the reptiles are Senegal softshell turtle, terrapin, and crocodile. The bird assemblage is comprised of cormorants and anhinga darters, two species of geese, white egret and white-neck stork. The consistently frequent cormorant and darters are precisely those divers frequently caught in fishermens' nets. Crow, quail, kite, and hawk are in the minority. Domestic chicken appears only after the end of Phase I/II. Its appearance at that time reinforces the impression of a growing population forced to rely more on domestic animals and less on hunted meat.

Jenne-jeno's population consumed fish in large quantities and in significant variety throughout the 1600-year occupation of Jenne-jeno.[51] Jenne-jeno yielded over 5,000 identifiable fish of 25 taxa. The fish can be sorted by three habitats of preference. Nile perch (*Lates*) and *Synodontis* and *Bagrus* catfish are large fish requiring the open, well-oxygenated channel conditions that apparently obtained despite the comparatively dry conditions of Phase I/II. They were probably caught by a variety of techniques, including net, harpoon, and spear. The frequency of *Lates* rises significantly in the second half of the first millennium AD. Very probably the rejuvenated hydrology of the Upper Delta included frequent high floods and multiple, permanently flowing floodplain channels. The longer flood season may have disturbed the shallow pond habitat of other catfish (*Clarias*) or tilapia (*Tilapiini*). A more active fluvial regime probably disturbed the permanent swampy (paludial) conditions prefered by *Heterotis* (osteoglossids) and the eel-fish (*Gymnarchus*). The frequencies of these species decline especially in Phase IV (AD 850–1400). By the end of this phase, the annual inundation was probably both reduced and much more variable from year to year and decade to decade.

Archaeologists have systematically collected big fauna and fish

[51] Wim van Neer, "Analysis of the fish remains," in S. McIntosh, *Excavations*, pp. 319–47.

samples at only two other sites, at Dia in the Macina[52] and Akumbu in the Méma.[53] Because of poor preservation in the lower levels, we possess adequate information from Dia only on the subsistence economy from the sixteenth to nineteenth centuries. These data close most of the gap between the last, Phase IV deposits at Jenne-jeno and the present. True to form, the Dia assemblages are mixed wild and domestic and are very aquatic in suggestion. Bushbuck and Kob were eaten. So were domestic chicken, cow, and non-dwarf sheep and goat. Local fishermen took turtle, catfish, tilapia, and Nile perch; hunters bagged cormorant, darters, geese, and duck.

The evidence at the deep basin sites of Jenne-jeno and Dia tells of variations within a consistent wetlands ecology. Contrast this with the ecological history from Akumbu in the Méma. Here we have a history of progressive and severe drying. The earliest well-dated iron age deposits excavated at the site have hints of continuity with the aquatic economy at Kobadi. As during the late stone age, the inhabitants herded small stock. Hunters could still find swamp-adapted antelope (Kob and reedbuck). There is, however, only a little duck and crocodile (significantly, no hippo, turtle, or diving birds) – and a negligible yield of fish throughout the sequence.

The lack of fish is curious. To what degree have fish bone not been preserved? Were the massive perch and catfish not available, even during the optimal centuries of the first millennia AD? Or were the fisherfolk living elsewhere, in a cultural landscape of occupational specialists? With time, the marsh around Akumbu turned into pro-gressively drier grasslands. Hunters turned to elephant, warthog, weasel, civet, and Patas monkey and, by AD 1000, to two dry Sahelo-Saharan antelope (red-fronted gazelle and Dama gazelle). By AD 1400 desiccation was nearly complete. Faunal remains in the site's termi-nal deposits show only the cattle and (non-dwarf) sheep and goat one would expect at a dying settlement of transhumant pastoralists.

Lastly, samples of soil from Jenne-jeno were processed by flota-tion to recover remains of plants.[54] The mix of wild and domestic is

---

[52] Kevin C. MacDonald, "Preliminary faunal analysis for the 1986 Survey at Dia, Mali, in *Archaeological Reconnaissance in the Region of Dia, Mali*, Helen W. Haskell, Roderick J. McIntosh and Susan K. McIntosh (eds.) *Archaeological Re-connaissance in the Region of Dia, Mali*, Final report to the National Geo-graphic Society, 1988, 152–69.

[53] Kevin C. MacDonald, "An initial report on the fauna of Akumbu," appendix to Téréba Togola, *Archaeological Investigations of Iron Age Sites in the Méma, Mali*. PhD dissertation, Rice University (1992), pp. 215–32.

[54] S. McIntosh, *Excavations*, pp. 348–53.

repeated in the ancient floral remains. The wild millet *Brachiaria ramosa* predominates throughout, from 250 BC to AD 1400. This comes as no special surprise, because *Brachiaria* and a large suite of wild grain and legumes are regularly collected today by the inhabitants of the floodplain[55]. They also gather the *bourgou* grasses, *Echinocloa* and *Panicum laetum*, and wild rice, *Oryza barthii*. From the founding of the settlement, the inhabitants ate domestic African rice (*O. glaberrima*), wild rice, bulrush millet (*Pennisetum glaucum*), and at least two forms of sorghum. Fonio appears in Phase III, although its absence before may simply be a problem of sampling or preservation. Fonio, of course, is today a critical element to Bozo ritual.

Taken in total, the plant and animal remains recovered from throughout the Jenne-jeno sequence give a strong impression of a generalized subsistence economy. These broad spectrum floral and faunal assemblages have a strong aquatic bias. Does that mean that all inhabitants were generalized (three grain) farmers and eclectic gatherers? Were they all herders and hunters, also? Did they fish indiscriminately the open rivers, shallow ponds, and the backswamp marshes? Probably not. With an active daily or weekly market and without strong "ethnic" food avoidances, one would expect the degree of homogenization of food remains.

To what degree was the community a gathering of specialist producers? We have a hint of an answer at two smaller sites between Jenne and Mopti. Here Rogier Bedaux documented a strong segregation of cereal remains from early second millennium (contemporaneous late Phase IV) deposits.[56] Togguéré Galia on the floodplain has a nearly exclusive yield of rice and fonio. Inhabitants at Doupwil on a river terrace relied heavily upon millet. Bedaux attributes these differences to occupation by different ethnic groups with specialized economies. The unexpectedly tiny yield of fish bone from Akumbu may mean that fishing was avoided. The negligible fish that was found may have been procured from fishermen who lived elsewhere. Are there other hints in the settlement pattern of early specialization in subsistence activities or other aspects of the economy?

---

[55] Youssouf Boré, *Recensement des Graminées Sauvages Alimentaires (Céreales Mineures) Utilisées en 5ème, 6ème, et 7ème Régions*, (École Normale Superieure, Bamako, 1983); see Harlan, "Wild grain seeds," pp. 72–4.

[56] Rogier Bedaux, T. S. Constandse-Westermann, L. Hacquebord, L. Lange, and J. D. van der Waals, "Recherches archéologiques dans le Delta intérieur du Niger," *Palaeohistoria* 20 (1978), pp. 170–80.

Finally, if subsistence production was, at the founding of Jenne-jeno, in the hands of specialists, why do we not find evidence of concentration on high yield crops or on labour-intensive irrigation or barrage projects? Susan McIntosh remarks: "Perhaps the most remarkable aspect of this economy is its stability through time at the site, despite major demographic changes and significant climatic variability. . . . In view of the staggering population increase that took place in the immediate vicinity of Jenne in the first eight centuries of our era, the lack of any sign of subsistence intensification is astonishing."[57] Perhaps, rather, this persistence is more evidence of the very deep roots to the central theme of this book: heterarchy and the resistance to monolithic trends (be they political or economic) crowns the early history of the Middle Niger. By keeping their economy specialized (for the efficient exploitation of many micro-environments) yet heterarchical (generalized, with an abiding respect for wild resources) the earliest population of the Middle Niger's deepest basins kept all options open in case of the very predictable interannual and interdecadal swings of climate. Further insurance (and encouragement to rapid population growth) would have come in the form of early long-distance commerce in food staples along the riverine networks. Let us turn, now, to the physical evidence for the population growth and social complexity.

Settlements of the First Colonists

Archaeologists have looked in comparable detail at the regional picture of earliest Iron Age settlement in three regions of the Middle Niger. Two of these regions differ enormously in the natures of the background environment. The western Méma and the Dia hinterland in the Macina differ in details of their settlement evolution, it is very true. However, the parallelisms in major theme are perhaps more remarkable. In both cases, early settlement is broadly comparable in radiocarbon dates and ceramic affinities to the Phase I and II occupation at Jenne-jeno. Early penetration into these basins was vigorous.

Archaeologists have developed a rich menu of ways to reconstruct changes in human ecology, population dynamics, and in social and political organization. On this menu, regional survey is the potatoes and gravy to the meat of excavation at deeply stratified

---

[57] S. McIntosh, *Excavations*, p. 377.

sites. The normal course of action is to anchor a sequence of ceramics or other artifacts onto a well-dated stratigraphic sequence.
Such sequences are best recovered at one or more deeply excavated
sites. Then one combs the surfaces of sites in the hinterland of the
anchoring sites for artifacts and features. Only then can one slot
that surface material into the temporal artifact sequence.

In the Méma, the anchoring site was a series of mounds collectively known as Akumbu.[58] According to the oral traditions, this
site played a role in the founding of the kingdom of Wagadou at
the end of the Empire of Ghana. The AK-3 mound at Akumbu has
not yet been excavated to the basal levels, where late stone age
materials erode out of the sides of the mound. However, the excavators Togola and MacDonald have dug 7.5 meters into deposits
with a ceramic quite similar to Jenne-jeno Phase I. AK3 provides a
radiocarbon date of the fifth century AD from a point just below the
transition to that fineware, from material that resembles Jenne-
jeno Phase III. The excavators term the lower material "Early Assemblage". What has come as a surprise is the extent of Early
Assemblage material on the Méma floodplain.

These young archaeologists completed surface examination of a
sample of the archaeological sites in the region. Their sample area
covered approximately 20 percent of a 50 by 25 kilometer block.
In that part of the western Méma, the density of sites was easily
comparable to that in the Jenne-jeno or Dia regions. Of the 109
Iron Age sites they recorded, 94 were habitation sites. And of these
settlements, 49 (or over half) had only Early Assemblage material
on the surface.[59] Many of these early abandoned Iron Age sites
nevertheless had had a long history of occupation. People lived
there long enough to build up the mound in some cases to a height
of five meters. It is very probable that occupation of such mounds
goes right back to the late stone age. It is reasonable to assign a
very broad date to the Méma Early period sites of the end of the
last millennium BC to beginning first millennium AD. That is, these
sites were occupied contemporaneously with the Upper Delta Phase
I and II sites. If it was curious to find a majority of "dead delta"
sites dating to the presumed driest centuries of post-neolithic times,
the distribution of these earliest iron age sites was even more curious.

[58] T. Togola, *Archaeological Investigations*, pp. 65–103 and "Iron Age occupation."
[59] Ibid., pp. 38–57.

Most Méma sites are found on the banks or near vicinity of the now senescent palaeochannels. For their survey region, the archaeologists selected the vicinity of the distributaries called the Niakené Maoudo and Bras de Nampala. Not surprising for a dry period, the inhabitants avoided dunes and degraded dune edges. What very much amazed the archaeologist was the degree to which the Early sites bunched together.[60] Late stone age sites dating to some centuries earlier (some perhaps even occupied contemporaneously) are known from the Méma levees. We have discussed MacDonald's hypothesis of early clustering. His belief is that these latest of the late stone age occupations represent hamlets or seasonal camps of specialist groups. However, nothing prepared Togola and MacDonald for the explosion of this bunched, or clustered effect in the Early Iron Age.

Almost all Early sites are clustered. They evolve during the Méma Early period along three paths. In some cases, many small Early sites implode into one or, at most, two very much larger sites by the beginning of the later Middle Assemblage period. This pattern is found, for example, at Niakaré Ndondi, Boundou Boubou Nord and Sud where, respectively, six, 21, and 10 separate Early sites implode into one large mound. Alternatively, a cluster of many Early sites, each less than one hectare, is abandoned wholesale by the end of the period. This happens at Bourgou Silatigui and Niessouma, site clusters that began with six and nine sites respectively. The single exception to the rule of settlement reduction is at Akumbu, where the isolated AK3 mound gives birth by the seventh century AD to seven later settlements.

In the heart of prehistoric Macina, the hinterland story was quite similar. However, the history of the focus, or anchoring cluster of mounds at Dia was significantly different. The regional survey near Dia covered a two-kilometer radius around the modern town of that name. Twenty-one sites, or half of the prehistoric sites (selected at random), were surface recorded. Again, before survey began, the archaeologists were obliged to conduct excavations at two of the several sites immediately surrounding modern Dia. Excavations at these sites, named Shoma and Mara, anchored the survey ceramics onto a radiocarbon-dated sequence.[61] The ceramics and their dates are nearly identical to those from Jenne-jeno and, at both, the same phase designations are used. At both sites, ex-

[60] Ibid., pp. 42–5, table 3.2, pp. 45–7.
[61] Haskell, et al., *Archaeological Reconnaissance,* pp. 43–8.

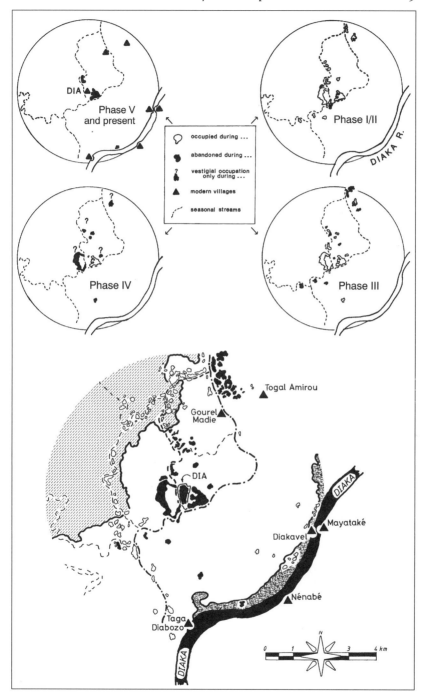

Map 6.3 *Prehistoric settlement dynamics in the Dia hinterland*

tensive lower deposits are littered entirely with Phase I and II wares (to depths of 1.7 m at Mara; 1.4 m at Shoma). Both mounds were more extensively occupied during this early period than at any time afterwards. Exposures of fineware outcrop on the surface of Shoma up to a full kilometer from the most distant excavation unit. We conclude from this ceramic evidence that, within centuries of initial penetration of the Macina, the settlement could very well have been as large or larger than contemporaneous Jenne-jeno. Interestingly, Phase I and II deposits are not identical. Those at Shoma show continuous, uninterrupted occupation. However, the early Mara levels are thick with pottery, fish bone, and ash. Here the levels are interrupted again and again by markers of temporary abandonment. Such markers include the presence of weathered sherds and surface disturbance by flood, river, and sheet wash. The differences make one think of the remains of a stable agricultural village versus repeated occupation by camps of fishermen.

The Dia survey shows some evidence of high density of population during the initial centuries after the first inhabitants penetrated the Macina. There was then a precipitous decline in rural fortunes.[62] The founders of Dia selected a locale of ecological diversity. In the near vicinity the pioneers had access to two distinct floodplain soils and a nearby high levee. Easy access to these three landforms is provided by a network of *marigots*. These *marigots* are now senescent. They display all the signs of having been quite active and maybe even flowing permanently in the last millennium. Mounds in Dia's hinterland were on occasion isolated, but the majority within a two-kilometer radius can be grouped into five clusters. These clusters took the form of long linear and tightly packed alignments along the banks of the *marigots*. The attraction of the *marigots* is logical if, at the time of 300 BC to AD 300 dry period foundation, settlements had to crowd close to permanent water. Three-quarters of the sites had extensive or exclusive surface exposures of the earliest artifacts. However, by c.AD 850 (end Phase III) over half of all sites were abandoned. Only one-third of the sites would have (the most attenuated) evidence of occupation lasting into the present millennium. As at the Méma clusters, it is hard to prove that all member mounds of the same cluster were occupied simultaneously. On the other hand, the ceramic sequence is finely enough tuned that we could probably discern at least a hint of a pattern of

[62] Ibid., pp. 107, 114–18, 121–39.

sequential occupation along these 10–20 member, strung-out clusters. The ceramics would differ from site to site had each mound been inhabited for perhaps two centuries and then abandoned for another a few hundred metres away. Subsequent replacement is not, as of now, the preferred hypothesis.

The apparent mid-first millennium AD population implosion (and possible population loss) at Mara and Shoma is reproduced in the hinterland. The explosion of population upon the first colonists' entry into the deep basins appears more pronounced here in the Macina than in the Upper Delta. However, the sustained first-millennium population increases of the Jenne-jeno hinterland are not seen here. Why should the demographics of two region of such similar ecologies differ so much?

The answer may lie in the floods. After AD 300, the rains over the Niger headwater improve and the deep basin inundation increases in height and length of season. The effect was beneficial at Jenne-jeno. The effect may have been devastating in the Macina. Higher floods and a greater bedload of sand probably strangled the aforementioned *marigots*. Climatic improvement may have changed the Macina floodplain hydrology from a network of distributaries to a single, bed-incising channel – the Diaka. Without the network of feeder *marigots*, far less land was available for rice cultivation. Without a multiplicity of permanent channels, settlement concentrated around available bodies of water. Dia lost its network of channels to carry boats to the far corners of the Niger floodplain. Without a teeming population and commercial routes, Dia lost its economic power to the soaring commercial hegemony of Jenne-jeno. The town retained its prestige as the parent of many Middle Niger cities, but its star was in the decline.

But before this decline, when population increases prevailed, clustering of communities was a feature of the first centuries after penetration into both dry and live basins. Why this particular settlement form? In neither environment is there any particular compulsion to clustering in the geomorphology. The answer has to lie in the economic or social lives of those early inhabitants. The form rather compellingly recalls (in elaboration) the landscape of separate but nearby and articulated camps and hamlets of specialists of the late stone age of the Azawad and Méma.[63] The surface remains of later clusters near Jenne-jeno also indicate occupational differences dis-

---

[63] Chapter 2, and Roderick McIntosh, "The pulse model."

tinguishing the inhabitants of the various satellites.[64] It is more than a bit of a mystery why the inhabitants should have elected to live on many small neighboring mounds rather than to live together at one site. With the latter option they would more rapidly have built up the occupation level about unusually high floods. On one mound, defense would have been easier. Perhaps these concerns of environmental stress and competition with neighbors were not the driving logic of settlement?

There is as yet no final solution to the mystery: however, more clues appear very soon with the emergence of true urbanism at Jenne-jeno. For the final word on clustering, let us return to the Upper Delta. It is very likely that the majority of the 69 sites packed within four kilometers of Jenne-jeno share a settlement history similar to that of Hambarketolo. Many of the elements that we have come to call the Jenne-jeno Urban Complex might have been founded simultaneously with or soon after the first colonists stepped onto the principal site. We will never be sure of such simultaneity until we can excavate into the basal levels. These satellites are built up tall. And the population explosion of the following phases has probably caused more recent deposits to cover and spill out over earlier deposits. With these issues in mind we developed a new research strategy during further excavations in the early 1980s. We returned to investigate whether there was a similar logic to the evolution of Jenne-jeno itself.

The hypothesis to be tested was that the earliest colonists first selected the low east levee of the Senuba. Hypothesis disproved. We then tested the suggestion that Jenne-jeno began as a set of small sites that later merged. The testing was done by standard deep units sunk in 1981 and in 1996–7 and, in 1994, by a dozen mechanically sunk cores at various parts of the mound as yet untouched by excavation.[65] Hypothesis partially disproved. Hambarketolo retained its independence to the end of the 1,600-year sequence (if one ignored the umbilical causeway between the mounds). However, from the very first days of the settlement, Jenne-jeno was one contiguous, large community. It was very quickly to become larger.

The situation was complicated enormously by the sinking of 36

[64] Roderick J. McIntosh, "Early urban clusters in China and Africa: The arbitration of social ambiguity," *Journal of Field Archaeology*, 18 (1991), pp. 203–6, 208–9.

[65] R. McIntosh, et al., "Exploratory archaeology at Jenne," pp. 19–28.

cores deep into modern Jenne. Archaeologists and historians had always favored the local oral traditions that claimed a foundation and growth of modern Jenne at the demise of Jenne-jeno (and the rest of the Jenne-jeno Urban Complex). The cores at Jenne were ambiguous, but suggestive: there is evidence for several centuries of overlapping occupation of these mounds, but no unambiguous evidence for settlement at Jenne before *c.*AD 800. That is the conservative position: the Jenne cores did sample one or two meters of deposits below the last datable ceramic. And these unaccounted deposits cover much of the town. A significant overlap during earlier centuries of the Present Era is not impossible, but will only be confirmed or disproved by proper excavation into the heart of the living town.

Right from the start, then, the Middle Niger settlement data from sites such as Akumbu, Dia, and Jenne-jeno are the local histories of the process introduced in the first chapter of this book: the evolution and long survival of autonomous, overlapping and competing interests in a political landscape of factions and multiple lines of authority that can effectively resist more coercive or monolithic forms of the state. In the separate, but articulated component communities of these urban clusters we perhaps see the factions spun by history and necessity into the horizontal web of authority and economic exigency in which each node is interconnected but also autonomous in their appropriate sphere of authority. Early clustering is a proxy measure of heterarchy. The spectacular expansion in number (and specialization) of these urban clusters in the first centuries of the Present Era is a measure of the success of the local integrative rules. When an archaeologist sees this kind of urban form, in the absence of marks of hierarchy (kings, palaces, ideologies of despotism and absolutism, and standing armies), he looks rather for a clue to the "contract" for peaceful access to services within a highly complex, generalized regional economy. This interpretation of the settlement pattern is so central to the thesis of this book that we must look a bit further at Middle Niger clustering as an urban organizational principle.

Along the two axes of temporal analysis (diachronic/synchronic), clustering evolves not as a dense agglomeration of population focused upon a single locale – as would be predicted by a long Western tradition of thinking about the origins of the preindustrial city. Rather, these towns are networks of specialized parts. Clustered cities as networks of physically distinct communities can cover impressive areas (greater than fifty kilometers-square in the case of

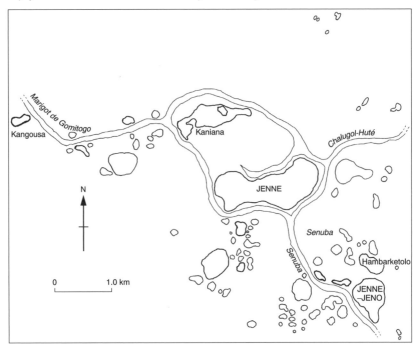

Map 6.4 *Jenne-jeno urban cluster*

the Jenne-jeno Urban Complex). Clustered cities can form a (peculiar) localized settlement hierarchy within a classic urban regional site hierarchy.[66] Who lived in these cities? We presume we can detect corporate, ethnic, and class differences amongst those who left behind evidence of varied subsistence tasks (net weights, cattle bones, sub-Saharan Africa's earliest *Oryza glabberima, inter alia*), of their artisan prowess (iron smelting furnaces, spindle whorls, fineware ceramics, *inter alia*), and of their (self-reflective?) inter-group differences (burial customs, architectural styles, forms and themes of the sadly famous Middle Niger terracottas, *inter alia*). But when looking for the antecedents to "civil society," the critical question is who made decisions in these populous, brazenly heterogeneous communities? Sadly, for the archaeologist, the individuals who moved community opinion, who had the mandate of the clan or

[66] Susan Keech McIntosh, "A tale of two floodplains: Comparative perspectives on the emergence of complex societies and urbanism in the Middle Niger and Senegal Valleys," in *Urbanism in Africa from a Global Perspecive*, P. Sinclair (ed.) (Societas Archaeologica Upsaliensis: Uppsala, forthcoming).

lineage to represent it in disputes with others, will always and forever be anonymous. That is why the function explanation for clustering has great appeal.

What is going on at these clustered towns? During 20 years of research in the Middle Niger we have tended to a functional and ecological definition of urban clustering: segmented communities of specialists or distinct corporate groups who voluntarily come together to take advantage of the services of others and a larger market for their products, but who make a demonstrable effort to preserve their separate identity by strategies of physical separateness.

In this view, the clustered city was a stable solution to the complementary ecological problems of the Middle Niger. The unavoidable reality was of a rich environment, but one marked by variable rain and flood regimes. One solution to this problem would be to remain perpetually generalized in subsistence regime, perpetually able to move on to more welcoming locales, perpetually the passive pawn moved about the ecologically checkered landscape by virtually chaotic outside forces. An alternative – and the one I believe hit upon by the inhabitants of these clusters – was to combat unpredictability by many (and increasingly) specialized artisan and subsistence producers linked into a generalized economy.

If this thesis is correct, the clusters needed mechanisms of integration. I have, in the past, relied frankly upon present-day canons of cooperation and ethnic reciprocity that maintain the modern ethnic mosaic of the Middle Niger. Extrapolated back into later prehistory, the occupation of separate mounds would be a strategy of physical segregation to complement foundation myths and ritual practices of integration.[67] These might include: (1) privileges of "first arrivals" – certain decisions vital to one group can be made only by another, linking everyone in a network of reciprocity; (2) bonds of fictive kinship – myths and legends of common origin and rules of obligatory common labor; (3) undischargable debt – lore of extraordinary sacrifice by one group for another under conditions of ecological stress – linking everyone in a tissue of expectations for future behavior.

This functional-ecological explanation leads to a prediction of cultural innovations leading to true urban clustering: late stone age communities will be encouraged to specialize (including those new habits that led to domestication of African rice, sorghums, millets,

[67] R. McIntosh, "Pulse Model," pp. 206–12.

and fonio, *inter alia*) if they have a season of joint occupancy of a shared locale with other (emerging) specialist groups. If peaceful, predictable reciprocity succeeds among these groups, further specialization will be encouraged, as will an eventually lengthening of the period of joint occupancy. In time, the season-round component of seasonality withers away. This may be the process we see in the late stone age clustered sites of the Azawad and Méma (chapter 2). The security of the generalized economy encourages further inmigration (and the normal population increases of sedentarism, if under salubrious conditions). Eventually the tiny seasonal, componential hamlets of the second and first millennium BC in the Méma evolve into the Akumbus and the Boundou Boukous and, with the eventual penetration of the deep basins, into Jenne-jeno and Dia of undisputed urban status.

In this scenario of emergent heterarchy, authority in the early clustered cities is shared amongst many corporate groups rather than being the monopoly of a charismatic individual (with a police force at his back) or of a wealth, elite, bureaucratic lineage. In an earlier age hunters may have pioneered notions of authority that gave their corporation the right to make decisions in certain realms. By the time these first cities appear on the Middle Niger landscape, another corporate group has augmented these notions of authority.

Specialists in a Realm of Their Own

We have delayed until now the discussion of a critical class of artifacts found in abundance at Middle Niger sites of this period. We turn now to the evidence of metallurgy (and iron smelting, most particularly). These remains come in the form of worked iron, furnace slag, chunks of lateritic ore, fragments of furnace and blow pipes (*tuyères*). Furnace parts and chunks of a 54 percent reducible-iron laterite ore are distributed throughout the entirety of the Jenne-jeno stratification. Residues of smelting (reduction of ore) are found in the lowest levels of Jenne-jeno and Hambarketolo. So, too, is evidence of smithing (reheating and working of the reduced bloom to make usable iron, repair of implements). Smelting slag (and presumably smithing slag also) comes from the earliest levels at Shoma, Mara, and Akumbu. Only the last site is anywhere near a source of abundant, good-quality ore. From these settlements' first days, smiths were importing ore. They conducted short (considering the density of slag), shifting (hence the lack of *in situ* furnaces) on-site smelts.[68]

What must the neighbors have thought? It must have been intolerable to live nearby with all the heat, dust, all-night stoking, the shouting, the roar of the furnace, the pounding on a chorus of anvils. And there may have been another, if nascent, reason why the smiths were becoming unwelcome neighbors. Their knowledge of the transforming arts – earth to metal, insubstantial fire to the mass of iron – was the key to a secret, occult realm of immense power and immense danger. In this, of course, we have to extrapolate back to Jenne-jeno broad principles of Mande power reckoning from ethnohistoric and ethnographic beliefs. Let us follow the many lines of evidence that suggest that this is permissible.

For these smiths to have selected Dia or Jenne for their smelts is extraordinary in itself. Far from primary sources of ore and fuel, the sites must have held some other advantage. Perhaps, as legend says, the sites were already of high occult power (due to the proximity of many *faaro*, the water spirits, in the case of Jenne-jeno?). A successful smelt at such a location would create not just strong metal, but a high cast of social power. Such power makes smiths revered, but also feared and the history of occupation groups in Mande (*nyamakalaw*) is one of that very same ambiguity of position in the greater society.[69] The smith lore credits them not only with the invention of iron working, but (along with hunters) with the creation of the (secret) power societies. With so much power to do social good and to cause unintended consequences, with so much noise and pollution (of all manner) to their creative acts, is it any wonder that society wished to keep them at arm's length?

Indeed, sometime during the middle to later half of the first millennium AD, we see revealing changes. Smiths appear to be removed to arm's length: In the Jenne-jeno hinterland,[70] at sites in the Lakes Region,[71] the Niger Bend,[72] and Méma,[73] production of iron shifts to permanent, possibly exclusive quarters at the edges of set-

---

[68] S. McIntosh, *Excavations*, pp. 267–79, 380–4.

[69] David Conrad and Barbara Frank, (eds.), *Status and Identity in West Africa: Nyamakalaw of Mande*, (Indiana University Press, Bloomington, 1995).

[70] S. McIntosh, *Excavations*, p. 381.

[71] Chieze, "Métallurgie," pp. 449–51.

[72] S. McIntosh and R. McIntosh, "Archaeological reconnaissance," pp. 313–15.

[73] Randi Haaland, "Iron production, its socio-cultural context and ecological implications," in *African Iron Working. Ancient and Traditional*, Randi Haaland

tlement. Alternatively, smelting shifts to associated, but separate satellite mounds. Typically, fewer than 20 percent of sites in a region have concentrations of furnace parts, *tuyères*, or mounds of the distinctive, dense "flow" slag of smelting furnaces. From mid-millennium, much pre-smelted iron must have been imported in the form of blooms, to be forged by local smiths. The activities of these smiths were spatially restricted. It is entirely likely that the smiths (and their potter-wives)[74] formed an organized artisan group. It is reasonable to view such groups as the prototype of the casted, segregated corporate groups of Mande occupational specialists (*nyamakalaw*). Working with the historical and linguistic evidence, Tal Tamari[75] claims that their corporate and casted status had taken form well before the fourteenth century. The archaeological evidence may prove a very deep antiquity for the *nyamakalaw* and for their secret power societies.

Does the development of the prototype corporate group begin with the appearance of these specialized metallurgical sites? Most archaeologists are aware of a long formative stage in the emergence of any institution. Often the earliest stages are centuries old before unequivocal physical manifestations are recognized in the dust and broken pottery. One such clue is the correspondence of major changes in the social and political structures of West Africa with the spread of the knowledge of iron.[76] These profound changes to society are particularly profound in the Mande lands. Many of the ideological and symbolic associations of secret knowledge and power in the social or political realms may have grown out of very ancient soil. The rich mystical earth of West Africa nurtured the earlier ideas of hunters. Hunters initiated and smiths later elaborated the core beliefs about how to control and transform the supernatural or occult power (*nyama*) of the natural world. Traditions[77] of itinerant, explorer and colonizing hunters and their secret power associations (*donso ton*) are reminiscent of the prehistorian's reconstruction of the late stone age transformations.

and Peter Shinnie (eds.) (Norwegian University Press, Bergen, 1985), pp. 64–6; Randi Haaland, "Man's role in the changing habitat of Méma during the old Kingdom of Ghana," *Norwegian Archaeological Review*, 13(19) (1980), pp. 31–46; Togola, *Archaeological Investigations*, pp. 52–7.

[74] Brooks, "Ecological," p. 28.
[75] Tamari, "Caste systems," pp. 221–35.
[76] S. McIntosh, "Blacksmiths."
[77] Cissé, "Notes," pp. 175–226; Dieterlen and Sylla, *L'Empire*.

The adaptation of these ideas of *nyama* by blacksmiths would have taken place gradually between the end of the last millennium BC. and perhaps (well before?) the eighth century AD.[78] By this last date, the casted status of specialists and the cult institutions of *Komo* (the smith-led initiation association) are in recognizable form.

The core concept of most powerful knowledge underwent a slow evolution. As that evolution progressed, the secret technical knowledge of the smiths become instrumental to the control of occult forces, *nyama* , the "agent that vitalized the world".[79] Specialist knowledge becomes more restricted by practices such as marriage restricted to within smith lineages. Secrecy is reinforced by the adoption of fearsome symbols that are dangerous for the uninitiated. Restricted knowledge leads to monopoly and uneven distribution of materials and production. Increased trade and the coalescence of the specialist group emerged as secondary effects. This may be why, during the earliest days of Jenne-jeno, smiths took costly and, on the face of it, inane production decisions. Why would they choose to import ores from over 75 kilometers away? Why would they choose to perform the smelt in a floodplain largely devoid of trees for fuel? One cannot help wonder what was so special, so vital about the location of the site *before* its foundation to make smiths go to such lengths.

The process led later in the first millennium AD to the emergence of the *Komo* society and its role as repository of social values in Mandé society. The process led to the accumulation in smiths' hands of dangerous amounts of *nyama*. It led also, early in the following millennium, to the development of smith kings and the Mandé political forms that could not exist without access to *nyama*. By this date, there had very likely been a long association of these ideas of power with smiths' esoteric knowledge and symbols of cult. Over wide regions of Mande one finds the privileging of these symbols: snakes, water, metals (especially copper and iron), and certain types of masks.

McNaughton[80] has recently begun to look at common elements

[78] George Brooks, *Western Africa to c. AD. 1960: A Provisional Schema Based on Climatic Periods*. Indiana University African Studies Program Working Papers Series, no. 1, (Indiana University Press: Bloomington, 1985), pp. 16, 19–31, 43–54, 77–153; Susan McIntosh, "Blacksmiths," pp. 20–1, 29.

[79] McNaughton, *Mande Blacksmiths*, p. 3.

[80] Patrick McNaughton, "Is there history in horizontal masks? A preliminary response to the dilemma of form," *African Arts* 24 (2) (1991), pp. 40–53, 88–90; and "From Mande" pp. 76–85, 99–100.

of form and context of use of one class of smith-crafted art, horizontal masks. This has led to some rather audacious, but very welcome speculation about the antiquity of the meaning of this art. In the ethnographic record, such masks are intimately linked in the Mandé mind with the Komo and smiths' manipulation of *nyama*. The masks are used in most smith-founded cults. As McNaughton puts it, the masks "articulate the nature of the world from its occult underbelly."[81]

In his opinion, the canon of production of these masks is simply too restricted. A handful of basic elements are repeated over and over. They are spread over too great an area (some 4,800 kilometers of West and Central Africa). They are found among too many ethnic groups (78 from eight language families). There must have been a deep shared history. McNaughton displays an art historian's caution when dealing with "the difficult question of history." He refuses to speculate on just how deep this history may go. The origin was probably Mande. Their use today is consistently among cults that impose mandated secrecy upon their members. In the early iron age, it was most probably the Mande blacksmiths who engaged in commercial migrations. The purpose of these trade diaspora was to control access to ores and even to found settlements in locations advantageous for the trade in manufactured metals. Over and over one hears of penetration of new territory with the new metal tools. Jealously guarded secrets of the smiths provided the new power to control the forces of the land. These are the consistent themes of legends about the spread of horizontal masks. Perhaps the masks provide a window upon the motivations behind the diaspora of those early Mande.[82]

In the train or in the fore of the first communities to penetrate the deep basins of the Middle Niger were blacksmiths who transformed iron out of ore. In the process they transformed themselves into enviable, if dangerous, positions of mediation within society. By working with fire and earth to make iron they transgressed into an altogether separate realm of supernatural energies. They pioneered the definition of "corporate group" and other specialists adapted a useful form of social definition. They became the agents of evolving social stratification and emergent political forms.

Many of the smiths' reinventions of authority, expressed eventually in resistance to centralized states and in clustered cities derived

---

[81] McNaughton, "History?," p. 50.
[82] Ibid., pp. 49–51; S. McIntosh, "Reconsideration," pp. 154–7.

from the new opportunities of sedentarism in a rich, diverse, yet unpredictable landscape. If corporate belonging had emerged, even in nascent form, in antecedent communities before the great drought of 300 BC, penetration of the deep basins would have sharpened focus upon potential points of conflict amongst those presuming to make decisions. Who had the authority to lay claim permanently to territory? Who said "We stop here!" when colonists saltated across the floodplains of the Niger (and Senegal) during the last centuries BC? When Jenne-jeno and Dia in the Middle Niger became true cities – who regulated relations between the growing number of artisan corporations defined by occult mysteries?

By mid-first millennium BC, smiths had begun a long process of appropriating key ideologies and symbols from a deeper Symbolic Reservoir. Smiths invent early expressions of *Komo*, *Ntomo*, and *Poro* (or any other initiation or power association) in order to resist attempts by anyone, including other smiths, to build vertical power . But smiths are just the most visible of several competing power associations acting as overlapping agencies of cooperation and competition, creating in greater Mande a landscape of highly complex, non-centralized polities. If not by mid-first millennium AD, then soon afterwards, other occult-charged corporations such as the *griots* (*jali*)[83] and even leatherworkers (*garankew*)[84] set in to fill up the interstices of the political and sacred landscape. Their authority derived from occult-sanctioned persuasion, rather than coercion. Collectively, they invented an original civil society.

---

[83] See Thomas Hale, *Griots and Griottes of West Africa*, (Indiana University Press: Bloomington, 1997); and Conrad, "Blind man," pp. 86–132.

[84] See Barbara Frank, *More than Objects: An Art History of Mande Potters and Leatherworkers*, (Smithsonian Institution Press: Washington, DC, 1988) and "Soninké *Garankew* and Bamana-Malinke *Jeliw* : Mande leatherworkers, identity and the Diaspora," in Conrad and Frank, *Status and Identity* , pp. 133–50.

7

Historical Imagination: AD 400

The last chapter ended with great optimism: the invention of an original civil society. Persuasion rather than coercion glues together a horizontal political landscape of independent, but interlocked segments of society. Peace prevails. Overall this is my basic belief about the Middle Niger of the early first millennium AD. But archaeology is a science of cautionaries. All prehistorians know the story of the great Mayanist, Eric Thompson, who wrote of the Maya as peace-loving original democrats. In fact, we know now that they (no less than most other peoples) – or at least their elites – pinned their hopes on the fortunes of war and worshipped quite blood-thirsty gods.[1]

The danger for any archaeologist with a deep affection for the long-gone peoples of his site and an equally strong friendships among their living descendants, is that the past will be written in terms far too rosy. Heterarchy, as seen in this historical imagination from the Roundé Sirou levee in the year AD 400, must have had its own share of tensions. After all, the stakes were becoming higher all the time:

Never before has it turned quite so nasty. It need never have been so. Of all the newcomers, smiths are the most welcome. Of all smiths, the welcome should have been especially warm for these three families. Large families, all with the highest training in the smelt, at the forge, and with long grey snakes of clay. They have been lodged since their arrival three months ago with the principal smith, and never have the anvils rung so loud and so long into the

---

[1] Jeremy A. Sabloff, *The New Archaeology and the Ancient Maya*, (Scientific American, New York, 1990).

night. Never have the furnaces belched flames so high. The night sky has been aflame since their arrival. The charcoal gatherers have had to double their daily journeys to find enough fuel. And the neighbors are furious – soot and cinder falling in the cook pots, animals and small children with shattered nerves, never a sound sleep with the din of hammers and the rumble of the furnaces.

It is said, in furtive whispers, in muffled voices, that never has there been such a disruptive meeting of the most secret of the smiths' conclaves, that gathering too powerful, too terrible to have a name. Called to discuss the new families' residency, all turned to chaos when the five elders of the new families opened the long leather bags in which were hidden their objects of power. Many guesses were made as to what was drawn from the bags – masks, iron staves, chains with links in the form of intertwined python? All that is known for certain is that no words were spoken for many hours until the objects were replaced from sight. Terrible indeed must have been the skill and power of that hidden disputation.

Of all the smiths, these families should have been most welcome. They come most recently from Dia, that most revered of towns. Like the many others newly arrived from Dia, they tell of years of terrible floods followed by years in which, for six, eight months, no water flows in the streams nearby. The land is furious and the people are confused as to why – but the whole town fears what offense could have been given to those most ancient spirits. More and more leave each year. But these new arrivals not only tell of the wonders of Dia. Their elders still recall old stories of when the families lived the itinerant life in the dry land to the west, moving year by year vast distances from village to hamlet. Those old men love to see the fear on the children's faces as they tell of the terrible serpents that rule those lands and of the yellow stones that fall with the rain.

These new families have brought many secrets from their wanderings. In the short time since their arrival, they have cured many foot and ankle wounds from hoe and ax by sprinkling on their iron shavings. Many infants would now be dead of the bowels that run water had they not sipped from the liquid in the pot in which these smiths thrust red-hot iron. And their wives are greatly respected, even though they have never learned to make the thin-walled bowls and cups that are the pride of potters here. Rather, they excel in mixing white, black, and deep red paints and in applying these to just-fired vessels for a look that is becoming the rage. All the town's potters are delighted with a new skill to make their masterpieces desired in greater numbers and even further down the great river than they are today.

It is a question to be resolved tonight, of where the newcomers will be permitted to live. This Roundé Sirou levee is much as it has always been; fishermen and their families camp here almost every year. But great happenings are going on to the south. The hamlet founded by farmers and smiths between the Huté and the Senuba, the one most call Jaboro out of respect for sacred Dia, has prospered. Scores of families come each year to settle there.

Now the old people complain that they live in a land of strangers. They see few in market whom they can call uncle or sister, niece or nephew. It grew quickly from camp, to hamlet, to village and is now far too proud to call itself a mere village. Most who arrive build their compounds close to older immigrants known from their old homes or, like the new smiths' families, nearby to members of their own professions – fishermen with fishermen, those who work leather with tanners and leatherworkers, smiths with smiths. But the new smiths have made an extraordinary request. It has turned the town upside down.

On the face of it, it is a simple request. The new smiths have, quite properly, asked permission of the gathering of principals of the professions to move their families to a new site on the high floodplain. This site is just across the great Mayo Manga *marigot* from the levee on which we stand. And it is a good half hour walk from the Jaboro settlement on the Senuba. This is the first problem.

This request has pushed relations with their host, the oldest and most respected elder of all the smith families, to the point where even insults might fly. To the new smiths, this is a simple request for room. For their host, it is evidence of how power can warp the minds and morals, even of smiths. No little envy is at work here. Custom has it that immigrant smiths will merge freely with the old, that through alliances of work and marriage they will add their thread to the complex web of kinship, workshop duties, and secret roles in the secret associations – and so soon loose their identification as an outsider. The principle smith had the expectation that these powerful newcomers, too, would gratefully share their skills at the forge and secrets of the life forces of the world – and identify with the town. The host's workshop would, not coincidentally, become ever richer, ever more feared.

This request to live separately, with its promise of secrets kept from the secret-keepers, of new powers born and alliances made with the spirits of which other smiths can just dream, this request has infuriated the principal smith. Blacksmith families throughout the town are divided, family against family, son against father, wife against husband. To be sure, there are ample precedents for the occupation to be apart. Between where we stand today and the town Jaboro there are dozens of smaller mound-villages. Several are occupied by farm families, another near here by the families of the builders of the big boats, and the sprawling sand flat just across this marigot is home, in the hot season, to the long-distance tenders of the herds.

The problem is not the desire to live apart, but rather the promise of distance to keep secrets – secrets of the craft, secrets of power. That is why, when the principals of the town meet tonight, the request of the newcomer smiths will stoke the passion of the head of their own craft, their host, who would normally be their main advocate. It will be a gathering of old men, the venerables of the town and most respected of their respective crafts, cults and corporations. Mason sits next to head of oldest farming clan. The latter sits next to smith, who is next to the representative of the family that sacrificed one of their own, the virgin Tapama at the founding of the town. All sit as equals, together plotting the future. Many gatherings before this were devoted to the dizzying growth of the population: what to do with all the newcomers arriving from the north and west? Which of the new professions and crafts that develop to service all these people to recognize as an association worthy of adding a new principal to the assembly?

Long ago, at a gathering just like tonight's, the venerables agreed to the principle of satellites in orbit about the town. After all (argue their neighbors), push a smith onto a satellite and your rice and fish is no longer seasoned with cinder. However, now the head of the smiths argues that this would be a satellite with enough arrogance to force the town in orbit about itself. And it is very true that the newcomers have shown, in hints of terrible knowledge gathered at sacred Dia and, before that, in the desert Serpent Land, that they possess new power perhaps without bounds. The argument that they intend harm is met, generally, with polite derision and calming, good-natured guffaws.

The issue soon would be closed and accord given to build at the Mayo Manga site, were it not for the sullen fury of the head of the hunters' cult who, for this year's gathering, is the first of the principals. A predictable complication, this. The hunters are unforgiving of the new respect and fear that all show for the smiths' mysteries. Those of the hunters are undiminished, simply somewhat eclipsed. Anything to divide the smiths and to slow down their ascent.

For many, the charges of arrogance stick. The newcomer smiths have made a gesture that they must have known would be seen by all as an insult to the authority of the first of the smiths, to the first of the principals, and to the collective authority of the assembly itself. Once started, this gesture could not be stopped. No one had the courage. What the immigrant smiths had done was to construct a building, a tiny round hut of clay and thatch in a grove of trees, just to the far side of the site to which they wish to relocate.

But this is no simple hut. This is the sacred of all sacreds. Travellers from the west, following the *marigot*, will be forced to loop far to the opposite bank at this point in order to avoid even looking at it. Some say they have seen a giant serpent with horns of iron on guard in the thatch and rafters. All know about the terrible lines and squares and zig-zags in white, black, and red paint on the outside of the walls – patterns that make many think of the new skills in decorating pots introduced by the women of these families. Those who lie even claim to have peeked inside and seen a tall, half-egg altar set with an iron chain of seventeen links, a tiny anvil and the revered water beasts – crocodile, manatee, hippopotamus – fired in clay.

Most unsettling still to most is the rumor that, hidden by the night, the new smiths spirited in a keeper of these objects, a man with ghostly pale skin who hides from light and only emerges from the hut when the sun has been down for hours.

No one doubts that great mysteries occur in that hut. No one doubts that it was inexplicably bad form to construct it without asking the head of the hunters to call a gathering of the principals. They will argue all night and perhaps for several nights following: hunter and smith – strange allies – against the majority. The majority will certainly be led by the elder of the Tanapo fishermen. He consulted the water spirits of the *marigot* about the wisdom of this new satellite. He received what was, clearly, an enthusiastic response.

So, the newcomer smiths will probably receive permission in the end. The majority will finally be swayed by that very power of the newcomers that is now being used in arguments against them. Everyone agrees that each new smith adds to the fortune, future, and promise of the town. A topic of incessant conversation in the market is the observation that the recent influx of immigrant blacksmiths over the last 20, 40, even 60 years has coincided with the beginning of the good-harvest rains and a steady rise in the level of the annual floods. Children now have to listen to their grandmothers' tales to know of times long past, when the floods came but went again before the rice could mature and before the fish could breed – or when the floods never came at all. All the smiths use their mighty knowledge to help the rains and the floods. Everyone agrees that the newcomers are equally enthusiastic in this role.

For those last hesitant ones, this enthusiasm of the new smiths will dissipate concerns about arrogance. It is widely known around town that they recently invited the Tanapo elder to their sacred hut on the *marigot*, not to enter, but to add some grains of fonio and plates from the tail of crocodile to the consecration of the sandstone altar just outside. Smiths have made rainmaking altars before, but never quite like this. The largest boat in the town, filled with slabs of sandstone from the cliffs far to the east and followed (up to a point) by hundreds of the curious, was pulled to on the bank of the *marigot* at the beginning of construction. Slab was piled upon slab; incantations with each handful of ore or iron waste thrown on the growing construction, pots with raised figures of snakes, and yet more slabs, until the top was higher than a herdsman's chest. This is power. The rains will surely be even more abundant. The floods, too. The rice farmers are already preparing extra seed and the fishermen weaving new nets for the promised deep water. And all those who trade know the boats filled with the oil, the reeking smoked fish, and the great baskets of rice from the town will go father than ever before to the hungry markets of the dune land to the north. This is power. The town will thrive.

By mid-first millennium BC, smiths had begun a long process of appropriating key ideologies from a deeper symbolic reservoir. By the time of this chapter's exercise in historical imagination, set as much as a millennium later, smiths have become the most powerful of many occult experts.[2] And smiths invent early expressions of

---

[2] There is a truly vast literature on Mande smiths, Komo, and on the instrumentality of their acts – see Bird and Kendell, "Mande hero," pp. 13–26; Brooks, *Landlords*, pp. 39–46, 73–7; Dieterlen and Cissé, *Les Fondements*; McNaughton, *Mande Blacksmiths*.

extremely potent power associations, *Komo* and *Poro*, in order to resist attempts by anyone, including other smiths, to build vertical power.[3]

McNaughton observes that smiths fashion art, especially horizontal masks, to "articulate the nature of the world from its occult underbelly."[4] One hears references to animal spirits of *nyama*-filled places in his interpretation of these masks as a dangerous secret masquerading as a composite animal. Masks mark the geographical expansion throughout much of West Africa of smith's associations. That spread is propelled largely by the search for ore and entrepreneurial knowledge.[5] *Komo* functions to rid society of criminals, sorcerers, and other sources of social deviation. Power associations also stand between the community and wilderness spirits.[6] Have they appropriated the hunters' special roles, or do they simply supplement them?

There are very real differences in roles. This is perhaps the source of continuing tension between smith and hunter and the reason why the latter will always refuse initiation into *Komo*. *Nyama* is transformed. For the hunters, the life-force of the world was extracted at the death of guardian animals or spirits. Smiths now experiment with a transformative vision of *nyama*. By transforming earth and fire to iron, smiths add significant value to the lifeforce. By taking the guardian snake into the *Komo* hall to serve as a secret familiar (a variation on the hunters' reluctance to kill python or vulture), smiths have shifted the symbolic tense of *nyama* from extractive to the active "*nyama ardent*" – fiery *nyama*.[7] This has everything to do with power of place.

Like hunters, smiths want to settle and smelt at places of supernatural power. They expand and transform the Middle Niger symbolic landscape. Indeed, there is no economic reason for early smiths

[3] This process is not confined to the Mande. For example, the smith chiefs of the Namandiru (central Senegal), who take a vow of humility and poverty, in H. Bocoum, "Contribution à la connaissance des origines du Takrur," *Annales de la Faculté des Lettres et Sciences Humaines* (Dakar) 20 (1990), p. 168; also see Brooks, *Landlords*, pp. 84–5.

[4] McNaughton, "History?," pp. 40–53, 88–90; McNaughton, "From Mande"; see also, M. Nooter, "Secrecy. African art that conceals and reveals", *African Arts* 26 (1993), p. 59.

[5] McNaughton, "From Mande," p. 81.

[6] McNaughton, *Mande Blacksmith*, pp. 130–1.

[7] Cissé, Notes, pp. 201, 207; see also Dieterlen & Sylla, *L'Empire* , p. 53 and McNaughton, *Mande Blacksmiths*, p. 11.

to be on a floodplain, far from fuel and ore. Yet they leap to places such as Dia or Jenne-jeno as soon as the alluvium opens for colonization. Smiths have invented an advantage in the scramble for power locations.[8] Rather than kill the animal guardians of these sacred places, as is the hunters' habit, smiths employ them (again) to *add* significant value to the *nyama* of the locale. The sacred landscape evolves and becomes richer with the smiths' transformations. With the ability to add value to or to augment the earth's life force, new smiths' associations proliferate. So, too, will new corporations devoted to other occupations and other dimensions of the occult.

Hunters' *dali-ma-sigi* adventure, smiths' entrepreneurial-quest – and in the future, royal pilgrimage – are all acts reflecting a core definition of the Middle Niger peoples that has persisted, transformed but recognizable, for millennia. No single symbol or constellation of symbols defines Mande. Rather, Mande is a many-tiered network of power localities. At some level, surely, the settlement archaeology of the Middle Niger reflects that network. The problem is how to investigate it empirically.

At some essential level, the historical disciplines can ally to study the Mande symbolic landscape as the spatial blueprint for the covenantal assimilation and restoration of power. The Mande epics and symbols can reveal the deep-time network of power locations for the Mandeist – although historians, archaeologists, and political scientists have just begun to look at historical processes in these terms. Most layers of the power locality network may be accessible to open scholarly search. However, in keeping with profound Mande concepts of secrecy, the most powerful tier or tiers will forever be hidden. More immediately accessible, however, many be the distinctively horizontal flow of authority and political power in early Mande, including the Middle Niger. In this environment rich in surplus resources and peoples, in this land beset by periodic climate stresses and, increasingly in the second half of the first millennium, by the social disturbances of migrations, why do classic kingdoms and early despotic states not appear?

And if such expressions of political centralization are hesitant to appear, what is the alternative? Smiths joined together in residential, kin, or power associations are just the most visible of several competing but overlapping agencies of cooperation and competition, creating in greater Mande a landscape of highly complex, non-

---

[8] E.g., Conrad, "Searching," pp. 155, (166), 169, 180, 183; McNaughton, *Mande Blacksmiths*, pp. xv, 43–4, 148; "From Mande," pp. 79, 80–3.

centralized polities.[9] Their authority is derived from occult-sanctioned persuasion, rather than coercion. As smiths' influence grows in assemblies, such as the imaginary council of this chapter, they still rarely rule in any formal sense. Rather, their genius is in "shaping cultural space" – defining the community's debates about action in response to crises (loosely defined to include opportunities as well as stresses) because of their ability to "come between individuals and the forces of the Mande universe."[10] Groups that harness mystical energy can effectively resist power asymmetries. Mande, and the Middle Niger as its engine of surpluses, were non-centralized.

[9] In historical treatment, these pre-Sunjata polities are usually described as "small kingdoms" or "statelettes" ruled by smith-kings or hunter-kings" – see Cashion, *Hunters*, p. 81; McNaughton, *Mande Blacksmiths*, p. 9; Conrad, "Searching for history," pp. 171–83 and Bathily does a particularly thorough job of inventorying these polities in *Portes de l'Or:*, pp. 66, 76–83, 96, 127, 134–7, 189–91, 221, 231–2. One of the great challenges for archaeologists and historians will be to find a label and vocabulary adequate to describe this non-state, horizontal complexity without the universalist, neo-evolutionary overtones of most discussion of the rise of vertical power structures.

[10] McNaughton, *Mande Blacksmith*, p. 41.

8

Prosperity and Cities

Smiths were active participants in the settlement of the Lakes Region and Niger Bend also. In the northernmost of the active Middle Niger basins, the location of their activities takes a dramatic shift at about the same time as in the Upper Delta and Méma, at about the mid-first millennium AD. These sites provide support for the inference that, as part of the process of coalescing specialization, smiths' noisy and dirty – and secret – activities move away from inhabited areas. As interesting as the metallurgical evidence is, however, it is just one aspect of settlement pattern that sets the sites of the Niger Bend and particularly the Lakes Region, in a class by themselves. The period that corresponds to Phase III at Jenne-jeno (beginning c.AD 400 and ending around AD 850) sees here the establishment of sites of unprecedented height, arrangement, speed of accumulation, and novelty of uses. During the middle and later centuries of the millennium, sites of the Upper Delta will grow larger and be more classically "urban." Contemporaneous sites of the Méma will demonstrate a more voluminous iron industry. But the northern sites will always astound for their raw monumentality.

Mounds of the Lakes Region and Niger Bend

Late stone age peoples seem genuinely to have avoided even the permanent highland parts of the Lakes Region. After a decade of extensive regional surveys as part of the Malian government's Archaeological Sites Survey Program, we can be confident of only the most fleeting presence of non-iron using peoples.[1] Avoidance changes to excess after the first centuries AD. Only three[2] of the thousands of high Lakes Regions mounds have been excavated to modern, scientific standards, and not all of these down through all the deposits.

Mouyssam II (KNT 2)[3] is a good example. The site is rather modest for the region at 110 meters on its longest dimension. But it soars to 9.6 meters high! As at Jenne-jeno, slag and furnace parts abound in the earliest levels (AD fourth century), but soon drop out of the sequence. The change in blacksmiths' activity area must have evolved quickly, because the entirety of the mound's 9.6 meters accumulated during about four centuries (*c.*AD 300–680).[4] The build-up of deposits at another site west of Soumpi, Toubel,[5] was equally as rapid: over four meters from the fourth to fifth or early sixth centuries. We will see that Akumbu in the Méma repeats this pattern of rapid accumulation, but compare this with Jenne-jeno, where 5.6 meters accumulated over 1,600 years of continuous, intensive occupation. Jenne-jeno spread out; these sites went up.

---

[1] A handful of stone tools were collected from one of the putative "tumuli" near the Tondidaro megalithic field - Fontes et al., "Prospection," p. 41. There is a good size late stone age site, Mobangou, near Lake Faguibine – Mamadi Dembélé, "Les recherches organisées par la Division du Patrimoine Culturel," in Raimbault and Sanogo, *Recherches Archéologiques au Mali,* p. 66, and several late stone age sites (with ceramics reminiscent of Kobadi) in the Daounas depression – Michael Raimbault, "Prospection dans les Daounas et environs," in Raimbault and Sanogo, *Recherches Archéologiques,* pp. 203–9. See Mamadi Dembélé, *Entre Débo et Faguibine, Etude sur la Morphologie et la Typologie des Sites Archéologiques d'une Région Lacustre au Mali.* 3ème Cycle Thesis (Ecole des Hautes Etudes en Sciences Sociales; Paris, 1986), pp. 128–9.

[2] Mouyssam II (KNT 2) west of Soumpi, Kawinza (KWZ 1) on the east shore of Lake Kabara, and Toubel (GMB 1) also west of Soumpi. At Bangou Bongo (SMP 3) north of Soumpi, furnaces were excavated for metallurgical analysis.

[3] Michel Raimbault, "La fouille sur la butte de Mouyssam II (KNT 2), Campagnes de 1985 et 1986," in Raimbault and Sanogo, *Recherches Archéologiques,* pp. 185–9; Michel Raimbault and Kléna Sanogo, "Les données de la fouille sur la butte de Mouyssam II (KNT 2), Campagnes de 1985 et 1986," in Raimbault and Sanogo, *Recherches Archéologiques,* pp. 301–71; Dembélé, *Entre Débo et Faguibine,* pp. 165–93; C. Rolandq and Michel Raimbault, "Vegetation associated with the protohistorical mound of "Mouyssam II" (KNT 2) in the Malian Sahel," *Palaeoecology of Africa,* 23 (1992), pp. 57–66.

[4] Raimbault et Sanogo, "Les données de la fouille sur le butte de Mouyssam II," pp. 321–2; (but see Rolandq and Raimbault, "Vegetation," p. 60).

[5] Michel Raimbault, "La fouille sur la butte de Toubel (GMB 1)," in Raimbault and Sanogo, *Recherches Archéologiques,* pp. 410–12.

They built up very high indeed, and yet most remain of almost derisory area (or must have appeared so to a contemporary visitor from the Upper Delta). Of 56 sites in the Léré-Faguibine region for which mound height is given, 32 are over 10 m high (several recorded at 15 m) and 15 are 5 m or higher. Of 40 sites near Diré, eight equal or exceed 10 m in height and 11 equal or exceed 5 m. Raimbault complains that the height of sites he surveyed in the Daounas, averaging more than 7 meters, are disappointingly "more modest" than those of the rest of the Lakes region![6] It is the rare site, however, that exceeds what would be considered a site of modest area (say, 500 meters along an axis) in the Upper Delta or Macina. Lakes Region sites can, exceptionally, grow to behemoths: Arham-Jeno north of Diré weighs in at 100 hectares.[7]

Where the sites of the several parts of the Middle Niger do fall into accord with larger Middle Niger patterns is in their arrangements. Consistently, a respectable number of sites are single mounds. However, up to twice as many are comprised of paired sites (usually two higher-than-average mounds) or clusters of as many as ten. In the last case, as we saw in the Méma, smaller satellites are situated in orbit around one or two very high principals. Unfortunately, we do not know whether the small satellites are abandoned before the large mounds in clusters, as they tend to be in the Méma. Lacking systematic surface ceramic collections, we do not know whether all sites in a cluster were occupied simultaneously, as they tend to have been in the Upper Delta. And we do not know when, in the course of occupation, the small, peripheral specialized iron smelting sites fissioned off of habitation mounds.[8]

We possess radiocarbon dates of varying conviction for the last

---

[6] Léré-Faguibine in Dembélé, "Les recherches organisées", pp. 69–80; Diré in Samuel Sidibé, "Reconnaissances archéologiques aux environs de Diré" in Raimbault and Sanogo, *Recherches Archéologiques,* pp. 199–202; Daounas in M. Raimbault, "Prospection dans les Daounas et environs," in Raimbault and Sanogo, *Recherches Archéologiques,* p. 205. Note, however, that low mounds (and superficial scatters in particular) are very probably underrepresented in these surveys designed to find "important" sites (that is, sites known to informants, recorded in the oral traditions, or most visible).

[7] Pascal Schmit, *Les Sites de Buttes de la Région de Diré (Mali).* D.E.A. Thesis (Université de Paris I: Paris, 1986), p. 9.

[8] For example, in the most systematic survey (of the Diré region) one-third of the habitation sites have furnaces and slag exposures, but the four sites with furnaces have those features removed at a distance of several dozen meters from the inhabited precincts – Pascal Schmit, *Sites de Buttes,* p. 29.

levels of half a dozen sites; abandonment is in some cases as early as the late seventh to late eighth centuries (KNT 2 and Toubel). But the epoch of serious demographic shift (apparent precipitous decline) came between the early tenth and twelfth centuries. The happiest days for the peoples of the Lakes Region coincided with Jenne-jeno Phases III and early IV, a time in the Upper Delta of great prosperity and social change. There are some human-induced ecological hypotheses for the decline of the Lakes Region – deforestation due to high-volume ceramic production[9] or general vegetation decline due to over-grazing by goats.[10] Whatever the cause, and on present imperfect data, the causes of significant demographic stress (or reorganization) appear in the Lakes Region some centuries before the Upper Delta.

We can think of no climatic or hydrological reason why the Lakes Region should not have seen its first colonists as early as Dia or Jenne-jeno. It does appear that first occupation was delayed as much as a half millennium in the vicinity of the left bank lakes. (For lack of basic survey, we know virtually nothing about who might have been showing interest in the right bank lakes and in the duneland of the Bara.) The earliest history of the Niger Bend supports this general picture. Nothing even approaching Upper Delta Phase I/II fineware has ever been reported from the many surveys and several colonial or later, more professional excavations. But by the later part of the first millennium, when population density was highest around the lakes, we witness the dawn of oral traditions of great states and paramount kingdoms (Ghana, Takrur, Soso, and Méma), and of the little polities (one yearns to call them statelettes) spun off from them. But before looking at the monuments that may give the archaeological side of the historical transformations of Lakes Region society, let us travel north and east.

The Niger Bend has never been as extensively surveyed for sites. But the two sectors, and the town of Timbuktu itself,[11] for which we have information were recorded fully, without regard for size of site or for the abundance or splash of the surface materials, or for geographical placement. Like the Jenne region, the Niger Bend

---

[9] Rogier Bedaux and Michel Raimbault, "Les grandes provinces de la céramique au Mali," in Réunion des Musées Nationaux, *Vallées du Niger*, p. 280.

[10] Rolandq and Raimbault, "Vegetation," p. 65.

[11] Pers. com., Tim Insoll, 1997; also, Raymond Mauny, "Notes d'archéologie sur Tombouctou," *Bulletin de l'Institut Français d'Afrique Noire (B)*, 14 (1952), pp. 899–918.

around Timbuktu has suffered abandonment as the historian's orphan.[12] Timbuktu has, of course, been the object of the most languid romanticism.[13] Because of the associated legends of great wealth, it became the magnet for European penetration into the heart of West Africa. The legends and local histories[14] recognized Timbuktu as the sister-city of Jenne in the riverine trade, the place where 60–ton displacement cargo boats off-loaded gold for the trip north by camel and onloaded salt and the finely worked metal and sacred Islamic manuscripts for the four-day voyage to Jenne.

However, the same source that celebrated the blessings brought to Timbuktu by Jenne did the town a disservice by too firmly linking its fortunes to the trans-Saharan trade. Es-Sa'di (himself an Imam of the Friday mosque at Timbuktu) and historians to follow composed a standard history that had Timbuktu in a marginal zone between the two earliest Saharan commercial zones. This standard treatment of the gold trade focussed on the routes between Awdaghost and Ghana to the west and Tadmekka and Gao-Koukia to the east.

In this received history, the Middle Niger would not come into its own until the opening of the Akan gold fields in the thirteenth or fourteenth century.[15] Timbuktu would remain a peripheral summer camp of the Toureg until as late as the fifteenth century, when it replaced Walata as the southern terminus of the newly expanded Teghaza and Taoudenni salt route. This late reconstruction retarded archaeological interest in the whole of the Niger Bend. Arab chroniclers and travelers, since al-Bakri and Idrisi in the eleventh and twelfth centuries, had detailed trade caravan itineraries that stopped at important towns, Awgham, Safankû, Tirekka, Bûghrat – most likely located along the Niger Bend.[16] But the idea has stuck that Timbuktu functioned late and for all times as a "port city," isolated on a

[12]   S. and R. McIntosh, "Archaeological reconnaissance, Timbuktu," pp. 302–5.
[13]   Eugenia Herbert, "Timbuktu: a case study of the role of legend in history," in *West African Culture Dynamics* B. K. Swartz, Jr. and Raymond E. Dumett (eds.) (Mouton: The Hague, 1980), pp. 431–54.
[14]   al-Sa'di, *Tarik'h es-Sudan*, p. 22–3.
[15]   Cissoko, *Tombouctou*, p. 23 and E. Saad, *Social History of Timbuktu* (Cambridge University Press: Cambridge, 1983), p. 31; John Hunwick, *Shari'a in Songhay: The Replies of al-Maghili to the Questions of Askia al-Hajj Muhammad*, (Oxford University Press: London, 1985), p. 16.
[16]   J. M. Cuoq, *Recueil des Sources Arabes Concernant l'Afrique Occidentale du VIIIe Siècle* (Editions du Centre National de la Recherche Scientifique: Paris, 1975), pp. 105–6.

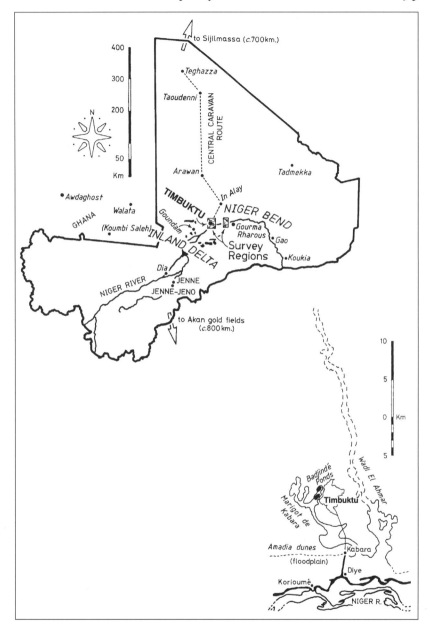

Map 8.1   *Timbuktu and Gourma Rharous surveys*

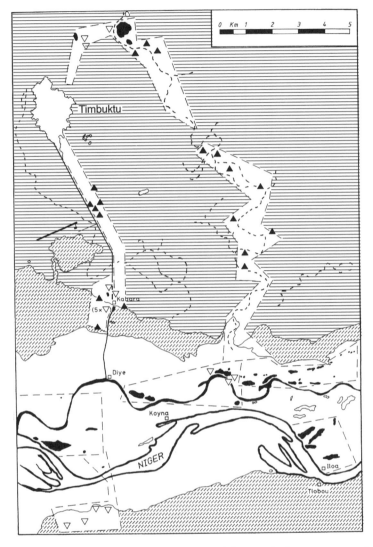

Map 8.2 part 1: *Sites and landforms of the Timbuktu survey region.*

Sahelian shore of the great desert, hanging onto existence by a golden thread of short historical length. Archaeological survey cautions us, once again, to be skeptical of documents pertaining to rich cities that, in later times, become highly contested political prizes.

Survey covered two segments of the Niger Bend: 260 km² of floodplain, degraded dune apron, and palaeochannel (the lower 13 kilometers of the Wadi El Ahmar) cutting through dunefields east

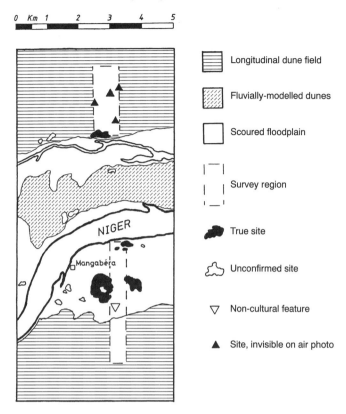

Map 8.2 part 2:   *Sites and landforms of the Gourma Rharous survey region.*

and south of Timbuktu and 50 km² about 90 kilometers down-stream near Gourma-Rharous. There have been no excavations to anchor the chronology of surface materials from the astonishing number and variety of sites discovered.[17]

This was not an area of particular interest to late stone age peoples. Early iron age sites with ceramics with indisputable affinities to Upper Delta Phase I and II wares (the Niger Bend Early period, which we guess to be 500 BC to AD 500) are small, rarely built-up to any appreciable degree, and are almost exclusively found in the channel of the major palaeochannels. Sites of this period probably represent tiny, still-semisedentary communities attracted to the seasonal streams or surface ponds. Then, as early as mid-first millennium, things explode.

[17] S. and R. McIntosh, "Archaeological reconnaissance, Timbuktu," pp. 305–17.

Seventeen of the 33 Timbuktu-vicinity sites and all ten sites downstream have surface ceramics with clear affinities to pottery found at Upper Delta sites dating to the mid-first millennium to early second millennium. These Niger Bend Middle period sites can sometimes be simple surface scatters. But the majority in both survey regions were of significant accumulation, of great density of surface artifacts, and could be very large in area. Five Timbuktu region sites were larger than 10 ha. Most of these were on the bank of the El Ahmar, where the largest surface scatter (Wadi-3) was greater than 50 ha.(little vertical accumulation) and another full-blown *tell* (Wadi-13) was 24 ha. This last site, of course, is where our observer for several historical imagination chapter stands. Perhaps more surprising, near Gourma-Rharous where the floodplain has contracted to a few kilometres, dune-side and floodplain sites are permanent, built up to significant heights (implying some length to the occupation), and are very large. A Gourma-Rharous clustered pair were 47 and 19 hectares!

Clearly, by mid-first millennium, the flood and palaeochannel hydrologies had changed for the better. More land along the floodplain flanking degraded dunes had been put to crops. The El Ahmar had emerged from a senescent state during the 300 BC to AD 300 desiccation to enjoy flow for several months of each year (or even to be permanent during the best decades). The source of all this water was a higher Niger flood. The beneficiary was the network of interdunal ponds and rejuvenated lakebeds of the southern Azawad. For at least 30 kilometers north of Timbuktu, Togola and Jacobberger[18] found an unexpected density of superficial, but extensive post-late stone age (probably Middle period) sites crowding the mid-slope fringe of nearly every interdunal depression. Even the long-dead southern Azawad had its final day in the sun (or rather, would soon thereafter have too many days to bleach in the sun). Presumably the lesser palaeochannel along which modern Timbuktu is found, the Marigot de Kabara, was similarly recharged. The foundation of the present town may have been at the turn of the first millennium, if not earlier.

These picked-over sites tell little of the occupations of their inhabitants. We know from the ceramics that communities of the Timbuktu hinterland had commercial contacts with the Upper Delta during the first millennium AD. The inhabitants of the Gourma-Rharous vicinity were much more closely allied to the Songhai city of Gao. The size and density of sites suggests a very

---

[18] Téréba Togola and Patricia Jacobberger, pers. com.

large population that could probably feed itself (which the inhabitants of Timbuktu could not do in historical times). The vast smelting slag exposures adjacent to these sites indicates both that there was greater market for iron and that rainfall had to have increased enough to keep the smiths in fuel, at least for a while. Again we have to ask: Why were the smiths electing to carry out their smelts in a region lacking in ore and marginal, at best, in terms of the slow-growing, slow burning tree species preferred for charcoal-making? The smiths' decisions were not based upon conventional optimizing economy; were they based upon the sacred and the occult?

The transformed social dynamics of the Middle Period Niger Bend are best seen in comparison with what happens after the sixteenth or seventeen century, at latest. Population implodes towards Timbuktu town and perhaps drops off significantly. It is difficult to say how much of this change is due to climatic deterioration or how much is due to the increasingly unsettled political and ethnic situation. The contrast, however, is between the later isolated, "port" function of the city and Timbuktu's earlier status as just one of many large settlements in a regional settlement hierarchy.[19] Not only were these town-like in size, they were clustered in the now familiar Middle Niger manner. The 24 ha. site (Wadi-13) far up the El Ahmar not only commands the point at which the palaeochannel flows into a field of ponds and dendritic *marigots*. It not only commands the last leg before Timbuktu of the camel route from the salt sources. It also commanded a galaxy of five satellite sites in near orbit. Here along the Niger Bend we have only the sketchiest information on why urbanism developed. We must return to Jenne-jeno to understand the process in detail.

Mature Jenne-jeno

When we left the Jenne-jeno region in chapter 6, it was with the lament that we have little knowledge of which satellite sites were occupied before mid-first millennium. There are just too many sites with later deposits that cover deeply interred earlier material. The picture of regional settlement and the evolution of the central settlement itself comes into better focus after that date. The most recent (1996–7) excavations show that, by the end of the earliest

---

[19] S. and R. McIntosh, "Archaeological reconnaissance, Timbuktu," pp. 317.

two phases of occupation, the western (Senuba-side) periphery is occupied. Soon after the turn of the Present Era, Jenne-jeno is at 25 ha. or more.[20] By the end of this occupation phase (Phase III: AD 400–850), Jenne-jeno and nearby Hambarketolo have begun to merge and together are 41 ha. Jenne-jeno is fully one kilometer long north to south.

This is the time of greatest depth of deposits and most generous yield of exotic items, diversity of local manufactures and ceramic heterogeneity, a situation that archaeologists label a "positive demographic period."[21] This is a classic understatement. At its heyday of *c.*AD 800–900, occupation covered the entire Jenne-jeno mound. At least three-quarters (and perhaps all) of the 69 satellites in a 4 km radius vicinity were occupied as well. Archaeologists have any number of estimators of population – site size, numbers and size of houses, size of necropoli – and are happy with none of these. Conservative estimates of between 7,000 and 13,000 persons for Jenne-jeno and between 15,000 and 27,000 for that site plus the 25 satellites within a one-kilometer radius just begin to tell the true story of mid-to-late first millennium population density.[22] If most of the *tells* of the Urban Cluster were occupied simultaneously, the total occupied area could have been in excess of 190 ha. A conservative guess might put total population at 42,000. Complicating matters is the result of the coring programme at modern Jenne: the settlement at the close of the first millennium might have added another 45 ha. to that total. Is an estimate of 50,000 persons an unreasonable *minimum* for the Urban Cluster at its moment of greatest prosperity?

Phase III is defined partially by the addition to the stable Upper Delta ceramic corpus of distinctive carinated pots, an increase in the size and diversity of vessels, new types of cooking pots (cuisine may change from baking and grilling to a new interest in stews and boiled grains), and a high incidence (20–50 percent) of black-and-white or geometric polychrome painting, especially superimposed over channels. There is a fascinating addition. A geometric white paint on red slip marks a pottery made clearly for conspicuous consumption. This was the elite ware of its day, because the paint was applied after firing and would disappear if ever washed. A new

---

[20] S. McIntosh, *Excavations*, pp. 61–4. The most recent excavations are as yet unpublished (these data are from the units TK and CP-2).
[21] Butzer, *Archaeology*, pp. 90–1.
[22] S. McIntosh, *Excavations,* pp. 374–7; S. and R. McIntosh, "Cities without citadels," p. 633.

prosperity and confidence is marked by the exuberance of these new wares. More interesting still: these "fugitive-paint" wares are everywhere on the mound, not just concentrated in the homes of the elite. And contrary to other early cities with rigid social ranking, all the skeletons from this time show robust good health.

An evolving cosmopolitanism is marked by the increase in the overall heterogeneity of all artifacts and by the addition of new practices. We now find the import of exotic beads and metals, public works such as the building of a 2 km long, 3.6 metre wide city wall, burials in a variety of postures (but especially in large urns either in residential quarters or in separate cemeteries), building houses of cylindrical mud brick, use of terracotta brick, decorative plaques, and the construction of pavements of potsherds.[23] It is the period of greatest influences (two-way, to be sure) to other parts of the Middle Niger and beyond. Phase III ceramics, urns, architecture, and the city wall at Dia are identical to those at Jenne-jeno. So are the ceramics of Tiebala, 20 kilometers off the floodplain to the south.[24] The pottery of the late first millennium sequences of KNT 2, Toubel and KWZ 1 in the Lakes Region and on the surface of Middle Period sites around Timbuktu are not as identical in assemblage composition, but are surely close enough to say that contact was intensive, sustained, and mutually beneficial.

Palaeoclimatologists tell us that rainfall increased from AD 300 to about AD 700 to something on the order of +20 percent of the 1930–60 average. The minor pluvial lasted until AD 900–1000. Climate was generally wetter until 1200, but West Africa had by then entered a phase of unpredictability and oscillation – and hence of great stress. Perhaps this is a contributing explanation for the changes in site and region that we begin to see at the Phase III/IV transition. The inhabitants of Jenne-jeno and of Dia build massive city walls (as defense against others or against wildly fluctuating flood levels?). While Jenne-jeno is not abandoned for several centuries yet, there are new thick levels of ash, house levelings and disruptions of domestic quarters that had been stable for nearly a millennium before. One has to be receptive to the idea of new, and less pleasant social and political realities.

The settlement is not dying. At the beginning of Phase IV (AD 850 to 1400), the Upper Delta should not be confused with Dia –

---

[23] Susan McIntosh, *Excavations at Jenne-jeno*, pp. 154–6, 215–16, 364–8.
[24] Phillip Curdy, *Tiebala, Mali: Etude de la Céramique*. Diplôme d'Archéologie Préhistorique, (Université de Geneve: Geneva, 1982).

poor prophetic Dia. Dia was the first in the Middle Niger to glory, but also the first to show the demographic agonies that will take a few centuries to overtake other areas. There is still a vigorous population at Jenne-jeno. Trade and artisan production is still expansive. There is a confident resistance to "North African" influences, the oil lamps and glass weights, *gargoulettes* (water bottles) and occuli (eye) design on the pottery, that sweep areas like the Middle Senegal and southern Saharan Teghdoust and Koumbi Saleh. But change is in the air. A new ceramic enters the sequence: fine channeled and impressed ware often with stamping, or humans or animals appliquéd on clearly non-domestic pots, as well as a decline in painting. There is an explosion of terracotta statuary.

After about AD 1100, contraction sets in. The peripheries of Jenne-jeno are abandoned or set to funerary or "ritual" uses. A more densely compacted population in the central residential quarters indulges in a flurry of building and tearing down of houses (in one unit, three houses are razed sequentially in the course of 100–200 years). Influence to areas outside the Upper Delta diminishes in subtle ways. Indeed, these areas, too, are in decline. Most of the Lakes Region sites have long been abandoned (or are in a secondary, sporadic occupation) and the Niger Bend and Méma are depopulated by c.AD 1300. There is rapid rural depopulation in the Jenne-jeno hinterland after AD 1200. This decline of population is accompanied by a shift in focus of occupation, from deep basins (rice lands) to the highland dunes and sand levees now favored by (Bambara?) millet growers. By AD 1400 Jenne-jeno and its satellites are just a recent memory.

Whereas we once believed that the population shifted from Jenne-jeno and its satellites to the present town of Jenne, it is now more likely that population was in very real decline. We once followed the local oral traditions in the belief that Jenne-jeno and Jenne were successive. After the coring programme at Jenne, however, when it became clear that much or most of that town's area was occupied simultaneously with later Jenne-jeno, we just have nowhere to put the refugees from the prehistoric sites. Perhaps there was a mass migration out of the Upper Delta, for which we have no traditions. Perhaps these refugees were the founders of sites on the eastern border of the Middle Niger, such as the eleventh to seventeenth century mounds of Galia and Doupwil.[25]

[25] Bedaux et al., "Recherches archéologiques," 91–220; Bedaux, et al., "L'archéologie entre," p. 42; see Fontes et al., "Prospection de sites," pp. 32–4.

Why this severe demographic decline or reshuffling? There is no evidence here or in the Ghana heartland of a political and social catastrophe in the form of the long hypothesized Almoravid "conquest"[26] of the late eleventh century. These are still the centuries of archaeology and oral tradition, before documentary sources gain our full confidence. But the story these diverse sources tell of the early centuries of the present millennium for the drier parts of West Africa as a whole is one of growing warfare and slave raiding (certainly in the Middle Senegal, but no evidence yet here in the Middle Niger), of changes to family structure and land rights (due to conversion to Islam or the effects of slaving), of migrations (recall the martial Bambara and Fulani, who are beginning to trickle into the Middle Niger) and of new forms of social stratification.

The Middle Niger was immune to none of these later changes. These will be put in a context of climate change in chapter 10. Before trying to understand the politics of decline, we need to return to what was perhaps the stellar contribution to West African prehistory by the Middle Niger. That is a precocious, indigenous, and highly individual form of urbanism.

Precocious Urbanism

Why can one presume to call Jenne-jeno a city? Until research began in the 1970s, many would have thought it preposterous to speak of Middle Niger urbanism, in any form, as early as the mid-first millennium. We face a paradox. Cities and towns are home to a heterogeneous population and have usually been called fully urban only when evidence is unambiguous of monumental (elite) architecture (city walls, palaces, temples) and of the privileged classes who had extraordinary power over the lives of the majority of inhabitants. Even very recent syntheses of the founding conditions of urban society are (from an africanist's perspective) obsessed with their presumed *sine qua non* of centralized, redistributive economy directed from above: "I consider an urban society as one with complex division of labor, that is, the existence of specialists in activities different from the production of subsistence goods; with

---

[26] S. McIntosh, *Excavations,* pp. 10–18; Pekka Masonen and Humphrey J. Fisher, "Not quite Venus from the waves: The Almoravid conquest of Ghana in the modern historiography of Western Africa," *History in Africa,* 23 (1996) pp. 197–231.

institutions that coordinate economic processes; and finally, with specialists in decision-making that live in an urban center providing specific services to the surrounding region, such as the distribution of a large variety of goods."[27] Yet, increasingly, archaeologists in Mesopotamia, along the Nile, in northern China have found that these criteria render invisible the all-important *circumstances* of development, the many centuries leading to these artifacts of a later aspect of urbanism. The earliest cities are best revealed, paradoxically, not (solely) by what is happening in the city, but by its relations with the countryside. That is why systematic regional survey is critical.

The best surveys are a mix of the intensive (concentration on the immediate vicinity of the city) and the extensive (a large region, ideally covering the entire territory or hinterland of an ancient city). Both are searched fully or sampled in such a way that all types of sites, the true proportions of sites of different types, and the placement of sites by landform are known. Without the extensive survey one never knows the regional ecological and social context, the "macro-dynamics" of the city's evolution. Without the intensive there will always be questions about why the city was located there in the first place and what were the sustaining advantages of its placement. The extensive survey of the Jenne-jeno hinterland covered 1,083 km² north, west, and south (deep into the Pondori rice basin, the dunes and high levees, and the *bourgou-serro* land to the north). There are 404 sites (predominantly floodplain) in a region now with 48 villages overwhelmingly located on the 7% of the region permanently above annual flood.[28] All 69 satellites within a 4 km radius around Jenne-jeno were recorded during the intensive survey.[29]

A complementary, overlapping extensive survey of some 2,000 km² to the north and east of this Jenne-jeno hinterland revealed a consistent density of sites (834 in total.)[30] These surface finds data

[27] Quote from Linda Manzanilla, "Early urban societies: Challenges and perspectives," in *Emergence and Change in Early Urban Societies*, Linda Manzanilla (ed.) (Plenum Press: New York, 1997), p. 5; the intellectual history of how we have looked at the early city is developed in Roderick McIntosh, "Early urban clusters" and "Western representations of urbanism and invisible African towns," in S. McIntosh, *Beyond Chiefdoms*, (forthcoming).

[28] S. and R. McIntosh, *Prehistoric Investigations*, II, pp. 346–432.

[29] Roderick McIntosh, "Early urban clusters," pp. 203–6. The 1994 survey will be published with the results of the 1996–7 excavations at Jenne-jeno.

[30] Dembélé, et al., "Prospection des sites archéologiques," pp. 218–32; Bedaux et al., "L'archéologie entre," pp. 41–53.

are in accord with that of the Jenne-jeno hinterland survey: 70 percent of sites have funerary urns; 69 percent have slag although only 3 percent have surface furnaces; differences in occupation can be inferred by relative presence of objects such as spindle whorls (weaving) or fishing net weights; and only 6 percent of all sites have tobacco pipes (presumed to have been introduced a few centuries after Phase IV closes in about AD 1400). The Dutch team conducting this survey also test-excavated two sites, Ladikouna on the Bani and the 6.9 meter-high Diohou. The lowest levels of the latter yielded the fineware ceramics so diagnostic of the earliest occupation of Dia and Jenne-jeno and, surely suggesting regional integration and long-term economic contact. The ceramics and settlement form are similar over the surveyed half of the Upper Delta.

Similar, but not uniform: the regional trends towards clumping and accommodation of diverse communities are intensified in the immediate vicinity of Jenne-jeno. Settlement density was far higher than today, at least at the Phase III/IV transition (one or two centuries either side of the turn of the present millennium). This settlement maximum happens just before a wave of abandonment began on the deep soils most removed from Jenne-jeno and continued until even that focal site lost its last inhabitant. From the height of deposits it would appear that the vast majority of near and far sites were founded by mid-first millennium (if not significantly earlier). But confirmation of that suspicion awaits excavation.

Ancient sites are strongly clustered (be they rural or within sight of Jenne-jeno), whereas modern villages are isolated (87 percent) or, exceptionally, paired ethnic hamlets. Of the 404 sites in the western Jenne-jeno hinterland, 23 percent of ancient sites are isolated, 62 (15 percent) sites are paired and the remaining 62 percent cluster in 47 groups of up to 16 satellites. Clustering intensifies as one approaches Jenne-jeno. Indeed, the division into separate clusters of the shotgun distribution of sites within the 4 km radius is a rather arbitrary exercise. The overwhelming impression from the surface ceramics is that sites within clusters near or far from Jenne-jeno were occupied simultaneously, and not sequentially. Again, only excavation of many, many sites will tell.

How do we explain these patterns? In the first place, the early abandonment of deep basin soils and remote channel-side hamlets may be related to the onset of violent and unpredictable floods, alternating with years of insufficient inundation. This is a subject to which we will return in chapter 10. Briefly, the resulting strangulation of channels and beginning of deep incision by the consolidated *marigots* would, in very short order, have changed the floodplain hydrology. Security concerns cannot be dismissed. The prosperous population of Jenne-jeno might have proved attractive to predators as yet unspecified (in oral traditions as in hard evidence). Oral traditions claim that old settlements were abandoned because they were polluted by pagan practices. Many are still recognized as the home to spirits loathed (or thought best avoided) by those newly converted to Islam.

However, the greatest survey surprises have to do with the size distribution of sites and with the nature of occupations represented on the surface of sites crowded about Jenne-jeno. Geographers working in many parts of the world in which indigenous urbanism can be documented have remarked upon a formulaic or predictable relationship between the size (that is, population) of a settlement and its rank within a city's territory.[31] Before urbanism, the landscape is populated by villages of roughly the same size. Each sports roughly an equivalent population doing roughly the same things. But as an urban region matures, sites can be placed on a logarithmic plot (log-log) – settlement rank (largest = number 1; second largest = number 2, and so on) against the log of population (in the case of archaeological sites, site area) – and a straight line is produced.

This relationship of size to rank in an economically and administratively mature urban territory is observed so frequently that the rank–size distribution is accepted as an urban signature. Curiously, it obtains for the ancient sites of Jenne-jeno's immediate hinterland, but beyond about a 4–kilometer radius (still Jenne-jeno's hinterland), the site sizes become more uniform and much smaller. Throughout the extensive survey regions, we also see the corollary effect that sites higher in the rank–size hierarchy will have on their surfaces evidence of a more heterogeneous population producing a greater diversity of goods for distribution down the regional system to their rural neighbors.

These lines of evidence support a claim for full Upper Delta urbanism by mid-first millennium AD. The same can be said for the Macina (Dia, amongst others?) and probably also for the Méma.

---

[31] B. J. Berry, "City size distributions and economic development," *Economic Development and Culture Change* 9 (1961), pp. 573–87; P. Haggett, A. Cliff and A. Frey, *Locational Analysis in Human Geography* (Wiley and Sons: New York, 1977); Rank-size in the Upper Delta is explained in S. McIntosh and R. McIntosh, "Cities without citadels," pp. 625–7.

Still, the process is best known for Jenne-jeno: the principal site had grown enormously and was populated by a dynamic population engaged in many industries, many crafts, and services. The manufactures of the principal town (or the style of ceramics, metal goods, terracotta items of functional and sacred uses) were spread widely throughout the region. The hierarchical distribution of settlements in this urban region implied a long history of integration, exchange, and prosperity. (At some point we will have to explain the Upper Delta twist on the rank–size rule: that only that part of the hinterland immediately focussed on the town displays the classic strength-line distribution, yet the entire region shows the classic homogeneity of economic integration.) With foods grown and gathered to surplus and with artisanal prosperity came high population densities. It is very likely to this period that es-Sa'di[32] referred (contrasting it to his own unsettled seventeenth century) when he wrote that 7,077 villages surrounded Jenne, and that

> If, for example, the sultan [Jenne-Weré] required the presence of an inhabitant of one of the villages near Lake Débo, his messenger would simply go to one of the gates of the city wall and, from there, cry out the summons. The people of village after village along the way would repeat the message, and so the summons immediately reached the concerned party, who hastened to the interview. Nothing further is required to show how heavily populated was the territory of Jenne in those days.

As mentioned briefly above, central to the claim of mid-first millennium urbanism is the nature of the goods and services provided by Jenne-jeno to its larger hinterland. Analysis of the components of the clustered satellites in the immediate vicinity shows a highly diverse population, doing highly diverse things. It supports a hypothesis of the emergence of clustering as a signature of Middle Niger urbanism[33].

The 80 artifact and feature classes recorded at contemporaneously occupied Jenne-jeno satellites occur in distinct patterns that provisionally imply specialist occupation of these sites by fishermen, weavers, peasant farmers, and blacksmiths. Others are occupied by those with access to imports and empowered to make or use items of a presumed ritual or sacred symbolism. Sites larger than 1.5 ha. usually have several crafts or subsistence occupations represented in the furnace parts, loom or net weights, copper pins or fragments of

[32] al-Sa'di, *Ta'rikh es-Sudan* (1900 edn), pp. 24–5.
[33] R. McIntosh, "Early urban clusters," pp. 203–9.

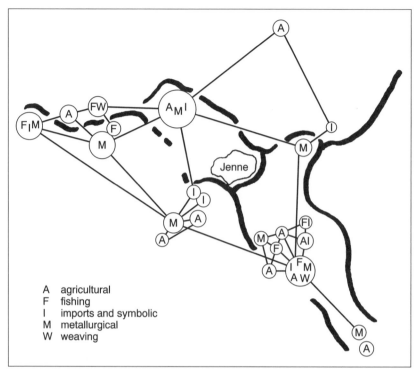

Map 8.3   *Clustered specialist settlements within 4 km of Jenne*

terracotta figurines recorded on the surface. Sites smaller than 0.5 ha. rarely demonstrate strong evidence of specialization. Medium-size sites (0.5–1.5 ha.), the majority in any Middle Niger cluster, show clear artisan or "ethnic" exclusivity. This tendency towards exclusivity is more pronounced if several medium size sites coexist within the same cluster. The intensive survey has revealed a hierarchy of very small peasant hamlets, modest but exclusively artisan-based or ethnic-based satellite villages and larger settlements where several specialists lived together. This near Jenne-jeno hierarchy is superimposed upon the more extensive urban region hierarchy.

The hypothesis for the evolution of clustering presumes that specialists have had a very long history of viewing themselves (and acting) as special interest groups. These groups, which anthropologists call corporate groups, define themselves in terms of shared activities (specifically, their craft or subsistence activity), a shared and usually mythological history, and ownership of shared property. In the modern city of Jenne, even today, several groups recall an origin from (and ritual ownership of) the satellite sites. An influential group of merchants claim origin from a site called Wangaradaga; several families of Somono smiths do likewise from Kongouso, four kilometers to the west. Membership in distinct corporate groups is reinforced by distinct dress, hairstyles, scarification, and the like. In the early first millennium AD, when population is growing and in the apparent absence of a coercive or despotic king or institutions that elsewhere keep the peace and reduce social tensions between an increasingly heterogeneous population, it is likely that the satellite sites come to serve as physical and symbolic property of the specialist groups. By living on separate mounds (or at least by claiming them), specialists can come together for the benefits of a larger market and to tap the services of others – and yet keep their separate identities. They can eat the cake of more-or-less equal status and, at the same time, savour the delights of city life. In this heterarchical spirit they will avoid the nasty (and signature) aspects of the eponymous early state (namely, centralized decision-making and enforced stratification).

This hypothesis rests upon frank speculation about the function of clustered elements, speculation that holds on present evidence, but could topple with expanded research at the satellite sites. Does the equation of specialists as corporate groups extend back sufficiently in time (to the late stone age perhaps)? Were relations amongst corporate groups essentially those of equals (as asserted in the traditions of Jenne, where the chief of the town (Jenne-Wéri) is a *primus inter pares* – first amongst equals – and the corporate heads of the masons, smiths, etc., retain enormous say over the day-to-day running of the city)? Whatever the fate of this particular explanation for its appearance, clustering came to be the dominating logic of settlement throughout the prosperous days of the Middle Niger.

This interpretation is based principally on the evidence from the Jenne-jeno hinterland, but the Méma and Lakes Region lend a novel slant. The chronology for these events is best in the Méma where, as we have seen, clusters of the mid-first millennium AD tend to be comprised of many small sites. We do not know whether these small satellites are already in orbit around a bigger focus, but it is likely that they were. By the second half of the millennium, however, abandonment of small habitation sites is complemented by the appearance of very large sites.[34] At several large clusters, one site only

[34] Togola, *Archaeological Investigations,* pp. 3.5–3.14; Togola and Raimbault, "Missions d'inventaire," pp. 87–92.

remains occupied through the Middle Period (e.g., Boundou Bougou Nord drops from 21 sites to one; Boundou Bougou Sud from 10 to one). Or, more exceptionally, clusters comprise a mere handful of medium to large sites and lack the swarm of tiny sites. One is left with the strong impression of population implosion and of a re-definition of the role of at least some satellites from habitation to special function (smelting appendage or funerary). Has population declined? Although far fewer in number, the later sites are far larger (now in the 10–20 ha. range). A few are exceptionally large: Taladié A, for which we have a fifth-century radiocarbon date is 80 ha.; Péhé is 30 ha.

It is tempting to extrapolate a similar trend from raw sizes of inventoried sites in the Lakes Region where, unfortunately, the chronology of site abandonment is non-existent.[35] The majority of sites are quite small (longest dimension between 50 and 150 meters). But perhaps two dozen inventoried sites reach 500 m long and a half dozen exceed Jenne-jeno in area (e.g., Arham-Djéno near Diré, estimated at 100 ha.).

Size, of course, does not a city make; very different occupation practices might have made the population density at a large Méma settlement, for example, far higher or lower than at contemporaneous Jenne-jeno. Diversity of population is a better marker of a site's place within an emerging regional settlement hierarchy. We have already looked at evidence of a heterogeneous population in the Jenne-jeno region in the form of diversity of occupations at the principal site and at nearby clusters. We close with a brief mention of two other proxy measures of that diversity, ambiguous though they may be: burial diversity and production in terracotta and small bronzes of free-standing and raised relief representations of animals and humans.

These particular proxy measures provide very inferential, highly indirect support for an interpretation of significant diversity in the Jenne-jeno population by the latter part of the first millennium. Burial practices and presumed ritual art are, frankly, a headache for the prehistorian. We possess many instances in prehistory in which one ethnic or kinship group considered itself a unity, and yet practiced a chaos of rituals and different ways to inter their dead. Yet, it is also reasonable to believe that the inhabitants of an overgrown village (under pressure loudly to protest their homo-

---

[35] See, esp. Schmit, *Sites de Buttes*, pp. 4–5, 9; Dembélé, "Les missions Léré – Faguibine."

geneity and solidarity in the face of increasing anomie) would not happily tolerate the degree of creative expression of burial postures and modes seen in Phase III and IV levels of Jenne-jeno.[36] The only rule that seems to apply is: no grave goods. From all the burials, only four iron bracelets and a tiny copper ring have yet been recovered. There is little variability of child and infant burials: all are in carinated pots, generally in domestic contexts. Often they are buried a few centimeters beneath house floors. However, adults might be buried singly, cremated, or in multiple in urns. Urn burial might be primary or a reinterment after a period sufficient for most connective tissue to have decayed. Inhumation outside of an urn may be in a variety of postures or in specialized cemeteries or residential quarters (as, indeed, can urn burials). It is admittedly a long leap from less than a score of burials to an interpretation of urban population heterogeneity, but the overall impression of diversity remains.

Just as different groups in a heterogeneous population can use differences in burial practices to mark their individual identities (as they might have used hairstyles, dress, scarification, etc.), so can differences or nuances in the ritual system act as a proxy measure of emerging urbanism. In this case, inference is heaped upon inference because the presumed ritual terracottas from Jenne-jeno[37] and a single case from Doupwil[38] are the only instances out of the hundreds (or thousands?) of fired clay statuettes with claims to be from the Middle Niger for which we possess chronological or contextual information. We now possess over 70 animal or human representations from Jenne-jeno. The majority are rather crude animals (presumed childrens" toys), but the arguably ritual production of free-standing human representations and snakes, headless humans and crocodiles in appliqué are recovered from an impressive array of contexts. Archaeologists find them buried in

---

[36] S. and R. McIntosh, *Prehistoric Investigations,* pp. 97–110; S. McIntosh, *Excavations* , pp. 66–8.

[37] Roderick J. McIntosh and Susan K. McIntosh, "Terracotta statuettes from Mali, *African Arts,* 11 (1979), pp. 51–3; R. McIntosh and S. McIntosh, "Dilettantism and plunder," pp. 49–57; S. McIntosh, *Excavations,* pp. 214–15, 370; Roderick J. McIntosh, "Just say shame: Excising the rot of cultural genocide," in *Plundering Africa's Past,* Peter R. Schmidt and Roderick J. McIntosh (eds.) (Indiana University Press: Bloomington, 1996, pp. 47–50.

[38] Rogier M. A. Bedaux, "Des Tellem aux Dogon: Recherches archéologiques dans la Boucle du Niger (Mali)," in *Dall'Archeologia all'Arte Tradizionale Africana,* Gigi Pezzoli (ed.) (Centro Studi Archeologia Africana: Milan, 1992), pp. 98–99.

Plate 8.1   *Terracotta statuette.*

the wall of a metal worker's atelier or house, buried in the floor of a purposefully razed house, in a rain-making altar, and thrown into the dump at the town's periphery after (purposeful?) mutilation . The variety of statuary styles and contexts may have signaled different beliefs and different identities for the various groups that commissioned and employed them.[39] Additionally, because most of the art dates from the last centuries of Jenne-jeno, it may mark a retrenchment or revitalization of traditional practices in the face of growing conversions to an Islam intolerant of representations of the human form.

This art has the potential to tell us so much about the beliefs and organization of the prehistoric populations, yet the hundreds languishing in museums and private collections or published in art

[39] R. and S. McIntosh, "Dilettantism and plunder."

historical catalogues are utterly mute on these issues.[40] All these pieces have been looted in what is arguably the single most massive destruction of archaeological sites anywhere in Black Africa. The act of looting rips these pieces from the stratigraphic context that would allow the prehistorian to reconstruct context of use or circumstances of deposition. Looting removes any possibility of accurate dating.

Undated and out of context, this art is mute on a host of issues that go beyond reconstruction of belief systems, one of which touches directly upon the art historian McNaughton's thesis that art can indeed show us the deep history of migrations, contact between distant peoples, trade and exchange of ideas. Many have remarked upon the general similarity of the Middle Niger terracotta styles and the wooden art of the Dogon of the eastern periphery,[41] or even at a far greater distance, certain aspects of Nok (central Nigeria) or "Sao" (Lake Chad) terracottas.[42] Under the circumstances of extreme abuse and destruction of this ritual and art evidence, conclusions about distant relations during the centuries of Middle Niger prosperity must rely upon data that is primarily economic. Much is the pity.

Distant Relations

The evolution of the Upper Delta cities' exchange and trade with other parts of the Middle Niger and with more distant lands was conditioned by the natural setting. These communities commanded a floodplain rich in staples (and in clay for pottery and terracottas). The floodplain was, however, absolutely lacking in other criticals, including stone, minerals and ores, salt, and fuel. The peoples of the Middle Niger responded by creating an early riverine network of commerce, with tentacles reaching to distant West African partners.

Again our most secure sequence of evidence comes from Jenne-

---

[40] E.g., Bernard de Grunne, *Ancient Terracota Statuary from West Africa*, (Université Catholique de Louvain: Louvaine-la-Neuve, 1980); Bernard de Grunne, *Divine Gestures and Earthly Gods. A Study of the Ancient Terracotta Statuary from the Inland Niger Delta in Mali.* PhD dissertation, Yale University, 1987; for a discussion of this issue, see a special issue of the art journal, *African Arts*, 28(4), Autumn 1995.

[41] Bedaux, "Des Tellem aux Dogon," pp. 99–100.

[42] Marla Berns, pers. com., 1985.

jeno, where the earliest colonists came with exchange relations already in place.[43] The site's lowest levels yield the slag that implies some volume of trade with ore sources at least 75 km distant (and purveyors of fuel, considering the climatic conditions?). Those sources were probably at the Bénédougou, along the eastern margin of the floodplain, the source of pre-smelted blooms until early in the present century.[44]

In those same levels one finds enormous numbers of sandstone grinders, rubbers, and hammerstones. They come in their hundreds and in such standardized shapes and sizes that it is a virtual certainty that they were manufactured to order at their source. The closest origins may have been the Bandiagara cliffs or lower Lake Débo sandstone hills. Materials sourcing methods may one day tell us if the commerce was at longer distances. What these materials were exchanged against we do not know. To what degree was there a reverse flow of the iron implements produced by Middle Niger smiths, first from locally smelted ores and, after *c*.AD 400, increasingly from blooms imported from the outside and worked in the new segregated ateliers at peripheries of communities? Perhaps most of the Middle Niger smiths worked for local markets. However, Boulel Ridge sites in the Méma have massive slag heaps of 30,000 m³ volume, Håland[45] interprets this volume of waste as evidence of short-term, intensive industrial production for export.

We can make a good guess that, featured prominently in the early trade, were the surplus staples – grains, smoked fish and meat, fish oil – with which the Upper Delta historically provisioned the Niger Bend and distant Sahelian and Saharan communities. René Caillié wrote of the trade in staples he witnessed first-hand in 1828:

> Timbuktu, though one of the largest cities I have seen in Africa, possesses no other resources but its trade in salt, the soil being totally unfit for cultivation. The inhabitants procure from Jenne everything requisite for the supply of their wants, such as millet, rice, vegetable butter, honey, cotton, Soudan cloth, preserved provisions, candles, soap, allspice, onions, dried fish, pistachios. Bousbehey and Toudeyni [Saharan towns] being only supplied with the grains which the merchants of Timbuktu receive from Jenne would of course be

[43] S. McIntosh, *Excavations*, pp. 246–7, 390–3.
[44] S. and R. McIntosh, *Prehistoric Investigations*, p. 19; Adria LaViolette, *An Archaeological Ethnography of Blacksmiths, Potters and Masons in Jenne, Mali (West Africa)*, PhD disseration, Washington University, 1987, pp. 133–4.
[45] R. Haaland, "Man's role," p. 42.

reduced to famine if the trade between these latter two cities should be interrupted.[46]

And we see already in a smattering of very early exotics the germ of first millennium AD prosperity. In the late centuries BC and first centuries AD, Jenne-jeno has access to beads and baubles of Saharan basalt, granites, quartzites, and to "Hambori marble" from south of the Niger Bend. Then there is the find of the curious Han-period Asian glass bead and a second pale-blue Hellenistic glass bead. It is most likely that these are incidental items in a low-volume trickle trade down the Sahara. Such a trade would have been necessary to provide Sahelian populations with precious salt and, increasingly with time, with other near invisible but highly valued items such as horses. The early development of this north–south trade is not at all surprising considering the natural latitudinal ecological zonation of West Africa.

At mid-millennium new items appear in the menu of exotics. There is a new organization to the production of other materials, and trade is voluminous. More Saharan stone turns up in excavations, but still in low numbers. What is the significance for hypotheses about distant trade relations of the apparent wide distribution through West Africa of one particular ceramic form? From as early as the sixth century (until perhaps the twelfth), three-footed or four-footed bowls are turning up from Mauritania (Koumbi Saleh) to Guinea, to Burkina-Faso and especially, in many Malian sites along the Niger and along the Bandiagara cliffs.[47] Have they spread by indirect diffusion or are they proxy evidence for a voluminous river and overland exchange network? Are these distinctive bowls just a first hint at a sub-continental exchange of elite or supercharged ritual objects, on analogy, for example, with the Hopewell Interaction Sphere of the Mississippi drainage?

Perhaps we will be able to say more in the near future about copper. The source of this new metal must have been at a considerable distance.[48] The nearest copper ores are at Gaoua, 350 km away

[46] René Caillié, *Travels Through Central Africa to Timbuktu and Across the Great Desert to Morocco: Performed in the Years 1824–1828.* 2 vols. repr. edn, (Colburn and Bentley: London, 1830), II, pp. 57–9.

[47] Bedaux and Raimbault, "Les grandes provinces," pp. 285–6.

[48] S. McIntosh, *Excavations,* pp. 384–90; Laurence Garenne-Marot and Loïc Hurtel, "Le cuivre: approche méthodologique de la métallurgie du cuivre dans les vallées du Niger et au Sud du Sahara," in *Vallées du Niger,* (Réunion des Musées Nationaux: Paris, 1993), pp. 320–3.

in Burkina Faso; the next after that are at Nioro-du-Sahel and Sirakoro over 500 km west of the Méma. Others known to have been worked in prehistoric times and still more distant are at Akjoujt in northern Mauritania, Gorgol Noir east of the Middle Senegal Valley, Tessalit along the upper Tilemsi Valley, and Azelik in Niger. Whatever the source, copper working goes through an evolution of alloying that reveals much about progress in production and changes in imports.

The earliest mid-first millennium Jenne-jeno copper is mixed with lead and arsenic. The metal is thus made more durable and malleable than native copper, but not so much as true bronze. Bronze, a true tin-alloy is cast on-site after *c*.AD 850 (evidence coming from bronze crucibles and moulds). By AD 1000 brass has made its way to the site from across the desert and it replaces bronze by the end of the sequence. Copper and its alloys turn up at many other Middle Niger sites of this period, as we will see when we next turn our attention in this chapter to the funerary monuments of the Lakes Region. Most significantly, however, copper-alloyed items dating to the last centuries of the millennium have quite different compositions (items from the Upper Delta (Jenne-jeno), the Méma (Akumbu, Kolima, Péhé), and Tegdaoust and Koumbi Saleh to the west in Mauritania). This is unexpected. These neighboring regions should have been included within the same trade and interaction sphere. Clearly, many different sources were being exploited simultaneously, and probably in some volume.

The other West African metal of high value and, later, sumptuary association was gold. It is not surprising that gold is rare in Middle Niger excavations. A single piece with a *terminus post quem* of AD 850–900 comes from secure context under the Jenne-jeno city wall. There are other ways to reconstruct the beginnings of long-distance trade in the metal. Garrard[49] argues that "it is not impossible that by the end of the third century a small, irregular supply of gold was becoming available [in North Africa] through trans-Saharan trade." If so, the earliest gold made its way north by way of the informal trickle trade one presumes was the source to the south of the Mediterranean glass beads, Saharan stone, and especially salt. Garrard goes on to argue from the appearance in North Africa of new currencies, taxes to be paid only in gold, and gold weighing systems that the gold trade becomes regular and quite

---

[49] Timothy F. Garrard, "Myth and metrology: The early trans-Saharan gold trade," *Journal of African History*, 23 (1982), p. 447.

significant in the fifth century. Still informally conducted, the Saharan commerce should best be considered an appendage to the voluminous exchange within the Middle Niger (demonstrated by the uniformity of ceramics and other artifacts of this period) and to contacts west of the Wagadou heartland of the Ghana kingdom and probably east down the Niger to Gao and beyond.

By the end of the millennium, the north–south offshoot of this more ancient, essentially east–west, Sahel–southern savanna exchange in commodities and small-scale luxuries[50] begins to exert its influence. Increase in production at source probably began by the fourth century. Those sources are far to the southwest (Bambuk, Buré) or south (Lobi or Akan fields) and it is not impossible that by mid-millennium, Soninké traders travelled annually to visit the wooded savanna and forest producers. This was the prototype of the later commercial networks of the itinerant *Dyula* (or Wangara) Soninké traders[51] that first has documentary mention in the fourteenth century. These same traders, who may very well already be calling themselves Wangara, inevitably come into contact with nomadic Berbers on the northern leg of their journey. This journey undoubtedly included a riverine passage through the Middle Niger. Perhaps they also made an obligatory visit to Wangaradaga, that near satellite of Jenne-jeno. The story of the transformation of this Saharan appendage of the ancient Middle Niger commodity exchange into the "Golden Trade of the Moors" that so excited European imaginations was a tale of one Berber or Arabo-Berber group after another wresting control of the Saharan routes from Soninké and other Berber rivals.[52] Integral to this transformation was the expansion to the north of markets for items such as kola and rare animal hides, in addition to gold. The greatly unappreciated element in this expansion of the trans-Saharan trade was the sad traffick in human souls.[53] North African, Berber Ibadism expands in the eighth century on the backs of enslaved peoples, as do the Ibadite

---

[50] Garrard, "Myth ", pp. 451–2; S. McIntosh, *Excavations,* pp. 390–2; cf., Jean Devisse, "L'or," in *Vallées du Niger,* (Réunion des Musées Nationaux: Paris, 1993), pp. 344–57.
[51] B. Marie Perinbaum, "Notes on Dyula origins and nomenclature," *Bulletin de l'Institut Fondamental d'Afrique Noire (B)*, 36 (1974), pp. 676–89; Philip D. Curtin, *Economic Change in Precolonial Africa* (University of Wisconsin Press: Madison, 1975), pp. 67–9; S. McIntosh, "Reconsideration," pp. 153–4.
[52] Cf., Brett & Fentress, *Berbers,* pp. 200–19.
[53] E. Savage, "Berber and blacks: Ibadi slave traffic in eighth-century North Africa," *Journal of African History,* 33 (1992), pp. 351–68.

commercial networks. The classic Golden Trade networks across the Sahara were in Ibadite hands. What relatively little we know about the earliest commercial relations slipped though the Ibadite wall of silence erected to maintain monopoly.

As the Saharan trade was reorganized (largely in Ibadite hands), new entrepôts (Awlil, Awqdaghust, Walata, Timbuktu, Tadmekka, Takedda) and new production centers (Taghaza, Taoudenni, Marandet) sprung up on the southern margin of the Sahara. The decline of Dia may in part have been caused by a post AD 500 devolution of the local hydrology, but was almost certainly also a response to these new commercial realities of a half-millennium later. The Dia-based Soninké trading clans realized the new potential of areas such as the Middle Senegal Valley, the vast plains between the Middle Senegal and the Middle Niger (especially Diara in the Diafunu and probably Koumbi Saleh in the Wagadou) and new river port towns along the Niger itself (Sansanding upstream of Jenne, perhaps Tirekka and Bughrat along the Niger Bend).[54] Foundation expeditions, in-migration to formerly sleepy outposts, abandonment of once proud cities such as Dia were parts of a millennium-long evolution of these distant relations of trade and exchange.

This second Soninké diaspora can be reconstructed, in the lamentable absence of archaeological fieldwork in pertinent places, only from the oral traditions. The Arab sources that celebrate the Saharan aspects of the trade (and that gave rise to the historical belief that the Golden Trade was imposed as late as the thirteenth century upon isolated, backwards tribes) only detail the commercial itineraries after the turn of the present millennium. By that time, the trans-Saharan graft onto the venerable Middle Niger trade had successfully taken. The new branch had a vigour all its own.

Of passionate interest for those Arab sources was the Island of Gold, the source of the desired metal south beyond the desert veil. To many later scholars, the Island of Gold refers to Bambouk and Buré, the gold workings at the Niger, Falemé and Senegal river headwaters. But a careful reading of the Arab descriptions and their cartographic details allows the alternative interpretation of the Island of Gold as *Bledd el Tibbr*, lands of gold, centers of the gold trade, where the metal was procured, amassed, and transshipped to a wider market.[55] Taking this interpretation, the description by

---

[54] S. McIntosh, "Reconsideration," pp. 154–7.

[55] Ibid., pp. 145–53.

al-Idrisi (1154)[56] of the Island of Gold, (the land of) Wangara, is a remarkably accurate portrait of the Middle Niger at the height of its prosperity:

> The country of the Wangara is a land of gold, celebrated for the purity and abundance of its gold. It is an island 300 miles long and 150 miles wide. The Nile [Niger] surrounds it on all sides throughout the year. In August, when the heat is extreme, the Nile covers the island, or at least the greater part of it, for the duration of the flood; then the waters begin to subside. Then, when the Nile has begun to fall, people from all the countries of the Blacks assemble at this island to look for gold during the days of the diminishing floodwaters. . . . Once the Nile has returned to its bed, the people sell the gold they have collected, trafficking among themselves. The greatest part is bought by the people of Wargla and Maghrib al-Aksa, who transport it to mints in their countries for striking into dinars. . . . The territory of the Wangara . . . contains celebrated places, the population is rich, the gold is abundant, and the merchandise imported by them comes from the furthest reaches of the earth.

If, in fact, the Middle Niger is the Island of Gold, then all that precious metal passing along its riverine byways poses one of those several challenges to historical orthodoxy that Africa loves to provide! Where are the elites and the emerging dynasties that should be maneuvering to monopolize this trade? Where are the states, with coercive police apparatus, that should be necessary to maintain the peaceful conditions for the expansion of trade? There is evidence from the Middle Niger of emerging social and political complexity before the turn of the present millennium. That evidence, however, turns on the unexpected.

Monuments and Emerging Polities

After the comprehensive economic and symbolic history of copper in sub-Saharan Africa by Herbert,[57] we should not be at all surprised by the lack of gold in the last class of sites of the prosperous millennium: monumental earthen burial mounds (tumuli) and megaliths. These monuments record several novelties recently appearing in Middle Niger society. From their size and apparent number, these

---

[56] Cuoq, *Recueil* , pp. 134–5.
[57] Eugenia Herbert, *Red Gold of Africa* (University of Wisconsin Press: Madison, 1984).

monuments represent the working of societies that can mobilize unprecedented amounts of labor for their construction. The only known earlier exceptions to the rule that communal engineering feats appear relatively late are the city walls at Jenne-jeno and Dia.

From the well-appointed principal burials in some, our natural first interpretation would be that the tumuli represent the efforts of communities in which an elite enjoyed unequal access to exotic items or to weapons. From the presence of multiple ritual murders (sâti) in some, these monuments might represent a society in which some had extraordinary control over the lives of others. But are these novelties enough to represent a political transformation to the true early state? In general archaeological theory, monumentality itself is often sufficient evidence of the centralizing tendencies and power-monopolization of the classic early state.[58] Monuments are, after all, the reinforcement to a class-enhancing or bureaucracy-celebrating state ideology – Thorkild Jacobsen's[59] "signposts to permanence" to over-awe a subjected population with a visual claim to god-given and posterity-promised right to rule with coercion.

Or, are the monuments of the Middle Niger just one of several wedges in the crack in that hoary theoretical edifice? Might there be alternative circumstances to explain their construction? Might they be more akin to the thousands of megaliths and tumuli of Senegal and The Gambia, where the prior condition of state formation is not at all certain? [60] We must always remember that, however grand and resource-wasteful, monuments are only a proxy measure of social condition. Might multiple political forms be expressed in the same material form? Similarly, are we justified in the *a priori* belief that the abundant copper and copper-alloy recovered from these monuments have already been successfully transformed from merely a rare exotic into the symbolic signifier, of a new order of power? This is the widespread socio-political function of Africa's red gold at the rise of the later, well-documented states of the Middle Niger's Imperial Tradition (chapter 10).[61] Are

[58] E.g., J. Friedman and M. Rowlands, *The Evolution of Social Systems*, (Duckworth: London, 1978), pp. 201–76; Brian Hayden, *Archaeology: The Science of Once and Future Things* (W. H. Freeman and Co.: New York, 1993), pp. 267–311, 331–6. Cf., R. McIntosh, "Early urban clusters," pp. 199–203.
[59] Thorkild Jacobsen, The *Treasures of Darkness* (Yale University Press: New Haven, 1976), pp. 180, 186.
[60] Susan McIntosh and Roderick McIntosh, "Field survey in the tumulus zone of Senegal," *The African Archaeological Review*, 11(1993), pp. 73–107
[61] Herbert, *Red Gold*, p. 302.

we there yet? The presence in the tumuli of copper (and iron) weapons, copper bracelets, rings, ornamental jewelry, and figurines is suggestive of a process by which the metal takes on a sumptuary and heightened power value. The skill of manufacture and "wasteful" consumption has traditionally suggested control over the artisans who work the metal. But has the state and this symbolic manipulation of copper for coercive control purposes really sprung out of an apparent political vacuum? Or do these monuments represent an earlier facet of a long development of centralized polities in the Middle Niger and neighboring lands?

The evidence is less persuasive than it might be, for emerging despotism or for alternative explanations. It is not always clear to some excavators whether their sites are true tumuli, erected for display, or high habitation mounds.[62] So, let us dive into that evidence, beginning with the Lakes Region megaliths. The most important, and most abused, of these is Tondidaro[63] on the banks of Lake Tagadji, 15 km northwest of Niafunké. The site is composed of three dressed-stone alignments (of 150, 50 and 30 stones respectively), two single monoliths, and two funerary mounds. The stones are of smoothed sandstone and many have a variety of incised or raised relief geometric designs (triangles, chevron, cross-hatching, circles, ovals) or figurations (sunburst, serpent, dagger, umbilici). Many are undeniably phallic in intent. The site was inexpertly scratched at during the earliest colonial years. Unfortunately, early recording was not done thoroughly enough to allow us now to reconstruct the position of the stones after they were utterly disturbed, and many carted away, during trenching in 1931–2 by a journalist for *l'Intransigeant*, Henri Clérisse.[64]

Frankly, it is hard to find anything nice to say about the man. He began the tradition of plunder for pleasure and cultural-heritage

[62] Dembélé, *Entre Débo et Faguibine*, pp. 144–58; M.Dembélé and M.Raimbault, "Les grandes buttes anthropiques," in Raimbault and Sanogo, *Recherches Archéologiques au Mali*; Schmit, *Sites de Buttes*, pp. 32–40.

[63] Alain Person, Mamadi Dembélé and Michel Raimbault, "Les mégalithes de la Zone lacustre," in Raimbault and Sanogo, *Recherches Archéologiques au Mali*, pp. 473–510; Fontes et al.; "Prospection de sites," pp. 37–41.

[64] Ibid., p. 39; Person et al., "Les mégalithes de la Zone lacustre," pp. 475–81; Henri Clérisse, "Les gisements de Tondidaro (Soudan Français) et les tumulis échelonnés le long du Niger de Niafunké au Lac Débo," *Actes du 15th Congrès International d'Anthropologie et d'Archéologie Préhistorique* (Paris, September, 1931), pp. 273–8; see various unpublished reports in the IFAN (Dakar) archives, drawer XV.4.MAL (Tondidaro).

Plate 8.2   *Tondidaro megalith field before its destruction at
the hands of Clérisse.*

rape as expression of the power of the civilized over the benighted
that continues today in the pillaging of Middle Niger terracottas
for the international art and antiquities trade. The site is now a
shambles. But it is impressive enough for Mauny[65] to deem it "West
Africa's most important centre of megalithism from the point of
view of scientific interest and of quality of stone-working" and for
recent researchers[66] to label the Lakes Region "one of African
megalithism's primordial zones."

The original alignments at Tondidaro are forever lost. The stones
were probably closely packed together in an ellipse of a very narrow
short axis. But we can make some general inferences about Middle
Niger megaliths. Unlike their counterparts in the Senegambia,[67] these
appear not to have been erected over burial sites. However, a sketch
map by Clérisse does mention three urns immediately east of his
trench into a bank of 300 (!) *phalliformes* megaliths. Were these

[65] Mauny, *Tableau Géographique*, p. 129.
[66] Person et al., "Les mégalithes de la Zone lacustre," p. 502.
[67] Gil Thilmans, Cyr Descamps, B. Khayat. *Protohistoire du Sénégal I: Les Sites
Mégalithiques*. Mémoire de l'Institut Fondamental d'Afrique Noire, no. 91 (1),
(IFAN: Dakar, 1980).

burial urns, which are as rare north of Lake Débo as they are common to the south, or were they simply big ceramic jars? Other megalithic arrangements are incompletely recorded. They are sometimes found in association with tumuli (Tondidaro, Kouga), but more often with habitation mounds. The majority recorded to date are on the left bank of the Niger, between Lake Tanda to the west, Faguibine to the north and Diré to the east. However, there is a major linear alignment of undressed megaliths c.10 km north of Korienzé in the eastern sector of the Erg of Bara (which remains the least explored of the all the Middle Niger basins).

The dating of these monuments remains difficult. The single radiocarbon date for the Tondidaro monuments, an AD seventh century date,[68] was obtained from charcoal near the isolated Tondidaro *mégalithe-polissoir* (large stone tool-sharpener) and may come from yet another context disturbed by Clérisse. The date does accord with seventh–ninth century dates obtained from the larger of two funerary tumuli (150 and 80 m diameter) with associated megaliths less than 100 m south of the Tondidaro megaliths (unfortunately, disturbed by no fewer than five of Clérisse's trenches). None of the 22 other reported megalithic sites are yet dated.

At present, funerary mound clusters are known from the Douentza (two fields of earthen and stone mounds, late stone age in date) and of later construction from the Lakes Region (Djim-Djim – 10 mounds, Goubo – 1 (?), Koï Gourrey (also known as Kili or Sinfassy) – ≥5, Kouga – 3, El Oualadji – 1, Tondidaro – 2).[69] The other dated tumuli are Kouga (cal AD 900–1250) and El Oulaladji (cal AD 1030–1120). Unfortunately, these dates represent one determination apiece from material that may but does not necessarily date to the moment of construction. The clusters can be quite complex. The Kouga site, in addition to tumuli of two size classes, has at least three habitation mounds, dressed and undressed megalithic arrangements, several deliberate stone piles resembling the ancient burial mounds of the Sahara (*basinas, tumulus pierriers*), and specialized metallurgical localities.[70] Lamentably, neither in the Kouga case (many types of sites clustered together), nor at Djim-Djim (clusters of many

---

[68] Person et al., "Les mégalithes de la Zone lacustre," p. 483.

[69] Fontes et al.; "Prospection de sites," pp. 263–4, 270.

[70] Mauny, *Tableau Géographique*, pp. 95–111; Dembélé, *Entre Débo et Faguibine*, pp. 115–16; Louis Desplagnes, "Etude sur les tumuli du Killi dans la région de Goundam," *L'Anthropologie*, 14 (1903), pp. 151–72; Piere Fontes, Mamadi Dembélé, Michel Raimbault, and Samuel Sidibé, "Prospection archéologique de

presumed true tumuli) do we know whether the clusters' components were erected simultaneously or sequentially over perhaps a great span of time.

In fact, El-Oualadji is unusual in its isolation from other tumuli or ancient settlements. The site was dug early (1904) and by an amateur, Lt. Louis Desplagnes[71] – who has put the lie to the claim that early colonial period research could not be conducted carefully (if not to modern standards of provenance recording) and with respect for the materials recovered (for only some of the material, to be sure). El-Oualadji has provoked extraordinary interest because of the similarity of Desplagnes' description of his finds to al-Bakri's eleventh-century description of the burial of kings of the Soninké kingdom of Ghana:

> Their religion is paganism and the worship of idols. When the king dies, they build a huge dome of wood over the burial place. Then they bring him on a bed lightly covered, and put him inside the dome. At his side they place his ornaments, his arms and the vessels from which he used to eat and drink, filled with food and beverages. They bring in those men who used to serve his food and drink. Then they close the door of the dome and cover it with mats and other materials. People gather and pile earth over it until it becomes like a large mound. Then they dig a ditch around it so that it can be reached only from one place. They sacrifice to their dead and make offerings of intoxicating drinks.[72]

Desplagnes describes the construction stages at El-Oualadji thus:

(1) Into the original sand of the left-bank dunes at the confluence of the Issa-Ber and Barra-Issa, the builders dug a depression and filled it with pounded clay, which was then covered with a bed of red sand.

(2) They constructed a southeast–northwest oriented, roughly oval funerary chamber (13 by 6.5 by 2.9 m high, of palm trunks

---

tumulus et buttes tumuliformes dans la région des lacs au Mali. Datations par le radiocarbone," *Comptes Rendus de l'Académie des Sciences de Paris, Série III.* 301 (5) (1985), pp. 207–12.

[71] Lt. Louis Desplagnes, *Le Plateau Central Nigérien.* (Larose: Paris, 1907), pp. 57–66; Louis Desplagnes, "Fouilles du tumulus d'El Oualadgi (Soudan)," *Bulletin de l'Institut Fondamental d'Afrique Noire (B),* 13 (1951), pp. 1159–1173; Annie M.D. Lebeuf and Viviana Pâques, Archéologie Malienne. Collections Desplagnes. Catalogues du Musée de l'Homme. Série C. Afrique Noire. no. 1. *Objets et Mondes,* 10 (3, supplement) (1970), pp. 1–55.

[72] Nehemia Levtzion, *Ancient Ghana and Mali,* (Methuen: London, 1973), pp. 25–6.

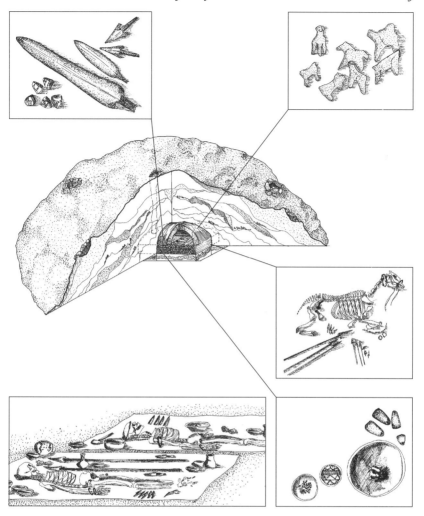

Figure 8.1 *Idealized tumulus and cross-section of El-Oualadji (Courtesy of Annatina Barbara Schneider)*

covered in mats or thatch and covered then by a fire-hardened envelop of clay.

(3) The bodies of two persons (whom Desplagnes interprets as a war chief and companion)[73] are interred (head to NE) on a bed of branches, with various vessels for food and drink, copper beads, bracelets, rings and ornaments, iron swards, knives,

[73] Desplagnes, *Plateau Central*, p. 62.

lance heads and arrowheads, beads of glass and semi-precious stone, bone needles and points.

(4) A 0.8m diameter pipe (*puits* or "well") leads from the eventual top of the tumulus, 10 m from the top of the funerary chamber, to penetrate the western side of the chamber and will be the conduit for sacrificial meals of beef, sheep, warthog (?), fish and tortoise in a "perpetuity" ritual.

(5) An unspecified number of food, material, and human sacrifices[74] were made, perhaps in succession much as an onion grows in layers, as the earth was heaped over the chamber to its final height of 12 meters above the surrounding dune.

(6) Finally, the surface of the mound was a patchwork of fire-hardened exposures (to retard erosion?) and "sacrificial hearths" that could reach 5 m in diameter.

Most interesting, but hard to interpret, are the patterns of artifact distribution. There appears to be a cardinal-point presentation of classes of materials offered in these ash-filled depressions: to the southeast, horses and their harnesses and ornamental trappings in iron and copper, along with many armaments, stone beads; to the west, terracotta beads and plaques, grindstones and groundstone axes; to the north, spindle whorls and arms and chunks of iron; to the east, much bone and seven terracotta figurines of humans and many of animals.

The El-Oualadji excavations leave many unanswered questions. To what degree is this cardinal-point orientation to sacrificed objects merely happenstance? Or is it a reflection of an ancient Middle Niger material culture *imago mundi*? To what extent had the copper and copper-alloy items assumed a special-power, sumptuary status? (Desplagnes[75] certainly regarded the copper-rich southeastern "hearth" to be the most important.) Desplagnes" description of El-Oualadji matches the much less satisfactory account by Clérisse[76] of the funerary chamber at Goubo (his descriptions of his Tondidaro tumuli probes are utterly unhelpful) and by Desplagnes[77] of a hurried excavation of one of the large Koï Gourrey tumuli. Mauny found no funerary chamber in his limited exposures into the small Kouga and Djim-Djim tumuli. Desplagnes, at one of the smaller Koï Gourrey

---

[74] Desplagnes, "Fouilles," p. 1172.

[75] Ibid., p. 1168.

[76] Mauny, *Tableau Géographique,* pp. 100–1; Rapport de Mission Clérisse, file XV.4.Mal. at IFAN, Dakar.

[77] Desplagnes, " Etude," p. 160.

tumuli, recovered 25–30 well-appointed skeletons (including children) in the center and a series of armed single and paired skeletons at various points in the earthen shell of the mound.

The excavators, colonial and recent, of these funerary monuments have been remarkably wary of over-interpretation. Desplagnes describes El-Oualadji as the burial of a warrior chief and Koï Gourrey as that of the women and captives of a local chief. In this Desplagnes is typical in resisting the temptation to follow al-Bakri and to call these royal burials. To do so would be to imply a state or advanced chiefdom with a fair degree of centralization. There is no need to go so far as to assume the presence of any political structure more complex than very local alliances of settlements (perhaps a prominent trade or production center and fissioned off daughter communities, or an autonomous town such as Jenne-jeno and its productive hinterland). The key to the emergence of these monuments is probably provided by a concept introduced when discussing the great uniformity of ceramic and other artifact fashions throughout the Middle Niger.[78] During second half of the millennium of prosperity, the Middle Niger had become a true sphere of intensive interaction of several interlocking culture areas.

What we have observed here may very likely be something akin to the peer polity interaction experienced, for example, by the islands and coastal settlements of the Aegean during the first millennium BC.[79] Here the term polities does not imply any specific degree of centralization or any necessary movement towards a vertical stratification of the population. The term designates autonomous socio-political units at any scale of territorial integration or politico-economic integration. Peer polities, however, have entered into a web of intensive, sustained and voluntary trade, exchange of ideas, communication. The interacting polities tend to be at about the same scale of organization. What sets this network, or sphere, of interacting polities apart from earlier interaction is that now when a significant technical innovation, increase in complexity, or more "efficacious" change to ritual or occult belief appears in one polity, it quickly and rather uniformly spreads to the other components of the

[78] S. and R. McIntosh, *Prehistoric Investigation*, ii, pp. 451–2; S. McIntosh, *Excavations*, pp. 360–72, 393–8.
[79] Colin Renfrew, "Introduction: Peer polity interaction and socio-political change," in *Peer Polity Interaction and Socio-Political Change*, Colin Renfrew and John F. Cherry (eds.) (Cambridge University Press: Cambridge, 1986), pp. 1–18; see Colin Renfrew, *Approaches to Social Archaeology*, (Harvard University Press: Cambridge, MA, 1984), esp. pp. 30–134.

interaction sphere. There need not be one center of innovation. Communication is so intensive and spontaneous that changes will appear to develop at roughly the same time at several places within the sphere.

In my view, the first millennium AD Middle Niger displays rather less of the first two of the five salient characteristics of a peer polity interaction sphere, namely (1) competition (including organized warfare) and (2) competitive emulation (leading to ever increasing displays of wealth or power so as to achieve greater status vis-à-vis other polities). (These essentially peaceful interactions will, sadly, pass within a very few centuries.) I believe future research will show that the Middle Niger at this time shares with Greater Mande, and indeed with much of West Africa, the peer polity interaction mechanisms of (3) symbolic entrainment (the tendency for a well-developed symbolic or belief system to be adopted when it comes into contact with a less well-developed one), (4) rapid flow of technological changes, and (5) increased trade and exchange (often encouraging more specialized production – thereby encouraging and spreading innovation). To one degree or another we have seen all these dynamics in the Middle Niger of the first millennium AD. This is, essentially, a retelling of the story of the smiths' rise to positions of authority and the emergence of the other *nyamakawlaw*.

The predicted effect will be the emergence in many places of new ways to display the legitimation of those who lead and make decisions. And here we have to deal with the challenge of the Middle Niger developments of this chapter – particularly the ballooning of trade networks, the growth of cities and (late in the game) the erection of monuments in the absence of other evidence of emergent states – to standard social science ruminations about the course taken by societies as they become more complex.

By the end of the epoch of prosperity, these Middle Niger "culture areas" are undoubtedly complex (as integrated mixes of various kin groups, ethnic clusters, and craft and occupation corporations, sometimes living together in large communities). And they are demographically impressive (more than the *c.*2500-person threshold used by neo-evolutionary theorists to indicate the point at which a "chiefdom" or other incipient coercive political structure must kick in to ensure the smooth running of society).[80] It is

---

[80] G. Feinman, "The emergence of inequality: A focus on strategies and processes," in *Foundations of Social Inequality*, T. D. Price and G. Feinman (eds.) (Plenum: New York, 1995), pp. 260–1; critiqued in S. McIntosh, *Pathways*, Introduction.

the very lack of traces pointing to institutions of despotic use of power, of widespread warfare, and of entrenched social and economic stratification that makes the first millennium AD Middle Niger so important. Research coming from the neo-evolutionary perspective would have looked for the managers of communication, trade, and strategic economic resources. These were the individuals (call them Big Men or Chiefs or early state dynasts) engaged in a struggle with an increasingly reduced number of competitors for increasingly centralized power. These are the individuals strategizing to expand their hold over social, economic, and religious activities and to restrict wealth and status symbols to themselves. They signal their success in translating increasing authority to new forms of power by conspicuous display (monumentality, invention of sumptuary rules, etc.) and by the elaboration of wealth and luxury differentials (access in life and grave goods in death) and by the exclusivity of rituals.

Unquestionably, the Middle Niger will, before too long, come under the sway of centralized, more-or-less coercive states and empires, such as Mali and Songhai (chapter 10). Before this, however, Middle Niger prosperity thrives on the advantages of peer polity interaction (amongst many other factors). Whereas society is increasingly complex and demographically intense, it is not at all clear that these processes march in lockstep with increasing economic inequality, hierarchical authority, new administrative machinery, and the like. It is equally unclear whether the regional polities came into a state of sustained interaction by consent, conquest, or unintended habituation. The Middle Niger appears, from the present admittedly extremely fragmented evidence, to be much closer to other examples from Africa of diffused authority.[81] Rather than look for a classic initial hierarchy of wealth and status leading to the early state, we might better look for heterarchy: power checked through a network of groups of competing, overlapping interests which in effect work together to create sustained resistance to centralizing tendencies.

It is precisely at this point that we may be able to speak of an early expression of "civil society" or public sphere authority. The overlapping and competing interests derive from a political landscape of factions: kinship, age sets, secret societies, cult groups, title societies, territorial and craft associations, and power associations such as *Komo*. The factions resist the tendency of charismatic

---

[81] See especially, S. McIntosh, *Pathways*.

individuals to monopolize or reinvent authority. They collectively check the aggression of other factions and resist the tendency to elaborate any emergent vertical control hierarchy.

This is, surely, a lot to pull out of the murky earliest oral traditions and spotty archaeology of the first millennium. And in some of the early tumuli (and megaliths) of the Lakes Region we might just have a glimpse of the first cracks in the edifice of resistance. Who were buried in vast mounds such as El Oualadji? These few might indeed have benefited from initial stages of unequal access to high value, exotic items (such as copper), and in time (through symbolic innovation and entrainment) some of these items might have status to become sumptuary props to the legitimation of increasing concentration of authority. Do we see in these monuments early inequality that, even at the low level hypothesized here, becomes institutionalized and accoutered with a set of symbols developed to express wealth and power? As the few become increasingly alienated from the majority of society, new legitimizing symbols are invented.

Yet we still must ask: are these monuments *exclusively* the proxy measures of increasing centralization? They can certainly be understood as the embodiment of huge amounts of labour, as monuments to the increasing call of some upon the decision-making prerogatives of the many. But might those some be other than the new power-elites celebrated by neo-evolutionary theory? These new symbols will be all the more powerful if they call on older elements of the local belief symbols (such as the phallic cult of river fecundity hypothesized for the Tondidaro megaliths[82]). This is the beauty of fluid symbols and of the porous symbolic reservoir. Symbols can be called upon, manipulated, and reinvented by anyone, nascent dynasts, senior members of secret societies, or leaders of artisan collectives.

So we return to the dynamism of polity interaction spheres. Calling on older beliefs and metaphors will only aid the process by which various polities linked within a peer polity interaction network will tend to ratchet themselves to more (horizontally) complex levels of socio-political organization. Undeniably, the dressing of the stones and erection of large megalithic fields such as Tondidaro do imply the call on much labor or a sustained exertion of effort for the expression of monumentality – but we simply do not know in whose interest. Similarly, exotics can be manipulated in the same process that links status of ritual authority with that of symbols of that authority. In whose interest? We cannot simply assume that all this was

---

[82] Dembélé, *Entre Débo et Faguibine*, pp. 506–7.

done exclusively under the control of elite patrons. It would be hard to argue that the numbers of sâti locked within tumuli such as El Oualadji and Koï Gourrey do not imply a component of fear to the workings of these polities or to activities of factions therein. As we know from the Igbo Ukwu burial (not of a chief, but of a presumed title holder in a secret society) in Nigeria, however, human sacrifice and mass disposal of luxuries can celebrate an efficient *heterarchy* dedicated to the suppression of centralized power.[83] The changes to society reflected in new interest in monumentality need not (at the beginning, at least) even imply new levels of warfare, destructive competition, and slave raiding between polities – although this is undeniably a feature of some peer polity interaction zones.

I end this chapter with the suggestion that the concept of the interaction sphere might be expanded west beyond the Middle Niger. This provides some inferential support to the above highly speculative interpretation of the function of multiple equivalent-scale polities in the Middle Niger. We know very little archaeologically about the emergence and nature of the Soninké kingdoms in the grasslands between the Middle Senegal Valley and the Middle Niger, of which a later aspect of North African-influenced Ghana is the most often cited in oral tradition and by the Arab chroniclers. But these same sources leave the overwhelming impression of Bovill's[84] "shadowy empires, . . . turbulent marches, . . . vigorous cities, . . . many isolated communities." Trimingham[85] provides the best characterization, loosely calling "empires" what we would here term polities:

> Empires were spheres of influence, defined not by territorial or boundary lines but by social strata, independent families, free castes, or servile groups of fixed status regarded as royal serfs. The ruler was not interested in dominating territory as such, but in relationship with social groups upon whom he could draw to provide levies in time of war, servants for his courts and cultivators to keep his granaries full. . . . These steppe empires give the appearance of structural weakness and instability.

These are issues that exercise Mandeists still, with an ongoing furious debate about whether an evolutionary sequence from egalitarian kinship structure, through "Big Men" to "chiefdom," to true

---

[83] C. Thurstan Shaw, *Unearthing Igbo Ukwu*, (Oxford University Press: Oxford, 1977).

[84] Bovill, *Golden Trade*, p. 54.

[85] J. Spencer Trimingham, *A History of Islam in West Africa*, (Oxford University Press: Oxford, 1962), pp. 35–6.

state ever applied even to the Mali "kingdom."[86] The theme these researchers return to over and over again is the dominance of segmentary structures (especially but not exclusively lineage) in the histories and genealogies of that expansionist polity.

A useful guide to future field research might be to describe the first millennium Soninké chiefdoms and "empires," including Ghana, as pre-Arab confederations, or "over-kingdoms" developing in extensive and mature regional interaction spheres. Interaction across the steppes would certainly have been facilitated by the arrival of the horse, hence perhaps its prominence among the sacrificial material at El-Oualadji. Tumuli, such as those described by al-Bakri and six purportedly located near Koumbi Saleh by Bonnel de Mézières in 1914,[87] were a potent symbol of power here also. Perhaps we can expand the model to include the thousands of roughly contemporaneous (late first, early second millennium) tumuli of the grasslands between the Senegal and Gambia rivers.[88] We then would have three communicating spheres of peer-polity interactions with a growing mass (critical mass?) of equivalent polities that can be reconstructed from oral traditions.[89] In all three regions, the monumental funerary mound may mark the burials of elites and chiefs. But they may also serve multiple functions: markers of sacred locales, neutral places for meeting friends and enemies or for conducting exchange, lineage markers (symbols of group solidarity), or territorial markers on boundaries of polities. Hence we need not be surprised if tumuli happen not to have a rich burial with many unfortunates in attendance, as most do not.

If this model of late first millennium peer polity interaction can be demonstrated by field research, it will be done not necessarily at the monuments, but at the many habitation mounds in their environs. The settlements give the social context of communities be-

---

[86] See Stephen Bühnen, "Brothers, chiefdoms, and empires: on Jan Jansen's 'The representation of status in Mande'," *History in Africa*, 23(1996), pp. 111–20 and Jan Jansen, "Polities and political discourse: Was Mande already a segmentary society in the Middle Ages?," *History in Africa*, 23(1996), pp. 121–8, esp. pp. 125, 127.

[87] A. Bonnel de Mézières, "Recherches sur l'emplacement de Ghana et de Takrour," *Mémoires de l'Académie des Inscriptions et des Belles Lettres de Paris*, (1920), pp. 227–73; Mauny, *Tableau Géographique*, p. 73.

[88] Vincent Martin and Charles Becker, *Inventaire des Sites Protohistoriques du Sénégal*, (CNRS: Kaolak, 1984); S. and R. McIntosh, "From stone to metal," p. 118 and "Field survey."

[89] E.g., Brooks, *Landlords and Strangers*, esp. pp. 62–85.

coming more complex, population stratifying (horizontally before vertically), and the use of symbols of legitimation by multiple factions. If this model of confederations of polities can be shown to apply to the Middle Niger and to the Soninké heartland (the lands of Ghana and Kugha, and perhaps reaching far west to the Middle Senegal territories later known to Arab chroniclers as Takrur and Silla), then the situation will be remarkably similar to that hypothesized by K. C. Chang for the Neolithic socio-political context for the development of the Hsia, Shang and Chou Empires of Bronze Age China.[90] In this view the three great Bronze Age states are not born *de novo*. They emerge from a long-standing (back to the Lungshan Neolithic) interaction sphere of competing, emulating, communicating kin-groups and intervillage leagues (his "hierarchical segmentation") united by language and shared shamanistic traditions. The king is a confederation maker, molding alliances by manipulating and monopolizing an increasingly institutionalized form of "high shamanism" – the state cult centered on the royal lineage.

Thinking of the Middle Niger monuments in these terms, we should perhaps see in them experiments in symbolic form. They can be thought of as innovations in the manipulation of signs of legitimation, during a period of rapid political and social change. Perhaps what we will call the Imperial Tradition of the great states of the Western Sudan, (late Ghana?), Mali, and Songhai, and of all the minor states that developed on their fringes and in the vacuums left at their decline had long pedigrees and did not appear spontaneously and out of a vacuum. Perhaps they were the successful experiments carried over from the innovative, emulative, competitive centuries of prosperity of the first millennium AD and expanded to celebrate a newly emergent elite.

[90] Kwang-Chih Chang, "Sandai archaeology and the formation of state in ancient China," in *The Origin of Chinese Civilization*. David Keightley (ed.) (University of California Press: Berkeley, 1983), pp. 552–8; Kwang-Chih Chang, *Archaeology of Ancient China*, 4th edn, (Yale University Press: New Haven, 1986), pp. 365–6, 414–19. See Roderick J. McIntosh, "Clustered cites and alternative courses to authority in prehistory," in *Feschrift for K.-C. Chang*, Robert E. Murowchick, Lothar von Falkenhausen, Cheng-hwa Tsang, and Robin D. S. Yates (eds.) (Peabody Museum of Archaeology and Ethnology: Cambridge, MA, forthcoming).

9

Historical Imagination: AD 1,000

I have used the preceding historical imagination chapters to explore two themes: the Middle Niger as a symbolic landscape and the millennia-long evolution of a complex belief system. What of the material world? It is appropriate to follow a chapter on the high prosperity of the Middle Niger – on the rise of sophisticated urban production systems and on distant commercial relations – with a glance towards the north.

North Africans and the Saharan nomads have heard rumour of great wealth beyond the dunes. Timbuktu, as seen from our observer's vantagepoint at "Wadi 13," is a growing community. Some of the satellites of Timbuktu, such as our observer's home on the Wadi El Ahmar, are even longer established. Someday to be eclipsed by Timbuktu, these settlements have been in business longer as points of welcome for visitors from the Sahara and beyond. Ties with the grain metropoli south of Lake Débo are many centuries old. But, as gold circulates in greater volume through the riverine networks, relations with northern neighbors turn complex. Citizen-merchants of our imaginary town in the dunes make their own adventure-travels across the great desert. In the salt-mine hamlets and towns of the Maghreb, they found their own entrepôt – as commercial strategy. A merchant's version of *dali-ma-sigi* is no less important a device to gather information as is the hunter's quest.

However, trouble blows in from the north. These communities near Timbuktu are the first of the Middle Niger communities to feel the asphyxiating – for some, apocalyptic – breath of the new millennium:

The spark lights again in the eyes of swollen-bellied little girls and boys who

prance through the streets and crooked alleyways for the first time in months. One can feel a palpable relaxation in the market atmosphere. Old men who, not two days ago had followed angry words to each other with feeble blows of their walking stick, are now sitting side by side on mats in the shade, sharing gap-toothed jokes.

First the river rose past the level remembered even by those same old men in their youth. Then came word from downstream of the great lakes of a rice crop so abundant that, for want of enough harvesters, much had to be left for the birds. And today the first deep-draft rice boats arrived from Jaboro. One, two, three . . . six, seven, eight . . . one boat after another right up the canal, past dune after dune, to the edge of the town itself!

What better sign than the rice boats that the recent troubles have passed? Or so everyone hopes. The last boats to come arrived three long years ago and only then with deep stress to the keel from running up sand bars in the low Niger. The boat crew had to wade into the water and push the boat around and around to excavate a path through the barrier.

Much cargo was spoiled by the water that seeped into the sewn and caulked planks of the hull. Now, however, the boats groan with their load. From the inner keel to tops of the gunnels, some of the boats are stacked with pots filled with sweet *karite* butter used for soap, cooking, and for light at night. Other vessels are filled with fish oil, and especially with the great hemp-cloth sacks of rice. Of course, grain had arrived in past years in the small two-man canoes. But many of these were lost in storms on the great lake and the rice was so dear it broke many merchant houses. The poor simply did without. Now there will be enough for all and enough to send far to the north. The merchants can already hear the growls of the camels at loading time.

The lead boat, the strongest and longest, that of the boat owner, is always loaded with delights for the curious, who now crowd around it. Exclamations and heated assessments follow in the wake as each item is borne on the heads of porters along the plank to the shore. Baskets filled with kola nuts from far to the south. High stacks of animal hides, common ones to be prepared for sitting upon, certain antelope to be made into shields prized by the desert warriors, skins of the great cats with heads and claws still attached, and great squares of hippo, elephant, crocodile to be used in rituals. Then come tiny flasks filled with rare and precious liquids – musk from the civit, rank-smelling love potions made from the livers of certain fish, and always the secret special orders of smiths and other sorcerers. Raucous laughter as the crew off-loads bottle after bottle of the highly alcoholic hydromel made by the marsh-dwellers. Bottles of honey, bags of spices, cloth of cotton, local linen and wool brightly dyed deep blue and red. Hair ornaments, bracelets and rings in copper and iron. Stack upon stack of tools and weapons, hoe blades, knives, lance heads, and daggers. But everyone averts their eyes, upon a sign from the boat owner, when the town's sorcerers enter the boat to retrieve the sacks carrying the dangerous metals, long iron staves with birds along the shaft, crocodile and serpents in fine copper, other shapes in iron too potent to be given a name.

Last to emerge into sunlight are the hundreds of finely painted bowls filled with gold. Those experienced in the trade to the north nod knowingly. Never had the season's first boats brought so much of the metal so desired by those who live beyond the salt and desolation of the dunes. The towns merchant families are indeed fortunate. This much gold, this early in the season, after a speedy desert crossing, will cement the already cordial relations with the avid traders of Tuat. For many months those who walk the long trails to the south have returned to Jaboro with head pans filled with gold. The gold then went into the storerooms of the houses owned by merchant families with joint allegiance to Jaboro and this town on the El Ahmar. Now, after the long river journey, the gold is returned to the same families' storerooms in this town. There it will remain until loaded onto the back of camels.

But perhaps the most precious cargo spent the four-day boat trip in misery in the full sun, languishing on top of the grain sacks. These are the passengers. Not the unfortunates who will walk the length of the desert behind the camels, picking up the precious dung used as fuel for the evening campfires and wondering all the while about their fate when they are sold in far markets. These come on the later boats. The first passengers are far more important than the not inconsiderable profits brought by the slaves.

For these are the sons and nephews and uncles of the heads of the great merchant families of Jaboro and of this town. They have riches locked in their heads. The young men returning to this town of their birth have spent many years, some more than a decade, in the family's house at Jaboro. There they learned the family's business, made friends and acquaintances amongst the other families of that great town, observed the local craftsmen, and built up years of trust with the itinerant traders who travel each year to the sources of gold. Some even traveled themselves to where the gold is mined or panned from fast-moving streams. Others are scions of Jaboro families, come to live here for the next many years. All, however, have locked in their heads that most jealously guarded of merchant treasures – knowledge.

Knowledge of the waxing and waning fortunes and luck of competing families. Knowledge of discrete secrets passed on by trusted friends among the gold traders – new mines just discovered, rumors of desire to raid by others to the south, movements by populations of whole regions in response to the erratic rains, new infestations of flies causing river blindness, or other changes brought on by the unsettling changes in climate. Knowledge of new implements in iron invented by smiths to the south, new materials needed for new rituals that have exploded in these unsettled times, and knowledge of the spread to the south of the new religion that demands the destruction of all the old gods and of the sacred places where those gods deign to speak to men.

For centuries the enduring strength of the principal merchant families has rested with these networks of shared family members living in family-owned houses in the various trade towns between Jaboro and this, the northernmost town of the great floodplain. Lesser nephews go to lesser towns; orphans and others wishing that their children might one day be adopted by the families go to lesser villages. The pride of the families has always been the expansion of the networks. Those families that do not send their sons as far as trade and security will permit will wither until they become the disgraced clientèle of some other, more vigorous family.

For centuries the families saw their representatives penetrate the farthest villages of the great floodplain and beyond to the homelands of the many petty kings and the stone towns where Arabs and Berbers and Blacks live together on the grasslands to the west. The recent drive had been to establish new houses beyond the already old ones in each of the oasis stops on the way to the two great salt works in the middle of the desert. The hope had been to establish those houses right in the towns north of the desert, where all worship the single God. And there had already been considerable success, in places such as Tuat, among those more welcoming than their co-religionists. But recent events have banked the fires of those hopes.

The losses came in many forms. Many sons and daughters of the families were killed. Each of them represented a repository of knowledge, each potentially a respected elder to join the decision-making inner circle of the family. The raiders pillaged too many things: an entire caravan load of salt, much gold, many slaves driven off probably to die wretched deaths in the wasteland. But the losses were in the intangible sense also, especially in the hope of an enduring and ever expanding prosperity, hope that had rested on the plans to expand the families' houses north as far as the salty northern sea. Then the veiled camel raiders destroyed the oasis settlement on the extension of the El Ahmar channel north through the dunes, the first of the major water points on the caravan route from this town to the salt mines.

Those veiled raiders destroyed a confidence already badly shaken by the recent droughts, by the refusal of the river to rise, by the movement to the banks of the great river and the shores of the large lakes of unprecedented numbers of desperate and frankly hostile desert folk. And the oasis destroyed by the raiders is only the distance traveled by a heavily laden caravan in one day. That fact, the immediacy of mortal threat, has been the perpetual topic of conversation since the sole survivor of the oasis stumbled into the town six months ago.

Many of the family members newly arrived from the south must be fighting down feelings of panic. Some of them know they have been chosen to travel north, some to resettle the destroyed oasis, some to replace cousins or brothers recently returned from other oases and the salt workings, some even to settle amongst the Ibadites in Tuat and perhaps even Tahert. Despite the return of the rains and the generous river and of the grain boats from Jaboro, no one thinks the danger is forever over.

Why the *litham*-wearers chose such violence no one can say for certain.

There have been rumours that the disastrous early rains and, consequently, the meager pasturages have driven many nomadic families to the edge of the floodplain. There have been rumors of many raids between clans and of violent clashes with the cattle-herders who, in numbers that increase each year, spend the hot months roaming the dry marshes downstream of the big lakes. Relations between the veil-wearers and the merchant families have always been cool, but proper – both prospered from the cross desert trade, neither could conduct that trade without the other.

But now the losses of the oasis raid have been replaced by insidious suspicions. Merchants have needed the camel drivers to move their goods, but have been careful to keep from them the precious information about the sources of gold. Now there is the suspicion that trusted *litham*-wearers, men long in the employ of the merchants, told the raiders of the dates when salt from the north and gold from the south would be together at the oasis resting place. These rumors are fed by other suspicions that the camel drivers wish to take over the desert trade utterly, suspicions fed by the increasing refusal of merchants beyond the desert to trade with anyone but those who submit to the single God called Allah.

These suspicions have fed fears in recent years. Fear of those who inhabit the tent and pole-and-straw hut camps that have grown around this town. The town has always had satellites, many nearby hamlets each with three or four families of artisans, smiths, leatherworkers, and the like. And there has always been seasonal tent and pole-and-straw encampments of nomadic *litham*-wearers, and their servants and slaves. But those in the new camps have stayed month after month since they lost their herds when the rains began to fail many years ago. They remain in their poverty and pride, the resentment festering, looking for expression. Many believe the slaughter in the oasis was just the first expression.

These fears and suspicions have even led some of the leading merchant families to do unthinkable things. Some have deserted this town for the upstart town two hour's walk to the east. When this town along the El Ahmar was proud home to thousands, the upstart was just a seasonal camp of *litham*-wearers of the Madasa tribe, derisively named after one of their servile women. But as more adherents of the God Allah came across the desert, they refused to dwell in this town, a place so infused with the power of the river gods, the birthplace of so many powerful crocodile, snake, and iron priests. Rather, they settled with the upstarts and soon their local converts among the poor began to settle there too.

Since the rains and river have turned against the people, many ask if perhaps this new God has shown a sign of his powerful displeasure. It is a reasonable question for the heads of merchant families to ask. Some appear to have found their answer, risking the wrath of venerable patron spirits and their priests by turning to the new God who brooks belief in no other. Still, the night-shrouded dances and rituals of the old gods still receive visits by members of the merchant families who have abandoned this town for the upstart. This causes more amusement than resentment – shared loyalties can mean shared opportunities and double insurance against bad luck. Still, the times are unsettled and even the arrival of a flotilla of rice boats cannot drive away deep misgivings for the future. The old men already speak of the prosperity known in the days of their grandfathers as if those days are truly of the past.

10

The Imperial Tradition

It would be wrong to attribute to climatic changes all the dramatic social, demographic, and political developments of the first half of the present millennium. It would also be foolish to ignore climate. We now know that the first several centuries of the second millennium AD found many of the globe's peoples in conditions of extreme environmental stress. What is most interesting is the growing appreciation of the social memories that communities brought to bear on these times of climatic surprise.[1] The response was not one of passive adaptation.

Past communities filtered information about climate and about their own past responses to change according to their models of the environment. And we appreciate increasingly the power of heterarchy – the reigning organizational mode of the Middle Niger – to gather and process many bits of climatic information from many locales, from the perspectives of many, ecologically distinct groups. Heterarchies many not act as swiftly and directly as hierarchies. But in times when climate has "deteriorated into a chaotic disarray" (as J. Dean describes a contemporaneous time of stress in the North American Southwest)[2] broad information gathering and a deep social memory can be the more effective counter. But at times, the cumulative stresses are just too great.

[1] R. McIntosh, et al., *Global Change*.
[2] Dean, "Complexity theory."

Global Climate Turned Upside-Down

Strange and dramatic things were afoot in the global climate during the first few centuries of the present millennium. Archaeological sciences, palaeoclimatology, and space physics have merged their perspectives on regional weather histories, sunspot cycles, planetary orbital modulations, and anthropogenic contributions to provide a much improved (if still raw) view of the forcing mechanisms at work over the past two millennia.

The first point of consensus in these studies is that, for the millennia for which we possess records, the solar activity envelope around the earth was perhaps at its most stable during the majority of the first millennium AD and that discernible solar activity cycles nearly double in number during the present millennium.[3] This is not to imply utter stability of climate during the period of Middle Niger prosperity (chapter 8). Rather, the picture we see from lake level and other geomorphological studies is of gradual improvement in West African precipitation from c.AD 300 to 700 and minor "pluvial" stability from AD 700 to perhaps 1100.[4] Even the solar energy peaks (associated in the low latitudes with lower precipitation) and valleys (middle latitude cold, low latitude wet) of AD 0, 650 and 900–90 had restrained effects.[5]

This steady improvement in West African climate most likely ends with an event dated to AD 1128, called the Medieval Maximum (energy secular wave).[6] In the American Southwest, four centuries of providential weather and population increases end abruptly at around AD 1130, with a severe drought (1130–80) marking the beginning of oscillations and ever worsening drought lasting until sometime after AD 1450.[7] The Medieval Maximum represents an extreme of solar energy production and a phase jump of sunspot activity, weather change, and glacial advances and

---

[3] D. J. Schove, "Sunspot cycles and weather history," in Rampino, et al., *Climate. History, Periodicity and Predictability,* pp. 358–9; see Theodor Landscheidt, "Long-range forecasts of solar cycles and climate change," in Rampino, et al., *Climate. History, Periodicity and Predictability,* figure 25.13, p. 437.

[4] Brooks, "Ecological perspectives," pp. 30–3; S. McIntosh and R. McIntosh, "From stone," p. 94; see Landscheidt, "Long-range forecasts of solar cycles," figure 25.14, p. 438.

[5] Schove, "Sunspot, tables 21.3, p. 363 and 21.4, p. 364 (see table 21.2, p. 358).

[6] Landscheidt, "Long-range," pp. 433, 437 and figure 25.14, p. 438.

[7] Dean, "Complexity theory."

retreats of an intensity perhaps not experienced since *c*.1369 BC (the Egyptian Minimum, which began roughly a millennium of rapid oscillations).

We can take AD 1128 (dated from tree-rings) to mark the beginning of a new order of overlapping sunspot cycles, of incidents of climate change and of intensity of wet or dry episodes. The date accords well with the early second millennium dramatic decline (the most severe since *c*.13,000 BP) in Lake Bosumtwi[8] and with the conclusion drawn by Nicholson[9] that, after AD 1000–1100, West African lakes oscillate wildly and the very nature of summer and winter rainfall changed dramatically. Extrapolating from middle latitude tree-ring and sunspot records, we can expect there to have been wet periods in the Middle Niger, lasting a decade or more at AD 1050, 1300–50 and 1450. The wet episodes would have generally punctuated very dry centuries (particularly so after AD 1150 and during most of the thirteenth and early fourteenth centuries).

It is instructive to take just a moment to look at archaeological sequences elsewhere for the effect on society of these early second millennium oscillations. The most precisely dated settlement and human ecological sequences in an analogous semi-arid region are those of the American Southwest.[10] There we find a consistent pattern encompassing the complex cultural complexes known as the Hohokam, the Anasazi, and Chacoan. Adequate to abundant rains and unprecedented population densities obtain from *c*.AD 900 until *c*.1130, followed by population decline and mass movements and by virtual depopulation of many highland and marginal areas by AD 1300 and persisting until after 1450. Periodic droughts are documented from AD 1134 to AD 1181 and, especially from 1276–99, the prolonged "Great Drought".

---

[8] Talbot and Delibrias, "Pleistocene-Holocene," pp. 341–2.

[9] Nicholson, "Historical climate," pp. 39–42; Nicholson, *A Climatic Chronology for Africa*, pp. 76–97.

[10] Patricia L. Crown, "The Hohokam of the American Southwest," *Journal of World Prehistory*, 4(2) (1990), pp. 234–5, 244; Robert C. Euler, "Demography and cultural dynamics on the Colorado Plateaus," in *The Anasazi in a Changing Environment*, George J. Gumerman (ed.) (Cambridge University Press: Cambridge, 1988), pp. 194–210, 222–7.; Joseph A. Tainter, *The Collapse of Complex Society* (Cambridge University Press: Cambridge, 1988), pp. 179–85; Joseph A. Tainter and Bonnie Bagley Tainter (eds.), *Evolving Complexity and Environmental Risk in the Prehistoric Southwest*, (Addison Wesley: Reading, MA, 1996; J. Dean, "Cultural adaptation."

Environmental deterioration is not the sole cause for the collapse of these systems. Rather, unpredictability and cumulative stress undermines the "energy averaging" core,[11] in which an increasingly hierarchical, increasingly distant elite administered a diverse hinterland and encouraged production specialists as a strategy to average out local and interannual environmental fluctuation. Only as long as rainfall was generally good could an artificially high population and costly non-productive elite be sustained. Hierarchy failed where heterarchy might have sustained the day. Of further relevance to the Middle Niger developments of this chapter, these stresses also stimulated novel and in some cases exaggerated religious expressions (Katsina Cult, the Southwestern Cult, and new Anasazi tower kivas) and intergroup warfare and raiding.[12] A single drought did not cause this collapse, but under the weight of centuries of wild fluctuations, social memory failed and with it, former population densities.

Other low latitude, lowland tropic sequences are not nearly as well dated. However, the emerging picture shows that the effects on the Middle Niger of these revolutionary changes in the global climate are not at all unique. The Lowland Amazon suffered a drought lasting many centuries at the end of the last millennium BC, then a phase of "punctuated equilibria"[13] from AD 0 to 1500. For this millennium and a half, a generally warm, wet climate is punctuated by significant aridity (associated with mega-El Niño Southern Oscillation events) correlated with archaeological discontinuities. Pollen studies and archaeology document aridity at c.AD 500 and at 750 or 850, but these episodes tend to be less severe than the cataclysms of c.AD 1000, 1250–1350 and 1500–50.

During these second millennium episodes in the Amazon, the archaeological discontinuities appear as significant periods of abandonment on a regional scale and replacement of emigrant groups by intrusive linguistic elements. That these same dynamics of fragmentation and disruption were not repeated wholesale in the Middle Niger can in part be attributed to the stability of economic and social interactions established during the previous millennium.

---

[11] Tainter, *Collapse*, p. 148, see 185–7, 191.
[12] Dean, "Cultural adaptation," p. 19; George Johnson, "Social Strife may have exiled ancient Indians," *New York Times* August 20, 1996, pp. B5–B6.
[13] Betty J. Meggers, "Archaeological evidence for the impact of Mega-Niño events on Amazonia during the past two millennia," *Climatic Change*, 28 (1994), pp. 321–39 and "Biogeographical," pp. 97–110.

Population levels, however, appear to suffer enormously. And elsewhere in Greater Mande, environmental stress must surely have contributed to the emergence of the new forces of pan-regional power and state-building – the Imperial Tradition.[14]

Unfortunately, the lowland West African archaeological evidence dealing specifically with post-AD 1000 rainfall changes is extremely sparse. The best data are the deeply dug well and settlement sequences from the Tagant region and from Tegdaoust in the Hodh of Mauritania.[15] The southern Saharan settlements begin by the seventh or eighth centuries as part of an expanding rainfed agricultural "civilization" of the Gangara.[16] However, shallow wells at Tegdaoust are replaced by deeply dug ones in the eleventh and early twelfth century, when the regular precipitation changes to short-term torrential rains and irrigation farming must be expanded. Desertification leaves its traces in the streets and abandoned houses of the town by late twelfth century and the wells are abandoned altogether by the early fourteenth century.

For those historians who fix their sights on the waxing and waning of the grand empires, this is a golden age of West Africa. The field evidence from the Middle Niger, however, suggests that the prosperity of the first millennium was succeeded by massive migrations and depopulation on a breathtaking scale.

Demographic Cataclysm

In his authoritative synthesis of the Western Sudan during the apogee of the Ghana and Mali empires, the Guinean historian D. T. Niane presents the received view of Middle Niger population: "The

---

[14] The term is coined by David Robinson, who explores the persistence into the nineteenth century of its political expressions, in "The imperial state in Mali and Songhay." Paper presented at the School of American Research Advanced Seminar on Complex Society in Africa, Santa Fe, New Mexico, October, 1984.

[15] E. Ann McDougall, "The view from Awdaghust: War, trade and social change in the southwestern Sahara, from the eighth to the fifteenth century," *Journal of African History*, 26 (1985), pp. 1–31; Jean Polet, *Tegdaoust IV. Fouille d'un Quartier de Tegdaoust. Urbanisation, Architecture, Utilisation de l'Espace Construit*, Editions Recherche sur les Civilisations, Mémoire no. 54 (Editions Recherche sur les Civilisations: Paris, 1985), p. 238

[16] S. Daveau and C. Toupet, "Anciens terroirs Gangara," *Bulletin de l'Institut Fondamental d'Afrique Noire, B*, 25 (1963), pp. 193–214; Robert Vernet, *Préhistoire*; Bathily, *Ports de l'Or*, pp. 75–6, 83, 96.

river valleys of the Niger and the Senegal were virtually human anthills."[17] The archaeologist must differ. The evidence from all parts of the Middle Niger concurs on a wave of settlement abandonment beginning in the earliest centuries of the present millennium. The wave crested, by AD 1400. By that date, population was reduced far below the levels known during the era of prosperity.

That evidence is best developed in the Upper Delta,[18] where, Jenne-jeno is abandoned by AD 1400. As we have seen, excavation and regional survey at Jenne-jeno show population to have peaked in the late first millennium and to have remained high perhaps as late as AD 1100. Soon thereafter, however, the satellite settlements of Hambarketolo and Kaniana are abandoned. Other satellites follow. Occupation at Jenne-jeno beats a fast retreat from the site's periphery. In the densely packed central sector there is a flurry of building. What factors lie behind the radically transformed density of structures, frequency of house reconstructions (and possibly related phenomena such as the explosion in production of statuary art)?[19] There is no unambiguous evidence of warfare (but, what evidence might we expect of slaving expeditions or of raids on hinterland settlements lacking protective walls?) The archaeologist is always forced simply to infer social transformations such as changes to family structure due to conversion to Islam, to land rights or to status as society becomes more stratified. The effect of social and climate change is more evident in rural population dislocations and eventual depopulation.

The story becomes considerably more complex with the results of core testing at the modern town of Jenne.[20] We once followed local oral tradition in the belief that some of the populace of the abandoned archaeological sites removed to the present town. Now, however, we know that the *tell* of Jenne is made up of some seven meters of cultural debris in places and was occupied at least since the ninth century. A fraction of the communities of Jenne-jeno and its satellites might have crowded onto Jenne, but most appear just to have vanished.

---

[17] D. T. Niane, "Mali and the second Mandingo expansion," in *Africa from the 12th to the 16th Century,* D. T. Niane (ed.) UNESCO General History of Africa. vol. IV. (University of Californai Press: Berkeley, 1984), p. 156.

[18] S. K. McIntosh, *Excavations,* pp. 63–4, 372–7.

[19] R. McIntosh and S. McIntosh, "Dillitantism and plunder," p. 56.

[20] R. J. McIntosh, P. Sinclair, T. Togola, M. Petrèn, and S. K. McIntosh, "Exploratory archaeology at Jenne and Jenne-jeno, Mali," *SAHARA,* 8 (1996), pp. 19–28.

The decline of Upper Delta hinterland settlement runs parallel to the patterns we have already traced in the Dia vicinity,[21] although in the former basin high population levels were maintained several centuries longer. Two-thirds of archaeological sites in the greater Jenne-jeno region are abandoned soon after the turn of the millennium. This begins as a rapid wave in the low-lying, rich rice basins, such as the Pondori, progressing through the higher, lighter floodplain soils until, by c.AD 1400, virtually all the satellites packed around Jenne-jeno are abandoned.[22] The new rural preference for the sandy soils of sand levees and, especially, dunes, implies a shift in emphasis from rice to millet, probably because of the historically attested immigration of the Bambara. The shift in agricultural systems was probably not immediate. It is more likely that a changing flood regime (and political instability) created a wave of rural depopulation, retreat of communities to centers such as Jenne-jeno or to new towns such as the present Jenne, and movements of others in and out of the floodplain. The last may be seen in the relatively short occupation of communities such as Togueres Galia (eleventh to twelfth centuries) and Doupwil (thirteenth to fifteenth centuries)[23] in the Mopti region and in the so-called Tellem occupation[24] of the eleventh through fourteenth centuries of the easily defensible Bandiagara cliffs at the Upper Delta's eastern periphery.

Taken all together, the evidence points to a slowly building wave of dislocations, beginning early in the present millennium and cresting by 1400 in massive depopulation, migrations, and probable (but as yet invisible) unrest. Unlike those emigrants several centuries earlier from a declining Dia, these newly dispossessed had nowhere to go. The end of prosperity swept all parts of the Middle Niger.

The Méma enjoyed a density of settlement at least equal to that of the Upper Delta until the thirteenth or fourteenth centuries. But when present dry conditions set in, population evaporated to all intents and purposes.[25] By 1000–1200, wild fauna associated with permanent standing water or swamps disappears from the Akumbu sequence. Desiccation had become a reality of daily life and would only become worse. The date of the Méma cataclysm is known

---

[21] Haskell, McIntosh and McIntosh, *Dia*, pp. 43–6, 127–39.

[22] R. J. McIntosh, "Floodplain geomorphology," p. 195.

[23] Bedeaux et al., "Recherches Archéologiques," pp. 185–9.

[24] Bedaux, "Des Tellem," pp. 83–101.

[25] Togola, *Archaeological Investigations*, ch. 4.

imprecisely only from the upper levels of a few sites: the iron-producers' "B" site and Akumbu AK 4 (both late eleventh, twelfth), Kolima (late thirteenth) and Akumbu AK1 (thirteenth to late fifteenth). Whereas the large, clustered mounds of the seventh century to early second millennium crowd the channels and water-retaining depressions, more recent sites are significantly smaller (less than 3 ha.), isolated or (in rare instances) paired, and are now situated on the light sandy soils of the longitudinal dunes. If the oral traditions that attribute these recent sites to the newly intrusive Bambara are correct, the survey and excavation evidence points to a near-total abandonment of the Méma by its original population. If one can imagine such devastation, for several centuries this basin must have been even more moribund than it is today.

But the oral traditions and some of the earliest written sources for the Western Sudan have contradictory things to say about this period of undisputed environmental decline. There was still a welcome in the Méma for the traveller, Ibn Battuta, who passed through in the early 1350s and, earlier, the Mali empire's Mansa Musa travelled that way in 1324 on his golden pilgrimage to Mecca. According to oral tradition and to the *Ta'rikh el-Fettash*, the kingdom of Méma gained independence of Mali in 1433 and remained sovereign for a few decades until conquest by the Songhai empire. Even before that (at a time we know population was high, if beginning to decline), the ruler of the Méma kingdom succored Sunjata in his exile and aided him in the battle (Krina, c.AD 1240), in which he defeated the Soso oppressor, Sumaworo, and officially founded the Mali empire. When the end did come for the Méma, the fall was hard.

At this millennial close to the twentieth century, there has been a raft of serious popularizing books about the course through world history of plagues and chronic infectious diseases.[26] Through the stomach-turning tales of different disease courses and enumerations of mind-numbing demographic cataclysms, one theme appears again and again. Humans and van Leeuenhoek's "wretched beasties" are

[26] Just to mention two useful primers for Africanists: Andrew Nikiforuk, *The Fourth Horseman. A Short History of Epidemics, Plagues, Famine and other Scourges* (M. Evans and Co., New York, 1993) and Christopher Wills, *Plagues. Their Origin, History, and Future* (HarperCollins: London, 1996). These acknowledge their descent from the bibles of human disease ecology: Alfred Crosby, *Ecological Imperialism. The Biological Expansion of Europe, 900–1900* (Cambridge University Press: Cambridge, 1986) and William H. McNeill, *Plagues and Peoples* (Doubleday: New York, 1976).

caught in a complex and historical web of ecological mutuality. Specific stresses (natural or anthopogenic) periodically rend the fabric of the web, with catastrophic consequences. To quote the evocatively entitled *The Fourth Horseman*[27] on the long relationship of humans with germs: "Relatives, no matter how distant or ancient, don't generally go out of their way to murder other relatives unless they have a good reason and this characteristically is particularly true of the superorganism. It has only become a killing machine when people have kicked or trampled its frontiers violating unwritten bacterial codes." Did the peoples of the Middle Niger essentially trample those codes by the as-yet undiscovered responses of dense populations (legacies of the prior millennium of prosperity) as flood and rainfall deteriorated into Dean's "chaotic disarray"?

One cannot read these global tales of famine, war and pestilence without wondering how possibly the Middle Niger could have escaped the waves of Black Death, particularly of the early thirteenth century (when North Africa was badly ravaged) and the dreadful fourteenth, through the lingering epidemics of the sixteenth and seventeenth centuries. Sanitation and public health works at these early towns must have been beyond the primitive. Here was a population relatively isolated from the Mediterranean disease reservoir until that time. By the first centuries of the new millennium, however, they were coming into increasingly frequent and voluminous contact with the Maghreb by way of the trans-Saharan caravans. We now know that infected rats need not have hitched a ride by camelback. An infested traveller, once bitten anew by fleas at his southern destination, could start the infestation cycles quite nicely.

All this is speculation, and it is very true that a score of other chronic diseases of the urban tropics (the infantile diarrhoeals, cholera, typhoid, smallpox and the viral influenzas, to name a few) could have blossomed under the right conditions. On the one hand, we lack the death pits or other hard evidence of mass mortality one might expect with waves of plague (again, one *always* treats the negative evidence of archaeology with due caution). The Jenne-jeno burials suggest a well-nourished population (famine and epidemics often marching hand-in-hand). On the other hand, among the persistent traditions at Jenne about the abandonment of the ancestral town are those telling of the death of all male children by infection of the umbilical cord, groin, and torso. Hundreds of Mid-

[27] Nikiforuk, *The Fourth Horseman*, p. 3.

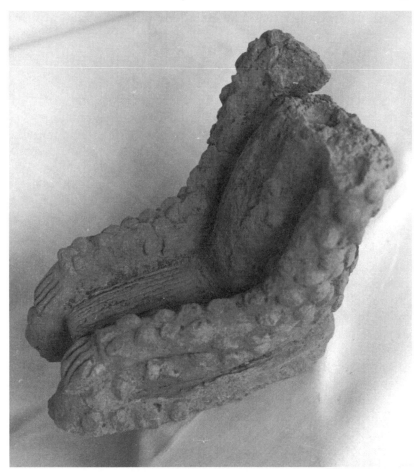

Plate 10.1   *Middle Niger statuette with buboes.*

dle Niger terracotta statuettes from this period depict buboes and pustules. To our great frustration, the historical evidence for famines and epidemics only appears in earnest in the late sixteenth century,[28] and really only becomes statistically trustworthy with European observers.[29]

How at odds with most reconstructions of social conditions at

[28] S. M. Cissoko, "Famines et epidemies," pp. 807–13.
[29] Philip D. Curtin, "Epidemiology and the slave trade," *Political Science Quarterly*, 83 (1968): 190–216 and "Disease exchange across the tropical Atlantic," *History and Philosophy of the Life Sciences*, 15 (1993), pp. 169–96.

the rise of the great Western Sudanese empires is this tale of disease and demographic collapse?

The Middle Niger and the Great Empires

If the preceding climatic and demographic reconstructions are even near the mark, how possibly could the late first millennium and early second millennium have witnessed the birth of the great so-called "medieval" empires of the Western Sudan? Arab geographers and travellers and, later, local chroniclers writing in Arabic begin in the eighth century to discuss the political structures of the lands of the Blacks south of the Sahara that they recognize as advanced chiefdoms, kingdoms, or multi-ethnic states.[30] We know from this new class of sources that major states dominate the political landscape: Mali of the Mande (Malinké) and Songhai of the Niger Bend peoples of that same name. Ghana (Wagadou) of the northern Soninké is more problematic. Some consider it a fully integrated, militarily mature state; others now consider it a more informally integrated confederation of essentially autonomous polities, an "overkingdom".

These empires are just the most relevant, for our purposes, of a new West African constellation of expansive, bureaucratic, and bellicose states (from Takrur along the Middle Senegal Valley and to Kanem on the shores of Lake Chad). These are just the most spectacular examples of a wider phenomenon of political reorganization. According to our observers from outside, they are territorially expansive and run by (warrior) dynasts and boast a formal bureaucracy. Many, many smaller polities appear in the umbra of the great empires. The aforementioned kingdom of Méma is one. Curiously, Arab visitors to the Middle Niger and local *ta'rikhs* do not mention centralized, hierarchical states (much less the "aristocracies of terror")[31] that dominate the scene elsewhere. Certainly long after the withering away of Mali, many polities appropriate as-

---

[30] For a general overview, see Susan Keech McIntosh and Roderick J. McIntosh, "West African savanna kingdoms," in *The Oxford Companion to Archaeology*, Brian M. Fagan (ed.) (Oxford University Press, Oxford, 1996), pp. 748–50. The classic source-book for the Arab narratives is Nehemia Levtzion and J. F. P. Hopkins, *Corpus of Early Arabic Sources for West Afrian History*, (Cambridge University Press: Cambridge, 1981).

[31] Bathily, *Portes de l'Or*, p. 232.

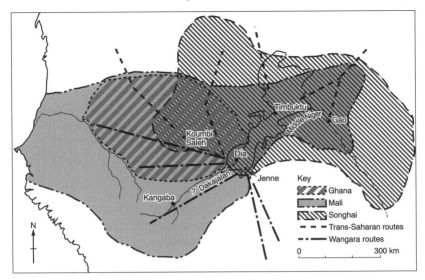

Map 10.1 *West Africa during the Great Empires with trans-Saharan and Wangara trade routes*

pects of that empire's legacy to legitimate their own growth.

Historians have long relied heavily upon the Arabic sources for their reconstruction of the circumstances of state formation in the Western Sudan. Indeed, with the prevailing low density of archaeologists and scholars of oral tradition, historians had little option but to rely upon these sources, both for the first mention of states and, most importantly, for the interpretation for why these polities appear where and when they did. The classic paradigm was "Arab stimulation":[32] West African communities were small-scale, economically isolated, and politically conservative until the idea of centralized states (and urbanism, bureaucratic control hierarchies, specialist production and long-distance trade) radiated from across the Sahara. New opportunities for the creation of an indigenous elite appeared in the form of the trans-Saharan (gold) trade.

The edifice of scholarship built around this paradigm of outside influence stood fast just as long as the principal (or only) sources were the writings of Arabs or arabicized Berbers. These authors came to their observations with, at best, a jejune and condescending view of their Black Sudanese neighbors across the desert. At

---

[32] See R. McIntosh and S. McIntosh, "From *Siècles obscurs*," pp. 146–7; S. McIntosh and R. McIntosh, "From stone to metal," pp. 111–14.

worst, they exuded virulent racial prejudices. One can see this atti-
tude clearly in the description by Ibn Hawkal (writing in AD 988)
of the political life of the Blacks, after he has just mentioned the
major states of Takrur and Ghana!

> We have not mentioned the land of the Sudan in the west, nor the
> Buja nor the Zanj, nor the peoples with the same characteristics,
> because the orderly government of kingdoms is based upon religious
> beliefs, good manners, law and order, and the organization of settled
> life directed by sound policy. These people lack all these qualities
> and have no share in them. Their kingdoms, therefore, do not deserve
> to be dealt with separately as we have dealt with other kingdoms.[33]

We see the long reach of those who would relegate Africans to a
People Without History. Beyond obvious questions about the ob-
jectivity or perceptiveness of Ibn Hawqal and his ilk, there are many
other questions of political process in the late first millennium and
early second millennium. If stimulation from the north were truly
the defining reason for new scales of political organization in the
Sahel and savannas of West Africa, why do states such as Ghana
(and Takrur and Kawkaw-Gao) appear on the scene simultaneously
with or even before the Islamic invasion and reorganization of North
Africa in the seventeenth century? Why do these early polities appear before the expansion of the trans-Saharan trade? Did West
Africa really pass from statelessness to Empires without intervening (indigenous) phases of evolving social and political complexity? And how can we even speak of rapidly evolving statecraft at a
time of severe climatic stress, presumed agricultural and pastoral
decline (or, at the very least, adjustments), and demographic dislocations (if not disaster)? Certainly, the dominant social science paradigm of social evolutionism would predict that the new scales of
political centralization represented by a Ghana or Mali should occur only in response to ever-larger populations living in circum-
scribed regions or, for whatever reasons, having increasingly regular
contact with each other.[34] Can it be that demographic cataclysm
itself stimulated new vertical orders of political organization?

At the moment we do not have an answer to any of these questions. We can say, however, that current scholarship and the growing contribution of field archaeology and newly recorded oral
traditions has led to the rejection of the "Arab stimulation" para-

---

[33] Levtzion and Hopkins, *Corpus*, p. 44.
[34] E.g., Johnson and Earle, *Evolution*.

digm. The paradigm has not yet been replaced by an entirely satisfactory *monolithic* theory of state formation. The emergence of
complex society and polities is far too diverse a process. Also, the
earliest polities that impinged in one way or another upon the Middle Niger probably looked very unlike the highly centralized and
bureaucratized, military-based, despotic states of the Western expectations for the pre-industrial state.[35]

Ghana itself is increasingly looking less like a unity than (at least
at its beginning) a confederation of roughly equivalent polities.
Various elements of this confederation (particularly those farthest
from the court) spin off into nominal independence at each periodic weakening of the dynasty or of its military will. There appears
to have been an earlier and much more complex, but essentially
unstable, process of transformation from an uncentralized landscape of small-scale polities (discussed at the end of chapter 8) into
a succession of dynastic states. An important part of this process is
the appropriation of the glory of an older empire to legitimate the
expansive claims of ambitious dynasts. This legitimation strategy
is one part of what we will call the Imperial Tradition. In order to
understand the process, let us first review the impact upon the Middle Niger of the three giant empires of the Western Sudan.

In truth, most sophisticated historians had long rejected a too-
literal reading of the "Arab Stimulation" model. Such a reading
would have the benefits of civilization diffusing across the Sahara,
spreading ineluctably by wave propagation, to a passive but na-
ively receptive population. While most historians' view of the
circumstances of Western Sudanese state formation is less uni-
dimensional than this, the emphasis is still upon those external influences without which, things would have just gone on as before.
Underdeveloped in the historiography of West Africa are those internal dynamics pushing local societies to greater complexity.

It is exactly such internal dynamics that led to expansive Middle
Niger commerce and specialist production and to the burgeoning
of cities such as Jenne-jeno and Dia, as we have seen. Before these
archaeological data became available, however, much emphasis had
been put upon the earliest Western Sudanese states as a response to
the long-distance contacts with North Africa. That is, state forma-

---

[35] The principal source for this section is Nehemia Levtzion's *Ancient Ghana*. The
approach to the great empires is heavy influenced by discussions with Nehamia
Levtzion, David Conrad, and Susan Keech McIntosh in advance of a joint rewrite
of that classic.

tion emerges as adaptation to pressures or new opportunities created by the western and southern expansion of the Islamic world. Secondarily, historians considered the need of southern communities to organize themselves into defense against nomadic incursions when the always tentative armed peace[36] with the Berbers of the southern Sahara (Sanhaja or Tuareg) eventually broke down. In this external-push paradigm, new local technologies such as agriculture, iron use, and perhaps even a prior experimentation with cavalry organization may have served as internal prior conditions for the success of outside stimulation. But internal demographic pressures or new developments in the internal political economy are not ascribed a particularly important role.

Given the traditional histories' emphasis on external influences, it is interesting that Jenne and Dia are so preeminent in traditions about the very beginning of Ghana and (in the case of Jenne) the very end of Mali. In the foundation myths of the northern Soninké, the origin and ranking of clans is reckoned by the order of patrimony from Dinga. The myths' most critical figures are Dinga, as eponymous ancestor of the clans and first to define the nature of authority in the Ghana Empire, and his son Diabé Cissé, the first king of Ghana and first to be invested with the sacred regalia.[37] Most of these legends deal with the consolidation of power in the Wagadou heartland (generally placed around Koumbi Saleh, in modern Mauritania), and thus outside the immediate purview of this book. But the beginning of the story places us squarely in the Middle Niger.

Dinga is generally given an invented birth from Biblical parents (Job, Solomon, David) or emigration from sacred lands (Mecca, Yemen, Aswan) very familiar to scholars from many other Western Sudanese foundation myths. As we shall see, these tales are devices for the appropriation of the Islamic legitimation within the Imperial Tradition. However, upon his arrival in the Sahel, Dinga does things that are decidedly pre-Islamic. All versions agree that he first travels to Jenne. This first stop bothered historians until the excavations at Jenne-jeno showed that, indeed, there was an important settlement of southeastern Soninké-speakers (Bozo and Nono) in place centuries before the presumed mid-first millennium consoli-

---

[36] Trimingham, *A History of Islam*, pp. 20–33, 37–60. See also, Webb, *Desert Frontier*, pp. 14–26

[37] Germaine Dieterlen and Diarra Sylla, *L'Empire de Ghana. La Wagadou et les Traditions de Yéréré*, (Karthala: Paris, 1992).

dation of Ghana. At Jenne, Dinga settles (for 27 years in some versions, 20 in others) and takes a wife.

They have no issue, unfortunately. So Dinga moves on. During the Jenne interlude, however, he acquired his power over rain and learns how to acquire power over ponds and wells by ritually killing the water genies or guardian beasts. These will be sources of authority exploited fully at the founding of Ghana. After Jenne, Dinga spends an unspecified number of years at Dia (alternative versions have him settling the region of [west of the] "Diaka," which would include Dia and most of the Macina, but would also encompass the Méma). There, his new wife, Assakoulé Soulouro, gives him three children (ancestors to three important clans of the Macina and Méma). From there, Dinga travels northwest to the Wagadou heartland. At the dangerous well of Dalangoumbé (south of Nioro), he fights and eventually vanquishes the female protector spirit. He marries the three lovely daughters of the vanquished genie, one of which is the mother of Diabé and of his twin, Bida, the snake of Wagadu. We have already met Bida travelling from Wagadou to the Niger along the subterranean Vallée du Serpent.

These various marriages establish the origin and hierarchy of the Soninké clans, but what reading can we give to the sterile years at Jenne? Although founded by Soninké-speakers, no accounts of Ghana claim that the city and its immediate hinterland were ever actually incorporated into the Empire. Cordial relations must have been maintained between the two entities. Ghana's direct rule extended into the Méma and, less certainly, to Dia at a time when the archaeology of these regions leaves no doubt of the close commercial and cultural ties between them. It is entirely possible that Dinga's long stay at Jenne describes the forging of solid alliance relations between Ghana and the Upper Delta. The latter region need not have been incorporated into the formal, hierarchical clan organization at the empire's root.

Dia and the Méma probably rested at the periphery, as compared to the territories of the clans issuing from the daughters of Dalangoumbé. What appears to be described in the legends is a classic process of non-coercive political agglomeration. This was a process that probably took place independently a hundred times and in a hundred places in the Western Sudan throughout the first millennium. Ghana (and Takrur and Gao) may be just the first known of these political agglomerations because of the accident of first contact by Arab chroniclers. J. Spencer Trimingham describes the process as being the slow superimposition of chiefly lineages over uncentralized village groupings. In his view, the ruler was "not interested in dominating territory, per se, but in relationships with social groups."[38]

I have presented a model of Ghana, not so much as a despotic conquest state, but as a slowly consolidated confederation of many "chiefdoms" in various relations to the core (from nominal, tribute-paying parity to fully administered). This reconstruction is more consistent with recent thought about the origins of states out of an earlier landscape of small-scale polities. Ghana was unquestionably concerned to tax the trade in gold and in other items that passed through its territories. The state unquestionably maintained a cavalry-based army. The military base was probably of fluctuating size, used to deal with its truculent camel nomad neighbors to the north.

However, as we will see with the later Mali and Songhai empires, during times of dynastic struggles or other sources of political turmoil at the core, the elements of the periphery slipped easily into states of greater or lesser political autonomy. During the ascendancy of the Ghana state, parts of the Middle Niger, such as the Jenne region, probably maintained their status as fully self-administering, independent, and friendly polities. The Méma and Lakes Region, however, were integrated more closely. They were still allowed a measure of self-rule, probably because of the iron-production within the former (recognized at "industrial" sites along the Boulel Ridge, dated to cal AD 690–970)[39] and because of the latter's critical role in the expanding northern Sahelian and trans-Saharan camel routes.

The process of confederation probably had begun by mid-first millennium. By the late ninth century, when the Arab sources begin to provide details, Ghana is recognized as a powerful kingdom. Its easternmost province of "Safanqu" probably included most of the Lakes Region and its administrative center was somewhere north of Ras-el-Ma. The Méma was so thoroughly integrated that we will see it play the intermediary role in the transfer of legitimacy from Ghana to Mali. The administered lands extended southeast to the left bank of the Niger west of Segou (al-Bakam) and southwest to the goldfields of Bambouk. Ghana gold was minted in North African (Sijilmassa) early in the tenth century. By the next century,

---

[38] Trimingham, *History of Islam*, p. 35.
[39] S. McIntosh, *Excavations*, pp. 383–4; Håland, "Man's role," p. 42.

the state's prosperity and military power incited the jealousy of neighbors to the north. Its northern Sahelian location left it exposed to the inevitable climatic stresses.

This, of course, is the orthodoxy about the Ghana heartland. The reader should be made aware of a persistent (but still minority view) that the heartland was, in fact, within one of the western basins of the Middle Niger itself. This speculation is encouraged by the disappointing results of archaeology (at least, to date) at the remains of Koumbi Saleh. Colonial and post-colonial period work at the site focussed overly upon the Islamic and North African aspect of the site's artifacts and architecture.[40] Still, a dedicated search of the surroundings of Koumbi Saleh's extensive stone-built ruins has failed to reveal either the indigenous "royal" quarter or (more disturbingly) the elite tumuli burials described by al-Bakri.[41] Speculation about a quite different location of the Ghana capital is encouraged also by ecological considerations. Koumbi Saleh at the extreme north of the Sahel would have had great difficulty provisioning itself in locally grown grain. Perhaps this would have been less of a concern, given our favorable reconstructions of the late first millennium climatic improvement. Further, there has always been a certain discomfort with the site of Koumbi Saleh based on alternative readings of information in the Arab chronicles about the camel caravan routes leading to the Ghana capital. Al-Idrisi, for example, places the capital on the Nile (Niger) (or a major tributary).[42]

The dissenters look naturally to the Middle Niger, both because of economic potential for centralized state formation and because of the superabundance of spectacular sites. The Malian archaeologist, Téréba Togola, is betting on the Méma.[43] He bases this belief

---

[40] Colonial period: de Mézières, *Recherches*, pp. 227–64; and Raymound Mauny and P. Thomassey, "Campagne de fouilles à Koumbi Saleh (Ghana?)," *Bulletin de l'Institut Fondamental de l'Afrique Noire* (B), 13 (1951), pp. 438–62; Post-Colonial: Denise Robert and Serge Robert, "Douze années de Recherches archéologiques en République Islamique de Mauritanie," *Annales de la Faculté des Lettres*, Dakar, 2(1972), pp. 195–233.; S. Bethier, *Recherches archéologiques sur la capitale de l'Empire de Ghana. Etude d'un Secteur d'habitat à Koumbi Saleh)Mauritanie)*, Cambridge Monographs in African Archaeology, no. 680, BAR: Oxford, 1997; Jean Devisse and Boubacar Diallo, "Le seuil du Wagadu," in Réunion des Musées Nationaux, Valleés du Niger, pp. 107–14.

[41] Levtzion and Hopkins, *Corpus*, pp. 80–1.

[42] Ibid., pp. 107, 109.

[43] Téréba Togola, pers. com., 1995.

only partly upon alternative readings of caravan itineraries. His reconstruction relies also upon the exclusive use of the title for the king of Wagadu, *Tunka*, by later kings of Méma, and upon the fact that later Western Sudanese kings (most notably Sunjata, founder of the Mali empire) travel to the Méma (not to the still extant Koumbi Saleh) if they wish to be invested with the symbols and living legacy of Ghana kingship. This last act is a central tenent of the Imperial Tradition. Togola believes archaeologists will find the capital in one of the many large sites (some up to 80 ha. in area; several accompanied by apparent funerary tumuli) in the region he surveyed along the Fala de Molodo. He reserves particular hope for the massive site of Péhé.

Others stake equally high hopes upon the ancient Soninké precinct of Tendirma in the Lakes Region.[44] Here the presence of several massive habitation sites, as well as the elite tumuli burials such as El-Oualadji and Killi, fan the spark of speculation lit by Idrisi. Some go so far as to call the Lakes Region (and Macina, and Méma?) the kingdom of the Wangara that functioned not only as the true heartland of Wagadou, but as the ancestral state to Mali ("Old Mali" and as Zarma, the homeland of the first Songhai dynasties). The sub-text of this minority hypothesis is that southern termini of the trans-Saharan trade routes have been assigned an unwarranted role in the political formulation of the Western Sudan only because of our overreliance upon the Arab texts. Thus one dissenter reassesses Koumbi Sahel and Gao: "In fact, these market towns were hardly more than outposts and windows of the powerful kingdoms of Inner West Africa on the Mediterranean world."[45] Only a great deal of future archaeology will resolve the issue. We leave the controversy by saying there is nothing specified in the ambiguous Arab accounts used by historians at the start of this century to make the initial identification of Koumbi Saleh as the capital of Wagadou that would necessarily preclude a location in either the Lakes Region or the Méma.

Limited as it has been, recent scholarship and archaeology does demonstrate reasonably convincingly that the late eleventh century exchanges between Ghana and the militant Islamic reformists, the

---

[44] Dierk Lange, "The Almoravid expansion and the downfall of Ghana," *Der Islam*, 73(2) (1996), pp. 122–59 and "From Mande to Songhay: Towards a political and ethnic history of medieval Gao," *Journal of African History*, 35 (1994), pp. 275–301.
[45] Lange, "From Mande," p. 299.

Almoravids, did not result in the extinction of the Empire.[46] The established view, not long ago, was that the southern Almoravids called for *jihad* against all Western Sudanese Blacks (except their allies from Takrur along the Middle Senegal), under their leader, Abu Bakr, who was himself killed by the Soninké of Taghant in 1087. Two principal objectives were to win back the southern Saharan entrepot of Awdaghost from Ghana (accomplished in 1055) and to conquer the pre-eminent symbol of truculent infidelism, the Wagadu capital (achieved in 1076–77, according to al-Zuhri).[47] However, by 1084 the empire musters sufficient resources (and orthodox Islamic motivation) to join with the Almoravids to remove the heretical Ibadiyya merchants from Tadmekka.

For the next two centuries, the external sources generally paint a picture of a reasonably prosperous state. The archaeology of Koumbi Saleh proves that occupation continues essentially unabated until the settlement withers in the late fourteenth or fifteenth centuries (as opposed to ending in the eleventh century in a natural or bellicose cataclysm).[48] By that late date, southern Sanhaja camel nomads are no longer united behind the Almoravid banner. Some Sanhaja tribes are even tributary to the Wagadou. Others provide troops for its army. By this time, however, Walata has superseded Koumbi Saleh as the principal terminus of the western trans-Saharan trade. Timbuktu is the trading partner on the Middle Niger.

In the end, what are we to make of the mid-twelfth century report by al-Idrisi that Ghana's capital sits astride the Nile/Niger? Is he just wrong (as the proponents of a western Middle Niger location would argue), or has the capital shifted? Or is al-Idrisi describing not old Ghana, but a successor state, such as the Méma, that has appropriated the prestigious name? Anything is possible in the Imperial Tradition.

Perhaps we have here an alternative reading of the famous Wagadou oral tradition of the killing of the protector snake, Bida, and the consequences for the state.[49] Dinga's son Diabé Sissé is able

---

[46] David C. Conrad and Humphrey J. Fisher, "The conquest that never was: Ghana and the Almoravids, 1076, I, the external Arabic sources," *History in Africa*, 9 (1982), pp. 21–59 and "The conquest that never was: Ghana and the Almoravids, 1076, I, the local oral sources," *History in Africa*, 10 (1983), pp. 53–78; cf., Sheryl L. Burkhalter, "Listening for silences in Almoravid history: Another reading of 'The conquest that never was'," *History in Africa*, 19 (1992), pp. 103–31.

[47] Levtzion, *Ancient Ghana*, p. 45.

[48] S. McIntosh and R. McIntosh, "Recent," p. 429.

[49] Conrad and Fisher, "Conquest that never was, II," pp. 63–9.

to found the Wagadou state only when he enters into a pact with his brother, the fearsome snake Bida. Bida will ensure sufficient rains and access to gold (of Bambuk) only so long as he is provided each year with the kingdom's most lovely virgin. One fateful year, the virgin's suitor, a young man with a Muslim name, lops off Bida's head and brings destruction to the state. In some accounts, the head bounces seven times to land in Buré (shifting the gold production to the sphere of Mali and away from Ghana's traditional source, Bambuk). The land is wracked by seven years of drought and famine – ending the empire. This tale has been interpreted as describing the destruction of the traditional religion and the state by Muslim invaders (the Almoravids in 1076–7). But it may also describe the situation centuries later, perhaps in the late twelfth to fourteenth centuries, when climatic disasters took their cumulative effect. The weakened empire then dissolves into many (seven?) successor states.

Indeed, at this time the Western Sudan reverted back to a condition in some ways approaching the landscape of interacting, competing small polities in place when Wagadou established itself as head of the confederation in the mid-first millennium. The great differences now were the presence of Islam and the ever evolving Imperial Tradition. The latter ensured that the multiple successor states would vie for the mantle of Ghana. They competed for the right to claim themselves as the proper inheritor, the imperial right to rule by divine condescension. Hence the need for historians to treat with extreme caution reports of sighting of "Ghana" by the alien, often far distant Arab chroniclers. What better way to wrest that Imperial mantle from competing neighbors that to claim the name of Ghana (or Wagadou) or the name of the faded empire's king.

That appears to be precisely what the strongest claimant does. Méma will serve the historical role of transmitting the Imperial Tradition from Wagadou to Mali. By the late twelfth or thirteenth century, the king of Méma presumes to call himself *Tunkara*. This was one of the traditional labels of the king of Ghana. Méma is always one of the strongest of the successor states and it has the strongest claim to direct continuity from Wagadou, on the increasingly accepted principle of shifting capitals.[50] However, Méma is

---

[50] Change of hegemony from one polity to a neighbor may not necessarily be abrupt, but may be ambiguous because of the tendency of the political focus, the "capital" to shift frequently, David C. Conrad, "A town called Dakajalan: The Sunjata tradition and the question of ancient Mali's capital," *Journal of African History*, 35(1994), p. 362.

not alone. Far to the west, in the Kolimbiné valley, the Diafunu and (to a lesser extent) the Guidimakka and Gadiaga have their day in the sun. Between the Kolimbiné and the southern Hodh, the Diara kingdom flourishes, as does the Kusa around Nioro and Goumbou, but both are eventually overwhelmed by the expansive southern Soninké Soso state.[51] All claim legitimacy from Ghana.

Soso expansionism is impressive, particularly under the early thirteenth-century magician, blacksmith king Sumaworo (Sumangourou). Soso picks off or threatens all these successor states, expanding south among the tiny Soninké statelettes among the Marka east of Segou, the Niare chiefdoms of the Bamako region and, most fatefully, among the Malinke chiefdoms of what is now considered the heartland of Mande. It is out of this clash between the last-gasp of Soninké expansionism and the recent ascendancy of the Malinke that the Mali empire is born.

The Sunjata legend of the rise of the Mali empire is vast in its scope and literary sophistication. The Sunjata legend is super-Homeric in the richness of its variations and in the role it plays in local and national statecraft in contemporary Mali and Guinea. Most of the action in the legend takes place far to the south of the Middle Niger, so Sunjata's rise to power will only be briefly summarized here. Some of the central actors do pass critical episodes of their careers in the Middle Niger. Thus it is important to see how the Méma, Jenne, and the Niger Bend figure in the evolution of the Imperial Tradition.

The legend tells the story of the consolidation and rise to imperial power of small chiefdoms, particularly Do and Malal, in the Mande savanna. This was the country of the Lamlam. These were Malinke, subject to raids and slaving by their better organized northern neighbors, particularly by the Middle Senegal peoples and Ghana, according to al-Idrisi.[52] The northern Malinke appear to have been organized into a small chiefdom, comprised of a few villages under a noble clan (the Konate for the Do and the Keita for early Mali). Oral traditions record at least ten Keita rulers before Nare-Maghan, the father of Sunjata.

Historians ascribe the rise of Mali to several underlying changes in the political economy of the Malinke territory.[53] Gold production began in the eleventh century in the nearby Buré fields. Wangara

[51] N. Levtzion, *Ancient Ghana*, pp. 48–51.
[52] Levtzion and Hopkins, *Corpus*, p. 108.
[53] N. Levtzion, *Ancient Ghana*, pp. 53–6.

from the Middle Niger (particularly Dia) pioneered extensive trade routes through the savanna and into the forest, linking "Old Mande" to rather more evolved polities west and north and to the cosmopolitan centres of the Middle Niger. And internecine struggles amongst the waning southern Soninké created the kind of turmoil in a political vacuum that would be the proving ground for a charismatic leader such as Sunjata.

The larger-than-life Sunjata did more than prevail militarily over the Soso forces under the clan Kante chief Sumaworo. Sunjata did more than to create or formalize a new social order based upon a hereditary cavalry-grounded nobility and a socially restricted classification of craftsmen (*griots*, leatherworkers and, especially, blacksmiths – the *nyamakalaw*). And he did more than borrow Islamic conceptions of supernatural power (*baraka*) and statecraft that had been percolating into the Mali heartland long before this time. Sunjata's genius was in the invention of a new legitimation tradition out of older traditions of hunters" authority, supernatural powers of Wangara and of the *nyamakalaw*, and out of inventing a claim to the imperial tradition of Ghana.

Into a scene of petty rivalries among the northern Malinke chiefdoms and succession disputes within those tiny states, steps the avaricious, evil, power-mad blacksmith king of the Soso. Sunjata had been forced into exile by the jealous king, his half-brother, when the Soso arrive to ravage the Mali countryside. A desperate call to lead the resistance brings Sunjata back from the Méma, where he had been living as honored guest of the *Tunkara*. From that transmitter state he brings the blessings of the king (legitimacy from the direct descendant of Ghana), new concepts of administration, and (not the least) a force of cavalry provided by the Méma king and from Wagadou. Sunjata's first act, however, is to establish himself (or reassert his lineage right) as the Hunter King.[54] He creates elite army corps out of the hunters" associations.

Little of the legends recounts actual battles. Far more volume of recitation is devoted to proving Sunjata's control over ancient and dangerous symbols of hunters (and of blacksmiths and *griots*) and to proving him the master of manipulating the Mande life-force, the energy of action and statecraft, *nyama*. He not only reinvents these ancient concepts and symbols of authority to serve the exigencies of the time, but he reinvents the very structure of Mande society. He provides the key by which secular dynasts control, but

[54] Conrad, "Searching," pp. 173–9; Cissé, "Notes," pp. 176, 190, 203.

are not themselves polluted nor undone by the terrible powers of *nyama* that are the purview of blacksmiths. The blacksmith king Sumaworo as possessor of absolute power is corrupted absolutely.

Of equal importance, Sunjata allies himself with Mande translators into African idioms of Islamic power and institutions, such as his lieutenant, N'Fatigi, who brings back from Mecca the *nyama*-filled power bundles called *boli*. The sub-legend of N'Fatigi has him making a ceremonial return by magic canoe along the river from Timbuktu to Jenne (sucking up the power of these venerable localities into his boli and into the canoe as he goes). The *faaro* are not to be ignored.

Sunjata's power is far more than the sum of these individual parts. Still, he is barely able to prevail over Sumaworo in the definitive magician's confrontation, the battle of Krina. Sumaworo is killed or disappears; the allies of the Soso are mopped up, and the Soso themselves (or at least their ruling clans) are forced into permanent exile. During the remaining 25 years of Sunjata's rule, his kingdom expands mightily into an empire. Here begins again the story of Middle Niger – strange that the prosperous live basins are so relatively absent from the story so far.

Mali is much more than the alliance of quasi-independent chiefdoms, as Ghana may have been. The Keita heartland was the undisputed core of the empire, later creating a hierarchy of dependencies. At one end of the hierarchy were the nominally independent Méma and Wagadou (probably paying tribute). Next came the variously autonomous, but heavy tribute-obliged provinces (some with local rulers and others with imperial governors). Was this the status of the Jenne and Dia regions? And at the shifting frontiers of the Empire were the garrisoned (and often resentful) fringe states such as Takrur and Silla along the Middle Senegal or Songhai immediately downstream of the Niger Bend (first conquered in *c*.1320).

The last were always waiting for a weakening of Mali's imperial will. They dreamed of the opportunity to rid themselves of royal governors or of local puppet dynasties. The shift in Songhai from the (much debated) Dia dynasty to the Sonni may represent just such a shedding of Mali's rule. Mali was strong and expansive for the remaining 25 years of Sunjata's life. Likewise, under his son Mansa Uli and, then, another son, Mansa Wali, the emperor and state were strong. Then followed a series of weak-minded, unlucky, usurping *mansas*, and the empire unraveled. The golden-age reigns of Mansa Musa (1312–37) and his son, Muhammed, brought Mali back to its former glory. Frontier states such as Gao, that had taken advantage of the political vacuum, were now shepherded back into the fold with punitive attention. Mansa Muhammed, however, is overthrown by his uncle, Sulayman in 1350. Conditions decline rapidly. By 1360–90 the core weakness is apparent to all vassal states, with the predictable result that Mali's territorial sway ebbs.

There is remarkably little mention of Middle Niger localities in the chronicles of the Mali empire. This indirectly encouraged the influential colonial reconstructions of a late foundation for the towns of Timbuktu (twelfth century) and Jenne (AD 1250). For some historians, these infant towns were just too insignificant to attract attention. Alternatively (since we know now that the towns and their commercial networks were very much older and very much wealthier), non-mention may imply that the towns settled into a peaceful, semi-autonomous relationship with the empire. Sunjata and his immediate issue may have had the uncommon wisdom (in ambitious dynasts) to let well enough alone.

Timbuktu was probably taken during the early expansion of the empire and would likely have been loath to join Gao in its periodic rebellions. By the later fourteenth century, Timbuktu had superseded Walata as foremost terminus of the western trans-Saharan trade route. Prosperity brought the unwanted attention of Mossi and Maghsharen Tuareg raiders. In 1433 the last vestige of Mali's authority was removed, to be replaced by Tuareg rule for 40 years. Then history was rewritten with the arrival of Sonni Ali Ber of Songhai.

Likewise, the Méma was conquered by the Songhai by 1464, after several decades of independence from the severely weakened Mali. For the Méma to have so asserted itself shows that, by the late fifteenth century, Songhai conquests were largely a matter of lurching into a political vacuum. This was no battle of the titans between the vital, opportunistic Songhai and the tired old man of the Western Sudan.

Jenne plays a doubly ambiguous role in the Mali ascendancy. The most reliable of the great indigenous *ta'rikhs* (Arabic chronicles), es-Sa'di's *Ta'rikh es-Sudan* of 1655, puts forward the claim that Mali never conquered Jenne, even after 99 attempts.[55] The other major chronicle, the *Ta'rikh el-Fattash*, however, says that the chief of Jenne was one of the most humble (and purposefully humiliated) servants of the Mali emperor.[56] Two perspectives, per-

---

[55] N. Levtzion, *Ancient Ghana*, p. 82.
[56] Ibid., p. 81.

haps, on the town's (voluntary?) tribute-paying fiefdom status.

Add to that conflicting view this mystery: during the thirteenth and fourteenth centuries, as a production center within a unified, peaceful, generally well administered empire, Jenne(-jeno) surely should have enjoyed superb conditions for prosperity. Yet we know from the archaeology that this and the following century were times of dramatic settlement pattern turmoil and very probably of dramatic depopulation, both in the town itself and in the floodplain hinterland. These demographic revolutions appear to have preceded the assertion of Jenne's independence of Mali early in the fifteenth century, at which time Jenne controlled most of the upper Inland Delta. These changes appear also to have preceded the devastation of the Mossi incursions of the 1430s, 1470s and 1480s into the vacuum left by a chronically weakened Mali.

Into this vacuum stepped the Songhai. Independent of Mali by the end of the fourteenth century, Songhai steadily grew in strength. In the reign of Sonni Silman Dama (d. 1464), the upstart empire took the Méma. This move might appear strange, given that the intervening Timbuktu region was not conquered until 1468. Stranger still – the archaeology of Méma sites such as Kolima and Akumbu demonstrate that desiccation had virtually depopulated this dry basin by that date. However, the move into Méma was perhaps understandable when we consider the long-term role of the Méma as the legitimizing descendant of Wagadou (and, even more so, according to the argument of some, that the adjoining Lakes Region was Tendirma, the real seat of Wagadou).

Whatever Silman Dama's motivation, his successor Sonni Ali Ber is considered the true expansive force of Songhai. He begins his reign fighting a succession of threats to the Gao heartland and Niger Bend (at the hands of the Mossi, Fulani, Tuareg, and a reascendant Mali). He takes Timbuktu in 1468. He deals as harshly with the Islamic notables of that town as with the hated Fulani of the Middle Niger. After a siege reported to have lasted seven years, seven months and seven days, Sonni Ali Ber takes Jenne. The town is treated remarkably leniently, reportedly at the behest of the town's protector *faaro*! He then goes on to attack Mali twice, although (according to Leo Africanus in 1512) the Songhai are generally content with the southern edge of the "kingdom" of Jenne as the frontier with the attenuated Mali.[57]

---

[57] Ibid., p. 87.

Songhai goes through another expansionist period under Askiya Mohammed. The empire expands to Galam along the upper Senegal by 1508, through the Middle Senegal in 1512–13 and east to Agadez two years later. But Askiya Mohammed is deposed in 1528 and Songhai begins the now familiar cycles of strength (during which errant provinces are forcibly reintegrated and Mali harassed, but never conquered) and of internal turmoil.

With weakened imperial rule, the latter half of the sixteenth century cannot have been a happy time in the Middle Niger. Added to the environmental misery of the rural population is the increasing evidence of significant influxes of Fulani, coming in from Mauritania and western Mali, and of non-Muslim, martial Bambara from the south (chapter 4). Increasingly, Songhai military action is directed toward stemming the intrusion of these peoples. Fulani and Bambara peasants and state-builders will soon be at each others throats as well. However, with the facility of convenient memory, the author of the *Ta'rikh es-Sudan* looks back upon the Songhai period as one of peace and prosperity in the Middle Niger.[58] The source of es-Sa'di's anguish is the covetousness of a ruler from far across the great desert.

In one of the signal years of world history, 1591, the Moroccan king sends a force of musketeers under Judar Pasha. The Moroccans defeat the Songhai army at the battle of Tondibi. The Moroccans then proceed to garrison Gao and the principle towns of the Middle Niger (Timbuktu and Jenne). They intermarry with the locals to create a local aristocracy, the Arma. The rule of the Arma, however, is restricted to those towns and to their most immediate hinterland, leaving the interior open to the Fulani raids and mass Bambara immigration. The Bambara, particularly, invested the Upper Delta and Erg de Bara. Interestingly, into the Moroccan vacuum steps a new power – and an old friend.

The collapse of Songhai and the imposition of Arma garrison rule coincides with the last hope of Mali. In the 1590s, the vigorous Malian Mansa Mahmud concludes alliances with the Fulani of Macina against Jenne. Together these forces invest the city and almost prevail. Mansa Mahmud, however, has to divert attention to the Bambuk region, where he is at war with the local Fulani. Moroccan reinforcements from Timbuktu arrive and the Jenne siege is lifted in April of 1599. Bambuk is lost in the same year. Mali disintegrates for the last time.

---

[58] Ibid., p. 91.

And for the next 300 years, the Middle Niger submits to the avarice and bellicose will of Fulani, Bambara, and Tukulor invaders from the Middle Senegal. But were the pre-Tondibi (1591) years of imperial hegemony really times of prosperity? Es-Sa'di had no love for the Arma and so, understandably, blames the chaos of his time on the Moroccan invasion. Archaeology at Jenne-jeno, Jenne, Dia, Akumbu, and Timbuktu, however, unequivocally shows that rural depopulation and enormous urban demographic stresses set in by AD 1200 (if not a century or two earlier). The settlement dynamics of the upper Upper Delta, Macina, and Niger Bend were, by AD 1400, radically altered from the long-stable, first millennium patterns of urban and village communities. By AD 1500, permanent settlement in the Méma is reduced to a smattering of pitiful hamlets.

So, to what period in Jenne's past does al-Sa'di refer when, in 1655, he writes his famous passage about the density of villages in the town's hinterland? Is he recalling a more immediate past under Songhai rule? Or perhaps he has tapped a deeper, collective Middle Niger memory of a pre-Mali prosperity when he writes of a time when the chief of Jenne took unusual advantage of a compliant hinterland of 7,077 closely packed villages:

> If the chief of Jenne, for example, wished an audience with an inhabitant of a village living along the banks of Lake Débo [160 km distant], his messenger would simply walk to one of the city gates. There he would call out his message. His call would be repeated by the inhabitants of village after village and the message would immediately reach the intended. He, then would immediately travel to Jenne for the audience. Nothing else could so clearly demonstrate how highly populated the Jenne region was once.[59]

Island of Gold

Inertia afflicts scholarship as surely as it does mass in motion. Inertia has its purposes. It keeps objects flying and impetuous scholars from studies in the ozone. At times it can, however, dictate that an initial, best guess of a long-departed researcher, often based upon highly fragmentary source material or upon assumptions or prejudices peculiar to the social milieu in which that scholar operated, becomes an unexamined foundation of the canon. Sometimes

[59] al-Sa'di, *Ta'rikh es-Sudan*, pp. 24–5.

subsequent scholars simply fail to return critically to those initial sources. Sometimes new discoveries in peripheral areas or adjacent disciplines render the old track unmaneuverable. There is perhaps no better example of this than the shift in scholarly opinion about the location of the famous Wangara, "Island of Gold" of the Western Sudan.

The reconsideration of what was essentially an historian's issue was occasioned by an archaeologist. With the change in perspectives created by the initial excavation results from Jenne-jeno on the period by which long-distance trade networks began, Susan Keech McIntosh claims[60] that the Wangara may not have been where we had all learned it was. Subsequent archaeological and historical work has only strengthened the case. The placement of the Island of Gold is a fascinating story of a scholarly debate of the early colonial period. Initially the debate was resolved in favor of one of several equally attractive alternatives because of the authority of one very distinguished, very thorough scholar – whose interpretation just happened to be underpinned by an assumption no longer unassailable.

The case of Wangara, Island of Gold, is by no means unique. David Conrad documents the underlying assumptions about the location of the early capital of the Mali Empire.[61] In a strikingly similar process, the authority of colonial scholarship, plus that of the popular telling of the Sunjata story by Djibril Tamsir Niane, threw the weight of scholarly opinion towards the Guinean site of Niani. No lone historian's voice[62] calling for a reassessment of the vague (not to say perversely contradictory) Arabic sources upon which the identification of Niani rested could shake the consensus faith in a permanent, monumental capital. No yawning gap in the radiocarbon dates from the site, a lacuna covering the span of the Mali Empire, could shake the faith that the modest compounds of Niani were, in truth, palaces befitting one of the world's great emperors.[63] The great irony is that one of the authorities who favored Niani, Maurice Delafosse, is the central authority on the story of the Island of Gold. Delafosse remains, in my mind, one of the heroes of West African scholarship. He simply got these two things wrong.

---

[60] S. McIntosh, "Wangara/Palolus."

[61] Conrad, "Town called Dakajalan."

[62] John O. Hunwick, "The mid-fourteenth century capital of Mali," *Journal of African History*, 14 (2)(1973), pp. 195–206.

[63] S. McIntosh and R. McIntosh, "Early city," pp. 85, 87–8, 92.

The will to possess the wealth of the Island of Gold was a major stimulus of Muslim and European imperial ambitions in the Western Sudan. This was an attraction that would "cost kings their thrones, peoples their freedom, and thousands their lives."[64] Little wonder that such covetous attention was turned upon what was presumed to be the source of perhaps two-thirds of the entire world production of gold in the early fourteenth century.[65] As we shall see, the word "source" is the sticking point. We enter the debate about the position of this fabled land during the early decades of European dominance, when scholars were turning their newly acquired facts of West African geography to the interpretation of extremely imprecise Arab references to towns, states, and gold regions.

The contrast could not be more striking between the tone of debate during early colonialism and recent decades. More recently, scholarly consensus has been almost universal in its identification of the Island of Gold with the goldfields of Bambouk and Buré. Earlier scholars were divided. On one side of the divide were those who believed that, like al-Fazari's "Ghana, Land of Gold," terms such as "land of gold" or "island of gold" did not necessarily refer to the regions of mines.[66] Rather, these terms were used for centers of the gold trade, where the foreign chroniclers or, more likely, their informants, first came into contact with those selling the metal. Opposed was the more literally inclined, including Delafosse, who believed in the primacy of production:

> Wangara . . . very likely represented the regions between the Falame and the Niger made famous by the auriferous districts of Bambuk/Buré. We still find this name, in the form Gangaran, applied today to one of the provinces in the country.[67]

According to Idrisi, Wangara forms an island surrounded on all sides by the "Nile." This description, applied to the districts enumerated above, is fairly exact; in effect, a river belt is formed around the gold producing country by the Senegal river to the north, the Faleme to the west, the Bakhoy to the east, and the Niger and Tinkasso to the south.[68]

---

[64] Bovill, *Golden Trade*, p. 191.
[65] N. Levtzion, *Ancient Ghana*, p. 132.
[66] See S. McIntosh, "Reconsideration," p. 146, note 8.
[67] Delafosse, *Haut-Sénégal-Niger* II, p. 55 (translated by S. K. McIntosh).
[68] Ibid., p. 45 (translated by S. K. McIntosh).

Bambouk and Buré, being in the higher elevations of the Futa Jallon, where the rivers have negligible floodplains, look nothing like an island. However, Delafosse was swayed to support their identification as the Island of Gold because of the presumption that the Middle Niger gold-transport centers of Jenne and Timbuktu did not come into existence until centuries after the first mention of Wangara by Mas'udi in the tenth century.

Susan McIntosh punched holes in both assumptions. She showed that Arab and European authors, writing at great distance from the Western Sudan, assumed that the gold trading centers were located near production sources.[69] She then pointed out that the archaeological evidence of a deep occupation sequence at Jenne-jeno, with evidence of early long-distance trade (e.g., copper at the fifth century), gives the lie to the assumption that the annually water-surrounded island towns of the Middle Niger were not economically developed until the fourteenth century.[70] The subsequent find of gold by AD 850–900 at Jenne-jeno, and early occupation at Dia and the Timbuktu vicinity, only strengthen her argument that the Arab sources deserve a second look.

Mas'udi, in the tenth century, only mentions that the Island of Gold is in a river that forms large islands inhabited by Blacks.[71] We must wait until 1154 for a lengthy description by al-Idrisi of this island. He describes it as 300 miles long by 150 wide, formed by a vast August inundation. It is where peoples from all countries of the Blacks assemble to "look for gold" as the floods diminish.[72]

Do peoples from all countries, including Berbers from the Sahara, "look for gold" at the production source? Or do merchants from all points of the horizon congregate at the sources of the intra-continental gold traders, the great Middle Niger assembly and transshipment centers later indelibly famous because of the Wangara? The former just does not square with the knowledge, revealed as some of the very first information about the Western Sudanese gold trade and known even by the Europeans on the periphery, that the peoples of the Bambouk and Buré source regions were pathologically private.[73] As early as Herotodus, and repeated

---

[69] S. McIntosh, "Reconsideration," p. 147.

[70] S. McIntosh, "Reconsideration," pp. 147–8.

[71] Cuoq, *Recueil*, p. 62.

[72] Ibid., pp. 134–5; S. McIntosh, "Reconsideration," p. 148.

[73] Levtzion, *Ancient Ghana*, pp. 153–5; Téréba Togola, "Traces et techniques anciennes d'exploitation aurifère dans la zone de Sadiola, Bambouk," paper presented at the 3rd International Meeting of the Mande Studies Association, March, 1995.

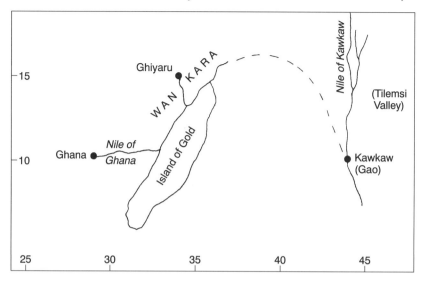

Map 10.2   *Ibn Sa'id's Island of Gold*

by the early Arab chronicles, we hear of the so-called "silent trade" in which the traders from outside would lay out their goods on the ground, hoping that the gold producers would leave in that place an equivalent quantity of the metal. Berber traders were never thought to have penetrated as far south as the goldfields. Even at its height, when they controlled all the surrounding lands, the Mali emperors resorted to a policy of non-interference in Buré and Bambouk because of past experience that the producers would simply halt the mining if outsiders infringed upon their prerogatives. Further, the Middle Niger floodplain is inundated in August; but the Bakhoy, Bafing, Falemé and upper Senegal swell within their banks months earlier. Susan McIntosh argues that in his many details, including overall size, al-Idrisi provides an accurate, if slightly garbled, account of the Upper Delta of the Middle Niger and of the seasonal gold trade at entrepôts such as Jenne.[74] Al-Idrisi places the Island of Gold in the correct position of the Middle Niger on his map of the Western Sudan (even with its many distortions). Even stronger support for that location comes from a reconsideration of Ibn Sa'id's 1240 map.[75]

[74] S. McIntosh, "Reconsideration," pp. 148–9.
[75] Ibid., pp. 150–1.

The implications of accepting the Middle Niger, and not the Bambuk/Buré goldfields as the fabled Island of Gold are that the commercial networks of the specialized Soninké-speaking long-distance traders, the Wangara, began to evolve in very distant times. They are present long before they are extensively mentioned by Arab travelers such as Ibn Battuta in the fourteenth century. Many historians attributed Ibn Battuta's knowledge of the trade to a new peak in the trans-Saharan gold trade created by the Wangara's (newly elaborated) networks of routes and centers.[76] This idea must be rethought. The second implication is that Wangara corporate organization and population movements recorded in oral tradition are early as well. Let us look first at how this reconsideration of the Island of Gold hypothesis changes our appreciation of the Golden Trade of the Moor, the classic trans-Saharan luxury commerce. Then we will reassess the archaeological traces of the Wangara and their diaspora.

The gold miners and traders of the Western Sudan were not the only ones obsessed with secrecy. Secrecy piled upon secrecy, and upon secrecy. All segments of the long-distance trade had their own, very sound commercial reasons for wanting to control the flow of information about their source of wealth: the gold miners about the position and production of the fields, the Western Sudanese agents of transshipment and artisans adding value to raw materials who lived in the great cities of the Middle Niger and in the caravansary and savanna and sahelian entrepôts and, finally, the Berber transshippers in the classic caravan trade. Let us speak briefly about the last of these, and especially about how their practices and relations with their Muslim brethren in North Africa affect what we know of trade south of the Sahara. Then we will turn to the traders of the Island of Gold.

Present best guess is that we have tended to underappreciate the volume of early first-millennium commodities crossing the Sahara, but that commerce was poorly organized until the later part of that millennium. We have already heard the argument of Garrard that considerable amounts of sub-Saharan gold were being minted in North Africa during the first few centuries AD. We know that the Punic colonies and then the Romans obtained semi-precious stones (for example the exotic carbuncles) and wild animals from trading partners such as the Libyan Garamantes.[77] Until we know from

[76] E.g., Levtzion, *Ancient Ghana*, p. 132.
[77] Brett and Fentress, *The Berbers*, pp. 65–7, 217.

archaeology more about the Berbers of the Carthaginian *chora* (administered, tribute-paying hinterland) and about the hostile Roman-period Mauritanii, we simply will not know much about the so-called proto-Berber predecessors of the trans-Saharan caravan leaders.

Until we have this knowledge, information that archaeology can alone provide about these peoples and their activities on the occluded periphery of the then literary Classical world, it is impossible to assess the standard presumption that a well-organized, voluminous trans-Saharan trade had to await the appearance on the scene of Islam and large-scale Western Sudanese empires.[78] Islam was the common religion that would overwhelm centuries-old antagonisms of Berber neighbors based upon territory and kinship. The second, imperial peace, would provide a secure, regular flow of luxury goods to the new Muslim, Berber entrepôt at the great desert's southern fringe.

In some important ways, however, the quality of our information about the workings of the trans-Saharan trade does not appreciably change during the early Islamic period. There is a vast need for gold in the Mediterranean and Near Eastern Muslim monetary systems. The desire for a regular influx of gold made the orthodox Sunni governors of Ifriqiya encourage, or at least to turn a blind eye to, the activities of independent schismatic Kharijite principalities and city-states (from Jabal Nafusa in the east to Sijilmasa in the west) that were the northern termini of the trans-Saharan routes.

Two Kharijite sects established themselves in the eighth century in the pre-Saharan steppes and mountains of North Africa, the Ibadiyya (from Jabal Nafusa in Tripolitania to Tahert in Algeria) and the Sufriyya (principally in Sijilmassa).[79] Religion was a form of political and spiritual rebellion against the orthodox hegemony. The threat of extermination hung closely over their heads (and was realized by the Fatimids in the early tenth century). So it is not surprising that our reconstruction of the trade's organization has had to be pieced together from scattered details from non-Ibidite travellers who were, by definition, not a party to the structure of authority and decision-making of these communities. In the back of scholar's mind is the hope that these outsider-travellers did not broadcast deliberate misinformation. Misinformation would, after all, have served the commercial aims of monopoly and information

---

[78] E.g., Levtzion, *Ancient Ghana*, p. 124.
[79] Brett and Fentress, *The Berbers*, pp. 87–98.

control of Ibidite traders. Disinformation would have served to protect aims of the Kharijite communities.

We have what appears to be a fairly coherent history of that trade.[80] In the last few centuries of the first millennium, the principle routes were from Tahert to Gao, by way of Wargla and Tadmekka and from Sijilmassa to Awdaghost. The volume of trade was vast. In 951, Ibn Hawqal at Awdaghost sees a cheque for 42,000 dinars.[81] There were reports of Ibadite communities (outlyers of that at Awdaghost) as far to the south as Ghiyara, the town closest to the goldfields. This has been taken by some to refer to a Wangara town in Bambuk. However, following the logic of the argument of this chapter, it is more likely that Ghiyara refers to one of the principal Wangara centers of the Middle Niger. It is entirely likely that Ghiyara may be another name for Dia (in which case, the presence of a Ibadite Berber quarter would not be remarkable). It is considerably less likely that Berbers would be allowed anywhere near the jealously guarded mines.

Changes in the routes are occasioned by political events in North Africa and by the state-building turmoil within the Western Sudan. Aghlabid Ifriqiya and Ibadite Tahert and Sijilmasa are overthrown by the Fatimids in 909. Wargla becomes the dominant terminus of the route to Gao. Under the Fatimids minting increases, especially around the time of their conquest of Egypt in 969. Minting in Spain peaks at about the same time. After a brief decline in the early eleventh century, trade booms with the Almoravids. Gold imports are generally high, but fluctuating (eg., declining under the Almohads) – as a new player from across the Mediterranean arrives on the scene.

European demand is low but rises to an insistent plateau in the early fourteenth century. By the 1480s, the amount of gold arriving at European factories along the Barbary coast declines as Portuguese caravels (1440s) and later ships from other European nations set up gold and slaving forts along the West African coast. These forts drain the gold (particularly from the Akan and Lobi sources) from the trans-Saharan routes.

---

[80] Bovill, *Golden Trade* ; Jean Devisse, "Commerce et routes du trafic en Afrique occidentale," *Histoire Générale de l'Afrique* (UNESCO, Paris, 1990), vol. III, pp. 397–483 and "Routes de commerce et échanges en Afrique occidentale en relation avec la Méditerranée," *Revue d'Histoire Economique et Sociale*, 50 (1) (1972), pp. 42–73 and 50 (3) (1972), pp. 357–97; Levtzion, *Ancient Ghana*, chs. 12–14

[81] Ibid., p. 140.

Until that happens, there is plenty of gold and other forest products to feed the fabled desert commerce. The route from Wadi Dar'a to Awdaghoust or from Wadi Dar'a through the al-Majaba al Kubra to Awdaghost flourished in the eleventh century (the last dramatically recorded by the lost caravan previously discussed).[82] By the thirteenth century, the Tlemcen–Sijilmasa–Walata network was important and Walata was fast replacing Awdaghost as a principal southern terminus (particularly early in that century when the Muslims of Ghana fled the conquering army of Sumanguru). The salt source of Taghaza (Tatental) grew in importance in the fourteenth century and with it, the Sijilmasa–Taghaza–Walata route. During the periodic weakening of Mali during that century, trade shifted east from Walata to the Taghaza–Tuat route, but new routes and opportunities appeared with the Mali–Egypt link established by the pilgrimages of the strong kings such as Mansa Musa. Timbuktu finally supersedes Walata in the later half of the 14th century, bringing ruin to Walata. After the Tondibi battle (1591), so much gold booty goes to the Moroccan ruler, Mawlay Ahmad al-Mansur, that he adds the honorific "al-Dhahabi" to his name. However, by that time the trans-Saharan trade is in a long decline because of competition from Latin American gold and the inability of the Moroccan expeditionary force and their Arma descendants to maintain security along the Saharan routes and, especially, within the Island of Gold. For the story of internal routes, we turn now to the role of the venerable Western Sudanese traders, the Wangara.

If it was to the advantage of the Ibadite Berber traders to manipulate information received by the rest of the world about the organization of the gold trade and the nature of the entrepôt communities servicing that trade, commercial secrecy would have been doubly advantageous to the Western Sudanese middlemen. Later Wangara (or Dyula as they will be known to the European chroniclers) communities were ferociously inbred and clannish. There is no reason to think that this was not a long-established pattern of dealing with a world of potentially dangerous neighbors. Because of the nature of those later sources (and their negligible mention in the earlier arabic chronicles), we know relatively more about their entrepôt "colonies" among non-Soninké-speakers and even among non-Mande peoples than we do about their traditional heartland – the Middle Niger. For this, we rely upon archaeology.

The most curious aspect of the history of Jenne is its non-men-

---

[82] Monod, "Ma'den Ijafen."

tion in any of the historical sources – Arabic or European – until 1447. Then, a Genoan commercial agent (and spy), Antonio Malfante, writes home from Tuat of the various *civitates* (city-states) of the Land of the Blacks, including Chuchian (Gao), Thambet (Timbuktu), Meli (Mali) and Geni (Jenne).[83] Imagining the reasons for this neglect to mention what we know from archaeology to be a millennium-and-a-half old commercial powerhouse is easier than absorbing the implications of that non-mention. The implications are deeply disturbing for the relative importance we tend to assign to written sources versus archaeology (and oral tradition), for the early history of the Western Sudan.

Might there be alternative names for Jenne-jeno? For example, Dia may also have been known as Yeresna, Diagha, or even Ghiyaru? Or, if it was late to adopt Islam, might the town have been ignored by Muslim chroniclers (who, nevertheless, did mention other pagan settlements). Given the Saharan copper, beads, and stone in the first millennium levels at Jenne-jeno, it is highly unlikely that Jenne participated in an internal Western Sudanese commercial network entirely divorced from the nascent trans-Saharan routes.

More likely there was a successful policy by the merchants of Jenne, or by the early Wangara moving goods along the Middle Niger riverways, to withhold information about the southern sources of the gold and about the wealth of the city itself. From their family bases in the Berber-built southern termini of the camel routes, to the near-forest trading camps near to the gold and kola producers, the Wangara were in a position to control the flow of information in both north and south directions. As speculators have known though time, information is a critical commodity to trade. No one has ever accused the Wangara of ever being anything than extremely skillful, crafty traders. What, then, does this mean for confidence in our historical reconstruction of the origins and organization of the Wangara?

It means that confusion about the Island of Gold, its synonym and heartland, is understandable. It also means that archaeology has to play the deciding role in the debate between the two positions: Island of Gold as site of gold mining or site of the gold traffick. When the archaeologist Raymond Mauny suggests that the Yarisna of al-Bakri is the producer market in Buré,[84] he is using the

---

[83] R. J. McIntosh and S. K. McIntosh, "The Inland Niger Delta before the empire of Mali: Evidence from Jenne-jeno," *Journal of African History*, 22 (1981), p. 4.
[84] Mauny, *Tableau Géographique*, pp. 302, 365.

same logic of Arabic historiography that assigns Ghiyaru to the Bambuk region. But these sources are supremely contradictory. Al-Bakri's Yaresna is a center on the Niger, where gold from Ghiyaru is brought by the Banu Naghmarteh – our first mention of the Wangara (under any label by which we can recognize them). By Idrisi's time, the Wangara have control of the Niger Bend, especially the important centers of Barisa and Tiraqqa, east of Timbuktu.

By the early 16th century, according to V. Fernandes, Wangara from Jenne control a thriving gold and slave trade well to the south. They penetrated the Akan gold producing region at least by the fourteenth century, establishing the center with the evocative name of Yarse, between Jenne and Akan. At about the same time, they are known in Hausaland to the far east (Niger and Nigeria) and have established important towns and dynasties along the Middle Senegal and upper Niger and Senegal regions. They reach as far as the Kabu goldfields of present-day Guinea-Bissau and settle as the Diakhonké along the Gambia. As impressive as is this territorial reach, archaeology suggests (once again) that the chronology for what has become called the Soninké (Wangara) diaspora may have been telescoped by several centuries.

In order to understand what the archaeology of towns such as Jenne, Dia, Timbuktu, and the Méma's Akumbu tell us about the Soninké diaspora, we must look once more at the evidence for interaction spheres or areal expressions of shared ceramics and other artifacts. We have already seen that through the ninth century (end of Jenne-jeno Phase III), Dia's Macina, Jenne-jeno's Upper Delta and Akumbu's Méma shared to a remarkable degree a coherent material culture and rules of settlement organization. The Lakes Region and Niger Bend represent a slightly different, but clearly related culture area. In the period of Imperial Tradition, specifically AD 850 to 1400 (Jenne-jeno's Phase IV) this coherence breaks down. Whether this process of areal devolution is due to climatic stress or to the political and social turmoil caused by attempts by the imperial states to dominate the cities' wealth is not clear at present. All are probably interwoven causes. The process of devolution has run its course by Sonni Ali Ber's investment of Jenne in 1468. The Moroccan victory at Tondibi twelve decades later finds a Middle Niger already compromised and balkanized.

These changes in regional integration are trumpeted in the ninth century by significant shifts in the signature ceramics of Phase IV

Jenne-jeno.[85] The Phase III painted ware is replaced by an equally distinctive fine-channeled and plastic impressed and stamped ware – representing change within a continuing tradition. New elements enter the Jenne-jeno assemblage: cylindrical mud-brick (*djenne-ferey*) architecture, zoomorphic and anthropomorhic terracotta statuary and ceramic appliqué, perforated terracotta plaques, ceramic drainpipes and bedrests. Other practices, such as the use of funerary urns continue as before. But some of the most dramatic changes (and eventually the most telling for the history of the Wangara) are in the settlement dynamics.

Before the ninth century in the Macina, the clustered urban settlement pattern recalled that of the Upper Delta as strongly as did their shared ceramic tradition. At Dia, however, of 21 sites surveyed, 18 have only Phase III artifacts on the surface and only eight have material from a later occupation.[86] There is almost none of the classic Jenne-jeno Phase IV comb-impressed and stamped ware at Dia. The Lakes Region and Niger Bend take a distinct deviation in their ceramic traditions to form a related but separate precinct, featuring slipped and highly burnished plus geometric comb-impressions. And the Méma region, holding on desperately as the environment does its worse, continues with a ceramic tradition little changed from the seventh or eighth centuries until permanent settlement essentially dies out between 1200 and 1400.

What the dry ceramics are telling us is that the intensity of contact that marked the Middle Niger during the first millennium is no more. The powerful Dia–Jenne axis weakens as the former becomes more and more peripheral. Méma is isolated. And the nature of links between the southern basins and the Timbuktu region alters, if not necessarily implying a diminishing volume of luxury and exotic goods transported between them.

The most curious aspect is that Dia looses population and cultural preeminence just at the time (or slightly before) that the oral traditions assign to the town its greatest glory. Again, we see an interesting (and apparent) paradox. Just as the Imperial Tradition claims to unite the Western Sudan (including the whole of the Middle Niger) in bureaucratically and militarily centralized empires, there is decreasing cultural contact between regions. Just as the centuries-old settlement logic of the Dia region unravels, the town is celebrated as the founder of innumerable far-distant Wangara colonies.

---

[85] S. McIntosh, *Excavations at Jenne-jeno*, pp. 360–72.
[86] Haskell, et al., *Dia*.

The Soninké diaspora is clearly tied to evidence of population peaks and declines just about everywhere. A recent (1994) archaeological coring project at modern Jenne[87] strongly suggests that most of that town was occupied during the upper Inland Niger Phase IV. Jenne may have been founded long before, but on present evidence we can at least say with confidence that most of the 45 ha. city was occupied simultaneously with Jenne-jeno at its demographic heyday (around 900) and with virtually all (if not all) of the 69 satellite sites. This pattern is stable until 1100 and perhaps as late as 1200. Ironically, considering the hoary "Arab Stimulation" model, decline appears just when we have the first evidence of the Berber trade – brass, spindle whorls and rectangular houses. Then decline sets in and Jenne-jeno itself is abandoned by 1400. The ancient town will claim one final moment of glory as the location of Sonni Ali Ber's garrison during the long Songhai investment of Jenne. Environmental stress may largely explain the declines in the first centuries of the present millennium in the Méma (Akumbu and Kolima, abandoned by c.1300), the Lakes Region (KNT2 and Toubel) as well as in the Soninké settlements of the Mauritanian Tagant, Adrar and Tichitt-Walata arc.[88]

Dia's earlier decline during an apparent climatic optimum is doubly puzzling. Susan McIntosh suggests that the decline might be attributable not to droughts, nor to strangulation of the local waterway networks, but to new commercial opportunities created by the founding of a southern Saharan Berber entrepôt such as Awdaghost. The trans-Saharan trade, though at first only grafted onto a much older east–west oriented trade maintained by the earliest Wangara, so increased in volume due to the quenchless Islamic and European lust for gold, that it ended up disrupting the older trade networks to which Dia was tied.[89] According to her hypothesis, from 900 to 1200, the commercial torch is passed to Jenne (increasingly in preference to Jenne-jeno as more of her population converts to Islam). We can also predict some significant migration from Dia to Jenne, as well as to points far to the west.

When the Arabic sources mention Wangara, the Island of Gold, they are really documenting Soninké trading centers along the Middle Niger. If this is so, then the precocious archaeological shift of settlement logic at Dia provides a proxy date and cause for the Soninké trade diaspora. This process is identified in the historical sources

[87] R. McIntosh, *et al.*, "Exploratory archaeology."
[88] S. McIntosh, *Excavations*, pp. 374–7.
[89] Ibid., p. 376.

only to the fourteenth century with travellers such as Ibn Battuta, but may go back to the very early second millennium AD or earlier.

In the oral traditions, Dia has a preeminent position over earlier, preliminary migration centers (Dioura) or later secondary nodes (Wagadu) as a focus of the Soninke dispersal. From these points, the Soninké moved east to settle as far as Bughrat, Timbuktu and Tiraqqa on the Niger Bend (and to trade as far east as Sokoto in modern Nigeria). They travel west to found the colonies of Silla, ("new"?) Yaresna, and Galambu along the Middle Senegal and (lower) Upper Senegal. Far to the west, a Soninké dynasty with strong memories of Dia, the Dia-Ogo, establish the first chiefdom in the Takrur (Middle Senegal Valley) region. Soninké are (still) in the north, as a strong commercial presence at Walata and as (struggling) farm communities in the Tagant, and other locations in the Hodh.

What is remarkable in the oral traditions of these communities is the degree of coherence of memory about their place of origin. There is always the danger, of course, that memory is being edited to establish a useful but fictitious tie to an illustrious ancestral town. In that case, why Dia whose commercial glory lost its burnish long ago?

I believe the answer may lie in the long memory of Dia as the beacon settlement on the Island of Gold for those plying the savanna gold routes, and before that, the east–west routes of the mid- or early first millennium. Whether it was symbolic or actual home to those Soninké-speaking traders matters little. The rich agriculture pastoral and fishing yields of the alluvium sustained the large artisan and merchant communities of Middle Niger towns such as Jenne(-jeno), Dia, Timbuktu and a hundred other towns whose ancient name or names have been lost to time and whose remains are now being lost to the pillaging of those hired by the European art syndicate to rip terracottas and bronze antiquities out of the ground.

If we can preserve these sites from their massive ongoing destruction at the hands of the heritage rapists, they will hold our only clues to the origin of the characteristic organization of Wangara commercial settlement. This organization is now known only from a far later time, usually by outsiders' (European) observations of Dyula (Malinke for Wangara) entrepôts strung along the trade routes within alien ethnic lands.[90] Here the Wangara/Dyula lived jealously guarded lives in separate quarters or hamlets, practiced Islam as their distinctive religion, provided long-distance trading and "magical" *marabout* services for the host community and very often served

---

[90] Perinbaum, "Notes," pp. 676–89; Curtin, *Economic Change*, pp. 67–9.

as councilors for the local chiefs. Their communities were local places of instruction in Islam and, more endogamously, in the esoteric practices that made them so respected by the local population. They enjoyed the very Mande privilege of long-distance travel for the purpose of bringing goods and (as importantly) intelligence from faraway places. Even if war raged between local polities, Wangara could generally travel unmolested. The Wangara are another example of the fertility of the Middle Niger for the creation of corporate genius and for broadcasting that genius to distant lands.

The earliest Wangara served the important purpose of transmitting over long distances a major constellation of Mande beliefs about the nature of authority and about the powers of the earth. Later, as the first long-distance Muslims, they provide the critical function of discovering a working synthesis of older traditions, symbols, and esoteric views of causation with the new religion. These are not just traders in gold. They traffick also in the power of beliefs and esoterica. Secret, peripatetic, competent in the occult, the Wangara provide an important role in the creation and transmission of the new canons of authority and new expressions of power that we call the Imperial Tradition.

The Imperial Tradition: Power from Authority

The historian David Robinson[91] coined the term Imperial Tradition to describe the final act in the millennia-long Middle Niger drama of symbolic and ideological synoecism: layered transformations of deep-time Mande values of authority. Robinson's interest was to understand a remarkable transformation in the claim by the theocratic state-builder, Sekou Amadou Lobbo, to authority over the peoples of the Middle Niger (that is, the claim to be the legitimate successor of the Mali and Songhai Empires) that took place in 1820. Before that time, as he built his army and his hegemony, he claimed legitimacy from a traditional Islamic source, the Sokoto Caliphate of northern Nigeria. However, once in his new capital of Hamdullahi (near Mopti in the Upper Delta)[92] by 1819, he turned

---

[91] Robinson "Imperial State." For the islamic input into a Sudanic "imperial cult," see Trimingham, *History of Islam*, pp. 34–7.
[92] Alain Gallay, Eric Huysecom, Matthieu Honegger, and Anne Mayor, *Hamdallahi. Capitale de l'Empire Peul du Massina, Mali. Première Fouille Archéologique, Etudes Historiques et Ethnoarchéologiques*, (Franz Steiner Verlag: Stuttgart, 1990).

instead to reinvent a variation on the Imperial Tradition of Mande statecraft that matured during the apogee of the Mali and Songhai empires (1250–1600) and that undoubtedly went through experimental phases during the times of Ghana and other emerging polities.

Robinson's core argument is that Sekou Amadou had to appropriate and manipulate an older tradition of Mande authority so as to "secure the imprimatur of the imperial tradition in order to legitimize his claim to the political economy of the Middle Niger."[93] Even in the unsettled centuries after the 1600 withering of a geriatric Mali, the prize was substantial. The merchants and intermediaries from the Middle Niger cities controlled the southern termini of the trans-Saharan routes by which salt, cloth, copper and brass, Mediterranean manufactures, horses, and the paraphernalia of the new religion entered the Western Sudan. To the south they controlled the forest and savanna networks bringing slaves, kola, spices, gold, wood, and hides. And the producers of the floodplain still created surpluses in grains, cotton, oil, fish, livestock, and many manufactures. Sekou Amadou's genius, and the key to control over the Middle Niger until his empire (the *Dina*) was overthrown by the Tukulor conqueror, El Hadj Umar, in 1862, was his appreciation (and ruthless promulgation – on which more later) of the Imperial Tradition.

As one might expect, much of the mature Imperial Tradition, was direct or slightly modified borrowings from the Islamic exterior. Travellers to the empire's courts, those who interviewed Western Sudanese pilgrims, and the local sources (*Ta'rikhs es-Sudan* and *al-Fattach*) give us a standard inventory: a courtly bureaucracy with retainers of differential privilege, "interpreters" mediating between the audience or supplicants and the king, announcing drums, rituals of obeisance (dust thrown on the head), large trousers and caps and turbans as sumptuary items, parasols and flags, obligatory pilgrimages, Islamic scholars, and Islamic jurists and court clerics. Each of these had a counterpart in the courts of extra-Saharan states, but the syncretistic ways in which these items and rituals were put together horrified many visitors from those same lands. But the real genius of synoecism was the ways in which the new dynasts reinvented older social and occult power practices.

At the base of synoecism were several subsequent transformations of values (as we have already traced in the Historical Imagi-

---

[93]   Robinson, "Imperial state," p. 2.

nation chapters of this book). An essential functionary at the new Imperial Tradition courts was an old Mande friend, the *griot*. His job is now to use *kuma koro* (the powerful "ancient speech") to create a legitimizing narrative of the genealogy and beneficence of his patron. Patron and *griot* still dispense power packages (*boli*), but now in the form of amulets and *grigris* (often with Islamic symbols or script). The king's role as Hunter King is reinforced by the ritual bow and quiver displayed at court. Court rituals can be recognizable variations on venerable hunters' and smith's rituals and the kings makes obligatory visits to ancient shrines to absorb the power of the mythical landscape. As for poor hunters: now impressed into the imperial armies, they witness their beyond-ancient symbols appropriated yet again. The bow and quiver become the imperial emblems of state. In a recent version of the Mali epic,[94] Sunjata demonstrates his powers to Fakoli by taking aim with his royal bow and arrows on a hunter's axehead stuck in a tree. Orthodox observers can only cringe at the masked dances (many of *Komo* origin). And critical to legitimation is the possession of a variety of musical instruments (lutes, drums, *balafons*, etc.) of inestimable Mande power.[95]

Beyond the court accoutrements and rituals, the evolving Imperial Tradition called upon a reinvention of social relations. In the idiom of this book, one way to look at these processes is as the final and much delayed – but ultimately only partially complete – triumph of hierarchy and coercion over heterarchy and civil society. It is very true that this was the period of the rise, in the Middle Niger and throughout an expansive Mande of the horse-warrior dynasts and of a mounted warrior elite, Bathily's "aristocracy of terror."[96] On the other hand, military power was notoriously unstable. Enduring hegemony and authority came when the skillful ruler found a balance between force and *Mansaya*, or astute statecraft.[97] *Mansaya* may be thought of as the accommodation by a state centralized in some domains, of heterarchical and centrifugal tendencies in other domains. *Mansaya* was the taproot of the

[94] D. Conrad, pers. com. 1996.
[95] Eric Charry, *Musical thought, History, and Practice Among the Mande of West Africa*, PhD dissertation, Princeton University, 1994.
[96] Bathily, *Portes de l'Or*, p. 232; the fullest treatment of the rise of the horse warriors and their role from *c.*1000–1600 in the expansion of Greater Mali is found in Brooks, *Landlords and Strangers*, pp. 2–4, 46–7, 97–114.
[97] Brooks, *Landlords and Strangers*, p. 101.

Imperial Tradition, drawing from the deep soil of Mande essential values of occult power and authority and the special relations with those groups skilled in the manipulation of *nyama*. The new dynasts had to learn an old lesson: *nyama* and occult power is too great, too dangerous and too corrupting to be held alone. True authority comes by establishing special (if asymmetrical alliances) with the corporate groups skilled in the garnering and augmentation of *nyama*.

In the Imperial Tradition, rulers invented a category of the ruled that is, frankly, despotic. Sekou Amadou was particularly concerned to establish his authority over the twelve "servile tribes" of the Middle Niger. These were, essentially, the peasant provisioners of empire; the grooms and fodder-gatherers for cavalry; the boatmen of the army's flotilla; the slaves or the semi-free working imperial plantations; armorers, messengers, headporters; and hereditary horse, foot and archer troops. But of more interest here is the relation of secular dynasts to the *nyamakalaw* (endogamous artisan and craft corporations, including bards, smiths, leatherworkers, and others) and to the power associations they headed. These were the traditional guardians of Mande values. These were the ones who, over the centuries and through countless transformations of occult concepts and practices, were privileged to deal in the overwhelming creative forces of the Mande world. These were the ones who knew how to harvest legitimate authority from the Mande power-grid.

The traditions of the early empires are narratives, not of battle and of kingly heroism, but of the absorption of traditional holders of Mande power into the new concept of empire.[98] The essential point for our exploration of the process of synoecism is that the role of the *nyamakalw* and of their power associations (*Komo, Poro, Nyakuruni* etc.) is not destroyed. It is transformed and, from the dynasts" perspective, tamed and brought into a subject or patron–client relationship. The bards and smiths might have legitimately seen things in a different light. Their powers were undiminished and, in fact, the structure of state was simply an overlay (generally an ephemeral one, at that) over greatly enhanced powers. After all, when empire wanes, the smiths are still there, and their secret societies are just the most visible of several competing power associations acting as overlapping agencies of cooperation and competition.

---

[98] Two classic examples by David Conrad are "Searching," pp. 147–200 and "Blind man," pp. 86–132.

Their authority derived still from occult-sanctioned persuasion, rather than coercion. Groups that harness mystical energy can effectively negotiate a new role in power asymmetries.

We could, perhaps, predict the ascendancy of hierarchy over traditional horizontal authority. We should not sniff at some thousand years of resistance, from the first glimmerings at centers like Jenne-jeno and Dia of the complex political economy that leads to state formation in other lands to the first spark of the Imperial Tradition. But, for the Mande, too, absolute power corrupts absolutely. There was surely nothing new in the charismatic individual trying to find ways by which symbols could be turned back to subvert traditions of horizontal authority. For centuries, structures of resistance held. However, we find in the Sumaworo figure, metaphor or real, the smith gone bad, corrupted by the awesome powers at his command. What are the secret symbols he transforms to sumptuary items: the (healers') medicine drum, the (*griots'*) balafon, the sword, and the spear (appropriated from the hunters)? His most fearsome fetish is a large snake secreted away in a huge pot of water . Sumaworo is just one of hundreds of local attempts to craft imperial traditions.

Those intent upon subverting horizontal authority also invented the new to go with the old. Al-Bakri's burial of the king of Ghana (chapter 8) and the spectacular tumuli concentrations in Mali and Senegal may very well be invented monuments to an emerging political elite. Nevertheless, the cardinal-point distribution of caches within eleventh–twelfth century El-Oualadji (figure 8.1) shows that the Mande symbolic reservoir was still a force to be tapped for elite legitimation. Eventually, the old landscape of roughly equivalent polities is undone, but some variation on that theme periodically reasserts itself during periods of Imperial weakness.

Sekou Amadou's Dina emerges from precisely such a landscape of collapsed centralization. Still, so powerful is the impulse of the Imperial Tradition, that he forges a prophesy that Askiya Mohammed of Songhai (rule 1493–1526) was the eleventh caliph of the Islamic world and that he, Sekou Amadou, would follow as the twelfth caliph. With the title of caliph came special rights over the Middle Niger's twelve "servile tribes." It is fitting that he should "appropriate" the pious Askiya Mohammed and not the more energetic empire-builder, Sonni Ali Ber. The latter was irremediably polluted by his membership of the guild of Songhai Sohance magicians. In a superb act of ideological appropriation and manipulation, Sekou Amadou has this invented history taught as official state history[99] throughout his caliphate and has it inserted into the *Ta'rikh al-Fattash*. The Imperial Tradition continues, transformed, through Mande history by means of, in Robinson's words, "one of the most elaborate inventions and forgeries in African history."[100]

[99] Brown, *Caliphate*, pp. 4–7, 133–4.
[100] Robinson, "Imperial state," p. 1.

11

Historical Imagination: AD 1472

Séku Amadou's forgery of a direct lineage for himself to the Songhai emperor, Askiya Mohammed, is really just part of the final stage of a long invention of Imperial Tradition. Earlier innovators, such as the blacksmith-king, Sumaworo, and Sunjata, the Mali founder, continue to receive the attention of many scholars. However, there is a Middle Niger anti-hero who serves as a bridge over an historical middle passage between these stages. The founder of the Songhai state, Sonni Ali Ber, is an empire builder and political genius of epic proportions. Yet he is curiously dismissed by the sources. Those *ta'rikhs* tend to represent him as the enemy of Muslims and of elites of conquered towns such as Timbuktu.[1] Yet there were other dimensions to the man.

Sonni Ali Ber, the great sorcerer-king, invested Jenne for seven years, seven months and seven days, so the sources tell us. Yet, when the town's gates finally open, king and Jenneans reconcile without retribution. Was there a secret history to the end of the siege? Our observer from Roundé Siru catches sight of passing strangeness in the waters of the guardian *marigots* encircling the great town:

---

[1] According to tradition, Sonni Ali Ber succeeded in taking Jenne after a siege of seven years, seven months, and seven days. During that time Jenne-jeno was occupied by his troops. At the end of the investment of the city, he was so impressed by the bravery, honor, and pride of the inhabitants of Jenne that he treated them with mercy. At Timbuktu in 1468, his troops ransacked the city and he had many members of the Islamic and learned community put to death. For that he earned the permanent enmity of pious Muslims of the Western Sudan.

The investment began seven years ago to the day. When the great king, Sonni Ali Ber, was still occupied with crushing Timbuktu, he sent an expeditionary force to Jenne. A harassing force really. To see if the impotent Mansa would reply to the danger on his doorstep. To test the lie of the land and, more importantly, to test the powers under the water and in the wind in this country far beyond the normal carry of Songhai spirits, the *daali*. Then the siege began.

For such was the nature of warfare for Sonni Ali Ber. Overwhelm the mortal forces above the waters with a flotilla of thousands of loyal Sorko. Sorko whom he had years earlier freed from their servitude to the Mansa. Overwhelm the mortal forces crawling over the surface of the earth with a deadly, disciplined cavalry. Hit hard from out of nowhere. Harass any enemy on foot or awkward camel. Surprise and ruthlessness.

But all the while, the more dangerous struggle goes on with the spirit-masters, the *tooru* of the thunder, of the wind devils, of the still *marigot* waters, and of the land.[2] Sonni Ali Ber can join them all for the silent conversation. At least he could at Timbuktu and at places far beyond visited while in his invisible state. But here, far from the ally *tooru* of the Songhai heartland, his eye is occluded and his heart heavy with foreboding. For seven years he has sent his flotilla against the town at high waters. For seven years his cavalry has ravaged the countryside in the dry season. But, seven years without the necessary sorcerer's contest with the master *tooru*, the chief *faaro* as she is called here, who would reveal the secret to conquest of this land.

Far to the south, the ancient town – once called Joboro or Jenne-jeno – lies abandoned now for a century or more. Houses melted by a hundred years of rain. Brick and potsherd and other discards of the humble and the proud, now trampled under the hooves of a thousand Songhai horse. For Jenne-jeno is now garrison to the siege army. When the floods are in decline, as they are now, the flotilla is drawn up on the slopes of the deserted town to await the next flood, the next season to surround the town with a continuous chain of animal carcasses to foul the water, to launch volleys of arrows into the town from the safe distance of the boats. Garrison and stable, too, to the vast cavalry grown sick at heart of the long siege. Sick at heart, too, at the undiminished pride and confidence of Jenne's townspeople.

Pride is undiminished, even though the town itself is smaller somewhat, now, than several centuries ago. Then, Jenne, and the ancient town, and innumerable neighboring workshop villages bustled with activity. No longer. Gone long before the disruptions of this siege. But the town is still a rich prize, still worth sending the dry-season cavalry round and round the sturdy

---

[2] For the world of Songhai sorcery in which Sonni Ali Ber was initiated, see Paul Stoller and Cheryl Olkes, *In Sorcery's Shadow: A Memoire of Apprenticeship among the Songhay of Niger*, (Chicago University Press: Chicago, 1987).

walls in the hopes of choking off that irrepressible pride and quiet defiance in a wall of dust.

No luck; still the siege goes on. The townspeople know, too, what the great king knows. And this is why he has at last made his pilgrimage to the banks of the Huté *marigot*.

He has laid down his quilt-armor and his poison-tipped arrows and long iron blade. He is dressed in a simple cloth shift. He carries hollow horns of dried plants, powders, and all the armory of his sorcerer's legacy. He knows this will be the challenge of his life. None of his Sorko boatmen, none of his cavalry can help him. Unlike Timbuktu, where the abused local spirits of the narrowing Niger and the high dune actively called upon him to join in alliance, here he must spend his full energies just to glimpse the mistress of the master-spirits that he knows to live deep in these waters.

So, the great king comes defenseless to this bank. He sits and takes a pinch of each powder, each potion. Each pinch in careful order and careful quantity; and then he begins the dosing cycle again. He will sit and stare and touch the powders to his tongue for days, if that is what it takes. Until the mistress reveals herself. Pray he has enough strength, then, to engage her, sentient human to sentient spirit, in order to find the key to alliance.

In possession comes clairvoyance. She comes to him as he sits on the bank. She emerges slowly, slouching from the water, steaming and reeking with the reeds and organic debris of the *marigot* bottom. She takes his hand and leads him to the water's edge. And slowly in – as he knew she would the moment he saw her flickering forms.

Visible to the king in her multiple states, she is at once very familiar and terribly odd. He knows her as Harakoy Dikko, the Niger's spirit queen of his Songhai heartland. And in another form she is the two-headed snake, Sadyara, who guards Harakoy Dikko's underwater village. Yet other forms are completely alien. He knows them, nonetheless, as his vision of Faara-Huté. Sometimes Faara-Huté is the poisonous boa; at other times, the great crocodile. Other times still she takes on the long-striding form of the first hunter who saw the future greatness of this place almost two millennia ago.

Sonni Ali Ber, the great sorcerer, has at last met the protector spirit of the town he intends to squash as he has Timbuktu five years earlier. Now he has consigned himself to the care of this spirit as the waves of the Huté lap over his head. Because the spirit has come to his sight initially as the Songhai sorcerer's familiar, Harakoy Dikko, he is not surprised when her fabulous city underwater appears before him. A step closer and an ironic Sadyara, still holding his hand, bows before him as he enters the glittering, streaming city.

In the center of the Huté, deep beneath the black waters, is the genie's crystalline palace midst a riot of gleaming metallic spires, domes, arches and architectural fantasies. Sonni Ali Ber often went walking with impunity through the underwater city of Harakoy Dikko, where she leads to death by drowning poor fishermen and kings who fail to respect her authority over the waters.

Now, he walks the narrow streets of a perfect dream city, knowing they are on their way to a silent conversation. To a test of his right by intelligence and stratagem to be king. And to stay alive.

They arrive at her palace. She shifts now from her familiar Songhai forms to the manifestations of Faara-Huté. Protector of Jenne. Hers is the voice of the disquiet of all water spirits along the whole of the Middle Niger: we see this new force, this acknowledgment of a singular god, that has entered the land. We are tolerant and accepting and take more strength from every new spirit that enters this domain of the annual floods. But the outsiders who bring this new belief are intent upon banishing us forever. They wish to end the sacrifices to all the *tooru* of the sky, of the land, of the water.

The outsiders are unshakably hostile to our world. They do not wish to understand a power immeasurably older than they can imagine. You must find the means to accommodate and absorb. Your actions at Timbuktu, however, will forever be remembered by those who would exterminate us. All would understand your fury at the followers of this new god, who joined with the men of the desert to oppress your people. But your act of killing the 30 virgin innocents will only force more fanaticism.

Here, you have no choice but to find a wiser path to accommodation. You must use you power to bring the old and this new way together and, by so doing, you will tap forces far more powerful than either of the two alone.

During this thought-conversation, it came to Sonni Ali Ber: those who would use the new religion to resist his authority would know his wrath. But those willing to let others believe as they wish would be unharassed. And his symbol of his resolve would be to decree that, henceforth, the new faith's sacrifice of Tabaski would be observed in his royal court as a sacrifice, also, to all *Zin*, all the Middle Niger's genies, from the mother of all *tooru*, Harakoy Dikko, to the most middling *holey*.

With this, Sonni Ali Ber was led to back to the bank and told of his reward. And the price. The resistance of Jenne would last another seven months and seven days. On that last day, a prince of the city would throw open the gates and come himself to lead Sonni Ali into this new prize. To consolidate his new empire against implacable enemies, especially the Tuareg and the Fulani, he would have command of the cold power of destruction and death of *Hargay* who lives in the Jenne cemetery just outside the walls of that town. But at a cost. Should he elect to ally with these cold, hard spirits, then in 20 years to the day they shall again lead him back to the city under the waters.[3]

One of the big-picture questions for historians of the Middle Niger concerns the engine of the Imperial Tradition. Was a centralizing

---

[3] In late October of 1492, Sonni Ali Ber the great sorcerer-king drowns while returning from a successful campaign in the Gourma.

push inevitable with the prosperity, higher population, cross-Saharan influences,[4] and improved rains of the later first and early second millennia AD? Using a conflict model, were states inevitable as smiths and traders expand the borders of Mande between AD 700–1100?[5] Or were the climatic perturbations, the new potential of cavalry, the increasingly insistent Islam, and migrations of the first several centuries of the present millennium the essential drives? Whatever the answer, after the thirteenth century, the Middle Niger had to contend with a radical transformation of Mande ideas of authority and leadership. Sonni Ali Ber's career is an open window on that transformation.

Absolute power corrupts absolutely: for the new breed of Mande hero, the success of symbols could be turned back to be the undoing of traditional, heterarchical authority. Occult competence remains an integral part of leadership. Now, however, new economic and religious potentials seeping in from the outside and the reinvention of deep-time notions of authority provide the means to break down old traditions of resistance to power and wealth monopoly. There was surely nothing new in the charismatic individual trying to subvert traditions of horizontal authority. For centuries, structures of resistance held. However, we now begin to find in the Sumaworo figure, metaphor or real, the smith gone bad. Here is the hero corrupted by the awesome powers at his command. Sonni Ali Ber marches up the Niger Valley in possession of a similar corpus of Songhai powers – and with the intention to add ancient Mande spirits and high *nyama* – locales to his trophy case. Like other Mande Masters of *nyama*, he regularly travels widely in visible or invisible *dali-ma-sigi*.

Those intent upon subverting horizontal authority also invented or absorbed the new to go with the old. Al-Bakri's burial of the king of Ghana[6] and the spectacular tumuli concentrations in Mali and Senegal[7] are perhaps invented monuments to an emerging political elite. Nevertheless, the cardinal-point distribution of caches

---

[4] For the regions between the Middle Niger and Middle Senegal, Bathily convincingly shows that Islamic, trans-Saharan trade and the accompanying cavalry, slave-raiding, and exansionism were not state-forming as stated in the conventional histories, but were destructive of centuries-old polities: Bathily, *Les Portes*, pp. 11, 87, 122, 147, 157–9.

[5] Brooks, "Ecological perspectives," p. 33; *Landlords and Strangers*, p. 51.

[6] Al-Bakri in Levtzion, *Ancient Ghana*, pp. 25–6.

[7] Preliminary dating and speculation about their function in S. McIntosh and R. McIntosh, "Field survey," pp. 73–107, 104–5.

within the El-Oualadji monument[8] (figure 8.1) shows that the Mande symbolic reservoir was still a resource to be tapped for elite legitimation. In the new Imperial Tradition, legitimation derives, in part, from intrusive elements: turbans, parasols, Muslim clerics as councilors, and new legal canons.[9]

But the old reappears in interesting ways. Unhappy hunters: now impressed into the imperial armies,[10] they witness their beyond-ancient symbols appropriated yet again. Their signature bow and quiver become the imperial emblems of state and the hunters themselves are impressed by the state as *Totadyo* ("archers, slaves to the cause"), the elite army corps.[11] In a recent version of the Mali epic,[12] Sunjata demonstrates his powers to his lieutenant, Fakoli, by taking aim with his royal bow and arrows on a hunter's axehead stuck in a tree. Sonni Ali Ber uses the aquatic hunters of the Niger Bend, the Sorko, as his imperial shock troops.

These new secular leaders of Mande must also ally with smiths in order to have access to the vast quantities of *nyama* that remain the foundation of Mande authority.[13] Yet how can society prevent the kind of perversion of authority – leading, as the oral traditions remind us, to repression and cruelty – represented by Sumaworo? This is done by a radical redefinition of the smith's role: by the thirteenth century,[14] at least, a recognizable form of *nyamakalaw* is

---

[8] Desplagnes, *Plateau Central*, pp. 57–66; and "Fouilles," pp. 1159–73; Lebeuf and Pâques, *Archéologie Malienne*, pp. 1–55.; see R. McIntosh and S. McIntosh "From *siècles obscurs*," p. 155.

[9] Robinson, "Imperial state," pp. 16–20.

[10] Cissé, "Notes," pp. 176, 190; Cashion, *Hunters*, p.108; S. McIntosh "Blacksmiths," p. 20.

[11] Cissé, "Notes," p. 190.

[12] Recently recorded in Guinea by D. Conrad; pers. com., 1996.

[13] The alternative to accumulating vast amount of occult power – and the dangers attendant thereto – is to secure the loyalty of those who possess it in abundance; hence the story of crippled child Sunjata becoming whole (and a hunter) after grabbing an iron bar crafted by a master smith – see S. McIntosh, "Blacksmiths," pp. 5, 12, 30; Bathily, *Les Portes*, pp. 160–2, 220–3; McNaughton, *Mande Blacksmith*, pp. 130–1; Conrad, "Searching," pp. 150, 163, 167, 171–3 – where he argues convincingly that the epic figure of Fakoli represents the bridge between an older Mande smith authority and the new political order, a reconciliation that affords the smiths enormous spiritual respect, while allowing them limited political power.

[14] Tamari argues that the *nyamakawlaw* "caste system" appears among the Malinke no later that 1300 ("development," pp. 221–50 and McNaughton similarly argues for a thirteenth century date (*Mande Blacksmiths*, p.1); see Robinson, "Imperial state," pp. 11–14.

in place. That is, some dangerous occupations are boxed into rules that effectively preclude their members from political ambition. The new order respects smiths as preeminent masters of the occult, yet constrains them as separate and fearsome.

Lastly, one of the key legitimation devices of the Imperial Tradition, the royal pilgrimage, derives from another deep-time ideal. Leaders enhance their authority by visiting the power-places of Islam as well as of their traditional lands.[15] Sunjata makes pilgrimage to the Méma to receive his birthright from ancient Ghana. Later kings of Mali make golden pilgrimages to Islam's holy places. Now we are told that the smiths" original *boli*, and even the very notion of *Komo*, were brought to Mande from Mecca![16] No wonder, then, that the founder of the Songhai empire, one of the world's great Islamic states, must ritually visit the occult power locations of lands he wishes to conquer.

This is the beauty of the Imperial Tradition: old occult practices and recently imported religions, all simmering together in a great symbolic cauldron for the new charismatic elites to season to taste. But as the great empires of Mali and Songhai weaken their hold over the Middle Niger, successor states such as Séku Amadou's *Dina* present a new challenge to the notion of horizontal webs of authority.

[15] Robinson, "Imperial state," pp. 16–20; P. F. de Moraes Farias "Pilgrimages to 'pagan' Mecca," in K. Barber and de Moraes Farias (eds.) *Discourses and its Disguises*, (Centre of West African Studies: Birmingham, 1989), pp. 152–69; Conrad, "Searching," pp. 152–3, 186.

[16] Ibid., p. 153.

12

Epilogue: Resilience of an Original Civil Society?

It is the strangest phenomenon; it is almost as if the memory of 66 years of French occupation has evaporated from Jenne's memory. Certainly, if pressed, the Jenneké elite recall the April 1893 extractions of the conquering colonel, Louis Archinard. These punishments for resistance were official (bar salt, all the town's horses, and an annual tax of one million cowries)[1] and clandestine (and perhaps apocryphal – terracotta ancestor statues). Certainly inhabitants of the most ancient quarter, Djoboro, recall the corvée labor that emptied that quarter's streets and courtyards of several meters of deposits to fill in the ancient ponds in front of the mosque.[2] This was represented as a magnanimous act of sanitary engineering – that also just happened to create a fine field of fire in front of the French garrison. Still, there is little enduring emotion, hot or cold, about the colonial period.

For me, the best measure of the resilience of Middle Niger peoples and institutions is the fact that the several bloody battles of penetration and the subsequent military occupation by the French are largely forgotten. Similarly, it is almost as if, before them, the Tukulor (Futanké) Umarian state, the theocratic Dina of Sékou Amadou's Fulani fanatics, the Bambara of the Segou state, and the

---

[1] Bernard Gardi, "Djenné et la conquête du Soudan," in *Djenné, Il Y A Cent Ans*, Bernard Gardi, Pierre Maas, and Geert Mommersteeg (eds.) (Institut Royal des Tropiques: Amsterdam, 1995), p. 18.

[2] R. McIntosh et al., "Exploratory archaeology," p. 26; see Arie van Rangelrooy and Pierre Maas, "L'historique et la morphologie de l'ancienne ville" (ch. 11) and "Le diagramme rituel" (ch. 12) in *Djenne, Chef-d'oeuvre Architectural*, eds Pierre Maas and Geert Mommersteeg, (Université de Technologie: Eindhoven, 1992), pp. 159–71 (ch. 11) and 173–7 (ch. 12).

Moroccans marching triumphant throughout the Middle Niger after Tondibi (1591) are largely off the inhabitants' emotional radar.
Resilience is the key word.

In the longer chronological perspective of this book, the deeper
structures of authority, inter-group relations, and occupations that
had emerged in the Middle Niger over the millennia persist remarkably in the face of three and a half centuries of warrior-state chaos.
This is not to diminish the changes wrought by the Moroccan, Segou,
Fulani, Tukulor, and French hegemonies. This is not to diminish
the hateful acts committed against individuals and families. However, compared to the utter devastations of society and human ecology experienced under analogous circumstances of predatory
warfare and expansive slaving at, for example, the southern
Mauritanian desert fringe[3] or in the Galam and Kolimbiné regions
of the Senegal-Mali frontier,[4] the Middle Niger enters the middle of
the present century as a testimony to the strengths of a profoundly
heterarchical society.

Make no mistake. The effects of political transformations after
the eclipse of Songhai are no mere gloss upon the economy and
political life of the Middle Niger.[5] In the historian, Richard Roberts's
opinion, violence and predation were the *raison d'être* of the various states that, since 1591, alternated between greater – or – lesser
degrees of state-sponsored plunder. Before the French, the state was
more often simply a loose umbrella sheltering undisciplined local
warlords. Slaving took place on unprecedented scales. No parts of
the Middle Niger went unaffected by slavers, although few were as
badly devastated as the dryland frontier (Sarro) between the Upper
Delta and the core of the Segou Kingdom or the Bani River's middle course. The Middle Niger may not have had the slave plantations of the Marka towns near Segou,[6] but the villages of servile
Rimaïbe bound to the Fulani elite of Sekou Amadou's *Dina* functioned in analogous ways.

The construction of this new ethnic group, the Rimaïbe, is just
one of several undeniable changes to the ethnic calculus. The influx
of Bambara to the high, light soils of the Middle Niger accelerates,
as do their conflicts with Fulani clans newly arrived out of the west.
Tuareg and Moorish populations shift and more permanently pen-

---

[3] Webb, *Desert Frontier.*
[4] Bathily, *Portes de l'Or.*
[5] The best overall source for these challenges remains Roberts, *Warriors.*
[6] Ibid., pp. 25, 47–50.

etrate the Lakes Region/Niger Bend and the Méma. The latter settle and trade as far south as Bamako. The Somono boat-tenders increase in importance (and undoubtedly in numbers) as cavalry and footmen need transport throughout the floodplain. And new "ethnic groups-*cum*-social classes," such as the Jenneké (a Muslim, Songhai-dialect speaking artisan/merchant elite in Jenne) and the Arma come into existence. From the 1790s, Islam takes on a new militancy. The nineteenth is the century of Theocracies.

Finally, New World crops (especially maize and tobacco) must have had an enormous effect on landuse, commercial patterns, and have created new ecological conflicts among producer groups.

The list could go on. By 1655, when es-Sa'di sits down to write the *Ta'rikh es-Sudan*, effects of warfare as the primary expression of imposed state power[7] are all too evident:

> When the Moroccan army arrived in the Western Sudan, they found this land to be one of God's most favoured with riches and fertility. Peace and security prevailed in all provinces. All that changed with the conquest: danger replaced security, misery replaced opulence, trouble and calamities and violence replaced tranquillity. Everywhere the people ruin each other, everywhere pillage prevails and everywhere war devours life, well-being, and the peoples' economic circumstances. Disorder is everywhere. It spreads and grows to the highest degree of intensity.[8]

Yet there is another story beyond the domains of the well-being and political life of traditional elites and of Wangara (now the Muslim Dyula) organized long-distance trade in and out of the Middle Niger. These last were clearly es-Sa'di's concern. Nevertheless, the theme of resilience pervades most analyses of *local social and economic relations* during these unsettled centuries. I quote Roberts:

> I shall argue that the state played an important role in determining the structure and performance of the economy...I do not, however, wish to portray the economy merely as an amorphous terrain in which the state materializes its presence. The regional economy of the Middle Niger valley had distinct characteristics that had nothing to do with political factors. . . . Some patterns of trade and production proved resilient, despite fundamental changes in the conditions in which the economy operated and in the forms of labor.[9]

[7] Ibid., p. 3.
[8] Es-Sa'di, *Ta'rikh es-Sudan*, p. 223 (translated by R. J. McIntosh).
[9] Roberts, *Warriors*, p. 3.

To Roberts' trade and production I would add essential relations within the mosaic of ancient ethnic groups, ecological relations of production and exchange between those groups, and settlement pattern. For all these, the upheavals of the millennium's first centuries were of greater or equal consequence to the new diminished political economy backed by state terrorism.

The historian's perspective on long-distance, capital-intensive trade and upon elite political economy tends to an emphasis upon the fragility of economic and social relations in the Middle Niger. However, on the other plane of history – that of webs of relations between groups and corporations, of accommodations of producer specializations within an enduring generalized economy – the troubled centuries after the Moroccan invasion are times to be endured, rather than survived as utter social deterioration. Resilience – this is measured for most parts of the Middle Niger, as in Jenne, by the fact that the warrior states have largely slipped off the conscious radar. Some places, particularly Timbuktu, undeniably suffered badly. The population of the Méma never does recover. Yet I would argue that the profoundly heterarchical social relations and values of production and of authority of the Middle Niger allows this region a measure of deep-time strength envied by other Sahelian and savanna lands ravaged by similar predatory states and aristocracies of terror.

I know of no evidence that the Middle Niger population fell below the level of the fifteenth century. Each successive warrior state, the imperial French included, appeared to have found plenty of material inducement to their costly wars of conquest. Traditional towns such as Jenne retain the fundamentals of local forms of rule, even if garrisoned or temporarily hosting outsiders as governors. The Middle Niger rebounds from the prolonged drought and famines of, for example, 1738 to the 1760s and of 1833–66 (and shorter, albeit severe droughts of 1591–1610, 1639–44, 1668–71, and the first decade of the eighteenth and nineteenth centuries.[10] In fact, the West African meteorological counterpart of the Little Ice Age, AD 1570–1730, should have generated somewhat better rainfall and climatic stability overall.

I would like to argue that this local-scale Middle Niger resilience is predicated upon millennia of layered transformations of social interactions into flexible, pluralistic complexes of relations. In times

---

[10] Cissoko, "Famines"; Nicholson, *Climate Chronology*, pp. 104, 106, 257–63, Faure and Gac, "Sahel drought."

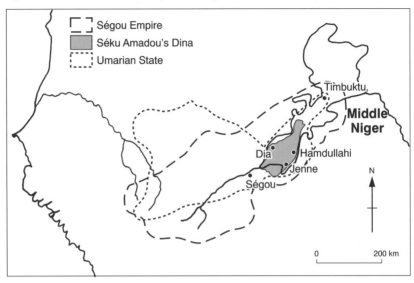

Map 12.1   *Successor states to Songhai*

of political chaos or state-terrorism, as in times of climatic stress and surprise, communities need ecological (social and environmental) diversity. Hierarchical states tend to reduce ecological diversity as part of their strategies of administrative control. But hierarchies are a brittle model. Ecological flexibility is needed for stability and sustainability.

Heterarchy, as the deep-time Middle Niger alternative, would have served the region well in its proven ability to meld together many competing interests (farmers of dune and paddy, smiths and leatherworkers, swamp dwellers and desert transhumans, town dwellers and mobile fisherfolk). Heterarchy would have served the region well in its collorary tendency to challenge the power-seeking impulses of the state. This is perhaps too simplified a view. But the common folk of Middle Niger towns and plains endured the centuries of political turmoil, their resilience providing a contributing passive resistance to the predatory states that, each in turn, soon fell apart of their own weight or because of the pressures of other states looking on enviously from the exterior.

Let us look briefly at each of these post-Songhai Empire states. We begin with the Moroccan proxy state begun with the 1591 invasion of Songhai by the mercenaries of the Sa'did Sultan Mulay al-Mansur. Lured by tales of the Island of Gold, the first military governor, Judar Pasha's troops trounced the hesitant Songhai army at Tondibi. Contained in this victory was the undoing of the victor: "The invasion swallowed up both the conqueror and the conquered."[11]

The story was to become a familiar one. The Moroccans defeat a weakened and overextended power. They greet the local populace with slaving, pillage, and harshly extractive garrisons and, consequently, preside over a steady diminution in the scale of trade within the Middle Niger and commerce with the exterior. Very soon the Moroccans are ineffective in the hinterland, restricted to garrisons in major towns. By 1612, the alien musketeers are ineffective against renewed (but ultimately futile) Songhai resistance. They have revolted against the legitimate *pasha* and against formal ties with the Maghreb. And they have begun a long assimilation into the "ethnic group-*cum*-elite social rank" called the Arma. During the long seventeenth century the Arma preside over a growing vacuum into which more martial Bambara and Fulani stream. Periodic droughts and attendant epidemics and famines undoubtedly accelerate the chaos. Tuareg plunderers run unchecked in the northern basins of the Middle Niger.

A century later in 1712, into the vacuum steps the Segou state.[12] At its promising start, the Bambara state aids an expansion of production (especially in the new, large-slave corps plantations south of the Middle Niger) and protects riverine trade. Regional economies expand for perhaps 150 years. Some Middle Niger towns, such as Jenne, pay tribute, but are excused of any direct rule from Segou. But direct control is slight, at best, north of Lake Débo. Timbuktu and the Lakes Region decline further into a battleground for the often-feuding Tuareg, Songhai, and Moors. It is at the peripheries of the Segou state that individual Bambara warlords first assert nominal independence, with disastrous effect.

By mid-eighteenth century, state control is tenuous. Already drought-stressed villages find themselves on their own against pillaging warlords, raids from independent pioneering Bambara villages, or from increasingly aggressive Fulani clans. Beyond the major Dyula overland and river routes, trade is becoming increasingly

---

[11] Lansiné Kaba, "Archers, musketeers and the mosquitoes: The Moroccan invasion of the Sudan and the Songhay resistance (1591–1612)," *Journal of African History*, 22 (1981), p. 475.

[12] Roberts, *Warriors*, pp. 21–75 and, esp. Adam Konaré Ba, *L'Epopée de Segou. Da Monzon: Un Pouvoir Guerrier*, (Favre: Paris, 1987).

difficult. Petty predations of Tuareg lead to a deserted landscape near Timbuktu.

Let us take a last look at our two vantagepoints for our Historical Imagination chapters. At the turn of the next century, an observer at the so-called "Wadi-13" locale northeast of Timbuktu would have seen nothing but desolate wastes – with that town just barely visible off in the hazy distance. And at our second vantagepoint, Roundé Siru, just north across the *marigot* from Jenne, an observer would have witnessed an unremarkable scene of revolutionary consequences for religion and society in the Middle Niger.

An undemonstrative, but increasingly fervent *talibe*, or young Koranic student, attends religious school at Roundé Siru. Lured by the promise of great learning at the university centre of Jenne so close, Sekou Amadou Lobbo instead comes to learn only deep disgust for the tepid Islam and (in his eyes, even worse) the behavior of the town's Islamic leaders. The late eighteenth and early nineteenth centuries, perhaps because of the instability of the times, was a time of religious revitalism throughout the Western Sudan. Out of his schoolboy disillusionment, and out of the general fundamentalist fever of the times, came the caliphate of Hamdullahi of 1818 to 1862 – the bellicose state called the *Dina*.

Sekou Amadou sets out to establish a theocracy of strict Islamic principles. But, as we have seen in chapter 10 (and as befits that only locally generated of our five warrior states), he subscribes still to the Imperial Tradition of the deeper Middle Niger. His brazen forging of a prophesy lineage to the Askiya Mohammed of Songhai is just part of a larger strategy of economic and social engineering.

Sekou Amadou's is a severe vision of the Middle Niger political economy.[13] In order to control and convert the still "wild" Fulani clans, he decrees the obligation of all pastoralists to have a permanent village in the *seno-bourgou* lands of the floodplain (see chapter 4). Bambara enemies in particular, but not exclusively, are enslaved and then transformed into the servile Rimaïbe. His presumed legacy from Askia Mohammed is direct control over the "servile" races, generally artisans and occupation specialists. Here is a master of hierarchy searching for a way to preserve a degree of human ecological diversity! His capital, Hamdullahi, between Jenne and Mopti is an architectural model of that vision.[14]

[13] The best study of this period remains Brown, *Caliphate*.
[14] Gallay et al., *Hamdullahi*.

And yet the outsider is struck by how tenuous, and ultimately how fragile, was Sekou Amadou's hold on the loyalties of the peoples of his *Dina*. Jenne submits early and easily, but soon the city's Arma are in revolt.[15] After a hard nine-month siege, Jenne is taken and the property of the elites confiscated and given to resettled Fulani families. A new elite is born. The traditional mosque is razed and a new austere version built nearby. There is perennial warfare with the southern Bambara of Segou and with the Bambara of the Erg of Bara to the north. The imperfectly converted rural Fulani are unhappy, as certainly are the rural populations of other ethnic groups. The Bozo slink further into their swamps and wait for the inevitability of change.

Change comes as a new Islamic vision from the far west. Sekou Amadou is not the sole theocratic genius attracted by the wealth in goods and people of the Middle Niger. El Hadj Umar of the Futa Toro (Middle Senegal Valley) invades the Segou Bambara in 1861 and takes Hamdullahi the next year. Jenne and neighboring villages resist until 1866, but all the Middle Niger eventually falls to the Umarian state. Here is perhaps the major exception to the general rule that these outsider, warrior states are not remembered in Jenne – for the memory of the Futanké (Tukulor) times is not a pleasant one. The riverine trade grinds almost to a halt. The Futanké garrisons and mobile troops support themselves by raids upon local communities. *Razzia* (lightning raids) especially against the domains of the ever-resisting Bambara warlords were replied to by Bambara *razzia* against villages under Umarian control (but not protection). Roberts documents how, on the eve of the French invasion, local producers (town and rural) had withdrawn in a passive revolt from the market, diminishing their tribute payments, hiding granaries, etc.[16]

It was into an almost feudal Middle Niger, a landscape balkanized between remnants of failed warrior states, that the French marched in 1893. Resistance at towns such as Segou and, especially, Jenne was stiff – but confined largely to Futanké holdouts. The locals had had enough of the politics of pillage and terror. But Jenne was scarcely exhausted economically. Colonel Archinard wrote on the eve of the town's investment on April 12, 1893:

---

[15] Bintou Sanankoua, "Aperçu historique de Djenné," in *Djenné, Il Y A Cent Ans*, Bernard Gardi, Pierre Maas, and Geert Mommersteeg (eds.) (Institut Royal des Tropiques: Amsterdam, 1995), p. 11.

[16] Roberts, *Warriors*, pp. 95–9.

The column's officers with experience in Tunisia said Jenne resembled Kairouan and the Senegalese soldiers compared it to Saint Louis. For me it is the richest and most commercially active city I have yet seen in the Western Sudan. It is the one which, for a European, most resembles a real city and, in that, it differs absolutely from the other centers of the Blacks with which we have become familiar.[17]

Jenne represented the last serious Umarian resistance in Mali. And, to the brutality of the French occupation (an example of which was given in chapter 1 in the description of recruitment of labor for the *Office du Niger*). The peoples of the Middle responded as they had to all hegemonies from the outside and to all episodes of environmental unpredictability. They relied upon their age-old strategies of diversity, of compartmental tasks within a generalizing economy. They relied upon ancient webs of interconnectedness of social, political and economic segments, each autonomous in its own sphere. They resisted a Progress that would have been, for the subjugated, no such thing.

Middle Niger resilience resided in the persistence of notions of local authority and in the resistance to domination inherent in heterarchy. Is it correct to call these Middle Niger social institutions an original civil society? These institutions enabled the populace to endure the depredations of the warrior states, as well as from 1968 to 1991 to survive the despotic, one-party statism of the Moussa Traoré dictatorship. We can quibble about definitions of civil society and about the applicability of the concept. What I hope this book has made clear, however, is that the reluctance of the peoples of the Middle Niger to submit to the promises of the Office du Niger, and other monolithic development schemes of the post-colonial period (such as USAID's Operations Riz or Mil) was not because of cultural perversity or shortsightedness. The peoples of the Middle Niger have had several millennia of experience with their abundant, but unpredictable social and physical environments. They have discovered the great resilience of heterarchy.

The monolithic statism (theocratic or imperial) and state terrorism of the three and a half centuries after the last great Western Sudanese empire came up against deeply grounded community values. These values prevailed in the times of chaos and sustained those communities through very significant decadal or multi-decadal droughts. These values ultimately prevailed over Monsieur Bélime's

---

[17] Quoted in Gardi, "Djenné," p. 17, (translated by R. J. McIntosh).

(the Office du Niger's "maître africain de l'eau") command to "break up that sterile economic cell that is the indigenous village." Here is the source: resilience and age-old accommodation to the requirements of sustainability in the Middle Niger by the componential corporate groups settled on that highly productive, yet changeable landscape. This has been a tale of the Middle Niger as, preeminently, social, economic, and political heterarchy – and of resistance to the arrogance of power hierarchies.

Glossary

city Heterogeneous settlement that provides a variety of goods and services to a larger, more or less integrated hinterland.

civil society Spontaneous emergence and evolution of multiple agencies of authority and local governance out of the many overlapping and competing interst groups in society. Together, these agencies challenge the power-seeking tendencies of the state and nation-state.

corporation Self-defined groups with a shared history and shared sense of belonging, among whose members some critical and defining property is held in common. These groups make decisions as a unit and attempt to establish well-defined domains of authority.

dali-ma-sigi In Mande, the hero's obligatory knowledge quest. He (or she) navigates over a symbol-charged, perilous landscape to harvest power, authority, and arcane knowledge.

heterarchy Complex organization in which the relations between elements are unranked vertically but may be highly stratified horizontally. In political heterarchies, the components derive authority from different sources and power can be counterpoised, resulting in local resistance to control hierarchies.

hierarchy Complex organization composed of several levels of dominant or subordinate elements. In control hierarchies, decisions originating at a higher level flow down to the lower ranks, whereas information, goods, and services flow upwards.

historical imagination An illustrative story or allegorical tale told in the style of local storytelling, in the hopes of revealing a way of looking at the world or core values very difficult to explain in a Western idiom.

Imperial Tradition Imposition of new mechanisms of centralized control over earlier heterarchical systems of authority without the total elimination of the latter. In Mande, a new secular elite reinvent and manipulate older notions of occult authority and liberally experiement with new agencies of power, such as horse-cavalry, Islamic methods of administration, new forms of piety, etc. Successful models are called up to legitimate successor states.

kuma koro "Ancient speech" – epics of the living ancestors; Mande perception of what animates their entire history.

Mande A language (Niger Congo) *cum* cultural group occupying large parts of West Africa west of the Niger Bend. Sharing a broad constellation of notions about the derivation of authority from an occult landscape, they can broadly be divided into a Northern (esp. Soninké) and Southern (esp. Bambara [Bamana] and Malinké) tier. Many neighboring peoples, such as the Dogon and Serer (and even, in restricted spheres of belief, Fulani and Songhai) share Mande cosmological and symbolic notions, such that it can be useful to speak of Greater Mande (of highly variable borders at different points in time).

mansaya Mande concept of astute statecraft, especially in the time of the Imperial Tradition. It describes the effective superimposition of the restricted centralized bureaucracy of empire over robust local governance.

nyama The highly-dangerous vitalizing force of the world that can be manipulated, bundled, and even augmented by Mande heroes and heroines. This is the energy of action released by transformative acts such as smelting or taking life. Occult energy is the source of all Mande authority.

nyamakalaw Professional classes of artists, artisans, and other occupationally defined specialist producers in Mande, such as smiths, leatherworkers, and bards. Often spoken of (perhaps misleadingly) as "casted," their status as society's unusuals derives from their close dealings with the potentially dangerous occult forces (*nyama*).

onomasticon A culturally-defined topography. The Mande landscape is conceived as a network of power locations, a spatial blueprint of power in three dimensions.

over-kingdom More-or-less loosely organized confederations of largely self-ruling, economically autonomous polities. Governance over one domain (e.g., foreign wars or taxation of the luxury commerce) may be controlled by a paramount entity. This paramount entity may derive its authority from a spiritual or symbolic source, but may be confused as a political sovereign by outside observers.

statism Philosophy of governance that decrees the superiority of centralized, nation-state administration over local institutions. In historical terms, there is an implied superiority (if not evolutionary inevitability) of the empire over the state, of the state over the chiefdom, etc.

symbolic reservoir That dynamic wellspring of symbols, legends, and ideologies that gives trajectory (structured dynamism) to cultural traditions. It is the place of mixing of symbols percolating from adjoining traditions and the always shifting archive transmitted from one generation to the next. Different sub-groups of a society dip into the reservoir to appropriate, reinvent, and display legitimation traditions that serve their own sectional interests. This is the never static source of appropriate strategies from the past used by peoples to deal, in new ways, with today's social or environmental stresses.

synoecism Process of spontaneous synthesis by which a novel organism or institution emerges from the combining together of diverse components. Novel scales and principles of organization evolve, and yet some remnant signature of the original components may persist. Often, but not exclusively, applied to "nested" urban or political landscapes or to layered transformations, with continuity of process or place.

Bibliography

Alpers, Edward A. "Africa reconfigured: Presidential Address." *African Studies Review* 38(2) (1995): 1–10.

Amblard, Sylvie, and J. Pernès. "The identification of cultivated pearl millet (*Pennisetum*) amongst plant impressions on pottery from Oued Chebbi (Dhar Oualata, Mauritania)." *African Archaeological Review* 7 (1989): 117–26.

Ba, Adam Konare. *L'Epopée de Segou. Da Monzon: Un Pouvoir Guerrier.* Paris: Favre, 1987.

Baa, Myeru, and Mahmadou L. Sunbunu. *La Geste de Fanta Maa. Archétype du Chasseur dans la Culture des Bozo.* Niamey: CELHTO, 1987.

Ballouche, Aziz, and Katharina Neumann. "A new contribution to the Holocene vegetation history of the West African Sahel: Pollen from Oursi, Burkina Faso and charcoal from three sites in northeast Nigeria." *Vegetation History and Archaeobotany* 4 (1995): 31–9.

Barnett, Steve. "Futures: Probable and plausible." *Anthropology Newsletter* 37(7) (1994): 52.

Bathily, Abdoulaye. *Les Ports de l'Or. Le Royaume de Galam (Sénégal) de l'Ere Musulmane au Temps de Nègriers (VIIIe–XVIIIe Siècle).* Paris: Harmattan, 1989.

Bazin, J. "A chacun son Bambara." *Au Coeur de l'Ethnie.* J.-L. Amselle, and E. M'Bokolo (eds). Paris: Editions la Découverte, 1985, 87–127.

Beaudet, G. R. Coque, Pierre Michel, et al. "Y-a-t-il eu capture du Niger?" *Bulletin de l'Association des Géographes Françaises* 445–6 (1977): 215–22.

Bedeaux, Rogier M. A. "Des Tellem au Dogon: Recherches

archéologiques dans la boucle du Niger (Mali)." *Dall'Archeologia All'Arte Tradizionale Africana*. Gigi Pezzoli (ed.). Milan: Centro Studi Archeologia Africana, 1992, 83–101.

Bedaux, Rogier, T. J. Constandse-Westermann, L. Hacquebord, et al. "Recherches archéologiques dans le Delta intérieur du Niger." *Palaeohistoria* 20 (1978): 91–220.

Bedaux, Rogier M. A., Mamadi Dembélé, Annette M. Schmidt, et al. "L'Archéologie entre Bani et Niger." *Djenné: Une Ville Millénaire au Mali*. Rogier M. A. Bedaux and J. D. Van der Waals (eds). Leiden: Rijksmussen voor Volkenkunde, 1994, 41–53.

Bedaux, Rogier M. A., and Michel Raimbault. "Les grandes provinces de la céramique au Mali." *Vallées du Niger*. Paris: Réunion des Musées Nationaux, 1993, 273–93.

Bedaux, Rogier M. A., and J. D. Van der Waals. *Djenné. Une Ville Millénaire du Mali*. Rogier M. A. Bedaux and J. D. Van der Waals (eds). Leiden, the Netherlands: Rijksmuseum voor Volkenkunde, 1994.

Berns, Marla. "Symbolic reservoirs, sacred ceramics, and linguistic complexity in the Gonola Valley, northeastern Nigeria." *Dynamic Symbolic Reservoirs in Deep Time*. Annual Meeting of the African Studies Association, Boston, Nov. 1993.

Berry, B. J. L. "City size distributions and economic development." *Economic Development and Cultural Change* 9 (1961): 573–87.

Bethier, S. *Recherches archéologiques sur la Capitale de l'Empire de Ghana: Etude d'un Secteur, d'Habitat à Koumbi Saleh (Mauritanie)*, Cambridge Monographs in African Archaeology, no. 680, Oxford: BAR, 1997.

Bird, Charles S. *The Songs of Seydou Camara*. Bloomington, IN: Indiana University African Studies Center, 1974.

Bird, Charles S., and Martha B. Kendall. "The Mande Hero." *Explorations in African Systems of Thought*. Ivan Karp, and Charles S. Bird (eds). Bloomington, IN: Indiana University Press, 1980, 13–26.

Blanck, J.-P. "Schéma d'évolution géomorphologique de la Vallée du Niger entre Tombouctou et Labbezanga (République du Mali)." *Bulletin de l'Association Sénégalese pour l'Etude du Quaternaire de l'Ouest Africain, Dakar* 19–20 (1968): 17–26.

——. *Projet d'Aménagement de la Vallée du Niger entre Tombouctou et Labbezanga (Etude Géomorphologique)*. Strasbourg: Centre de Géographie Appliquée, Université de Strasbourg, 1968.

Bocoum, Hamady. "Contribution à la connaissance des origines du Takrur." *Annales de la Faculté des Lettres et Sciences Humaines* 20 (1990): 159–78.

Boré, Youssouf. *Recensement des Graminés Sauvages Alimentaires (Céreales Mineures) Utilisés en 5eme, 6eme, et 7eme Régions.* Bamako: Ecole Normale Superieure, 1983.

Bourgeon, G., and R. Bertrand. "Evaluation du milieu naturel des plains alluviales de la Boucle du Niger (Mali)- II. Potentialités." *L'Agronomie Tropicale* 39 (1984): 208–15.

Bovill, E. W. *The Golden Trade of the Moors*, 2nd edn. Oxford: Oxford University Press, 1970.

Brasseur, Gérard. *Les Etablissements Humains au Mali.* Mémoire de l'Institut Fondamental D'Afrique Noire no. 83. Dakar: Institut Fondamental d'Afrique Noire, 1968.

Brent, Michel. "The rape of Mali." *Archaeology* 47(3) (1994): 26–31, 34–5.

Brett, Michael, and Elizabeth Fentress. *The Berbers.* Oxford: Blackwell, 1996.

Brett-Smith, Sarah C. *The Making of Bamana Sculpture: Creativity and Gender.* Cambridge: Cambridge University Press, 1994.

Brooks, George E. "Ecological perspectives on Mande population movements, commercial networks and settlement patterns from the Atlantic Wet Phase (*ca.*5500–2500 B.C.) to the present." *History in Africa* 16 (1989): 23–40.

—— *Landlords and Strangers. Ecology, Society, and Trade in Western Africa. 1000–1630.* Boulder, CO: Westview Press, 1993.

——. "A provisional historical schema for western Africa based on seven climatic periods (*c.*9,000 B.C. to the 19th century)." *Cahiers d'Etudes Africaines* 26 (1986): 43–62.

——. *Western Africa to c.A.D. 1960: A Provisional Schema Based on Climatic Periods.* Indiana University African Studies Program Working Paper Series no. 1. Bloomington: Indiana University, 1985.

Brown, William A. *The Caliphate of Hamdullahi, ca.1818–1864. A Study in African History and Tradition.* PhD dissertation. Madison: University of Wisconsin, 1969.

Brunet-Moret, Y., P. Chaperon, J. P. Lamagat, et al. *Monographie Hydrologique du Fleuve Niger.* Monographies Hydrographiques no. 8. Paris: ORSTOM, Institut Français de Recherche Scientifique pour le Développement en Coopération, 1986. 2 vols.

Bühnen, Stephen. "Brothers, chiefdoms, and empire: On Jan Jansen's 'The representation of status in Mande' " *History in Africa* 23

(1996): 111–20.

Bulman, S. "The Buffalo-Woman tale: Political imperatives and narrative constraints in the Sunjata epic." *Discourse and its Disguises. The Interpretation of African Oral Texts.* K. Barber, and P. F. de Moraes Farias (eds). Birmingham: Centre for West African Studies, 1989, 171–88.

Burke, K., A. B. Durotoye, and A. J. Whiteman. "A dry phase south of the Sahara 20,000 years ago." *West African Journal of Archaeology* 1 (1971): 1–8.

Burkhalter, Sheryl L. "Listening for silences in Almoravid history: Another reading of 'The conquest that never was.' " *History in Africa* 19 (1992): 103–31.

Butzer, Karl W. *Archaeology as Human Ecology. Method and Theory for a Contextual Approach.* Cambridge: Cambridge University Press, 1992.

Caillié, René. *Travels Through Central Africa to Timbuktu and Across the Great Desert to Morocco: Performed in the Years 1824–1828.* London: Colburn & Bentley, 1830.

Camps, Gabriel. "Beginning of pastoralism and cultivation in northwest Africa and the Sahara." *The Cambridge History of Africa.* John Desmond Clark (ed.), vol. 1. Cambridge: Cambridge University, 1982, 548–623.

——. "Extension territoriale des civilisations épipaléolithique et néolithique dans le nord de l'Afrique." *Acts of the Sixth Panafrican Congress of Prehistory and Quaternary Studies.* H-J Hugot (ed.). Chambéry: Les Imprimeries Réunies, 1967, 284–7.

——. *Les Berbères. Mémoire et Identité*, 2nd edn. Paris: Editions Errance, 1987.

——. *Les Civilisations Préhistoriques de l'Afrique du Nord et du Sahara.* Paris: Doin, 1974.

Cashion, Gerald. *Hunters of the Mande. A Behavioral Code and Worldview Derived from the Study of their Folklore.* Diss. Ph.D. dissertation. Bloomington, IN: Indiana University, 1984.

Centre International pour l'Elevage en Afrique, and Mark Haywood. *Evolution de l'Utilisation des Terres et de la Végétation dans la Zone Soudano-Sahelienne du Projet CIPEA au Mali. Document de Travail, no. 3.* Addis Abeba: CIPEA, 1981.

Chang, Kwang-Chih. *The Archaeology of Ancient China*, 4th edn. New Haven: Yale University Press, 1986.

——. *Art, Myth, and Ritual. The Path to Political Authority in Ancient China.* Cambridge, MA: Harvard University Press, 1983.

——. "Sandai archaeology and the formation of state in ancient

China." *The Origin of Chinese Civilization.* David Keightley (ed.), Berkeley: University of California Press, 1983, 493–521.

Charry, Eric. *Musical Thought, History, and Practice Among the Mande of West Africa.* PhD dissertation. Princeton: Princeton Univeristy, 1994.

Chevalier, A. *Le Sahara. Centre d'Origins de Plantes Cultivées.* Mémoire de la Société Biogéographie no. 6. Paris: Société Biogéographie, 1938, 307–22.

Chieze, Valérie. "La métallurgie du fer dans la zone lacustre." *Recherches Archéologiques au Mali.* Michel Raimbault and Kléna Sanogo (eds). Paris: Karthala, 1991, 449–72.

Childs, S. Terry, and David Killick. "Indigenous African Metallurgy: Nature and Culture." *Annual Review of Anthropology* 22 (1993): 317–37.

Cissé, Youssouf Tata. "Notes sur les sociétés de chasseurs Malinké." *Journal de la Société des Africanistes* 34 (1964): 175–226.

Cissé, Youssouf Tata and Wa Kamissoko. *La Grande Geste du Mali des Origines à la Fondation de l'Empire.* Paris: Karthala – ARSAN, 1988.

——. *Soundjata. La Gloire du Mali.* Paris: Karthala – ARSAN, 1991.

Cissoko, Sékéné M. "Famines et épidemies à Tombouctou et dans la Boucle du Niger du XVIᵉ au XVIIIᵉ siècle." *Bulletin de l'Institut Fondamental de l'Afrique Noire (B)* 30 (1968): 806–21.

——. *Tombouctou et l'Empire Songhay.* Dakar: Nouvelles Editions Africaines, 1975.

Clérisse, Henri. "Les gisements de Tondidaro (Soudan Française) et les tumulis échelonnés le long du Niger de Niafunké au Lac Débo." *Actes du 15th Congrés International d'Anthropologie et d'Archéologie Prehistorique.* Paris, Sept. 1931, 273–8.

Cohen, Ronald. "Endless teardrops: Prolegomena to the study of human rights in Africa." *Human Rights and Governance in Africa.* Ronald Cohen, Goran Hyden, and Winston P. Nagan (eds). Gainesville: University Press of Florida, 1993, 3–38.

COHMAP Members. "Climatic changes of the last 18,000 years; Observations and model simulations." *Science* 241 (1988): 1043–52.

Commelin, Dominique. "Céramique." *Sahara ou Sahel?* Nicole Petit-Maire and Jean Risier (eds). Marseille: Centre National de la Recherche Scientifique, 1983, 343–66.

Commelin, Dominique, Michel Raimbault, and Jean-François Saliège. "Nouvelles données sur la chronologie du Néolithique au Sahara malien." *Comptes Rendus de la Académie des Sciences, Paris. Série II* 317 (1993): 543–50.

Commissariat de l'Afrique Occidentale Française. *L'Aménagement Hydraulique et la Mise en Valeur de la Vallée Moyenne du Niger.* Paris: Commissariat de l'Afrique Occidentale Française, 1931.

Connah, Graham. *Three Thousand Years in Africa.* Cambridge: Cambridge University Press, 1981.

Conrad, David C. "Blind man meets prophet." *Status and identity in West Africa: Nyamakalaw of Mande.* David C. Conrad, and Barbara E. Frank (eds). Bloomington: Indiana University Press, 1995, 86–132.

——. "Mooning armies and mothering heroes: Female power in Mande epic tradition." *The Mande Epic as History, Literature and Performance.* Ralph Austin (ed.). Bloomington, IN: Indiana University Press, forthcoming.

——. "Searching for history in the Sunjata epic: The case of Fakoli." *History in Africa* 19 (1992): 147–200.

——. "A town called Dakajalan: The Sunjata tradition and the question of ancient Mali's capital." *Journal of African History* 35 (1994): 355–77.

Conrad, David C., and Humphrey Fisher. "The conquest that never was: Ghana and the Almoravids, 1076, I, the external Arabic sources." *History in Africa* 9 (1982): 21–59.

——. "The conquest that never was: Ghana and the Almoravids, 1076, II, the local oral sources." *History in Africa* 10 (1983): 53–78.

Conrad, David C., and Barbara E. Frank. "Contradiction and ambiguity in Mande society." *Status and Identity in West Africa: Nyamakalaw of Mande.* David C. Conrad, and Barbara E. Frank (eds). Bloomington, IN: Indiana University Press, 1995, 1–23.

——. *Status and Identity in West Africa: Nyamakalaw of Mande.* David C. Conrad, and Barbara E. Frank (eds). Bloomington: Indiana University Press, 1995.

Cornevin, Marianne. *Archéologie Africaine. A la Lumière des Découvertes Récentes.* Paris: Maisonneuve et Larose, 1993.

Crosby, Alfred. *Ecological Imperialism. The Biological Expansion of Europe, 900–1900.* Cambridge: Cambridge University Press, 1986.

Crown, Patricia L. "The Hohokam of the American Southwest." *Journal of World Prehistory* 4(2) (1990): 223–55.

Crumley, Carole L. "Heterarchy and the Analysis of Complex Societies." *Heterarchy and the Analysis of Complex Societies.* Robert M. Ehrenreich, Carole L. Crumley, and Janet E. Levy (eds). Archaeological Papers of the American Anthropological Association, no. 6. Washington, DC: American Anthropological Association, 1995, 1–5.

———. *Historical Ecology. Cultural Knowledge and Changing Landscapes.* Carole Crumley (ed.). Santa Fe, NM: School of American Research Press, 1994.

Cuoq, J. M. *Recueil des Sources Arabes Concernant l'Afrique Occidentale du VIIIe Siècle.* Paris: Editions du Centre National de la Recherche Scientifique, 1975.

Curdy, Phillip. *Tiebala, Mali: Etude de la Céramique. Diplôme d'Archéologie Préhistorique.* Diss. Diplôme d'Archéologie Préhistorique. Geneva: Université de Genève, 1982.

Curtin, Philip D. "Disease exchange across the tropical Atlantic." *History and Philosophy of the Life Sciences* 15 (1993): 169–96.

———. *Economic Change in Precolonial Africa.* Madison: University of Wisconsin Press, 1975, 67–9.

Curtin, Philip. "Epidemiology and the slave trade." *Political Science Quarterly* 83 (1968): 190–216.

Daget, L. "La pêche dans le Delta central du Niger." *Journal de la Société des Africanistes* 19 (1949): 1–79.

———. "La pêche à Diafrabe." *Bulletin, de l'Institut Fondamental d'Afrique Noire (B)* 18 (1956): 1–97.

Daveau, S. and C. Toupet. "Anciens terroirs Gangara." *Bulletin de l'Institut Fondamental d'Afrique Noire (B)* 25 (1963): 193–214.

David, Nicolas. "The archaeology of ideology: Mortuary practices in the Central Mandara Highlands, Northern Cameroon." *An African Commitment: Papers in Honour of Peter Lewis Shinnie.* Judy Sterner, and Nicolas David (eds). Calgary: Univesity of Calgary Press, 1992, 181–210.

———. "Early Bantu expansion in the context of Central African prehistory: 4,000–1 BC." *L'Expansion Bantoue.* L. Bouquiaux (ed.). Paris: SELAF, 1980, 609–47.

———. "History of crops and peoples in north Cameroon to A.D. 1900." *Origins of African Plant Domestication.* J. Harlan, J. M. de Wet, and A. B. Stemler (eds). The Hague: Mouton, 1976, 223–67.

Davidson, Basil. *A History of West Africa 1000–1800.* London: Longman, 1977.

de Grunne, Bernard. *Ancient Terracotta Statuatory from West Africa.* Louvain-la-Neuve: Université Catholoque de Louvain, 1980.

——. *Divine Gestures and Earthly Gods. A Study of the Ancient Terracotta Statuatory from the Inland Niger Delta in Mali.* PhD Dissertation. New Haven: Yale University, 1987.

de Mézières, André Bonnel. "Recherches sur l'emplacement de Ghana et de Takrour." *Mémoires de l"Académie des Inscriptions et des Belles Lettres de Paris* (1923): 227–73.

de Moraes Farias, P. F. "Pilgrimages to 'pagan' Mecca." *Discourses and its Disguises.* K. Barber, and P. F. de Moraes Farias (eds). Birmingham: Centre for West African Studies, 1989, 152–69.

Dean, Jeffrey S. "Complexity theory and sociocultural change in the American Southwest." *Global Change in History and Prehistory.* Roderick J. McIntosh, Joseph Tainter, and Susan Keech McIntosh (eds). New York: Columbia University Press, 1998.

Delafosse, Maurice. *Haut-Sénégal-Niger (Soudan français).* Paris: Larose, 1912, 3 vols.

Dembélé, Mamadi. *Entre Débo et Faguibine, Etude sur la Morphologie et la Typologie des Sites Archéologiques d'une Région Lacustre au Mali.* 3eme Cycle Thesis. Paris: Ecole des Hautes Etudes en Sciences Sociales, 1986.

——. "Les misions Léré–Faguibine (1981 et 1983)." *Recherches Archéologiques au Mali.* Michel Raimbault and Kléna Sanogo (eds). Paris: Karthala, 1991, 63–80.

——. "Les recherches organisées par la Division du Patrimoine Culturel." *Recherches Archéologiques au Mali.* Michel Raimbault and Kléna Sanogo. Paris: Karthala, 1991, 63–80.

Dembélé, Mamadi, and Michel Raimbault. "Les Grandes buttes anthropiques." *Recherches Archéologiques au Mali.* Michel Raimbault, and Kléna Sanogo. Paris: Karthala, 1991, 249–58.

Dembélé, Mamadi, Annette M. Schmidt, and J. D. Van der Waals. "Prospection de sites archéologiques dans le delta intérieur du Niger." *Vallées du Niger.* Paris: Editions de la Réunion des Musées Nationaux, 1993, 218–32.

Desplagnes, Louis. "Etude sur les tumuli du Killi dans la région de Goundam." *L'Anthropologie* 14 (1903): 151–72.

——. "Fouilles du tumulus d'El Oualadgi (Soudan)." *Bulletin de l'Institut Fondamental d'Afrique Noire (B)* 13 (1951): 1159–73.

——. *Le Plateau Central Nigérien.* Paris: Larose, 1907.

Devisse, Jean. "Commerce et routes du traffic en Afrique occidentale." *Histoire Générale de l'Afrique.* Paris: UNESCO, 1990, 397–483.

——. 'L'Or." *Vallées du Niger.* Paris: Editions de Réunion des Musées Nationaux, 1993, 344–57.

——. "Routes de commerce et échanges en Afrique occidentale en relation avec la Méditerranée." *Revue d'Histoire Economique et Sociale* 50(1) (1972): 42–73.

Devisse, Jean and Boubacar Diallo. "Le seuil de Wagadu." *Vallées du Niger*. Paris: Réunion des Musées Nationaux, 1993, 103–15.

Devisse, Jean and Samuel Sidibé. "Mandinka et mandéphones." *Vallées du Niger*. Paris: Edition de la Réunion des Musées Nationaux, 1993, 143–50.

Devisse, Jean and Robert Vernet. "Le bassin des Vallées du Niger: Chronologie et espaces." *Vallées du Niger*. Paris: Réunion des Musées Nationaux, 1993, 11–37.

Diallo, Boubacar. 'Les Soninko." *Vallées du Niger*. Paris: Editions de la Réunion des Musées Nationaux, 1993, 134–142.

Dieterlen, Germaine. *Les Ames des Dogon*. Travaux et Mémoires no. 40. Paris: Institut d'Ethnologie, 1941.

——. "The Mande creation myth." *Africa* 27(2) (1957): 124–38.

Dieterlen, Germaine, and Y. Cissé. *Les Fondements de la Société d'Initiation du Komo*. Paris: Mouton, 1972.

Dieterlen, Germaine, and Diarra Sylla. *L'Empire de Ghana. Le Wagadou et les Traditions de Yéréré*. Paris: Karthala, 1992.

Dramani-Issifou, Z. "Les Songhay: dimension historique." *Vallées du Niger*. Paris: Edition de la Réunion des Musées Nationaux, 1993, 151–62.

Dunbar, Robert. "Climate variability during the Holocene: An update." *Global Change in History and Prehistory*. Roderick J. McIntosh, Joseph Tainter, and Susan Keech McIntosh (eds). New York: Columbia University Press, 1998.

Dupuy, Christian. "Trois milles ans d'histoire pastorale au sud du Sahara." *Préhistoire et Anthropology Méditerranéennes* (1992): 105–26.

Durant, Will. *Our Oriental Heritage*. The Story of Civilization. New York: Simon & Schuster, 1954.

Earle, Timothy (ed.). *Chiefdoms: Power, Economy, and Ideology*. Cambridge: Cambridge University Press, 1991.

Echenberg, Myron, and Jean Filipovich. "African military labour and the building of the Office du Niger installations, 1925–1950." *Journal of African History* 27 (1986): 533–51.

Escudier, Denis. "Qui avait intérêt à créer l'Office du Niger?" *Afrique Histoire*.9 (1985): 31–6.

es-Sa'di. *Ta'rikh es-Sudan*. trans. Olivier Houdas. Paris: Leroux, 1900.

Euler, Robert C. 'Demography and cultural dynamics of the Colorado Plateaus." *The Anasazi in a Changing Environment.* George J. Gumerman (ed.). Cambridge: Cambridge University Press, 1988, 192–229.

Fabre, Jean and Nicole Petit-Maire. "Holocene climatic evolution at 22–23°N from two palaeolakes in the Taoudenni area (northern Mali)." *Palaeography, Palaeoclimatology, Palaeoecology* 65 (1988): 133–48.

Fage, John. *A History of Africa.* London: Unwin Hyman, 1988.

Fairbridge, Rhodes W. "Monsoons and paleomonsoons." *Episodes* 9(3) (1986): 143–9.

Falconer, Steve, and Stephen Savage. "Heartlands and hinterlands: Alternative trajectories of early urbanism in Mesopotamia and the southern Levant." *American Antiquity* 60(1) (1995): 37–58.

Fatton, Robert Jr. "Africa in the age of democratization: The civic limitations of Civil Society." *African Studies Review* 38(2) (1995): 67–99.

Faubion, James D. "History in anthropology." *Annual Review of Anthropology* 22 (1993): 33–54.

Faure, H. "Variabilité et pseudocyclicité du climat au Sahel aux échelles de temps de 10 à 10^5 ans." *Climat et Risques, Natureles.* Paris, June 1986. AFGP Colloquium paper.

Faure, Hugues, and Jean-Yves Gac. "Will the Sahelian drought end in 1985?" *Nature* 291 (1981): 475–8.

Feinman, G. "The emergence of inequality: A focus on strategies and processes." *Foundations of Social Inequality.* T. D. Price, and G. Feinman (eds). New York: Plenum, 1995, 255–79.

Fish, S. K., and S. Kowalewski. *The Archaeology of Regions.* Washington, DC: The Smithsonian Institution Press, 1990.

Folland, C. K., T. N. Palmer, and D. E. Parker, "Sahel rainfall and worldwide sea temperatures, 1901–85." *Nature* 320 (1986): 602–7.

Fontes, Pierre, Mamadi Dembélé, Michel Raimbault, et al. "Prospection archéologique de tumulus et buttes tumuliformes dans la région dec lacs au Mali. Datations par le radiocarbone." *Comptes Rendus de l'Académie des Science de Paris, Série III* 301(5) (1985): 207–12.

Fontes, Pierre-Bernard, Alain Person, and Jean-François Saliège. "Prospection de sites archéologiques de la région des lacs et du delta intérieur du Niger (1980)." *Recherches Archéologiques au Mali. Les Sites Protohistoriques de la Zone Lacustre.* Michel Raimbault, and Kléna Sanogo (eds). Paris: Karthala, Agence de Coopération Culturelle et Technique, 1991, 29–61.

Frank, Barbara. *More than Objects: An Art History of Mande Potters and Leatherworkers*. Washington DC: Smithsonian Institution Press, 1998.

Frank, Barbara E. "Soninké Garankew and Bamana-Malinke Jeliw: Mande leatherworkers, identity and the Diaspora." *Status and Identity in West Africa: Nyamakalaw of Mande*. David C. Conrad, and Barbara E. Frank (eds). Bloomington: Indiana University Press, 1995, 133–50.

Freidel, David, Linda Schiele, and Joy Parker. *Maya Cosmos. Three Thousand Years on the Shaman's Path*. New York: William Morrow and Co., 1993.

French, Howard W. "In a faraway place, living with fear." *New York Times* 30 Jan. 1995, A: 6.

Friedman, J., and M. Rowlands. *The Evolution of Social Systems*. Madison: University of Wisconsin, 1978.

Furon, Raymond, "L'Ancien delta du Niger." *Revue de Géographie Physique et de Géologie Dynamique* 2 (1929): 265–74.

Fussell, Paul. *The Great War and Modern Memory*. New York: Oxford: University Press, 1975.

Gabriel, Baldur. "Palaeoecological evidence from neolithic fireplaces in the Sahara." *African Archaeological Review* 5 (1987): 93–103.

Gabriel, Kathryn. *Roads to Center Place: A Cultural Atlas of Chaco Canyon And the Anasazi*. Boulder, CO: Johnson Publishing Co., 1991.

Gallais, Jean. *Hommes du Sahel. Espaces-Temps et Pouvoirs. Le Delta Intérieur du Niger 1960–1980*. Paris: Flammarion, 1984.

——. *Le Delta Intérieur du Niger. Etude de Géographie Régionale*. Mémoires de l'Institut Fondamental d'Afrique Noire no. 79. Dakar: Institut Fondamental d'Afrique Noire, 1967.

——. *Le Delta Intérieur du Niger et ses Bordures: Etude Morphologiques*. Mémoires et Documents du Centre de la Documentation Cartographiques et Géographiques no 3. Paris: Centre National de la Recherche Scientifique, 1967.

Gallay, Alain. "Quelques gisements néolithiques du Sahara malien." *Bulletin de la Société des Africainistes* 36(2) (1966): 167–208.

Gallay, Alain, and Eric Huysecom. 'Un site néolithique de l'Adrar Tabarbarout (Saharan malien oriental)." *Bulletin de la Société Préhistorique Française* 90(5) (1993): 357–64.

Gallay, Alain, Eric Huysecom, Matthieu Honegger, et al. *Hamdallahi, Capitale de l'Empire Peul du Massina, Mali. Première Fouille Archéologique, Etudes Historiques et*

Ethnoarchéologiques. Stuttgart: Franz Steiner Verlag, 1990.

Galloy, P., Y. Vincent, and M. Forget. *Nomades et Paysans d'Afrique Noire Occidentale*. Mémoire des Annales de l'Est no. 23. Nancy: CRNS, 1963.

Galloy, Pierre. 'Nomadisme et fixation dans la région das lacs du Moyen Niger." *Nomades et Paysans de l'Afrique Noire Occidentale*. Pierre Galloy, Yvon Vincent, Maurice Forget (eds). Nancy: Université de Nancy, 1963, 11–34.

Gardi, Bernard. "Djenné et la conquête du Soudan." *Djenné, Il Y A Cent Ans*. Bernard Gardi, Pierre Maas, and Geert Mommersteeg (eds). Amsterdam: Institut Royal des Tropiques, 1995, 13–23.

Garenne-Marot, Laurence, and Loïc Hurtel. "Le cuivre: Approache méthodologique de la métallurgie du cuivre dans les vallées du Niger et au sud du Sahara." *Vallées du Niger*. Paris: Editions de Réunion des Musées Nationaux, 1993, 320–43.

Garrard, Timothy F. "Myth and metrology: The early trans-Saharan gold trade." *Journal of African History* 23 (1982): 443–61.

Gautier, A. "Prehistoric men and cattle in North Africa: A dearth of data and a surfeit of models." *Prehistory of Arid North Africa: Essays in Honor of Fred Wendorf*. Angela Close (ed.). Dallas: SMU Press, 1987, 163–87.

Gerbeau, Herbert. "La région de l'Issa-Ber." *Etude d'Outre-Mer* 42(2) and 3 (1959): 51–8 and 91–108.

Gibbal, Jean-Marie. *Les Génies du Fleuve*. Paris: Presses de la Renaissance, 1988.

Grébénart, Danilo. "Les métallurgies du cuivre et du fer autour d'Agadez (Niger), des origines au début de la periode médievale." *Métallurgie Africaines. Nouvelles Contributions*. Nicole Echard (ed.). Mémoire de la Société des Africanistes no. 9. Paris: Société des Africanistes, 1983, 109–25.

——. "Relations inter-éthniques Saharo-Sahéliennes dans l'Ouest Africain durant la préhistoire finale et la protohistoire." *Prehistoire et Anthropologie Méditerranéennes* 4 (1995): 121–30.

Gregory, Derek. *Geographical Imaginations*. Oxford: Blackwell, 1994.

Griaule, M. 'l'Alliance cathartique." *Africa* 18 (1948): 242–58.

Grove, Anthony T. *The Niger and Its Neighbours. Environmental History and Hydrobiology, Human Use and Health Hazards of the Major West African Rivers*. Anthony T. Grove (ed.). Rotterdam: A. A. Balkema, 1985.

Grove, Anthony T., and A. Warren. "Quaternary landforms and climate on the south side of the Sahara." *Geographical Journal* 134 (1968): 194–208.

Guitat, Raymond. "Carte et répertoire des sites néolithiques du Mali et de la Haute-Volta." *Bulletin de l'Institut Fondamental d'Afrique Noire (B)* 34(4) (1972): 896–925.

Haaland, Randi. "Iron production, its socio-cultural context and ecological implications." *African Iron Working. Ancient and Traditional.* Randi Haaland, and Peter Shinnie (eds). Bergen: Norwegian University Press, 1985, 50–72.

——. "Man's Role in the changing habitat of Méma during the old Kingdom of Ghana." *Norwegian Archaeological Review* 13(19) (1980): 31–46.

Haggett, P., A. Cliff, and A. Frey. *Locational Analysis in Human Geography*. New York: Wiley and Sons, 1977.

Hale, Thomas. *Griots and Griottes of West Africa*. Bloomington: Indiana University Press, 1997.

Hama, Boubou. *Histoire des Songhay*. Paris: Présence Africaine, 1968.

Harlan, Jack R. "Wild grain seeds as food sources in the Sahara and Sub-Sahara." *Sahara* 2 (1989): 72–4.

Harlan, Jack R., J. M. de Wet, and Ann B. L. Stemler (eds). *Origin of African Plant Domestication*. The Hague: Mouton, 1976.

Harris, David R. "Traditional systems of plant food production and the origins of agriculture in West Africa." *Origin of African Plant Domestication*. Jack R. Harlan, Jan M. J. De Wet, and Ann B. L. Stemler (eds). The Hague: Mouton, 1976, 311–56.

Haskell, Helen, Roderick J. McIntosh, and Susan Keech McIntosh. *Archaeological Reconnaissance in the Region of Dia, Mali 1988.* Final report to the National Geographic Society.

Hassan, Fekri. "Abrupt Holocene climatic events in Africa." *Aspects of African Archaeology. Papers from the 10th Congress of the Pan African Associations for Prehistory and Related Studies.* Gilbert Pwiti and Robert Soper (eds). Harare: University of Zimbabwe Publications, 1996, 83–9.

——. "Population ecology and civilization in ancient Egypt." *Historical Ecology. Cultural Knowledge and Changing Landscapes.* Carole Crumley (ed.). Santa Fe, NM: School of American Research Press, 1994, 155–81.

Hassan, Fekri, and B. R. Stucki. "Nile floods and climatic change." *Climate. History, Periodicity, and Predictability.* Michael R. Rampino, John E. Sanders, Walter S. Newman, et al. (eds). New

York: Van Nostrand Reinhold, 1987, 37–46.

Hayden, Brian. *Archaeology. The Science of Once and Future Things*. New York: W. H. Freeman, 1993.

Hays, J. D., John Imbrie, and N. J. Shackleton. "Variations in the Earth's orbit: Pacemaker of the Ice Ages." *Science* 194(4270) (1976): 1121–32.

Hays, T. R. " 'Wavy Line' pottery: an element of Nilotic diffusion." *South African Archaeological Bulletin* 29 (1974): 27–32.

Hays, Thomas R. "An examination of the Sudanese Neolithic." *Proceedings of the 7th Pan African Congress of Prehistory and Related Studies*. A. Berhanou, J. Chevaillon, and J. E. G. Sutton (eds). Addis Ababa: Provisional Military Government of Socialist Ethiopia, Ministry of Culture, 1971, 85–92.

Herbart, Pierre. *Le Chancre du Niger*. Paris: Gallimard, 1939.

Herbert, Eugenia. *Red Gold of Africa*. Madison: University of Wisconsin Press, 1984.

——. "Timbuktu: a case study of the role of legend in history." *West African Culture Dynamics*. B. K. Swartz and R. E. Dumett (eds). The Hague: Mouton, 1980, 431–54.

Herzfeld, Michael. *Anthropology Through the Looking Glass. Critical Ethnography in the Margins of Europe*. Cambridge: Cambridge University Press, 1987.

Holl, Augustin. *Economie et Société Néolithique du Dhar Tichitt (Mauritanie)*. Paris: Editions Recherches sur les Civilisations, A.D.P.F., 1986.

——. "Subsistence patterns of the Dhar Tichitt, Mauritania." *African Archaeological Review* 3 (1985): 151–62.

Hunwick, John. "Gao and the Almoravids revisited: Ethnicity, political change and the limits of interpretation." *Journal of African History* 35(2) (1994): 251–73.

——. "The mid-fourteenth century capital of Mali." *Journal of African History* 14(2) (1973): 195–206.

——. *Shar'ia in Songhay: The Replies of al-Maghili to the Questions of Askia al-Hajj Muhammad*. London: Oxford University Press, 1985.

Imperato, P. 'Nomades of the Niger." *Natural History* 81 (1972): 60–8, 78–9.

Jacobberger, Patricia A. "Drought-related changes to geomorphic processes in central Mali." *Bulletin of the Geological Society of America* 100(3) (1988): 351–61.

——. "Geomorphology of the upper inland Niger delta." *Journal of Arid Environments* 13 (1987): 95–112.

————. "Mapping abandoned river channels in Mali through directional filtering of thematic mapper data." *Remote sensing of Environment* 26 (1988): 161–70.

Jacobsen, Thorkild. *The Treasures of Darkness*. New Haven: Yale University Press 1976.

Jansen, Jan. "Polities and political discourse: Was Mande already a segmentary society in the Middle Ages?" *History in Africa* 23 (1996): 121–8.

Johnson, Allen W., and Timothy Earle. *The Evolution of Human Societies, From Foraging Group to Agrarian State*. Stanford: Stanford University Press, 1987.

Johnson, George. "Social strife may have exiled ancient Indians." *New York Times* 20 Aug. 1996, B: B5–B6.

Johnson, John William. *The Epic of Son–Jara. A West African Tradition*. Bloomington, IN: Indiana University Press, 1986.

Johnson, John William, Thomas A. Hale, and Stephen P. Belcher. *Oral Epic in Africa: Vibrant Voices from a Vast Continent*. Bloomington, IN: Indiana University Press, 1997.

Kaba Lansiné. "Archers, musketeers, and mosquitoes: The Moroccan invasion of the Sudan and the Songhay resistance (1591–1612)." *Journal of African History* 22 (1981): 457–75.

Kaplan, Robert D. "The Coming Anarchy." *The Atlantic Monthly* 273(2) (February 1994): 44–76.

————. *The Ends of the Earth: A Journey at the Dawn of the 21st Century*. New York: Random House, 1996.

Kassibo, Ibréhima. "Histoire du peuplement humain." *La Pêche dans le Delta Central du Niger*. Jacques Quensìere, (ed.) Paris: ORSTOM, 1994, 81–103.

Keane John (ed.) *Civil Society and the State. New European Perspectives*. London: Verso, 1988.

Kemp, Barry J. *Ancient Egypt. Anatomy of a Civilisation*. London: Routledge, 1989.

Kense, François. "The initial diffusion of iron to Africa." *African Iron Working – Ancient and Traditional*. Bergen: Norwegian University Press, 1985, 11–27.

Kervran, L. "Le cours fossile du Niger." *Notre Sahara* 10 (1959): 53–8.

Kesteloot, Lilyan, Christian Barbey, and Siré M. Ndongo. "Les Peul." *Vallees du Niger*. Paris: Edition de la Réunion des Musées Nationaux, 1993, 173–89.

Kesteloot, Lilyan, C. Barbey, and S. M. Ndongo. "Tyamaba, mythe Peul." *Notes Africaines* 185–6 (1985): 1–72.

Killick, David. "A little-known extractive process: Iron smelting in natural draft furnaces." JOM: Journal of the Minerals, Metals and Materials Society 43(4) (1991): 62–4.

——. "On claims for "Advanced" ironworking technology in precolonial Africa." *The Culture and Technology of African Iron Production.* Peter R. Schmidt (ed.). Gainesville: University Press of Florida, 1996, 247–66.

Killick, David, Nikolaas J. van der Merwe, R. B. Gordon, et al. "Reassessment of the evidence for early metallurgy in Niger, West Africa." *Journal of Archaeological Science* 15 (1988): 367–94.

Kopytoff, Igor. *The African Frontier.* Bloomington, IN: Indiana University Press, 1987.

Kostof, Spiro. "Junctions of town and country." *Dwellings, Settlements and Tradition. Cross-Cultural Perspectives.* Jean-Paul Bourdier and Nezar Alsayyad (eds). Landam, MD: University Press of America, 1989, 107–33.

——. "Urbanism and polity: Medieval Siena in context." *International Laboratory for Architecture and Urban Design, Yearbook for 1982* (1982): 66–73.

Kuper, Rudolph. "Agypten am Rande des Sahel. Ausgrabungen in der Abu Ballas-region." *Archäologie in Deutschland* 2 (1989): 18–22.

——. "Sahel in Egypt: Environmental change and cultural development in the Abu Ballas area, Libyan Desert." *Environmental Change and Human Culture in the Nile Basin and Northern Africa Until the Second Millennium B.C.* Lech Krzyzaniak, Michal Kobusiewicz, and John Alexander (eds). Poznan: Poznan Archaeological Museum, 1993, 213–23.

Kutzbach, John E. "The changing pulse of the monsoon." *Monsoons.* Jay Fein, and Pamela Stephens (eds). New York: Wiley, 1987, 247–68.

Kutzbach, J. E. and F. A. Street-Perrott. "Milankovitch forcing of fluctuations in the level of tropical lakes from 18 to 0 kyr B.P." *Nature* 317 (1985): 130–4.

Lamb, Peter J., and Randy A. Peppler. "West Africa." *Teleconnections Linking Worldwide Climatic Anomalies.* Michael H. Glantz, Richard W. Katz, and Neville Nicholls (eds). Cambridge: Cambridge University Press 1991, 121–89.

Lambert, Nicole. "l'Apparition du cuivre dans les civilisations préhistoriques." *Le Sol, La Parole, et l'Ecrit.* C. H. Perrot, Yves Person, Y. Chrétien, et al. (eds). Paris: Société Française d'Histoire d'Outre-Mer, 1981, 213–26.

——."Nouvelle contribution á l'étude du Chalcolithique de Mauritanie." *Metallurgie Africaines: Nouvelles Contributions.* Nicole Echard (ed.). Mémoire de la Société des Africanistes no. 9. Paris: Société des Africanistes, 1983, 63–87.

Landscheidt, Theodor. "Long-range forecasts of solar cycles and climate change." *Climate. History, Periodicity and Predictability.* M. R. Rampino, J. E. Sanders, W. S. Newman, et al. (eds). New York: Van Nostrand Reinhold, 1987, 421–45.

Lange, Dierk, "The Almoravid expansion and the downfall of Ghana." *Der Islam* 73(2) (1966): 122–59.

——. "From Mande to Songhay: Towards a political and ethnic history of medieval Gao." *Journal of African History* 35 (1994): 275–301.

LaViolette, Adria. *An Archaeological Ethnography of Blacksmiths, Potters, and Masons in Jenne, Mali.* Ph.D. dissertation. St. Louis: Washington University, 1987.

——. "Women craft specialists in Jenne. The manipulation of Mande social categories." *Status and Identity in West Africa. Nyamakalaw of Mande.* David C. Conrad, and Barbara E. Frank (eds). Bloomington: Indiana University Press, 1995. 179–81.

Lebeuf, Annie M. D., and Viviana Pâques. "Archéologie Malienne. Collections Desplagnes. Catalogues du Musée de L'Homme. Série C. Afrique Noire. No 1." *Objets et Mondes* 10(3), Supplement (1970): 1–55.

Lepper, Bradley T. "Tracking Ohio's great Hopewell road." *Archaeology* 48(6) (1995): 52–6, 94.

Levtzion, Nehemia. *Ancient Ghana and Mali.* London: Methuen, 1973, 25–6.

Levtzion, Nehemia, and J. F. P. Hopkins. *Corpus of Early Arabic Sources for West African History.* Cambridge: Cambridge University Press, 1981.

Lézine, Anne-Marie. "Late Quaternary vegetation and climate of the Sahel." *Quaternary Research* 32 (1989): 317–34.

Lézine, Anne Marie and Joel Casanova. "Pollen and hydrological evidence for the interpretation of past climates in tropical West Africa during the Holocene." *Quaternary Science Review* 8 (1989): 45–55

Lézine, Anne Marie and H. Hooghiemstra. "Land-sea Comparisons during the last glacial-interglacial transition: pollen records from West Tropical Africa." *Palaeogeography, Palaeoclimatology, Palaeoecology* 79 (1990): 313–31.

MacDonald, Kevin C. "Analysis of the mammal, reptile and bird remains." *Excavations at Jenne-jeno, Hambarketolo and Kaniana.* Susan McIntosh. Berkeley: University of California Press, 1994, 291–318.

——. "An initial report on the fauna of Akumbu." *Archaeological Investigations of Iron Age Sites in the Méma, Mali.* Téréba Togola. Ph.D. dissertation. Rice University, 1992, 215–32.

——. "Preliminary faunal analysis for the 1986 Survey at Dia, Mali." *Archaeological Reconnaisance in the Region of Dia, Mali.* Helen W. Haskell, Roderick J. McIntosh, and Susan K. McIntosh (eds). Final Report to the National Geographic Society, 1988, 152–69.

MacDonald, Kevin Craig. *Socio-Economic Diversity and the Origins of Cultural Complexity along the Middle Niger (2000 B.C. to A.D. 300).* Cambridge: University of Cambridge, 1994.

——. "Tichitt-Walata and the Middle Niger: evidence for cultural contact in the second millenium BC." *Aspects of African Archaeology. Papers from the 10th Congress of the PanAfrican Association for Prehistory and Related Studies.* Gilbert Pwiti, and Robert Soper (eds). Harare: University of Zimbabwe Publications, 1996, 429–40.

MacDonald, Kevin Craig, Téréba Togola, Rachel Hutton MacDonald et al. "International news: Douentza, Mali." *PAST, The Newsletter of the Prehistoric Society* 17(4) (1944): 12–14.

MacDonald, Kevin Craig, and Win Van Neer. "Specialized fishing peoples in the later Holocene of the Méma region (Mali)." *Annales du Musée Royal de l'Afrique Centrale, Sciences Zoologiques, no. 274,* 1994, 243–51.

MacEachern, Scott. "Symbolic reservoirs' and inter-group relations: West African examples." *African Archaeological Review* 12 (1994): 205–24.

MacNeish, Richard S. *The Science of Archaeology?* North Scituate, MA: Duxbury Press, 1978.

Magasa, Amidu. *Papa-Commandant á Jeté un Grand Filet Devant Nous. Les Exploités des Rives du Niger 1900–1962.* Paris: François Maspero, 1978.

Mainguet, Monique M. "Les actions du vent au Sahara: un exemple de système éolien ouvert." *Sahara* 4 (1991): 7–12.

Maitre, J.-P. "Notes sur deux conceptions traditionelles du néolithique Saharien." *Libyca* 20 (1972): 125–36.

——. "Schémas d'evolution culturelle, I. Note sur la répartition régionale des décors céramiques néolithiques sahariens." *L'Anthropologie* 83 (1979): 584-601.

Maley, Jean. *Etudes Palynologiques dans le Bassin du Tchad et Paléclimatologie de l'Afrique Nord-tropicale de 30,000 ans á l'Epoque Actuelle.* Travaux et Documentation. Paris: ORSTOM, 1981, 129.

——. "Les variations climatiques dans le Bassin du Tchad durant le dernier millénaire: nouvelles données palynologiques et paléoclimatiques." *Acts of the 9th Congress of the International Union for Quaternary Research.* Christchurch: International Union for Quaternary Research, 1973, 175–81.

——. "Mise en évidence d'une péjoration climatique entre ca. 2500 et 2000 and B.P. en Afrique tropicale humide." *Bulletin de la Société de Géologie Française* 163 (3) (1992): 363–5.

Malzy, P. "Les Bozo du Niger et leurs modes de pêche." *Bulletin de l'Institut Fondamental d'Afrique Noire (B)* 8 (1946): 100–32.

Manzanilla, Linda. "Early urban socieities: Challenges and Perspectives." *Emergence and Change in Early Urban Socieities.* Linda Manzanilla (ed.). New York: Plenum Press, 1997, 3–39.

Markovitz, Irving Leonard. "Constitutions, Civil Society, and the Federalist Papers." Symposium paper to the Inter-African Group, Addis Ababa. *On the Making of the New Ethiopian Constituion.* May 1993.

——. "An uncivil and critical view of Civil Society in Africa, with some considerations of the formation of new social structures in Senegal." Unpublished conference paper. *Civil Society in Africa.* Jan. 1993. Truman Institute, Hebrew Univesity of Jerusalem.

Martin, Vincent, and Charles Becker. *Inventaire des Sites Protohistoriques du Sénégal.* Kaolak: CNRS, 1984.

Masonen, Pekka, and Humphrey J. Fisher. "Not quite Venus from the waves: The Almoravid conquest of Ghana in the modern historiography of Western Africa." *History in Africa* 23 (1996): 197–231.

Matthews, Victor H., and Don C. Benjamin. *The Social World of the Bible. 1250–587 B.C.E.* Peabody, MA: Hendrickson Publishers, 1993.

Mauny, Raymond. "Notes d'archéologie sur Tombouctou." *Bulletin de l'Institut Fondamental d'Afrique Noire (B)* 14 (1952): 899–918.

——. *Tableau Géographique de l'Ouest Africain au Moyen Age d'Après les Sources Ecrites, la Tradition, et l'Archéologie.* Mémoire de l'Institut Fondamental d'Afrique Noire 61. Dakar: Institut Fondamental d'Afrique Noire, 1961.

Mauny, Raymond, and F. Poussibet. "Nouveaux sites à harpons et faune subfossile de l'Azawad (Sahara malien)." *Notes Africaines* 93 (1962): 1–5.

Mauny, Raymond, and P. Thommassey. "Campagne de fouilles à Koumbi Saleh (Ghana?)." *Bulletin de l'Institut Fondamental d'Afrique Noire (B)* 13 (1951): 438–62.

Mazar, Amihai. *Archaeology of the Land of the Bible. 10,000 to 586 B.C.E.* New York: Doubleday, 1990.

McDougall, Ann. "The view from Awdaghust: War, trade and social change in the southwestern Sahara, from the eighth to the fifteenth century." *Journal of African history* 26 (1985): 1–31.

McIntosh, Roderick J. "African agricultural beginnings." *The Archaeology of Sub-Saharan African: An Encyclopaedia.* Joseph O. Vogel (ed.). New York: Garland Press, 1997, 409–18.

———. "Ancient terracottas before the Symplegades gateway." *African Arts* 22(2) (1989): 74–83, 103–4.

———, Archaeological research in francophone Africa. *Encyclopaedia of the History of Archaeology.* Timothy Murray (ed.). New York: Garland Press, (forthcoming).

———. "Clustered cities and alternative courses to authority in prehistory." *Festschrift for Kwang-chih Chang.* Robert E. Murowchick, Lothar Von Falkenhausen, Cheng-hwa Tsang, et al. (eds). Tapiei and Cambridge, MA: Academica Sinica and Peabody Museum of Archaeology and Ethnology, 1998, (forthcoming).

———. "Early urban clusters in China and Africa: The arbitration of social ambiguity." *Journal of Field Archaeology* 18 (1991): 199–212.

———. "Floodplain geomorphology and human occupation of the upper Inland Delta of the Niger." *Geographical Journal* 149 (1983): 182–201.

———. "From traiditional African art to the archaeology of form in the Middle Niger." *Dall'Archeologia al'Arte Tradizionale Africana.* G. Pezzoli (ed.). Milan: Centre Studi Archeologi Africana, 1992, 145–51.

———. "Just say shame: Excising the rot of cultural genocide." *Plundering Africa's Past.* Peter R. Schmidt and Roderick J. McIntosh (eds). Bloomington, IN: Indiana University Press, 1996, 45–62.

———. "The Mande weather machine and the social memory engine." *Global Change in History and Prehistory.* Roderick J. McIntosh, Joseph Tainter, and Susan Keech McIntosh (eds). New York: Columbia University Press, 1998, (forthcoming).

———. "Plight of Ancient Jenne." *Archaeology* 47(3) (1994): 32–3.

———. "The Pulse Model. Genesis and accommodation of specialization in the Middle Niger." *Journal of African History* 34(2) (1993): 181–212.

———. "Western representations of urbanism and invisible African towns." *Pathways to Complexity: An African Perspective.* Susan Keech McIntosh (ed.). Cambridge: Cambridge University Press, 1998, forthcoming.

McIntosh, Roderick J., and Susan Keech McIntosh. "Dilletantism and plunder. Dimensions of the illicit traffic in ancient Malian art." *UNESCO Museum* 149 (1986): 49–57.

———. "Early Iron Age economy in the Inland Niger Delta (Mali)." *From Hunters to Farmers. The Causes and Consequences of Food Production in Africa.* J. Desmond Clark, and Steven A. Brandt (eds). Berkeley: University of California Press, 1984, 158–72.

———. "From *siècles obscurs* to revolutionary centuries on the Middle Niger." *World Archaeology* 20(1) (1988): 141–65.

———. "The Inland Niger Delta before the Empire of Mali: evidence from Jenne-jeno." *Journal of African History* 21 (1981): 1–22.

———. "The Inland Niger Delta before the Empire of Mali." *Journal of African History* 22 (1981): 1–22.

———. "A la recherche du diagramme fondateur de la Djenné préhistorique." *Djenné. Une Ville Millénaire au Mali.* R. M. A. Bedaux, and J. D. Van der Waals (eds). Leiden: Rijksmuseum voor Volenkunde, 1994, 54–63.

———. "Les prospections d'après les photos aériennes: Régions de Djenné et Tombouctou." *Vallées du Niger.* Paris: Réunion des Musées Nationaux, 1993, 234–43.

———. "Terracotta statuettes from Mali." *African Arts* 11 (1979): 51–3, 91.

McIntosh, Roderick J., Susan Keech McIntosh, and Téréba Togola. "Archaeology of the 'People Without History'." *Archaeology* 42(1) (1989): 74–80, 107.

McIntosh, Roderick J., Paul Sinclair, Téréba Togola, et al. "Exploratory archaeology at Jenne and Jenne-jeno, Mali." *Sahara* 8 (1996): 19–28.

McIntosh, Roderick J., Joseph A. Tainter, and Susan Keech McIntosh. *Global Change in History And Prehistory.* New York: Columbia University Press, 1998.

McIntosh, Roderick J., Téréba Togola, and Susan Keech McIntosh. "The Good Collector and the premise of mutual respect among nations." *African Arts* 28(4) (1995): 60–9, 110–12.

McIntosh, Susan Keech. *Blacksmiths and the evolution of political complexity in Mande society: an hypothesis*. The School of American Research Advanced Seminar on Complex Society in Africa. Santa Fe, NM, Oct. 1984.

——. "Changing perceptions of West Africa's past: Archaeological research since 1988." *Journal of Archaeological Research* 2(2) (1994): 165–98.

——. *Excavations at Jenne-jeno, Hambarketolo and Kaniana in the Inland Niger Delta (Mali). The 1981 Season*. Susan Keech McIntosh (ed.). University of California Monographs in Anthropology 20. Berkeley: University of California Press, 1995.

——. *Pathways to Complexity: An African Perspective*. Susan Keech McIntosh (ed.). Cambridge: Cambridge University Press, 1998.

——. "A reconsideration of Wangara/Palolus, Island of Gold." *Journal of African History* 22(2) (1981): 145–58.

——. "A tale of two floodplains: Comparative perspectives on the emergence of complex societies and urbanism in the Middle Niger and Senegal Valleys." *Proceedings of the Second World Archaeological Congress. Intercongress, Mombasa*. Paul Sinclair (ed.). London: Routledge & Kegan Paul, 1998. (forthcoming)

——. "West African savanna Kingdoms; The Sahara, caravan trade, and Islam." *The Oxford Companion to Archaeology*. Brian M. Fagan (ed.). Oxford: Oxford University Press, 1996, 748–50.

McIntosh, Susan Keech, and Roderick J. McIntosh. "Archaeological reconnaissance in the region of Timbuktu, Mali." *National Geographic Research* 2(3) (1986): 302–19.

——. "Cities without citadels: Understanding urban origins along the Middle Niger." *Foods, Metals and Town in African History: African Adaptation in Subsistence and Technology*. C. Thurstan Shaw, Paul Sinclair, Basey Andah, et al. (eds). London: Unwin Hyman, 1993, 622–41.

——. "Current directions in West African prehistory." *Annual Review of Anthropology* 12 (1983): 215–58.

——. "Finding West Africa's oldest city." *National Geographic Magazine* 162 (1982): 396–418.

——. "From stone to metal: New perspectives on the later prehistory of West Africa." *Journal of World Prehistory* 2(1) (1988): 89–133.

——. "Initial perspectives on prehistoric subsistence in the Inland Niger Delta (Mali)." *World Archaeology* 11 (1979): 227–43.

——. "Finding West Africa's oldest city." *National Geographic Research* 2.3 (1986): 313–15.

——. "Pompei de l'Afrique noire." *GEO (France)* 47 (1983): 36–51.

------. *Prehistoric Investigations in the Region of Jenne, Mali.* Cambridge Monographs in African Archaeology no 2. Oxford: BAR, 1980.

------. "Recent archaeological research and dates from West Africa." *Journal of African History* 27 (1986): 413–42.

McIntosh, Susan Keech, Roderick J. McIntosh, and Hamady Bocoum. "The Middle Senegal Valley Project: Preliminary results from the 1990–91 field season." *Nyame Akuma* 38 (1992): 47–61.

McNaughton, Patrick. "From Mande Komo to Jukun Akuma, Approaching the difficult question of history." *African Arts* 25(2) (1992): 76–85, 99–100.

------. "Is there history in horizontal masks? A preliminary response to the dilemma of form." *African Arts* 24(2) (1991): 40–53, 88–90.

------. *The Mande Blacksmiths. Knowledge, Power and Art in West Africa.* Bloomington, IN: Indiana University Press, 1988.

------. "The semantic of *jugu.*" *Status and Identity in West Africa: Nyamakalaw of Mande.* David C. Conrad and Narbara E. Frank (eds). Bloomington: Indiana University Press, 1995, 46–57.

------. *Things change, but can they stay the same?*, 1993. Panel entitled "Dynamic Symbolic Reservoirs in Deep Time" at the Annual Meeting of the African Studies Association (Boston, Nov. 1993).

Meggers, Betty J. "Archaeological evidence for the impact of Mega-Niño events on Amazonia during the past two millennia." *Climatic Change* 28 (1994): 321–39.

------. "Biogeographical approaches to reconstructing the prehistory of Amazonia." *Biogeographica* 70 (1994): 97–110.

Miller, Duncan E., and Nikolaas J. Van Der Merwe. "Early Metal Working in Sub-Saharan Africa: A review of recent research." *Journal of African History* 35 (1994): 1–36.

Molina, Hélios, and Jean-Stéphane Vincent. "Trafic de biens culturels: Le Mali se rebiffe." *L'Aladin* October (1995): 20–8.

Monod, Théodore. *Majàbât-Al-Koubrâ. Contribution à l'Etude de l' "Empty quarter" ouest-saharien.* Mémoire de l'Institut Fondamental d'Afrique Noire 52. Dakar: Institut Fondamental d'Afrique Noire, 1958.

Monod, Théodore, and Raymond Mauny. "Découverte de nouveaux instruments en os dans l'Ouest africain." *Proceedings of the Third Panafrican Congress of Prehistory and Quaternary Studies.* Livingstone, 1955. London: Chatto & Windus, 1955, 242–7.

Monod, Théodore, and G. Palausi. "Sur la présence dans la région du lac Faguibine de venues volcaniques d'âge subactuel." *Comptes Rendus de l'Académie des Sciences de Paris* 246 (1958): 666–8.

Monteil, Charles. *Une Cité Soudanasie, Djenné. Métropole du Delta Central du Niger.* Paris: Société des Etudes Geeographiques Maritimes et Coloniales, 1932.

Monteillet, J. Hugues Faure, P. Pirazzoli, et al. "L'Invasion saline du Ferlo (Sénégal) à l'Holocène supérieur (1900 BP)." *Palaeoecology of Africa* 13 (1981): 205–15.

Mörner, Nils-Axel, Short-term paleoclimatic changes: observational data and a novel causation model. *Climate. History, Periodicity, and Predictability.* Michael R. Rampino, John E. Sanders, Walter S. Newman, et al. (eds). New York: Van Nostrand Reinhold, 1987, 256–69.

Munson, Patrick J. "Archaeological data on the origin of cultivation in the southwestern Sahara and their implication for West Africa." *Origins of African Plant Domestication.* Jack Harlan, Jan M. J. de Wet, and Ann B. Stemler (eds). The Hague: Mouton, 1976, 187–209.

——. "Debate about 'Economie et Société Néolithique du Dhar Tichitt (Mauritanie) (by Augustin Holl)'." *Sahara* 2 (1989): 106–8.

Muzzolini, Alfred. *L'Art Rupestre Préhistorique des Massifs Centraux Sahariens.* Cambridge Monographs in African Archaeology no 16. Oxford: BAR International Series, 1986.

——. "Les climats du Sahara et sur ses bordures, du Pléistocène final à l'aride actuel." *Empuries* 47 (1985): 8–27.

——. "A reapprasial of the 'Neolithic' of Tichitt (Mauritania)." *Journal of Arid Environments* 16 (1989): 101–5.

Nanda, S. *Cultural Anthropology.* Belmont, CA: Wadsworth, 1994.

N'Diaye, Bokar. *Groupes Ethniques au Mali.* Bamako: Editions Populaires, 1970.

Neumann, Katharina. "The contribution of anthracology to the study of the late Quaternary vegetation history of the Mediterranean region and Africa." *Bulletin de la Société Botanique de France* 139 (1992): 421–40.

Newman, James L. *The Peopling of Africa.* New Haven: Yale University Press, 1995.

Niane, Djibril Tamsir. "Mali and the second Mandingo expansion." *Africa from the 12th to the 16th Century.* Djibril Tamsir Niane (ed.). UNESCO General History of Africa. Berkeley: University of California Press, 1984. vol. IV: 117–71.

——. *Sundiata: An Epic of Old Mali*. London: Longman, 1965.

Nicholson, Sharon E. *A Climatic Chronology for Africa: Synthesis of Geological, Historical, and Meteorological Information and Data*. PhD dissertation. Madison, Wisconsin: University of Wisconsin, 1976.

——. "Climatic variations in the Sahel and other African regions during the past five centuries." *Journal of Arid Environments* 1 (1978): 3–24.

——. "The methodology of historical climate reconstruction and its application to Africa." *Journal of African History* 20 (1979): 31–49.

——. "Saharan climates in historic times." *The Sahara and the Nile*. Martin A. J. Williams and H. Faure (eds). Rotterdam: Balkema, 1980, 173–200.

Nicolaisen, J. *Ecology and Culture of the Pastoral Tuareg*. Copenhagen: The National Museum, 1963.

Nikiforuk, Andrew. *The Fourth Horseman. A Short History of Epidemics, Plagues, Famines, and other Scourges*. New York: M. Evans & Co., 1993.

Nooter, Mary H. "Secrecy. African art that conceals and reveals." *African Arts* 26 (1993): 54–69, 102.

Olivier de Sardan, Jean-Pierre. *Concepts et Conceptions Songhay-Zarma (Histoire, Culture, Société)*. Paris: Nubia, 1982.

——. *Les Sociétés Songhay-Zarma (Niger-Mali)*. Paris: Karthala, 1984.

Paris, François, Alain Person, and Jean-François Saliège. "Peuplements et environnements holocènes du bassin de l'Azawagh oriental (Niger)." *Vallées du Niger*. Paris: Réunions des Musées Nationaux, 1993, 378–92.

Park, Thomas K. "Early trends towards class stratification: chaos, common property, and flood recession agriculture." *American Anthropologist* 94(1) (1992): 90–117.

Peel, J. D. Y. *Herbert Spencer on Social Evolution. Selected Writings*. J. D. Y. Peel (ed.). Chicago: University of Chicago Press, 1972.

Perinbaum, Marie. "Notes on Dyula origins and nomenclature." *Bulletin de l'Institut Fondamental d'Afrique Noire (B)* 36 (1974): 676–89.

Person, Alain, Mamadi Dembélé, and Michel Raimbault. "Les mégalithes de la Zone lacustre." *Recherches Archéologiques au Mali*. Michel Raimbault and Kléna Sanogo. Paris: Karthala, 1991, 473–510.

Pestiaux, P., J.-C. Duplessy, and A. Berger. "Paleoclimatic variability at frequencies ranging from 10-4 cycle per year to 10-3 cycle per year – evidence for nonlinear behavior of the climate system." *Climate. History, Periodicity, and Predictability*. Michael R. Rampino. John E. Sanders, Walter S. Newman, et al. (eds). New York: Van Nostrand Reinhold, 1987, 285–99.

Petit-Maire, Nicole. "Homo climaticus: Vers une paléoanthropolgie écologique." *Bulletin de la Société Royale Belge d'Anthropologie et de Préhistoire* 97 (1986): 59–75.

——. "Interglacial environments in presently hyperarid Sahara: Palaeoclimatic implications." *Paleoclimatology and Paleometeorology: Modern and Past Patterns of Global Atmospheric Transport*. Margaret Leinen, and Michael Sarnthein (eds). NATO Advanced Science Institutes. Series C: Mathematical and Physical Sciences no. 282. Dordrecht: Kluwer Academic Publishers, 1987, 637–61.

——, (ed.). *Le Sahara Atlantique au Holocène: Peuplement et Ecologie*. Mémoires du CRAPE no. 28. Algers: CRAPE, 1979.

——. "Palaeoclimates in the Sahara of Mali." *Episodes* 9(1) (1986): 7–16.

——, (ed.). *Paléoenvironnements du Sahara. Lacs Holocènes à Taoudenni (Mali)*. Marseilles: Editions C.N.R.S., 1991.

——. "Recent Quaternary climatic change and Man in the Sahara." *Journal of African Earth Sciences* 12(1/2) (1991): 125–32.

Petit-Maire, Nicole, J.-C. Celles, Dominique Commelin, et al. "The Sahara in northern Mali: Man and his environment between 10,000 and 3,500 years BP." *African Archaeological Review* 1 (1983): 105–25.

Petit-Maire, Nicole, and Mireille Gayet. "Hydrologie du Niger (Mali) à l'Holocène ancien." *Comptes Rendus de l'Académie des Sciences de Paris, Série II* 298(1) (1984): 21–3.

Petit-Maire, Nicole, and Jean Riser, (eds). *Sahara ou Sahel? Quaternaire Récent du Bassin de Taoudenni (Mali)*. Marseilles: Centre National de la Recherche Scientifique, 1983.

Polet, Jean. *Tegdaoust IV. Fouille d'un Quartier de Tegdaoust. Urbanism, Architecture, Utilisation de l'Espace Construit*. Mémoire no. 54. Paris: Editions Recherche sur les Civilisations, 1985.

Portères, Roland. "African cereals: elusine, fonio, black fonio, teff, brachiaria, paspalum, pennisetum and African rice." *Origins of African Plant Domestication*. J. Harlan, J. M. de Wet, and A. B. Stemler (eds). The Hague: Mouton, 1976, 409–51.

——. "Vielles agricultures africains avant le XVIeme siècle. Berceaux d'agriculture et centres de variation." *L'Agronomie Tropicale* 5 (1950): 489–507.

Quensière, Jacques, Jean-Claude Olivry, Yveline Poncet, et al. "Environnement deltaïque." *La Pêche dans le Delta Central du Niger.* Jacques Quensière (ed.). Paris: ORSTOM. 1994, 29–80.

Raimbault, Michel. "Industrie lithique." *Sahara ou Sahel.* Nicole Petit-Maire, and Jean Riser (eds). Marseille: Centre National de la Recherche Scientifique, 1983, 317–41.

——. "La fouille sur la butte de Mouyssam II (KNT 2), Campagnes de 1985 et 1986." *Recherches Archéologiques au Mali.* Michel Raimbault and Kléna Sanogo. Paris: Karthala, 1991, 185–9.

——. "La fouille sur la butte de Toubel (GMB 1)." *Recherches Archéologiques au Mali.* Michel Raimbault and Kléna Sanogo. Paris: Karthala, 1991, 391–412.

——. "Le gisement néolithique de Kobadi (Sahel malien) et ses implications paléohydrologiques." *Changements Globaux en Afrique Durant le Quaternaire. Passé-Présent-Futur.* H. Faure, L. Faure, and E. S. Diop (eds). Paris: Editions de l'ORSTOM, 1986, 393–7.

——. "Les faciès néolithiques du Sahara Malien avant l'aridification." *Actes du 116e Congrès National des Sociétés Savantes.* Paris: Editions du Comité des Travaux Historiques et Scientifiques, 1992, 85–7.

——. "Les récentes missions du C.N.R.S. dans le Sahara Malien (1980–1985)." *Recherches Archéologiques au Mali.* Michel Raimbault and Kléna Sanogo (eds). Paris: Karthala, 1991, 121–40.

——. "Pour une approche du néolithique du Sahara Malien." *Travaux du Laboratoire d'Anthropologie et de Préhistoire des Pays de la Méditerranée Occidentale* (1990): 67–81.

——. "Prospection dans les Daounas et environs." *Recherches Archéologiques au Mali.* Michel Raimbault and Kléna Sanogo. Paris: Karthala, 1991, 203–14.

——. *Sahara Malien: Environnement, Populations et Industries Préhistoriques.* Diss. Thèse d'Etat. Aix-en-Provence: Université de Provence, 1994.

Raimbault, Michel, and Olivier Dutour. "Les nouvelles données du site néolithique de Kobadi dans le Sahel malien. La mission 1989." *Travaux du Laboratoire d'Anthroplogoie et de Préhistoire des Pays de la Méditerranée Occidentale* (1989): 175–83.

Raimbault, Michel, C. Guérin, and M. Faure. "Les vertébrés du gisement néolithique de Kobadi (Mali)." *Archaeozoologia* 12 (1987): 219–38.

Raimbault, Michel, and Kléna Sanogo. "Les données de la fouille sur la butte de Mouyssam II (KNT 2), Campagnes de 1985 et 1986." *Recherches Archéologiques au Mali.* Michel Raimbault and Kléna Sanogo. Paris: Karthala, 1991, 301–71.

——, (eds). *Recherches Archéologiques au Mali.* Paris: Karthala, 1991.

Renfrew, Colin. *Approaches to Social Archaeology.* Cambridge, MA: Harvard University Press, 1984.

——. "Introduction: Peer polity interaction and socio-political Change." *Peer Polity and Socio-Political Change.* Colin Renfrew, and John F. Cherry (eds). Cambridge: Cambridge University Press, 1986, 1–18.

Richardson, Robert D. Jr. *Emerson. The Mind on Fire.* Berkeley: University of California Press, 1995.

Riser, Jean, Anne-Marie Aucour, and Fousseyni Toure. "Niveaux lacustres et néotectoniques au lac Faguibine (Mali)." *Comptes Rendus de l'Académie des Sciences de Paris* Série II(10) (1986): 941–3.

Riser, Jean and Nicole Petit-Maire. "Paléohydrologie du Bassin du Araouane à l'Holocène." *Revue de Géologie Dynamique et de Géographie Physique* 27(3–4) (1986): 205–12.

Robert, Denise and Serge Robert. "Douze années de recherches archéologiques en République Islamique de Mauritanie." *Annales de la Faculté des Lettres (Dakar)* 2 (1972): 195–233.

Roberts, Richard. *Warriors, Merchants, and Slaves. The State and the Economy in the Middle Niger Valley, 1700–1914.* Stanford: Stanford University Press, 1987.

Robinson, David. "The imperial state in Mali and Songhay." *School of American Research Advanced Seminar on Complex Society in Africa.* Santa Fe, New Mexico, Oct. 1984.

Rognon, Pierre. "Essai d'interpretation des variations climatiques au Sahara depuis 40.000 ans." *Revue de Géographie Physique et de Géologie Dynamique* 18 (1976): 251–82.

——. "L'Evolution des Vallées du Niger depuis 20.000 ans." *Vallées du Niger.* Paris: Réunion des Musées Nationaux, 1993, 40–62.

Rolandq, C., and Michel Raimbault. "Vegetation associated with the protohistorical mound of Mouyssam II (KNT 2) in the Malian Sahel." *Palaeoecology of Africa* 23 (1992): 57–66.

Rothchild, Donald, and Naomi Chazan. *The Precarious Balance. State and Society in Africa.* Boulder, CO: Westview Press, 1988.

Rouch, Jean, (ed.). *Contribution à l'Histoire des Songhay*. Mémoire de l'Institut Fondamental d'Afrique Noire no. 29. Dakar: Institut Fondamental d'Afrique Noire, 1953.

———. *Les Songhay*. Paris: Presse Universitaires, 1954.

Saad, E. *Social History of Timbuktu*. Cambridge: Cambridge University Press, 1983.

Sabloff, Jeremy A. *The New Archaeology and the Ancient Maya*. New York: Scientific American, 1990.

Sanankoua, Bintou. "Aperçu historique de Djenné." *Djenné, Il Y A Cent Ans*. Bernard Gardi, Pierre Maas, and Geert Mommersteeg (eds). Amsterdam: Institut Royal des Tropiques, 1995, 9–12.

Sanderson, Stephen K. *Social Evolutionism. A Critical History*. Oxford: Blackwell, 1992.

Savage, E. "Berber and blacks: Ibadi slave traffic in eighth-century North Africa." *Journal of African History* 33 (1992): 351–68.

Schama, Simon. *Landscape and Memory*. New York: Alfred A. Knopf, 1995.

Schmidt, Peter R., and Roderick J. McIntosh, (eds). *Plundering Africa's Past*. Bloomington, IN: Indiana University Press, 1996.

Schmit, Pascal. *Les Sites de Buttes de la Région de Diré (Mali)*. D E A. Thesis. Paris: Université de Paris 1, 1986.

Schove, D. J. "Sunspot cycles and weather history." *Climate. History, Periodicity, and Predictability*. Michael R. Rampino, John E. Sanders, Walter S. Newman, et al. (eds). New York: Van Nostrand Reinhold, 1987, 355–77.

Schulz, E. "The Taoudenni-Agorgott pollen record and the Holocene vegetation history of the Central Sahara." *Paléoenvironnements du Sahara. Lacs Holocènes à Taoudenni (Mali)*. Nicole Petit-Maire (ed.). Paris: Editions du Centre National de la Recherche Scientifique, 1971, 143–58.

Shaw, C. Thurstan. *Unearthing Igbo Ukwu*. Oxford: Oxford University Press, 1977.

Sidibé, Samuel. "Reconnaissances archéologiques aux environs de Diré." *Recherches Archéologiques au Mali*. Michel Raimbault, and Kléna Sanogo (eds). Paris: Karthala, 1991, 190–202.

Smith, Andrew B. "Biogeographical considerations of colonization of the lower Tilemsi Valley in the second millennium B.C." *Journal of Arid Environments* 2 (1979): 355–61.

———. "Cattle domestication in North Africa." *African Archaeological Review* 4 (1986): 197–203.

———. "The neolithic tradition in the Sahara." *The Sahara and The*

Nile. Martin A. J. Williams and Hugues Faure (eds). Rotterdam: A. A. Balkema, 1980, 451–66.

——. "New approaches to Saharan rock art of the Bovidian Period." *Environmental Change and Human Culture in the Nile Basin and Northern Africa until the Second Millennium B.C.* Lech Krzyzaniak, Michal Kobusiewicz, and John Alexander (eds). Poznan: Poznan Archaeological Museum, 1993, 77–89.

——. "Origins of the Neolithic in the Sahara." *From Hunters to Farmers.* John Desmond Clark and Steven A. Brandt (eds). Berkeley: University of California, 1984, 84–92.

——. *Pastoralism in Africa: Origins, Development and Ecology.* Athens, OH: Ohio University Press, 1992.

Smith, Susan E. "The environmental adaptation of nomads in the West African Sahel: a key to understanding prehistoric pastoralists." *The Sahara and the Nile.* Martin A. J. Williams and Hughes Faure (eds). Rotterdam: Balkema, 1980, 467–87.

Songoré, Ibrahim. "Présentation géographique." *Recherches Archéologiques au Mali.* Michel Raimbault, and Kléna Sanogo (eds). Paris: Karthala, 1991, 217–27.

Spencer, Herbert. "Progress: Its Law and Cause (essay, 1857)." *Herbert Spencer on Social Evolution. Selected Writings.* J. D. Y. Peel (ed.). Chicago: University of Chicago Press, 1972, 38–52.

Spengler, Oswald. *The Decline of the West.* New York: A. A. Knopf, 1928.

Sterner, Judy. "Sacred pots and 'symnbolic reservoirs' in the Mandara Highlands of Northern Cameroon." *An African Commitment: Papers in Honour of Peter Lewis Shinnie.* Judy Sterner, and Nicolas David (eds). Calgary: University of Calgary Press, 1992, 171–9.

Street, F. Alayne, and Anthony T. Grove. "Environmental and climatic implications of late Quaternary lake-level fluctuations in Africa." *Nature* 261 (1976): 387–8.

——. "Global maps of lake-level fluctuations since 30,000 yr B.P." *Quaternary Research* 12 (1979): 83–118.

Street-Perrott, F. Alayne, and R. A. Perrott. "Holocene vegetation, lake levels, and climate of Africa." *Global Climates Since the Last Glacial Maximum.* H. E. Wright Jr, J. E. Kutzbach, T. Webb III, et al. (eds). Minneapolis, MN: University of Minnesota Press, 1993, 318–56.

Sundström, Lars. *Ecology and Symbiosis: Niger Water Folk.* Studia Ethnographica Upsaliensia 35. Uppsala: Institutonen för Allmän och Jämförande Ethnografi vid Uppsala Universitet, 1972.

Sutton, John E. G. "The aquatic civilisation of middle Africa." *Journal of African History* 15 (1974): 527–46.

Szumouwski, Georges. "Fouilles au nord du Macina et dans la région de Ségou." *Bulletin de l'Institut Fondamental d'Afrique Noire (B)* 19 (1957): 224–58.

Tainter, Joseph A. *The Collapse of Complex Soceieties.* Cambridge: Cambridge University Press, 1988.

Tainter, Joseph A. and Bonnie Bagley Tainter. *Evolving Complexity and Environmental Risk in the Prehistoric Southwest.* Joseph A. Tainter, and Bonnie Bagley Tainter (eds). Reading, MA: Addison-Wesley, 1996.

Talbot, Michael. "Environmental responses to climate change in the West African Sahel over the past 20,000 years." *The Sahara and The Nile.* Martin A. J. Williams, and Hugues Faure (eds). Rotterdam: Balkema, 1980, 37–62.

Talbot, Michael, and G. Delibrias. "A new late Pleistocene-Holocene water-level curve for Lake Bosumtwi, Ghana." *Earth and Planetary Science Letters* 47 (1980): 336–44.

Tamari, Tal. "The development of caste systems in West Africa." *Journal of African History* 32(2) (1991): 221–50.

Tauxier, Louis. *Moeurs et Histoire des Peuls.* Paris: Payot, 1937.

Thilmans, G., Cyr Descamps, and B. Khayat. *Protohistoire du Sénégal I: Les Sites Mégalithiques.* Mémoire de l'Institut Fondamental d'Afrique Noire no. 91(1). Dakar: IFAN, 1980.

Time-Life Books. *Africa's Glorious Legacy.* Lost Civilizations. Alexandria, VA: Time-Life, 1994.

Togola, Téréba. *Archaeological Investigations of Iron Age Sites in the Méma, Mali.* Diss. Houston, TX: Rice University, 1993.

——. "Iron age occupation in the Méma region, Mali." *The African Archaeological Review* 13(2) (1996): 91–110.

——. "Traces et techniques anciennes d'exploitation aurifère dans la zone de Sadiola, Bambouk." *Mande Studies Association, 3rd International Meeting.* Mar. 1995. Leiden, the Netherlands.

Togola, Téréba, and Michel Raimbault. "Les missions d'inventaire dans le Méma, Karéri et Farimaké (1984–1985)." *Recherches Archéologiques au Mali. Les Sites Protohisoriques de la Zone Lacustre.* Michel Raimbault, and Kléna Sanogo (eds). Paris: Karthala, 1991, 81–98.

Tricart, Jean. *Reconnaissance Géomorphologique de la Vallée Moyenne du Niger.* Mémoires de l'Institut Fondamental d'Afrique Noire no. 72. Dakar: Institut Fondamental d'Afrique Noire, 1965.

Trigger, Bruce G. *A History of Archaeological Thought*. Cambridge: Cambridge University Press, 1989.

Trimingham, J. Spencer. *A History of Islam in West Africa*. Oxford: oxford University Press, 1962.

Tylecote, R. F. "Furnances, crucibles, and slags." *The Coming of Age of Iron*. J. A. Wertime and J. D. Muhly (eds). New Haven: Yale University Press, 1980, 183–228.

Yves Urvoy. *Les Bassins du Niger*. Mémoire de l'Institut Fondamental d'Afrique Noire no. 4. Dakar: IFAN, 1942.

van der Merwe, Nikolaas J. "The advent of iron in Africa." *The Coming of Age of Iron*. Theodore A. Wertime and James D. Muhly (eds). New Haven: Yale University Press, 1980, 463–506.

Van Neer, Wim. "Analysis of the fish remains." *Excavations at Jenne-jeno, Hambarketolo and Kaniana*. Susan Keech McIntosh (ed.). Berkeley: University of California Press, 1995, 319–47.

——. "Holocene fish remains from the Sahara." *Sahara* 2 (1989): 61–8.

van Rangelrooy, Arie, and Pierre Maas. "Le diagramme rituel." *Djenné. Chef-D'Oeuvre Architectural*. Pierre Maas, and Geert Mommersteeg (eds). Eindhoven: Université de Technologie, 1992, 173–7.

——. "L'Historique et la morphologie de l'ancienne ville." *Djenné. Chef-D'Oeuvre Architectural*. Pierre Maas, and Geert Mommersteeg (eds). Eindhoven: Université de Technologie, 1992, 159–71.

Vansina, Jan. "Deep-down time: Political tradition in Central Africa." *History in Africa* 16 (1989): 341–62.

——. *Paths in the Rainforests. Towards a History of Political Tradition in Equatorial Africa*. Madison: University of Wisconsin Press, 1990.

——. "Western Bantu expansion." *Journal of African History* 25 (1984): 129–45.

Vernet, Robert. *Climats Anciens du Nord de l'Afrique*. Paris: L'Harmattan, 1995.

——. *La Mauritanie, des Origins au Début de l'Histoire*. Nouakchott: Centre Culturel Française, 1986.

——. "Le Néolithique récent dans le sud-ouest du Sahara." *Environmental Change and Human Culture in the Nile Basin and Northern Africa Until the Second Millennium B.C.* Lech Krzyzaniak, Michal Kobusiewicz, and John Alexander (eds). Poznan: Poznan Archaeological Museum, 1993, 91–101.

——, "Néolithique du Sahel: Problèmes spécifiques, éléments de synthèse et exemple du sud-ouest nigérien." *l'Anthropologie* 100(2/3) (1996): 307–55.

———. "Préhistoire des bassins affluents de la rive gauche du fleuve Niger." *Vallées du Niger*. Paris: Réunion des Musées Nationaux, 1993, 63–74.

———. *Préhistoire de la Mauritanie. Etat de la Question*. Paris: CNRS, 1993.

Vincent, Yvon. "Pasteurs, paysans et pêcheurs du Guimbala (Partie Centrale de l'Erg du Bara)." *Nomades et Paysans d'Afrique Noire*. Pierre Galloy, Yvon Vincent, and Maurice Forget (eds). Mémoire des Annales de l'Est no. 23. Nancy: Université de Nancy, 1963, 37–157.

Voute, C. "Geological and morphological evolution of the Niger and Benue Valleys." *Annales du Musée Royale de l'Afrique Centrale* 40 (1962): 189–207.

Webb, James L. A. *Desert Frontier. Ecological and Economic Change along the Western Sahel, 1600–1850*. Madison: University of Wisconsin Press, 1995.

Wheatley, Paul. *The Pivot of the Four Quarters*. Chicago: Aldine, 1970.

Wicklein, John. "Spirit paths of the Anasazi." *Archaeology* 47(1) (1994): 36–41.

Wills, Christopher. *Plagues. Their Origin, History and Future*. New York: HarperCollins, 1996.

Wilson, Robert R. *Genealogy and History in the Biblical World*. New Haven: Yale University Press, 1977.

Winters, Clyde A. "The migration routes of the proto-Mande." *Mankind Quarterly* 27 (1986): 77–96.

Wood, Ellen Meiksin. "The uses and abuses of 'Civil Society'." *The Socialist Register, 1990*. Ralph Miliband (ed.). New York: Monthly Review Press, 1991.

Wright, H. E., J. E. Kutzbach, T. Webb III, et al. (eds). *Global Climates Since the Last Glacial Maximum*. Minneapolis, MN: University of Minnesota Press, 1993.

Wright, Henry T. *The Administration of Rural Production in an Early Mesopotamian Town*. University of Michigan, Museum of Anthropology, Anthrolopology Papers no. 38. Ann Arbor: Museum of Anthropology, 1969.

Index

African rice (*Oryza glaberrima*), 3, 99, 151, 154, 165
agriculture
  on Erg of Bara, 115–19
  origins of, 43, 47–8, 83, 150–3, 164–5
  see also fonio; millet; rice growing; sorghum
Akumbu, 62, 154, 168
  ceramics, 63–4, 160, 167
  depopulation, 246–7, 265, 267
  fauna and fish, 164, 165, 246–7
  iron smelting, 176
Alestes leuciscus (fish), 98
Almoravids, 258–9, 260, 274
Amazon, 243
American Southwest, 241, 242
antelope, 162
Aqualithic culture, 50, 58
Arab stimulation model, 251–3, 279
Archinard, Col. Louis, 294, 301–2
Arma, 126, 266, 296, 299
art
  and antiquities, pillaging of, 22, 31, 212–13, 221–2, 280
  ritual, 210–13
  rock, 114, 128
articulated specialization approach, 55–7, 61, 63
Askiya Mohammed, 266, 285, 300
autochthonous communities, 15–16, 103
  of Upper Delta, 89–105
Azawad, 34–48, 86, 123, 151, 198
  lacustrine, 42, 75, 122

palaeochannels, 43–5
seasonal *playas* and marshes, 42–3
semi-arid steppe, 45–6
views of stone-using communities, 48–57

al-Bakri, 224, 227, 232, 257, 276–7, 291
Bambara, 299, 300, 301
  agriculture, 92, 115–19, 246
  relations with Fulani, 110, 112, 116, 117, 118, 266, 295
Bambouk, 31, 32–3, 218, 256, 269, 270–1
Bani River, 90–1, 94
Bara-Issa channel, 89, 116, 224
Bassikounou, 161
Bedaux, Rogier, 165
Bélime, Emile, 3, 4, 302–3
Bella (servile population), 128–9
Bénédougou, 89, 214
Berbers, 127–8, 148, 217–18, 254, 272–3, 274, 275
Besiedlungsgeschichte der Ost-Sahara (History of Population Dynamics in Eastern Sahara) project, 68–9
Bida (snake), 144, 255, 259–60
Black Death, 248
blacksmiths *see* smiths
boatmen, 97–8
boli (power bundles), 263, 283, 293
borcin (social class), 126
Bosumtwi, Lake, 68–9, 73, 75, 77, 242
Bourgou-Dialloubé, 106, 111

bourgou vegetation, 106, 107, 108, 110–12, 129, 165
Bourgou-Yallabé, 106, 111
Bovill, E. W., 231
Bozo fisherfolk, 96–9, 101, 102, 103, 104, 106, 254–5, 301
Bras de Nampala, 58, 64, 168
brass, 216
bronze, 216
Brooks, George E., 141–2
Buré, 31, 32–3, 218, 260, 261, 269, 270–1, 276–7
burials
    diversity at Jenne-jeno, 210–11
    monumental mounds, 219–33, 258
burti (paths), 110, 111

Caillié, René, 214–15
canal de Sonni Ali Ber, 122
ceramics
    in Azawad, 48, 52
    'chinaware', 63–4, 160
    at Dia, 160, 168–71, 201, 278
    'fugitive-paint' wares, 200–1
    from Hodh, 53–4
    at Jenne-jeno, 160–1, 200–1, 202, 277–8
    in Méma, 63–4, 160, 161, 167, 278
    trade in, 215
    wavy-line, 50, 51, 58
Chad, Lake, 75, 76, 77
Chang, K. C., 17, 233
Chevalier, A., 151
chiefs of cattle, 110
China, Bronze Age, 17, 233
cities *see* urbanism *and individual names*
city walls, 201, 220
Civil Society, 6–10, 229, 294–303, 304
Clérisse, Henri, 221–3, 226
climate
    and emergence of Imperial Tradition, 240, 241–4, 297
    mode-shift phases, 70–1, 140–1
    palaeoclimate and geomorphological events, 64, 66–80, 120–3, 140–1, 240, 241–4, 297
    in Upper Delta, 93–4
clustering, 168–76, 192, 205, 207–10
colonial period, 1–5, 294, 301–2
Conrad, David, 268

copper and copper alloys, 147, 215–16, 220–1, 226
corporate groups, 9–10, 142, 180, 208–9, 284, 303, 304
    see also nyamakalaw
Coulibali, Biton, 117

dali-ma-sigi (quest), 27, 28, 135, 234, 291, 304
Débo, Lake, 74, 89, 106, 115, 116
décrue (flood recession), 98, 118–19
deep basins, penetration of, 140–81
Delafosse, Maurice, 113, 116, 155, 268, 269–70
de Mézières, A. Bonnel, 232
demographic crisis, 202, 244–50, 252, 267, 279
Desplagnes, Lt. Louis, 224–7
Dia, 106, 125, 220
    ceramics, 160, 168–71, 201, 278
    decline, 171, 201–2, 218, 267, 278–9
    early settlements, 145, 154, 168–71, 177
    fauna and fish, 163–4
    founding, 161
    and gold trade, 274, 278–9, 280
    and Imperial Tradition, 254, 255, 267, 278
Diabé Cissé, 254, 259–60
Dina empire, 112, 282, 285, 295, 300–1
Dinga, 254–5
Djim-Djim, 223–4, 226
Dogon, 96, 101–2, 103, 213
domestication of plants and animals, 43, 47–8, 61, 83, 150–4, 162–3, 164–5
Douentza, 154, 223
doungou rains, 111
dry basins, 34–80
    palaeoclimate, 66–80
    views of stone-using communities, 48–57
    see also Azawad; Méma
dune systems, formation of, 71, 75, 91, 115, 122, 123
Durant, Will, 88, 104
dyi tuu (ritual chiefs), 98–9
Dyula, 217, 275, 280, 296

El-Ahmar palaeochannel, 43–4, 45, 129, 196, 198, 199, 234

Index

El Hadj Umar, 282, 301
El-Oualadji, 223, 224–7, 232, 258, 285, 291–2
Emerson, R. W., 26
epidemics, 247–9
eponymous and evolutionary approach, 49–51
Erg of Bara, 88, 89, 115–19, 122, 127, 223

faaro (water spirits), 99, 177, 263, 265, 288, 289–90
facies approach, 52–3
Faguibine, Lake, 121, 122, 123
Fairbridge, Rhodes, 67
Fala de Molodo, 62, 64, 65, 74, 258
farmer–pastoralist conflict, 109, 111–12, 116, 118, 129
farming *see* agriculture
fishing, 82–3, 96–9, 101, 103, 126–7, 158, 163–4, 165
floods, annual
    in Erg of Bara, 119
    in Upper Delta, 89, 94–5, 99, 100, 171
fonio, 99, 102, 151, 165
fossiles directeurs, 52
French colonial period, 1–5, 294, 301–2
Fulani, 106–14, 116, 117–18, 129, 266, 295, 300, 301
funerary monuments, 219–33, 258
Furon, Raymond, 64
Fussell, Paul, 26

Gabriel, B., 153
Gallais, Jean, 95–6, 99, 105, 113
Gallay, Allain, 39–40, 52
Gao, 125, 126, 198, 258, 264, 276
Garrard, Timothy F., 216
Ghana (Wagadou) empire, 31, 224, 250, 253, 254–61, 262
Ghiyara, 274
glass beads, 160, 215, 216
gold trade/production, 30–3, 155, 194, 216–19, 260, 261, 267–81
Goubo, 223, 226
Gourma-Rharous, 120, 196–7, 198–9
Gow, 125, 126
grandes pêches, 98–9
Great Empires, 250–67
grindstones, 47, 159, 160
griots (story tellers), 26, 30, 181, 283

gué (passageways), 110
guerriers libyens (Libyan warriors), 128

Haaland, R., 214
Hale, Thomas, 22
Hambarketolo, 158, 176, 200, 245
Harratine (former slaves), 128–9
Hassan, Fekri, 69
Herbert, Eugenia, 219
herding 61, 84, 106–14, 129, 153–4, 162–3
Herzfild, Michael, 13
heterarchy, 5–10, 166, 173, 229, 231, 240, 298, 304
hierarchy, 6–10, 243, 304
historical imagination, 22–30, 304
    4100 BP, 81–7
    300 BC, 131–9
    AD 400, 182–9
    AD 1000, 234–9
    AD 1472, 287–93
Hodh, 53–5, 161, 244
Holl, Augustin, 54, 55
Holocene wet periods (pluvials), 41, 44–5, 74, 75, 122
horizontal authority, 87
hunters, 83–4, 117, 132–3
    and Imperial Tradition, 262, 283, 292
    and *nyama*, 27, 28, 86–7, 135–8, 178, 187

Ibadites, 217–18, 273–4, 275
Ibn Battuta, 247, 272
Ibn Hawkal, 252, 274
al-Idrisi, 32, 218–19, 257, 259, 261, 270, 271
Imperial Tradition, 97–8, 220, 233, 240–86, 290–3, 300, 304–5
infectious diseases, 247–9
Institut des Sciences Humaines (Mali), 21
iron smelting technology
    and early settlements, 62, 159–60, 161, 164, 166–76, 214
    at Jenne-Jeno, 159–60, 176, 177, 179, 188
    transition to, 63–4, 145–50
    see also smiths
Islam, 100, 212, 273, 280–1
    and Imperial Tradition, 260, 262, 282, 293, 300, 301

Island of Gold (Wangara), 30–3, 218–19, 267–81
Issa-Ber channel, 89, 116, 224

Jacobberger Jellison, Patricia, 198
Jacobsen, Thorkild, 220
Jenne, 91, 97, 117
  corporate groups, 208–9
  founding, 143, 155–7, 172–3, 202, 245
  French occupation, 294, 301–2
  and gold trade, 275–6, 279
  and Imperial Tradition, 254–5, 264–5, 266, 267, 287–90, 301
  and Sonni Ali Ber, 265, 287–90
Jenne-jeno, 9–10, 23, 31, 154, 191, 220, 254
  burial diversity, 210–11
  ceramics, 160–1, 200–1, 202, 277–8
  decline, 202, 245–6, 248–9, 267, 279
  early economy, 161–6
  early settlements, 171–3
  exchange and trade, 160, 213–15, 216, 268, 270, 276
  founding, 155–61
  mature, 199–203
  precocious urbanism, 203–13
  ritual art, 210–13
  smiths, 159–60, 176, 177, 179, 182–6, 188
Jenneké, 294, 296

Karkarichinkat South, 152
Kélinga, 97
Kemp, Barry, 17
Kharijites, 273–4
Kobadi, 58–61, 62, 63, 160
Koï Gourrey, 223, 226–7
Kolima, 61, 62, 63, 247, 265
Komo (power association), 179, 181, 186–7, 293
Korientzé, Lake, 74, 89, 115
Kostof, Spiro, 18
Kouga, 223–4, 226
Koukya, 125
Koumbi Saleh, 257, 258, 259
Krina, battle of (*c.*AD 1240), 247, 263
kuma koro (ancient speech), 24, 138, 283, 305

lacustrine ecology, 42, 75, 122
Lake Bosumtwi, 68–9, 73, 75, 77, 242

Lake Chad, 75, 76, 77
Lake Débo, 74, 89, 106, 115, 116
Lake Faguibine, 121, 122, 123
Lake Korientzé, 74, 89, 115
Lake Paléo-Débo, 74, 89, 106
Lakes Region, 120–30, 202, 210, 295–6
  and Imperial Tradition, 256, 258, 278, 279
  iron production, 149, 177–8
  megaliths, 221–7, 230
  mounds, 190–9
landform organization principles, 42–6
late stone age communities, 140–5, 175–6
  in Azawad, 38–57
  historical imagination, 81–7
  in Lakes Region, 190–1
  in Méma, 62–6, 168
  transition to iron and origin of agriculture 63–4, 145–54
  views of, 48–57
layered transformations, 10–22, 36, 46, 281, 297
Libyco-Berber, 127–8
lithic assemblages, 48, 49, 50–1, 52
live basins
  penetration of Upper Delta and Macina, 140–81
  peoples of, 88–130
  see also Erg of Bara; Lakes Region; Macina; Niger Bend; Upper Delta

ma'at in Egypt, 17–18
MacDonald, Kevin, 15–16, 61, 62, 63, 144, 161, 167, 168
Macina, 74
  ceramics, 53–4
  Fulani and pastoral cycle, 106–14
  penetration, 76, 140–81
  see also Dia
McIntosh, Susan Keech, 32, 166, 268, 270, 271, 279
McNaughton, Patrick, 28, 179–80, 187, 213
Malfante, Antonio, 155, 276
Mali empire, 100, 250–1, 258, 260, 261–5, 282
  capital, 268
  decline, 254, 264–6
  and gold trade, 31, 261, 276
  and Sunjata, 247, 261–3

Malinké, 15, 250, 261, 262
Mande: defined, 305
Mande Onomasticon, 27, 29
mansaya, 283–4, 305
al-Mansur, Mawlay Ahmad, 275
marigots (creeks), 42, 45, 94, 98, 122, 123, 170
Marka *dié*, 100
Marka *pi*, 100
Marka rice growers, 89, 96, 99–100, 110
masks, horizontal, 180, 187
Mauny, Raymond, 31–2, 222, 226, 276–7
Medieval Maximum, 241–2
megaliths, 219–33
Méma, 2, 54, 57–66, 143, 176, 177–8
  ceramics, 63–4, 160, 161, 167, 278
  clustering, 209–10
  demographic crisis, 202, 246–7, 267, 279
  and Fulani, 110, 114
  Iron Age sites, 62, 146, 161, 164, 166, 167–8
  kingdom of, 247, 255, 256, 257–8, 260–1, 263, 264, 265
  palaeoclimate, 74, 76–7, 246–7
  see also Akumbu
Men (and Women) of Crises, 24, 26, 30, 86
metallurgy *see* copper; iron smelting technology; smiths
Middle Senegal, 66–7, 161
millet, 102, 111, 118–19, 124, 151, 152, 165, 246
Missions Paléoenvironnements du Sahara Occidental et Central, 40–2
mode-shift phases in climate, 70–1, 140–1
monuments and emerging polities, 219–33
Mopti, 93, 94
Moroccans, 266, 275, 296, 298–9
Moussa Traoré regime, 1, 302
Mouyssam II, 191
Munson, Patrick, 54, 55

Ndondi Tossokel, 103
neo-evolutionism, 11–12, 228–9
N'Fatigi, 263
Niakené Maoudo, 64, 168
Niane, D. T., 244–5, 268

Niani, 268
Nicholson, S. E., 242
Niger River, 90–2, 115–16
  floods, 89, 94–5, 99, 100, 119, 171, 198
  reorientation, 122–3
Niger Bend, 88, 202, 277, 278, 295–6
  mounds, 190–9
  palaeoclimate and geomorphological events, 120–4
  Songhai and Tuareg, 124–30
  see also Timbuktu
Nono, 100, 101–2, 104, 106, 143, 160, 254–5
Nono-Marka, 100
nyama
  defined, 305
  and hunters, 27–8, 87, 135–8, 178, 187
  and Imperial Tradition, 262–3, 283–4, 291, 292
  and smiths, 179, 180, 187, 188, 262–3, 292
nyamakalaw (occupational castes), 27
  emergence of, 142, 177, 178, 228
  and Imperial Tradition, 262, 284, 292–3
Nyansanare, 92

Office du Niger irrigation scheme, 1–5, 65, 302–3
Ogolian dunes, 71, 75, 115, 122, 157
onomasticon, 27, 29, 305
origin myths/hypotheses, 101–5, 113–14, 125, 127–8, 254
over-kingdoms, 232, 250, 305

palaeochannels, 76, 123, 144–5, 161
  in Azawad, 43–5
  El-Ahmar, 43–4, 45, 129, 196, 198, 199, 234
  in Méma, 58, 64
palaeoclimate *see* climate
Paléo-Débo, Lake, 74, 89, 106
Park, Thomas K., 66–7
pastoralism, 61, 84, 106–14, 129, 153–4, 162–3
peer polity interaction, 227–33
Péhé, 62, 210, 258
perch (*Lates niloticus*), 44–5, 75, 99, 163
Petit-Maire, Nicole, 40, 73
pirogues (canoes), 98

plague, 248–9
plant domestication, 43, 47–8, 83, 150–3, 164–5
playas (shallow lakes) and marshes, seasonal, 42–3
polities, emerging, 219–33
Pondori, 71, 91, 97, 100, 246
Pondo-Sorogo, 97
population crisis, 202, 244–50, 252, 267, 279
Portères, R., 151
power associations, 178, 179, 181, 186–7, 229, 284
power localities, mapping of, 27, 28–9, 136–8, 188
primary variation view of plant domestication, 151
proto-specializations, 104
pulse model, 58, 76

radiocarbon dating, problems with, 146
Raimbault, Michel, 41, 52, 57, 58–61, 192
rains, 111, 117–18
rank–size distribution and urbanism, 206, 207
'Red Men', 15, 103
regional survey, 166–7, 168, 204
rice growing, 3, 99–100, 119, 127, 151, 165
Rimaïbé, 106–7, 108, 112, 295, 300
ritual art, 210–13
Roberts, Richard, 295, 296, 301
Robinson, David, 281, 282, 286
rock art, 114, 128
Rouch, J., 125
Roundé Siru, 25, 182, 287, 300
royal pilgrimages, 293

sacred landscape, 28–9, 136–8, 144–5
sacrificed objects, cardinal-point orientation of, 226, 285, 291–2
es-Sa'di, *Ta'rikh es-Sudan*, 113, 155, 156, 194, 207, 264, 266, 267, 296
Sahara
  and Aqualithic culture, 49–51
  emergence of pastoralism, 153–4
  palaeoclimate, 66–80
  trans-Saharan trade, 30–3, 155, 194, 216–19, 267–81
Sahel

Drought, 66, 111, 123
  palaeoclimate, 66–80
salt caravans (*Azalaï*), 129–30
sâti (ritual murders), 220, 231
seasonality approach, 53–5
Sebi-Marigot channel, 89
Segou, 117, 299
Sekou Amadou, 25, 107, 112, 117–18, 281–2, 284, 285–6, 300–1
semi-arid steppe ecology, 45–6
seno (sand highland), 108
shamanistic authority, 17, 233
shell and bone middens, 47
shifting capitals principle, 260
'silent trade', 270–1
slaves, 217, 295
Smith, Andrew B., 153
smiths, 89, 142, 150, 176–81, 214
  historical imagination, 135, 137–8, 182–9
  and Imperial Tradition, 262–3, 284–5, 292–3
  at Jenne-jeno, 159–60, 176, 177, 179, 182–6, 188
  in Lakes Region-Niger Bend, 190, 191, 192, 198–9
  and *nyama*, 179, 180, 187, 188, 262–3, 292
  see also iron smelting technology; Sumaworo
Somono, 97–8, 296
Songhai, 34, 103, 125–7, 129, 263, 285
Songhai empire, 126, 250, 264, 265–7, 282, 287, 293, 298–9
Soninké, 15, 142–3, 217, 218, 232, 255, 261, 277, 279–80
Sonni Ali Ber, 126, 264, 265, 279, 285, 287–91, 292
sorghum, 119, 124, 127, 151, 165
Sorko, 103, 126, 292
Sorogo, 97, 100–1, 102
Soso, 261, 262, 263
Spengler, Oswald, 18–19
state formation, theories of, 251–4
statism, 305–6
Stoller, Paul, 22
stress hypothesis and plant domestication, 151, 152
Sumaworo (blacksmith king), 247, 261, 262, 263, 285, 291, 292
Sundström, L., 104, 127

Sunjata, 247, 258, 261–3, 264, 283, 292, 293
symbolic entrainment, 228
symbolic reservoir, 5, 14–17, 230, 285
  defined, 16, 306
synoecism, 10–22, 281, 282–3, 284, 306

Tamari, Tal, 178
Tanapo, 100
Taoudenni palaeolake region, 36, 42
Tapama myth, 104, 158
Tauxier, Louis, 113
tectonic activity, 120–1
tells (settlement mounds), 76, 100, 159
Tendirma, 258, 265
terracottas, 211–12, 213, 248–9, 278
Tiabel Goudiodié, 61, 62
Tichitt, 53–5, 152, 160
Tié, 97
Timbuktu, 120, 127, 193–9, 234, 276
  conflict between Tuareg and Songhai, 34, 126, 299
  and Imperial Tradition, 264, 265, 267
  trade with Jenne-jeno, 155, 194, 214–15
Tin Hinan, princess, 128
Togola, Téréba, 21, 61, 62, 63–4, 161, 167, 198, 257–8
Tondibi, battle of (AD 1591), 266, 275, 277, 298–9
Tondidaro, 221–3, 230
toubabou diongwou (captives of the Whites), 4
Toubel, 191, 201
trade and exchange, 56–7, 61, 63, 160, 213–19, 228, 234–9, 261–2, 296
  see also gold trade
transhumant cycle
  of Fulani, 108–13
  of Tuareg, 129
transition sites, 63–4, 145–6
trans-Saharan trade, 30–3, 155, 194,

216–19, 267–81
Trimingham, J. Spencer, 231, 255–6
Tuareg, 34, 111, 126, 127–30, 264, 295–6, 299, 300
Tukulor, 113, 114, 282, 301
tumuli, 219–33, 258

Upper Delta, 74, 88, 126, 255
  autochthones, 89–105
  ceramics, 53–4, 63–4
  demographic crisis, 245–6, 267
  penetration, 76, 140–81
  see also Jenne; Jenne-jeno
urbanism
  and clustering, 168–76, 192, 205, 207–10
  precocious, 203–13
  and prosperity, 190–233
  see also individual names of cities

Vallée du Serpent palaeochannel, 144–5, 161
Van der Merwe, N. J., 149
Vansina, Jan, 13
Vernet, R., 69
Vincent, Y., 119

Wadi-13, 25, 81, 198, 199, 234, 300
Wadi El-Ahmar, 43–4, 45, 129, 196, 198, 199, 234
Wagadou, 167, 250, 254, 255, 258, 259–60, 263, 265
Wangara, 217, 258, 261–2, 272, 274, 275, 276–7, 278–81
  land of (Island of Gold), 30–3, 218–19, 267–81
Webb, James L. A., 77–9
West Africa
  origins of agriculture, 150–4
  origins of iron smelting, 145–50
Western Sudan, Great Empires of, 250–67
Wheatley, Paul, 18–19
wild grasses, 43
Wright, Henry, 95